# Understanding Apocalyptic Terrorism

MW00650713

This book explores a cross-cultural worldview called 'radical apocalypticism' that underlies the majority of terrorist movements in the twenty-first century.

Although not all apocalypticism is violent, in its extreme forms radical apocalypticism gives rise to terrorists as varied as members of Al Qaeda, Anders Behring Breivik, or Timothy McVeigh. In its secular variations, it also motivates ideological terrorists, such as the eco-terrorists Earth Liberation Front or The Unabomber, Ted Kaczynski. This book provides an original paradigm for distinguishing between peaceful and violent or radical forms of apocalypticism and analyzes the history, major transformations, and characteristics of the apocalyptic thought system. Using an interdisciplinary and cross-cultural approach, this book discusses the mechanisms of radicalization and dynamics of perceived oppression and violence to clarify anew the self-identities, motivations, and goals of a broad swath of terrorists. As conventional counter-terrorism approaches have so far failed to stem the cycle of terrorism, this approach suggests a comprehensive "cultural" method to combating terrorism that addresses the appeal of radical apocalyptic terrorist ideology itself.

This book will be of much interest to students of apocalypticism, political violence, terrorism and counter-terrorism, intelligence studies, religious studies, and security studies.

**Frances L. Flannery** is Professor of Religion and Director of the Center for the Interdisciplinary Study of Terrorism and Peace (CISTP), James Madison University, USA, and author of *Dreamers, Scribes and Priests: Jewish Dreams in the Hellenistic and Roman Eras* (2004) and co-editor (with Rodney Werline) of *Experientia, Volume One: Inquiry into Religious Experience in Early Judaism and Early Christianity* (2008).

**Political Violence**
Series Editor: David Rapoport

This book series contains sober, thoughtful, and authoritative academic
accounts of terrorism and political violence. Its aim is to produce a useful
taxonomy of terror and violence through comparative and historical analysis in both national and international spheres. Each book discusses
origins, organizational dynamics and outcomes of particular forms and
expressions of political violence.

# Understanding Apocalyptic Terrorism

## Countering the radical mindset

**Frances L. Flannery**

Routledge
Taylor & Francis Group

LONDON AND NEW YORK

First published 2016
by Routledge
2 Park Square, Milton Park, Abingdon, Oxfordshire OX14 4RN

and by Routledge
711 Third Avenue, New York, NY 10017

First issued in paperback 2016

*Routledge is an imprint of the Taylor & Francis Group, an informa business*

*British Library Cataloguing-in-Publication Data*
A catalogue record for this book is available from the British Library

*Library of Congress Cataloging-in-Publication Data*
Flannery, Frances.
Understanding apocalyptic terrorism: countering the radical
mindset / Frances L. Flannery.
    pages cm. – (Political violence)
    Includes bibliographical references and index.
    1. Terrorism–Religious aspects. 2. Terrorism. 3. Political violence–
    Religious aspects. I. Title.
    BL65.T47F53 2016
    363.325'17–dc23                                    2015010689

ISBN 13: 978-1-138-28249-0(pbk)
ISBN 13: 978-1-138-77954-9(hbk)

Typeset in Baskerville
by Wearset Ltd, Boldon, Tyne and Wear

**For Harry, Sam, Lloyd, and Susie**

# Contents

**PART III**
**Conclusion**                                                      239

# Abbreviations

| | |
|---|---|
| AAA | American Anthropological Association |
| AAR | American Academy of Religion |
| ADL | Anti-Defamation League |
| ALF | Animal Liberation Front |
| AQI | Al Qaeda in Iraq |
| BATF | Bureau of Alcohol, Tobacco, Firearms and Explosives |
| BMIS | Black Mountain Indigenous Support |
| CIA | US Central Intelligence Agency |
| CSA | Covenant, Sword, and Arm of the Lord |
| CSCC | The State Department Center for Strategic Counterterrorism Communications |
| CENTCOM | United States Central Command |
| CISTP | Center for the Interdisciplinary Study of Terrorism and Peace |
| CSG | Counter-terrorism Security Group |
| CWC | Chemical Weapons Convention |
| ELF | Earth Liberation Front |
| DCI | Director of Central Intelligence |
| DIA | Defense Intelligence Agency |
| DOJ | US Department of Justice |
| EMETIC | Evan Mecham Eco Terrorist International Conspiracy |
| FAA | Federal Aviation Administration |
| FBI | US Federal Bureau of Investigation |
| GCI | Grace Communion International Church |
| HTS | Human Terrain System |
| HUMINT | Human Intelligence |
| IAFIE | International Association for Intelligence Educators |
| ICRD | International Center for Religion and Diplomacy |
| IPCC | Intergovernmental Panel on Climate Change |
| ISIS/ISIL | Islamic State in Iraq and Syria/Islamic State of Iraq and the Levant |
| JP | Joint Publication (of the US Military) |
| KIM | Kingdom Identity Ministries |

| KKK | Ku Klux Klan |
|---|---|
| MAK | Mektab al Khidamat |
| NATO | North Atlantic Treaty Organization |
| NCMI | National Center for Medical Intelligence |
| NGA | National Geo-spatial Intelligence Agency |
| NGO | Non-governmental Organization |
| NIC | National Intelligence Council |
| NPT | National Philanthropic Trust |
| NSA | National Security Agency |
| ODNI | Office of the Director of National Intelligence |
| OPCW | Organization for the Prohibition of Chemical Weapons |
| PALS | Portraits of American Life |
| PDB | Presidential Daily Briefings |
| POGO | Project on Government Oversight |
| PSI | Perfect Salvation Initiation |
| PSIA | Permanent Subcommittee on Investigations of the Committee on Governmental Affairs |
| RAMPS | Radical Action Mountain Peoples Survival |
| REAR | Radical Environmental and Animal Rights |
| REM | Radical Environmental Movement |
| SBL | Society of Biblical Literature |
| SEIB | Senior Executive Intelligence Briefs |
| SHAC | Stop Huntingdon Animal Cruelty |
| SPLC | Southern Poverty Law Center |
| SSSR | Society for the Scientific Study of Religion |
| START | National Consortrium for the Study of Terrorism and Responses to Terrorism |
| SWAT | Special Weapons And Tactics Team |
| UFO | unidentified flying object |
| UNEP | United Nations Environmental Program |
| UNICEF | United Nations Children's Fund (formerly United Nations International Children's Emergency Fund) |
| WMD | Weapon of Mass Destruction |
| WMO | World Meterorological Organization |
| ZOG | Zionist Organized Government |

# Acknowledgments

This field-crossing project marks a point in a long intellectual journey. I could never have arrived at these ideas without relying heavily on the work of a host of excellent scholars in myriad fields, including religion, biblical studies, political science, intelligence analysis, sociology, anthropology, philosophy and international relations. I am particularly indebted to those whom I cite (see p. i) throughout the book and hope that my appreciation is evident. Any mistakes are definitely my own.

I heartily thank the Department of Philosophy and Religion and the College of Arts and Letters at James Madison University for the educational leave grant in 2014–2015 that enabled me to finally finish this book, so many summer and winter breaks in the making. I appreciate the great direction and flexibility of the editors at Routledge, particularly Hannah Ferguson and David Rapoport. Special thanks go to my copy-editor, Anna Kelleher, for being tireless, careful, and funny. She might wish to reword that sentence. I must also thank Noel Hendrickson, at whose invitation the conceptual seeds of this project began with a grant sponsored by the Institute for National Security Analysis at JMU.

So many scholars and colleagues have informed my thinking on this topic over the years that it is impossible to mention them all, but a few deserve special mention. Reading Mark Juergensmeyer as a newly minted Ph.D. started me on this journey and his work continues to influence my thinking. I am gratified to be a part of a rich and innovative guild, the Society of Biblical Literature, which has proven to be a supportive home for a field-traversing biblical scholar. Several scholars of Apocalypticism, including George Nickelsburg, John J. Collins, Christopher Rowland, Michael Stone and Alan Segal have been my generous teachers, mentors, and conversation partners. They have sharpened my thoughts on apocalypticism in immeasurable ways. My attention to and understanding of the "moods and motivations" of religious experience, which forever transformed my approach to religion, emerged from conversations with my friend and main intellectual partner, Rodney Werline. Since he and I co-founded the Religious Experience program unit at the Society of Biblical Literature in 2005, I have benefited profoundly and repeatedly from interactions with other dear members of the "Experientia Group" and a small circle of highly cherished friends in the Society of Biblical Literature. These include Colleen Shantz, Angela Kim Harkins, Kelley Coblentz Bautch, Judy Newman, Bert Jan Lietaert-Peerbolte, Celia Deutsch, Robin Griffith-Jones, Daphna Arbel, James Davila, Daniel Falk, Anathea Portier-Young, and Jack Levison. My understanding of intelligence analysis has been greatly enriched by conversations with Timothy Walton, Mike Deaton, Ron Wulf, and Rick Gill.

I genuinely thank my students, especially those brave enough to take my "Apocalypticism, Religious Terorism, and Peace" course at James Madison University, the "Simulations of Outcomes of the Iranian Nuclear Program" course that I had the privilege of teaching with Timothy Walton for JMU and the University of Virginia, and my "Apocalyptic Thought and Movements course" at Hendrix University. It has been a genuine privilege to teach them and learn from them; without them I could not have hammered out my thoughts on radical apocalypticism over the last fifteen years. In particular, three students' teamwork on ELF changed my views of eco-terrorism, and I thank Amanda Wilson, Joshua Ryan Stairs, and Luke Manning.

My colleagues in the Center for the Interdisciplinary Study of Terrorism and Peace (CISTP) have been my invaluable conversation partners. Their continued influence on my thinking is undeniable and profoundly appreciated. These include David Owusu Ansah, Edward Brantmeier, Jennifer Connerley, Lennie Echterling, Glenn Hastedt, Shin-Ji Kang, Sallie King, Jonathan Miles, Maria Papadakis, Anne Stewart, and Timothy Walton, as well as the student interns James Prince, Christiaan Firmani, Katherine Hussey, Emily Spiwak, and Sidney Barton. Jonathan Jackson has lent insights from afar. At JMU I have been fortunate to work with great colleagues in two supportive departments, the Department of Philosophy and Religion and the Intelligence Analysis program. I profoundly appreciate the support of Dean David Jeffrey, Provost Jerry Benson, President Jon Alger, and the Office of Research and Scholarship, especially Ken Newbold, who understood my vision of CISTP and helped us get started. I also thank CISTP's intellectual partners, the Handa Center for the Study of Terrorism and Political Violence at the University of St. Andrews and the International Center for Religion and Diplomacy, especially Rebecca Cataldi and Doug Johnston. The work of the Kosovo Working Group at JMU and Eastern Mennonite University continues to inform my thinking on ways to achieve peace and stem extremism by improving the social lives of people. I thank my co-chair, Edward Brantmeier, for his extreme dedication to the Kosovo project, along with Ambassador Ahmet Shala, Hatixje Shala, and our partners in Kosovo. Their friendship means much to me.

A work such as this entails a deep emotional journey, even when I write in an academic style. It is difficult to read and think about the tragedies in this project. I would have experienced much more psychological wear and tear without the unfailing support of a network of friends, old and new.

Peg and Marv B. have been hearing about and reading pieces of my work since 2009, providing tremendous support and deep friendship. In addition, I wish to thank Emily C., Jonathan J., Liz B., Mike D., Jenny R., Sara T., Isabel D., Bev B., Elizabeth M., Jim M., Kay H., Kimberly D., Tom J., Jennifer C., Andrea V., Lisa T., Michael S., Kristen C., Tami K., Alan K., Chanel N., Tracy L., Perry N., Keli B., Chris M., Toni M., Daiken N., C.H.M., Valerie M., Cassie B., Joe B., Sue E., Maggie F., Buck F., and Casey F. I cannot name all of my cherished people here and I ask them to please forgive me for any omissions.

My family has made all of this possible. My mom Susie has been generous with time, food, and advice. My dad Lloyd is severely missed. Above all, I love and thank Sam and Harry, my heart walking around in other bodies. I dedicate this book to them.

# Introduction

On September 11, 2001, I watched the television coverage of the first plane hitting the World Trade Center tower in New York. I instinctively put my hand on my belly, which held my growing baby, and wondered what kind of world my son would grow up in. Like other Americans, I was terribly disturbed and saddened. No one could have imagined those specific scenes of devastation, those particular lives impacted, in scenes and memories that would become iconic.

However, to be honest, I wasn't completely surprised. I was a newly graduated Ph.D. in Religion who had just taught a course on Apocalyptic Movements at a small liberal arts college in Arkansas. In that course, which I've now taught multiple times at a big Virginia liberal arts university, I recognized something that not many in the media seemed to be discussing, even in the aftermath of 9/11. Put simply, the actions of many terrorists are not, in fact, nonsensical or irrational; they are repulsive, but also predictable. They make perfect sense within the context of the apocalyptic worldview.

The nature of terrorism has changed dramatically in the last thirty years. In 1980, only two of sixty-four active terrorist groups had an overtly religious self-identification or agenda (Hoffman 2006, 85).[1] By 2004, of 113 active terrorist groups, about half had explicitly religious self-identities and motivations (an assessment that depends on a narrow definition of religion and is probably conservative) (ibid., 86). More importantly *the attacks with the greatest number of casualties* have been conducted by religious groups or individuals associated with religious groups (ibid., 86–88).[2]

Despite the fact that such groups differ widely in their cultural contexts, as a scholar I find that they exhibit the characteristics of a thought system that biblical scholars call "apocalypticism," which has been around for thousands of years. However, apocalypticism in and of itself can give rise to either peace or violence. Those apocalyptic groups that do commit violence accept the basic apocalyptic worldview that others do, plus a steady set of other propositions, resulting in a reality map that I call "radical apocalypticism."

Hence, despite the dizzyingly complex global situation in what was once called "the War against Terror," we *can* shed some light on the overarching goals, ethics, and motivations of most terrorists. From the Islamist extremism of Al Qaeda to the seventy-seven murders of (mostly) children by Neo-Templar Anders Behring Breivik in Norway, the over-arching worldview that lies at the root of religious terrorism, radical apoca-lypticism, includes some consistent, trans-cultural propositions about reality. To non-believers these ideas seem entirely non-intuitive, yet for believers, a radical apocalyptic worldview organizes the whole of reality into a coherent portrait, accounting for every circumstance, including wars, social identities, political events, astronomical events, or even the weather.

## Definition of apocalypticism

As a biblical scholar as well as a scholar of religious terrorism, I am using the framework of "apocalypticism" in a technical sense that goes somewhat against the popularized meaning of "apocalypse" as the catastrophic end of the world. Indeed, this latter usage appears not only in media and popular culture, but also in scholarly treatments of terrorism. The fact that I have chosen to go against this enormous tide of usage is *not* simply because I am wedded to the jargon of my field! Rather, I have found that this limited equation of "apocalypse" and "apocalyptic" with the end of the world has prohibited a full understanding of the systemic relationship between terrorism and the symbolic universe or worldview that I am calling radical apocalypticism. My hope is that by grounding the full meaning of "apocalypticism" in the original texts of early Judaism, Christi-anity, and Islam, we can appreciate much more fully the potent draw of the apocalyptic worldview, which has proven to be so "sticky" that it has lasted approximately two and half millennia.

Hence, I follow a biblical studies and history of religions approach and define *apocalypticism* as the system of thought held by certain movements, the themes of which are first found in the early Persian, Jewish, Christian and Muslim *apocalypses* – literary texts such as the Avesta, *1 Enoch*, Daniel, the Gospel of Mark, the Book of Revelation, *4 Ezra*, and the Qur'an. Within biblical studies, many scholarly definitions of "apocalypse" and "apocalypticism" exist, each of which attempts to distill the few essential features of *apocalypse*, a literary genre, and *apocalypticism*, the socio-religious worldview of which it partakes and in turn generates (e.g., Collins 1979; Hanson 1962; Rowland 1982). Drawing on a rich body of scholarship, and updating these insights for the contemporary era, I define "apocalypti-cism" as: *an orientation to reality that maintains that the divine (or "tran-scendent") realm has sent a revelation to a select few persons, the righteous, disclosing the divine view through a transformative or meaningful experience. This revelation affirms that evil forces rule the mundane realm that the righteous now inhabit, but someday there will be divine intervention that will dramatically change the operation of the cosmos by overcoming this evil, allowing the righteous to partake more fully of the divine reality.* This transformation may or may not involve a catastrophic end to the world, but it does typically involve a dramatic, profound change to history as we know it, such that the experience of it is as a new world. Typically, this change rights a cosmic wrong that has affected an entire nation or cosmos (Sacchi 1990).

Apocalypticism does not always focus on a terrestrial, collective human salvation from doom. Sometimes the righteous escape the ordinary earthly realm altogether, and sometimes they must be transformed into a non-human or supra-human state in order to attain salvation. The key is that believers maintain they are the special recipients of revelation, aligned with the divine or transcendent will. They believe that the revelation – which is quite often an interpretation of an older, original revelation (such as the Bible or the Qur'an) – enables them to view reality from an ultimate, transcendent, or divine point of view.

While the anticipation of a dramatic change drives the apocalyptic worldview, the recipients of the revelation do not believe that they need to wait until the end of history to experience the rescue of the cosmos. In some small way, they believe that they are able to partake of that ultimate reality *now*. This might occur by creating a temporary corner of "paradise," such as a pure community, or by having mystical experiences, or simply by obeying the will of the divine (Flannery 2014). Eventually, they believe they will fully overcome the spatial, temporal, or ethical/purity/physical constraints of this world. Thus, as a starting point, they dismiss the values and importance of the mundane world in which we all live.

For some people, this world feels like it has gone awry and is broken. The apocalyptic worldview affirms the pain they feel and points to a clear culprit who is the cause of evil. Apocalyptic belief gives their suffering meaning and promises them a special place in a good and restored world to come. The more that they become fully committed to that utopia, their "real world," the more their care for the "temporary world" that the rest of us share fades away.

## Definitions of terrorism

In the literature on terrorism, there are hundreds of definitions, some emphasizing methods, others effect and others intention (Stern 2003, xx). Altogether, they cover an extensive range of aspects, including the intent to create broad psychological effects, victim–target differentiation, the planned nature of terrorist acts, extra-normality, the targeting of civilians and publicity (e.g., Hoffman 2006, 34). Hoffman has simply stated, "Terrorism is thus violence – or equally important, the threat of violence – used and directed in pursuit of, or in service of, a political aim," and he notes that it is "ineluctably political in aims and motives" (ibid., 2, 40). While he is correct that terrorism almost always has political dimensions, the question is whether dividing "political terrorism" from "religious terrorism" is appropriate in the case of apocalyptic terrorists, who conceptually fit the political realm into a symbolic universe that anticipates the imminent arrival of a divine form of governance.[3] Radical apocalyptic terrorism is a thought system that deeply intertwines theological claims with political and social dimensions.

Occasionally the view arises in scholarship and the media that terrorists use religion to mask their true political views. This implies that the terrorists' religious views are not genuine, which is not the same as saying that geo-politics and religion are inextricably combined, especially in apocalyptic systems.

Compounding the difficulty of arriving at a satisfying definition of terrorism is the fact that there is no internationally agreed-upon legal definition of terrorism. Even within the US government, different agencies have used different definitions, which continue to evolve. For instance, the US Code, used by the US State Department, the FBI, and other agencies, calls terrorism "premeditated, politically motivated violence perpetrated against non-combatant targets by subnational groups or clandestine agents, usually intended to influence an audience" (22 US Code, Section 2656 f(d)). Elsewhere, the US Code stresses that terrorism is intended "to intimidate or coerce a civilian population," "to influence the policy of a government by intimidation or coercion," or "to affect the conduct of a government" through various unlawful means (18 US Code, Section 2331). Again, while the issues of intent and motivation are essential to these legal definitions, the terrorists may not view "politically motivated violence" as distinct from their religious objectives, a point unaddressed by the legal definitions. In addition, not all terrorists (actors) are subnational groups or clandestine agents. Moreover, in cases of radical apocalyptic terrorism, there are instances in which the main or perhaps only "audience" that is meant to be influenced is God, making these definitions even more ill-fitting.

Since ascertaining motivation and intent is vital to prosecuting terrorism, it is important to understand the religious worldview of a radical apocalyptic terrorist for legal reasons, in addition to the host of counter-terrorism practicalities that I explore in this study. Thus, the agency definition that seems the most promising to me is that of the US Department of Defense (DOD), in use until 2010, which stated that terrorism is "the calculated use of unlawful violence or threat or unlawful violence to inculcate fear; intended to coerce or intimidate governments or societies *in the pursuit of goals that are generally political, religious, or ideological objectives*" (Joint Pub. 3–07.2, GL-4). Helpfully, this definition focuses on the intent to cause fear and recognizes that religion and ideology are paramount to many terrorists' objectives.

However, the DOD recently changed its definition, which now reads, terrorism is "the unlawful use of violence or threat of violence, often motivated by religious, political, or other ideological beliefs, to instill fear and coerce governments or societies *in pursuit of goals that are usually political*" (DOD *Dictionary of Military Terms*, italics mine). This revision actually reverts back to a more limited understanding of the goal of terrorist groups that fails to capture the worldview and intent of many radical apocalypticists.

For this study, I understand radical apocalyptic terrorism to be the act of employing violence or the threat of violence against victims who are themselves not the intended audience, for the purpose of achieving religious, political, and social goals framed within the symbolic universe of radical apocalypticism. It is that symbolic universe that this book seeks to unpack.

## Explanations regarding terminology

The terms "apocalypticism"/"apocalyptic" are often conflated with the terms "millennialism"/"millenarianism" by scholars of contemporary religious history and by those in other fields, such as political science. I have purposefully not adopted the terms "millennialism" or "millenarianism" in this book for numerous reasons. First, I seek to root the phenomenon that I am examining in the early apocalyptic texts and scholarship in this area uses the framework of apocalypticism, not millennialism. Second, scholars of "millennialism" have developed their own categories and approaches separate from those propagated by scholars of apocalypticism. These are not, in my opinion, as useful for differentiating between peaceful and violent believers in apocalyptic systems. Third, my central concern is that the original phrase "millennialism" refers to a long history of Christian interpretations of the thousand-year reign of the elect in the Book of Revelation. In fact, there are Jewish, Muslim, Buddhist, and secular interpretations of that image, therefore it is important to avoid being unnecessarily Christian-centric in nomenclature for phenomena that are trans-cultural. Worse yet is the use of the term "messianism" as an equation for apocalypticism,[4] a term with a clear resonance in Christian theology. My concern is that such terminology may prove to be a conceptual hindrance when applying the model to non-Christian groups. My hope is that "apocalypticism," rooted in scholarship on Persian, Jewish, Christian, and Muslim texts, will prove over time to be more neutral and better able to function cross-culturally.

Both apocalypticism and millennialism are external scholarly frameworks, heuristic devices for understanding the belief systems under scrutiny, but they sometimes notice different features. One could use a magnifying loop and a pair of glasses to inspect an object, but while they have a lot in common, the difference in approaches matters in terms of what one sees. My reasons for preferring the framework of apocalypticism should become apparent in this book, while my reasons for avoiding the framework of millennialism deserve an explanation, considering that much excellent work has been done on the relationship of "millennialism" to terrorism.

To be honest, many scholars use the term "millennialism" without much definitional clarity. A welcome exception is Catherine Wessinger's thorough scholarly analysis of millennialism and terrorism (Wessinger 2000). Wessinger defines millennialism/millenarianism as "belief in a collective terrestrial salvation," in which "limitations of the human condition such as illness, suffering, death, injustice, conflict, and war will be overcome" (Wessinger 2000, 2–3). While this overlaps with my definition of apocalypticism, it omits aspects essential to the formulation of the phenomenon of apocalypticism, such as the understanding of the world as an evil (and not simply a difficult) place, the self-identity of believers as those caught in a cosmic battle, and the believers' experiential sense of the divine plan and presence. The definition is also confusing given that Wessinger notes immediately that "millennialists also can expect the millennial kingdom to be heavenly or other-worldly," or have doubts as to whether it is terrestrial or heavenly (ibid., 3). However, her insights into an essentially dualistic worldview that aims at a collective transformation are invaluable in what proves to be a precise and insightful cross-cultural analysis of the religious aspects of terrorist groups.

Wessinger further divides the phenomenon of millennialism/millenarianism into two categories. "Progressive millennialism" has an optimistic view of humanity and society's ability to improve itself. "Catastrophic millennialism" is pessimistic regarding human society and envisions that the world must be destroyed and recreated by divine beings, perhaps with the help of humans (Wessinger 2000, 16–17). These categories are helpful and I will occasionally make use of them, but they are not able to distinguish between peaceful and violent forms of apocalypticism.

Every model has its limitations, including mine. I have grounded my definitions and approaches in the *earliest* historical examples of the phenomenon, which imperfectly limits me to texts, a literary genre that scholars call "apocalypse." The advantage is a truly cross-cultural framework based on themes found in early Persian, Jewish, Christian, and Muslim apocalypses, but the disadvantage is that these are idealized literary refractions that do not convey how people actually lived out the worldview. Moreover, this study is not a book on the ancient apocalypses; it is a sweeping analysis of radical apocalyptic groups and their worldview, as it is historically rooted in antiquity and the medieval periods. Thus, I have had to forego discussion of these ancient texts, instead choosing to begin with the Book of Revelation as a representative of the genre, because it is influential and conveniently illustrates many of the crucial characteristics that I wish to highlight. However, my model has not derived solely or even primarily from this text or from a scholarly framework limited to Christianity.

Another influence on my approach is a pragmatic concern that stems from my work in intelligence analysis. I have tried to arrive at a simple structural "formula of radical apocalypticism" for this conceptual map that operates cross-culturally, while still allowing for the particular cultural contours of each context. My goal in distilling matters down to a formula is usability by practitioners, especially law enforcement, public policy officials, and intelligence analysts. I am not trying for a comprehensive analysis of each individual group in this study (which would necessarily be much larger), but rather for an overarching analysis of the radical apocalyptic worldview that I see as operative in these groups. That means that some nuance in the analysis will be lost and practitioners extending the formula to other groups should be careful to conduct a thorough culturally specific analysis of a given group. Ideally, I would recommend generating a comprehensive "thick description" to capture relevant cultural details (Geertz 1973) alongside the use of this formula to recognize overarching patterns, estimate threat, and possibly make predictions.

A pre-emptive word about Chapter 7 is necessary, as scholars of ecological activist groups such as ELF or ALF may object that the conceptual model of apocalypticism is somewhat ill-fitting for a secular worldview. Since I follow Baird (who follows Tillich 1957) in defining religion as that which addresses *ultimate concern* (Baird 1991, 14), I find that viewing eco-activism as a religious system illuminates important aspects of the worldview. Also, from the point of view of intelligence analysis practitioners, I believe there is pragmatic value in viewing eco-activist groups against the spectrum of apocalyptic religious groups to facilitate analytic understanding of the distinctions between eco-activism, eco-activism with criminal behavior, and genuine eco-terrorism.

In this book I refuse to employ the term "cult," even in the extremely violent case of Aum Shinrikyo. For scholars of religion, "religion" is a value neutral term (Reader 2000). When a sect or group exhibits the traditional characteristics of other religions, such as an overall explanation of ultimate reality, sacred ethics, spiritual practices, and moods and motivations pertaining to the sacred realm, I refer to the group as a religion or, to convey a smaller scale, as a religious sect or group. Moreover, if such a group also expresses political dimensions in symbolic terms within a larger orientation to cosmic reality, I may also refer to them as a religion, religious group, or religious sect rather than as a political faction. Finally, worship of a particular deity is not a prerequisite for the label "religion"; hence, I argue that some eco-activist groups provide a secular or spiritualized experience of nature religion.

In addition, my use of the term "religion" or "religious group" as opposed to "cult" in this book is vital for other conceptual and pragmatic reasons. David C. Rapoport makes the point that religion itself has both violence-reducing and violence-producing dimensions (Rapoport 1992, 118). Recognizing this, I believe, is vital to comprehending how to approach counter-terrorism in a manner that is successful in the long term. Hence, limiting the term "religion" to non-violent groups and the term "cult" to violent ones, as the media and even some academics regularly do, is more than just unhelpful and inaccurate.[5] This terminology also obscures vital similarities between the groups under examination and more mainstream "religions" and implies that the sects' worldviews, ethics, and community-structures are so alien as to be closed off for understanding by both the public at large and by analysts. In turn, this mystery box approach to the groups under scrutiny casts the members inside as dangerous and creates impasses between law enforcement and intelligence analysis on the one hand, and the sects on the other. The label "cult" also inhibits critical understanding of a group's practices and theology for potential and current members of a sect by placing them in a defensive position. Most of all, it promotes a confrontational relationship between media/government/academia/analysts and the group in question, which in and of itself informs the dynamics of the apocalyptic believers' self-identities and orientation to the world.

Yet while we should refrain from the pejorative term "cult," it is also vitally important to recognize when the mainstream members of a particular faith community reject a group's identification with a parent religion. For example, while as a scholar I do not identify a phenomenon such as radical Islamist ideology as "false Islam," I *will* point out that it is a recent aberration or fringe interpretation that seems to deviate from traditional interpretations. Similarly, I don't call Christian Identity teaching "false Christianity," but I do note that it is a fringe racist interpretation that the majority of Christians reject. This language does not in any way indicate my acceptance of these doctrines as legitimate expressions of the parent religions. Rather it indicates my position as an analyst who respects the pernicious potential of religious interpretations and who is interested in the conceptual ties that these groups make as they situate themselves in relation to the parent religions. As the final chapter indicates, I think it is absolutely vital for the traditional adherents of the parent religions to reject these radical interpretations. Thus, I retain the labels "false Islam" for radical Islam or "false Christianity" for Christian Identity teaching when I am describing the views of mainstream Muslims and Christians.

## Methodological approach

My approach is thoroughly interdisciplinary, like most of religious studies. Any contribution I am able to make builds on the vast scholarship of numerous other researchers and stems from my bridging of several typically disparate fields. My specialty in ancient apocalypticism led me to a broader research specialty in general apocalypticism, which gradually led me to focus on religious terrorism over the last decade. This brought me into contact with the substantial amount of scholarship on intelligence studies and various strategic assessment tools, as well as with political science and international affairs. To my surprise, I also drew conceptually on my first degree in Environmental Science, which stresses a systems-wide approach that understands that parts of a system are related dynamically and affect one another.[6]

As I have said, I am first and foremost, in my training, a scholar of the Bible and the "Pseudepigrapha." Thorough reading of the earliest expressions of the apocalyptic worldview in the original languages (Hebrew, Aramaic, Syriac, Greek, Latin, Arabic) continues to inform my thinking on the phenomenon of apocalypticism as I turn to the contemporary period. I am also a scholar-researcher of apocalypticism throughout the ages and I have immersed myself in hundreds, if not thousands, of case studies of apocalyptic groups ranging from antiquity to the present day. My examinations of contemporary groups have included official scriptures and their interpretations, as well as fringe and mainstream transformations and adaptations in texts, ritual, material culture, popular culture, and social media.

As a biblical scholar, I have been trained in *form criticism*, a literary technique that recognizes *patterns and structures* in texts and traditions. This methodology enables me to see the patterns in the enormous mass of examples of apocalyptic groups that I have examined and to distill the formula for radical apocalypticism that I present in Chapter 3. Every good form critic must be able to respect the individuality of the source information while spotting overarching patterns and structures as not just coincidence, but as the consequence of cultural transmission.

Through form criticism, we are thus able to identify patterns in texts that appear quite different on the surface. My mentor, George Nickelsburg, illustrated form criticism with the example of various TV commercials that look quite different and sell different products, but use the same narrative pattern. A person has a problem (dirty laundry, body odor, dirty toilet). She/he is shunned, depressed, or frustrated as a result. Later, the person (or in one trope, a better looking friend), is contrasted when he/she uses Product X to address that problem. The person or friend is shown having lots of success in life (a happy family, an attractive partner, happiness, and self-fulfillment). The strength of form criticism is that it makes a pattern obvious and recognizable, once identified.

By applying form criticism to thousands of examples of apocalypticism from antiquity to the present day, I propose a formula for radical apocalypticism in Chapter 3. This formula does not address every detail of each case example analyzed, but rather seeks to lift up the overarching logic common to the examples as a whole. This method certainly has limitations, but also some great advantages in pattern recognition and predictive capability.

Over the years, I have taught the contents of this book to students of religion, international affairs, political science, justice studies, and intelligence analysis. I have presented lectures on this to the public as well as to analysts in various intelligence agencies from multiple allied countries.

Though over a decade has passed since 9/11, many intelligence analysts, university students, members of the general public, policy makers, and representatives of the media still only dimly understand the apocalyptic worldview that informs most religious and ideological terrorism. That is why I wrote this book.

## Plan of this book[7]

Apocalyptic thinking, in and of itself, can be a force for peaceful societal change. It has also led some groups in various societies to peacefully and patiently wait for this divine intervention to arrive. However, when this apocalyptic worldview combines with a particular set of beliefs that I outline in this book, it rather easily turns into a potent, violent myth that can translate into murder, terrorism, and even genocide. This dangerous form of "radical apocalypticism" has occurred across the globe, in various religions, for thousands of years.

This study is above all a comprehensive study of a phenomenon – radical apocalyptic terrorism. I begin in Chapter 1 by examining the parameters and key characteristics of apocalypticism as illustrated in the Book of Revelation, which influences every group that I examine in this book. In Chapter 2, I explore key changes that occurred in apocalyptic interpretation during the Middle Ages, transforming a pacifist ideology into a militant one. These medieval interpretations of apocalypticism, which are not original to the Book of Revelation itself, have influenced radical apocalyptic groups today. In Chapter 3, I propose a formula for radical apocalypticism and apply it to a few representative radical apocalyptic groups, beginning with the example of a Christian group, the Covenant, Sword, and the Arm of the Lord.

Certainly, the extremist Islamist variety of radical apocalypticism is of grave concern in the study of terrorism today. Thus I address the transnational terrorist organizations Al Qaeda in Chapter 4 and ISIS/ISIL in Chapter 5. Both happen to be mostly Sunni in membership. I do not discuss Shi'ite versions of radical apocalypticism, simply due to space limitations. Radical apocalyptic violence does occur in extremist Islamist Shi'ism: for example, in the Iraqi Mahdi Army, formed by Muqtada al-Sadr, and in Hezbollah, a state-sponsored terrorist group historically backed by Iran.

In spite of the image projected by today's media climate, terrorism is not limited to radical forms of Islam. Thus I would urge readers not to read these chapters in isolation, but to read the other chapters that contain case studies of radical apocalypticism in Christianity, secular environmental activism, and new religious movements. It is not Islam that provides the rationale for violence (quite the contrary), but rather the transcultural framework of radical apocalypticism, importable into any religion and many secular worldviews.

In Chapter 6, I examine the mindset of Timothy McVeigh, the Oklahoma City bomber, and several American domestic groups that cluster around the Christian Identity form of radical apocalypticism. In order to illustrate the importance of understanding peaceful versus violent forms of apocalypticism, I analyze the Branch Davidians and the Christian Identity affiliated Weaver family of Ruby Ridge. In Chapter 7, I investigate a form of radical apocalypticism represented by eco-terrorists such as James Lee, the Unabomber, and certain members of Earth Liberation Front. Positioning their actions along a spectrum of eco-activism provides an appreciation of real as opposed to manufactured threat, to stem terrorism and violence in the long term. In Chapter 8, I turn to an example of a violent New Religious Movement, Aum Shinrikyo, which applies a radical apocalyptic turn to Buddhism and Hinduism fused with New Age religion and apocalyptic Christianity.

These case studies are only a few possible examples of radical apocalyptic individuals and groups. Hundreds of examples exist. If space had permitted, it would have been ideal to also analyze radical Jewish apocalyptism, such as the Kach party or Yigal Amir, who assassinated Prime Minister Yitzhak Rabin for his compromises and peace talks with the Palestinians. Ideally, I would have liked to discuss radical apocalypticism in the cosmic worldview of numerous UFO groups, including Heaven's Gate and the Order of the Solar Temple. The non-white racist radical apocalyptic groups, such as the United Nuwaubian Nation of Moors and the original Nation of Islam would have added another dimension (Juergensmeyer 2003).[8] Hence, I offer this study as a starting point of exploration that others may continue.

Through these analyses, I repeatedly note missteps in approaches to counter-terrorism efforts that have not understood the radical apocalyptic framework, mistakes that have unintentionally fostered dangerous dynamics and made terrorism worse. In the last chapter of the book, I humbly propose a comprehensive, long-term approach to counter-terrorism and provide some concrete examples of programs that appear to be successful in promoting peace.

Radical apocalypticism can construct a total view of reality and propel adherents into committing shocking violence against their perceived enemies. To counteract terrorism effectively in the long term we must understand – and begin to transform – the radical apocalyptic mindset. In an information age, killing terrorists will not end apocalyptic terrorism. The ideology will survive and draw more adherents later. The only solution is to undermine the appeal of radical apocalyptic ideology by understanding it fully and addressing the roots of discontent. This involves promoting a full conception of peace that entails the physical, psychological, cultural, material and ecological well-being of peoples everywhere.

This is cultural counter-terrorism, in which we all can and must participate, to end apocalyptic terrorism.

## Notes

1 These were the Shi'a organizations al-Dawa and the Committee for Safeguarding the Islamic Revolution.
2 Studies stating that religious terrorism makes up a minority of terrorist acts miss the point. As Hoffman notes, "while al Qaeda perpetrated only 0.1 percent of all terrorist attacks between 1998 and 2004, it was responsible for nearly 19 percent of total fatalities from terrorist attacks during that time period" (Hoffman 2006, 88).
3 Hoffman does an excellent job of outlining the core characteristics of "religious terrorism" as follows: viewing violence as "a sacramental act or divine duty executed in direct response to some theological demand or imperative," a transcendental dimension, the goal of eliminating "broadly defined categories of enemies," large-scale violence, and a role for sacred texts imparted by clerics with authority. He also points out that religious terrorists, unlike secular terrorists, feel alienated from the social system they wish to change, and might dehumanize others (Hoffman 2003, 88–89).
4 See, for example, Cook, "Messianism in the Shi'ite Crescent" (2011). Despite my concerns with this terminology, I must state that I find Cook's scholarship to be excellent and an invaluable resource that I utilize heavily in this study.
5 Consider too, other pejorative terminology, such as the title of the reader by Ted Daniels (1999) *A Doomsday Reader: Prophets, Predictors, and Hucksters of Salvation*.
6 A profound thanks goes to my colleague Michael L. Deaton, who also contributed significantly to my thinking in this manner by tutoring me in systems dynamics modeling over the course of a year.
7 Although I know of no English work that takes a similar approach to mine, an important exception in Dutch is Bob de Graaff, who has written and taught on the history of fanaticism and on terrorism, grounding the phenomenon in the Book of Revelation and apocalypticism.
8 Excellent overviews of most of these groups are found in Juergensmeyer (2003).

## Bibliography

18 US Code, Section 2331. US FBI. Accessed July 4, 2014, www.fbi.gov/about-us/investigate/terrorism/terrorism-definition.
22 US Code, Section 2656 f(d). Legal Information Institute, Cornell University Law School. Accessed October 10, 2010, www.law.cornell.edu/uscode/text/22/2656f.
Baird, Robert. 1991. *Essays in the History of Religions*. New York: Peter Lang.
Collins, John J. 1979. *Apocalypse: The Morphology of a Genre. Semeia 14*. Missoula, MT: Scholars Press.
Cook, David. 2011. "Messianism in the Shiite Crescent." *Current Trends in Islamic Ideology* 11, 13: 91. Accessed September 10, 2011, www.hudson.org/research/7906-messianism-in-the-shiite-crescent.
Daniels, Ted, ed. 1999. *A Doomsday Reader: Prophets, Predictors, and Hucksters of Salvation*. New York: New York University Press.
Flannery, Frances. 2014. "Dreams, Visions, and Religious Experience in the Apocalypses and Apocalypticism." In *Oxford Handbook of Apocalyptic Literature*, edited by John J. Collins. London: Oxford University Press. Accessed July 11, 2014, http://dx.doi.org/10.1093/oxfordhb/9780199856497.013.007.
Geertz, Clifford. 1973. *The Interpretation of Culture*. New York: Basic Books.

Hanson, Paul D. 1962. "'Apocalypse, Genre' and 'Apocalypticism'." In *Interpreter's Dictionary of the Bible Supplementary Volume*, edited by Keith Crim, 29–34. Nashville: Abingdon.

Hoffman, Bruce. 2006. *Inside Terrorism*. Revised and expanded edition. New York: Columbia University Press.

Juergensmeyer, Mark. 2003 [2000]. *Terror in the Mind of God*. Berkeley: University of California.

Rapoport, David. 1991. "Some General Observations on Religion and Violence." In *Terrorism and Political Violence* 9, 3: 118–40. Accessed August 8, 2010, http://dx.doi.org/10.1080/09546559108427119.

Reader, Ian. 2000. *Religious Violence in Contemporary Japan: The Case of Aum Shinriyko*. Honolulu: University of Hawai'i Press.

Rowland, Christopher. 1982. *The Open Heaven: A Study of Apocalyptic in Judaism and Early Christianity*. New York: Crossroad.

Sacchi, Paolo. 1990. *L'apocalittica guidaice e la sua storie*. Brescia: Paideia. In English translation, 1997. *Jewish Apocalyptic and its History*. Sheffield: Sheffield Academic Press.

Stern, Jessica. 2003. *Terror in the Name of God*. New York: Ecco.

Tillich, Paul. 1957. *Dynamics of Faith*. New York: Harper & Row.

US Department of Defense. *Dictionary of Military Terms*. Accessed January 15, 2015, www.dtic.mil/doctrine/dod_dictionary/.

US Joint Publication. 1998. 3–07.2. 17 March. *Joint Tactics, Techniques, and Procedures for Antiterrorism*.

Wessinger, Catherine. 2000. *How the Millennium Comes Violently: From Jonestown to Heaven's Gate*. New York: Seven Bridges Press.

# Part I

# Roots of the apocalyptic worldview

# 1 The original Book of Revelation

> After this I looked, and there in heaven a door stood open! And the first voice, which I had heard speaking to me like a trumpet, said, 'Come up here, and I will show you what must take place after this.'
>
> (Rev. 4:1)[1]

When members of the Japanese Doomsday sect Aum Shinrikyo placed deadly sarin nerve gas on a Tokyo subway and sickened up to 5,000 people, they believed that they were hastening the advent of Armageddon through the instructions of Lord Shiva, god of destruction. Their religion, which prompted them to engage in fourteen attacks with both chemical and biological weapons, was a fusion of the Book of Revelation, Buddhism, Hinduism, and New Age religion. When leaders of the Christian militia group The Covenant, Sword, and Arm of the Lord trained around 1,500 armed soldiers in a military style camp for a future Armageddon that they believed would take the form of a race war in America, they too believed that they were fulfilling their role as foretold in the Book of Revelation. So did one person whom they influenced, Timothy McVeigh, when he blew up the Oklahoma City Murrah Federal Building just outside its daycare, claiming 168 lives, including nineteen toddlers. And, when Joseph Kony organized his followers to kidnap, torture, mutilate, and rape over 60,000 children in Uganda to force them into becoming the Lord's Resistance Army, he also believed himself to be acting out scenes from the Book of Revelation.

The Book of Revelation has arguably been responsible for more genocide and killing in history than any other. Yet that is not the vision of the book itself. In fact, the Book of Revelation tells the story quite differently.

According to Christian Scripture, sometime in the late first century CE John of Patmos received a series of visions in which he visited the Temple in Heaven and learned that the corrupt ways of the world on earth were going to be short-lived. The word "apocalypse" comes into use from his writings, the "*apokalupsis*" or "revelation" according to John. This word, from a Greek verb meaning "to reveal, unveil, uncover," claims that a visionary sees a new worldview unveiled. The revelation conveys reality from the divine perspective, outside of the limitations of ordinary human knowledge. Beyond the popular equation of apocalypse with "the end of the world," for scholars of antiquity an apocalypse is a narrative that relays a revelation, usually in a dream or vision, of what has been hidden from others about the true nature of the world.[2] It comes to a group in crisis, and gives them hope and new purpose.[3] It is therefore transformative.

Apocalypses first derived from ancient Persia, after which they were transmitted to early Judaism and then early Christianity. However, the Book of Revelation is so definitive of the literary genre "apocalypse" that this book alone has come to be called, simply, "The Apocalypse." It is full of visions that disclose a divine reality and, as the book makes clear, it is no less believable to its intended audience just because it is a visionary report (Hanson, J.S. 1980). We modern, post-Freudian people think of dreams as subjective, unreal fantasies that might tell the dreamer about his/her own psyche or past. We think of visions as akin to hallucinations or other unhealthy altered mental states and we certainly do not trust dreams or visions to reveal truths about the political future of the world. By contrast, the peoples of the ancient Near East and Mediterranean considered dreams and visions to be a kind of hypnagogic state that exists in between sleeping and waking, in which certain privileged people could receive real messages from God or the gods (Noegel 2007; Butler 1998; Flannery-Dailey 2004; Szpakowska 1999). Dreams and visions were a "change of reality level" that acted as "a cushion to soften the contact between god and man" (Oppenheim 1956, 192). By means of dreams and visions, a person might even interact with dangerous divine beings such as angels, but without dying as a result of the contact.

People in antiquity – whether in Persia, Mesopotamia, Egypt or Israel – did not "have" a dream or a vision; they "saw" it, as one sees something tangibly real (Szpakowska 1999, 16; Butler 1998, 31, 36). Many ancient Near Eastern cultures even lacked a verb for "dreaming." It was not an activity, but a noun, a real *thing to be seen* in special state of perception (Noegel 2007; Zgoll 2006, 55–82; Szpakowska 1999, 15).

According to the Book of Revelation, the visions that John of Patmos saw lifted the veil on reality.

## Blueprint for an apocalypse

The influence of the Book of Revelation on apocalyptic thinking across the world's religions is without parallel amongst apocalyptic texts. Although it is not the earliest Jewish or Christian apocalypse,[4] The Apocalypse provided a blueprint for thousands of years of interpretations and variations. Like a standard melody that undergoes years of improvisations, the motifs in The Apocalypse appear over and over in different examples of apocalyptic thought, from the Qur'an to *Left Behind*.

The book purports to be a record of the visions of John of Patmos "on the Lord's day" or the Sabbath.[5] In the first of these visions, John witnesses the appearance of a frightening "one like the Son of Man" (Rev. 1:13) who reveals to him that there are hypocrites in the Christian churches with whom God is displeased (Rev. 1:3). Still in a visionary state, the text next describes John's ascent to God's court in the heavenly Temple (Rev. 4:1). The original readers of the text, early Jews and Christians, considered God's real Temple to be outer space, the realm of the stars (Himmelfarb 1993). Thus, the text claims that John is granted a divine, angelic vantage point from which he is able to see further scenes that explain to him the true nature of evil and the course of past and future events.[6]

The author knew of a rich, powerful Empire that he symbolically calls "Babylon," the ancient standard for a vast Empire that oppressed the Jews. According to Revelation, most of the nations of the world love "Babylon" because it provides a high standard of material living. However, through his visions John learns that the Empire had come by its wealth through cruelty: it kills people and builds its economy on slavery (Rev. 18:13). John believes that this injustice will not go unpunished, for he "saw" in a vision an angel offering up, as sacrifices on the heavenly altar, the prayers of those whom the Empire had killed (Rev. 8:3–5).

In additional visions, John learns that the true source of power for this seductive, beautiful Empire is Satan, symbolized as a cosmic, giant red Dragon that hates the people of God (Rev. 12:1–18). This Dragon is the real force behind the Empire. In a stunning vision, John watches it come down to earth and stand on the shore of the sea – that ancient symbol of chaos from which unnatural monsters are birthed – to give rise to the Empire, symbolized as a "Beast" rising out of the sea (Rev. 12:3–13:1) (Beal 2002, 13–22, 25–28).[7] Next, John also sees a "second beast" arise that makes people worship the first beast. The second beast controls the Evil Empire's priestly and governmental operations, including its economy (Rev. 13:11–18) (Royalty 1998).

"Evil" here deserves to be capitalized. In The Apocalypse, it isn't just the case that people make bad choices, or do evil things, or even that terrible injustices are easily perpetuated by a vast institution like the Roman Empire – the original, historical referent for "Babylon" at the time of writing. Rather, the author of the Book of Revelation, like the authors of other apocalypses, defines "Evil" as a force that draws its power from Satan, the cosmic source of Evil opposing God and Goodness. In this book, the Empire is a monstrous, concretized Evil that aligns with other forces, like Death and Hades, perversions of the natural cosmic process that God has created.[8] The Universe is out of sync with what the Creator God has intended.

However, John doesn't just see the problem, he also sees the solution: this world ruled by Evil is not the ultimate one. Through his visions he learns that we live in a multi-tiered universe and that this earth is only a temporary shadow of reality. Through his revelations, John even visits the ultimate world, *God's world*, which is beyond the earthly plane. In a spirit journey, he ascends to the heavenly Temple, God's palace and court, and learns that God rules the universe from there, despite the Roman "Babylon" ruling on earth (Bauckham 1993a, 33 emphasis mine). Through these visions, John looks into the future to see that God's judgment will be meted out from this heavenly Temple onto those on earth. In fact, this judgment has already started. With the macro-view of reality gained from the divine perspective of his visions (Rowland 1982, 9, 14–17; Bauckham 1993b, 7), John recognizes that this terrible reign of Evil that he and his companions are experiencing on earth is going to be short-lived. For Revelation, the end of regular human-led history is coming "Soon!" (Rev. 22:7, 10, 12, 20).[9]

Scholars call endtime events "*eschatology*," from the Greek word *eschaton*, signifying "the end" in a temporal sequence. The endtime is such an important part of apocalyptic literature that in popular culture the word "apocalypse" has become synonymous with a cataclysmic "endtime" of history. However, John's "apocalypse" or "revelation" is not all about eschatology. Instead, through his visions, John gains a proper reorientation to the true nature of reality and knowledge of the gradually unfolding *coup d'état* of the Universe in which God will conquer Evil. The *coup d'état* will occur on all levels on which Evil operates, both on earth and in heaven, from the bottom all the way to the top.

Over the course of the Book of Revelation, John's visions unfold in multiple stages that describe the Universe's gradual transformation from a world partially ruled by Evil to one that will eventually be wholly ruled by Goodness. His early visions reveal that Evil reigns on earth. John sees what the rest of the world does not recognize: that so many people, including those in the Church,[10] partake in Evil and that the Empire and its priestly and governmental officers are fueled by the cosmic force of Evil, the Dragon Satan.

At the same time, according to the Book of Revelation, John gradually sees that God's judgment on Evil's reign is already unfolding in heaven. Christ/the Lamb is opening seven seals – seven heavenly decrees – and certain patterns in history are beginning to mete out God's punishment on the world. Angels, the intermediaries shuttling between God and humankind, pour out punishments in the form of natural plagues, environmental disasters, wars, disturbances to heavenly bodies, and famine on the earth (Rev. 6:16). These terrible occurrences are the harbingers of God's full intervention. They are an assurance that the Dragon, the first beast, and the second beast are all doomed (Rev. 12:13).

With the revelation of the sixth seal, John's visions reach beyond his own historical time period. That vision and his subsequent visions are truly *eschatological* in nature, involving a change to the world order that is so dramatic that it deserves to be called "the end of history." John experiences a time in the future when he can claim, "the sky vanished like a scroll rolling itself up" (Rev. 6:14). He knows that the "great day of wrath" is about to come.

John's subsequent visions predict that there will be a full-scale intervention by the angels in a battle against "Babylon" and her allies. According to the Book of Revelation, this will happen at Mount "Megiddo" (Rev. 16:16), from whence comes the name "the Battle of Armageddon" (from the Hebrew consonantal word m-g-d). Angels will bring an end to the mighty Empire and her vast armies of allies: Evil Babylon and the kings of the world who love her will fall (Rev. 18:2, 19:18, 19). More importantly, God's angels will also conquer the power fueling the wicked Empire, as an angel imprisons Satan for 1,000 years in a sealed, bottomless pit (Rev. 20:1–3).

At this point in John's visions, Goodness is spread over earth. This occurs in the form of a "millennial" 1,000-year-long reign of Christ and the righteous martyrs who had been beheaded by Babylon, but who are now resurrected (Rev. 20:4). This "millennial kingdom" replaces the scope and reign of the former, Evil Babylon. Yet however wonderful it is, it turns out that ultimate Evil is hard to vanquish! Hence, in his revelations John then sees even further into this eschatological future, and he finds that Satan will arise just once more (Rev. 20:7).

As the text continues to unfold the future, one final cosmic Battle ensues. Satan deceives the nations at the four corners of the earth, "Gog and Magog," and they march against the city of the saints who have just ruled in the millennial kingdom (Rev. 20:7–10). This time, though, there is no battle. Fire – the ultimate appearance of God throughout the Bible, as at Sinai – comes down from heaven and consumes them (Rev. 20:9). Satan is thrown into a lake of fire: God's presence simply overwhelms Evil. The dead are brought out of "Death and Hades" and they are judged according to their works (Rev. 20:12, 13). Finally, Death and Hades themselves are destroyed in the lake of fire, along with those who deserve this destruction according to whether they have done wicked deeds in their lives (Rev. 20:10–15). In the end, God's presence burns up all wickedness and anything not pure enough to withstand pure Good. The Universe is saved!

## The lost message

Christianity and Islam both consider the New Testament and the Book of Revelation to be Scripture, that is, authoritative teachings from or about God. For some interpreters in these two faiths but not all, the Book of Revelation is prophecy not for John's time but for their own time. For such interpreters, the fact that the eschatological events haven't come to pass simply means that past interpreters were wrong and that *their* group is the one that finally has the correct meaning; the eschatological events are unfolding in their lifetimes.

When added to other social factors that I discuss in Chapter 3, this method of interpretation has resulted in the Book of Revelation being responsible, directly or indirectly, for massive amounts of violence. In fact, it is arguably the bloodiest book in history. Even today, groups and individuals as diverse as the Oklahoma City bombers and radical Islamist groups affiliated through the Al Qaeda network have each updated the Book of Revelation to apply to their own period and causes, using it to justify violence and brutality.

Since the events in The Apocalypse are depicted in richly evocative visual symbols, such groups are able to lift specific symbols out of context and find the referents in their own unfolding scenario.[11] But in this "cut and paste" updating of the Book of Revelation, *its original message is lost.* This is true for all groups that make it serve their own needs and time period, whether or not they are terrorists.

As the biblical scholar Richard Bauckham has noted, interpreters who assume that the Book of Revelation is addressed to later generations and not to a first-century audience neglect an important fact. The Apocalypse is a letter, specifically addressed to the situations of seven churches in first century Asia. Bauckham writes, "The special character of a letter as a literary genre is that it enables the writer to specify those to whom he or she is writing and to address their situation as specifically as he or she may wish."[12] And in fact, when this original message of the Book of Revelation is understood in its own historical context, it may hold tremendous theological and intellectual insights for modern readers.

The original setting in which the author "John" composed the Book of Revelation was around 90–95 CE and the Evil Empire of "Babylon" that he envisioned was certainly the Roman Empire. Many clues in the text indicate to the original audience that the author really had Rome in mind, but did not state it explicitly due to a justified fear of serious persecution. According to the fourth- century Christian historian Eusebius, the author wrote his book while in exile on the island of Patmos during the reign of the Roman Emperor Domitian (Eusebius *Ecclesiastical Histories* 3.17–20). The identification of the Empire as Rome is clear in the image of a "great whore who is sitting on a scarlet beast ... with seven heads and ten horns" (Rev. 17:3, 5). In the text, just after John witnesses this vision, an interpreting angel of Jesus Christ (see Rev. 22:8, 16) imparts a deep meaning of the vision, saying: "This calls for a mind that has wisdom." The angel then reveals the secret identity of the symbol, explaining, "the seven heads are seven mountains on which the woman is seated" (Rev 17:9). This is a patent reference to Rome, known in antiquity as the City of the Seven Hills. Since symbols by their very nature have multiple meanings, the angel continues, "also, they are seven kings, of whom five have fallen, one is living, and the one has not yet come" (Rev. 17:10). Simultaneously, the symbol is both Rome and the emperors of Rome.

Biblical scholars use such clues to date the time period in which the author received his visionary oracles and the subsequent composition of the Book of Revelation. Many scholars (e.g., Aune 1993, 2330) understand the reference to the "seven heads" who are "seven kings" as follows:

- first head/king=Nero (54–68 CE)
- second head/king=Galba (68–69)
- third head/king=Otho (69)
- fourth head/king=Vitellius (69)
- fifth head/king=Vespasian (69–79)
- sixth head/king=Titus (79–81)
- seventh head/king to come=Domitian (81–96).

In this majority scholarly view, the reckoning of the seven emperors begins with Nero, the Emperor who is the most famous for killing Christians, and ends with Domitian, the other Emperor that ancient histories testify also persecuted Christians.[13]

It is the larger than life Nero who blamed and killed Roman Christians for starting the fires that burned Rome, fires that he himself may have ordered. On June 8 in 68 CE, the Roman Senate deposed Nero, declaring him to be a public enemy. Nero committed suicide the next day, but few ever saw his corpse. Hence, for decades and in John's lifetime, "Elvis-like" myths surrounded him, claiming that he had been sighted. Some believed the *Nero redux*, or "Nero returns" myth that maintained he was not dead, while others held to the *Nero redivivus* or "Nero living again" myth that claimed that although dead, he would come to life again to rule (Scullard 1976; Trudinger 1987). Writing in the early part of the second century CE, the Roman writer Dio Chrysotom noted, "Even now everyone wishes that Nero were alive and most people actually believe it" (*Orations* 21.10; Aune 1998a, 738). For decades, false Neros appeared here and there, and edicts were posted under his name that continued to threaten his enemies after his death (Scullard 1976, 332).

Contrary to popular opinion, the Roman Emperors did not systematically persecute Christians until 250 CE. However, both Nero and Domitian were cruel exceptions to the rule.[14] In the mid-second century CE, the Christian Melito of Sardis wrote to the Emperor Marcus Aurelius, "The only emperors who were ever persuaded by malicious men to slander our teaching were Nero and Domitian, and from them arose the lie, and the unreasonable custom of falsely accusing Christians."[15] Thus, in their historical context, John's visions seem to anticipate that Domitian would be the seventh emperor at the Battle of Armageddon, with a revivified Nero someday present at the eschatological Battle of Gog and Magog.

The infamous number "666" also indicates that John had the Emperors Nero or Domitian in mind when he wrote about the first beast. In the Jewish tradition of *gematria*, numbers were also codes for words, since

Hebrew letters possess numerical equivalents. The author "John," most likely a Palestinian Jewish Christian (Aune 1997, 1), draws on this Jewish tradition when he writes that "the number of the name" (Rev. 13:17) is a code for a name. The obvious candidate for the name is Nero Caesar, which yields "666" when translated from Greek into Hebrew. (In rough English transliteration, *qsr nrwn*, such that *qsr*=360 plus *nrwn*=306.) [16] In fact, some early manuscripts of the New Testament list "616" as the number of the beast because the Latin form of "Nero Caesar" transliterated into Hebrew is spelled *nrw qsr*, which adds up to 616 (*nrw*=256 plus *qsr*=360) (Aune 1998a, 770–771).

Alternatively, one scholar has proposed that "666" refers to Domitian, based on the Greek numerical equivalents. The full name of Domitian, with titles, is found abbreviated on coins in a Greek phrase that may be represented in English as "A KAI DOMET SEB GE," which also adds up to 666, with "DOMET" short for "DOMETIANOS" or Domitian (Stauffer 1947). If correct, it would be fitting that the author would choose a code from a coin to be the symbol of the oppressive, rich Empire that ruled the world's economy.

Whether the referent is Nero or Domitian, according to The Apocalypse, the numerical code of 666 or 616 is clearly associated with money. It is to be branded on "all, great and small," allowing them buy and sell goods (Rev. 13:16–17). In the Book of Revelation, perhaps the main characteristic of "Babylon" is its vast wealth, including:

> cargo of gold, silver, jewels and pearls, fine linen, purple, silk and scarlet, all kinds of scented wood, all articles of ivory, all articles of costly wood, bronze, iron, and marble, cinnamon, spice, incense, myrrh, frankincense, wine, olive oil, choice flour and wheat, cattle and sheep, horses and chariots, slaves – and human lives.
>
> (Rev. 18:11–13)

In other words, The Apocalypse takes the view that the success and wealth of the Empire are built on war, slavery and oppression, "horses and chariots, slaves – and human lives" (Rev. 18:13). The Empire appears to be bountiful, but that prosperity is built on cruelty.

Whether John had the Emperor Nero or Domitian precisely had in mind as the referent of "666/616," his visions gave hope to the Christians who felt oppressed under the exploitative Roman Empire. The Apocalypse promises that someday there will be a divine intervention that will end the Empire and replace it with God's. The assumption is that the scale of this violent, exploitative situation of the Roman Empire is so vast that it must be powered by cosmic Evil, the Devil himself. The apocalyptic worldview holds, at its root, that the problem with the world is much bigger than any human can fix.[17] Only Divinity itself can rectify the brokenness of the universe.

**Humans as victims, not avengers**

Throughout The Apocalypse, righteous persons are identified as those who have been martyred, killed by Rome, just like Jesus was (Rev. 5:9, 6:9, 7:14, 20:4). This point is so misremembered that it is worth rereading. The righteous are not the ones fighting God's battle. They are the pacifists who, like Jesus, went to their deaths under the cruelty of the Roman Empire and who, like Jesus, did not fight back. If this message is missed, then the core point of the author (or, if one so inclines, of the Scripture) is lost.

This original message of The Apocalypse is a powerful and perennial one that can still have meaning for the oppressed today, although it may not be the meaning that many desire. It is certainly not the message embraced by revolutionaries, advocates of social change or, for that matter, terrorists who deem themselves to be righteous. In Revelation, the oppressed suffer against an almost unimaginably powerful Empire that is well loved throughout the world. They don't stand a chance. The Apocalypse proclaims that someday in the eschatological future, God will end their suffering through divine agency. In the meantime, they suffer, but they do not fight. The righteous are the pacifistic martyrs who are like Jesus, symbolized as a Lamb about whom the angels sing, "Worthy is the Lamb that was slaughtered!" (Rev. 5:12). Like Jesus himself, the elect "were slaughtered and by [their] blood ransomed for God saints from every tribe" (Rev. 5:9). Their robes are now "washed in the blood of the Lamb," the sacrifice of martyrdom (Rev. 7:14).

But God will not let this situation stand. In an eschatological righting of injustice, Rome's power will be brought low, the Lamb will be elevated, and his followers will rule in the millennial kingdom. Who will receive thrones to rule for a thousand years? Again, they are "the souls of those who had been beheaded for their testimony to Jesus" (Rev. 20:4). With this, The Apocalypse turns our common understanding on its head, claiming that the real way to wage war against oppressors is to wage peace through passive sacrifice and not through violence. Only this pacifism deserves divine intervention.

This is what the terrorist interpreters whom I mentioned earlier miss in their reading of The Apocalypse. In this book, *God never appoints a human being to kill anyone in order to mete out His justice.* The Apocalypse only describes two eschatological Divine Wars: one at Armageddon and one at Gog and Magog. These two battles are the only cases in the Book of Revelation that may be justifiably called "Holy Wars," with forces fighting on God's side. In the original version, these wars are fought by the Word of God, and God; never by humans.

On one side of the Battle of Armageddon are demonic spirits that come from the mouth of the Dragon (Satan), the mouth of the Beast (the Roman emperor), and the mouth of the false prophet – the second beast or a leader of the Roman Imperial religious cult (Rev. 16:12–14). The spirits assemble "the kings of the whole world" (Rev. 16:14) for battle at Har-megadon or Mount Megiddo (the Greek megadon transliterates the Hebrew m-g-d, commonly called Megiddo in English). The reader knows that "the merchants of the earth" are allied with these "kings of the whole world" because they weep and mourn when the City of Babylon/Rome is crushed by earthquakes, hailstones, and fire (Rev. 16:20; 18:11, 18). Thus, the side pitted against God represents the whole imperial, military, and economic forces of the earth combined, since at the time of the Roman Empire there are no godly Empires, according to The Apocalypse. But who fights them on the other side?

Combing through chapters 16–19, only these act on God's side: God, nature (earthquakes, huge hailstones weighing 100 pounds), angels (who make decrees, show John visions and interpret visions), the Word of God (an avenging rider who is a martyr) and "the armies of heaven" coming down from heaven on white horses (Rev. 19:11–16). In Christianity, the Word of God is typically understood to be Christ, but in some Muslim traditions he is viewed as the Mahdi. Whoever the figure, he is a martyr whose "robe is dipped in blood" (Rev. 19:13) and has a name that no one else knows (Rev. 19:12). His eyes are fire; he rides a white horse, comes from heaven, and has a sword coming from his mouth to strike down the nations so that he will rule (Rev. 19:11–16).

The armies of heaven either represent angels or the dead martyrs, who earlier in the text were told to wait for God to avenge them (Rev. 6:9). In my view as a biblical scholar, the "heavenly army" that accompanies the Word of God at Armageddon is probably angelic. They wear "white, pure linen" (Rev. 7:14), like the seven angels who emerge from the heavenly Temple in "white shining linen" (Rev. 15:6), and they ride white horses, like the "four horsemen of the Apocalypse," who are clearly angels (as are their horses) (Rev. 6:2). Moreover, the image of an angelic army appears throughout texts in the Bible as well as in early Jewish Scripture (e.g., Josh. 5:13–15, 2 Kings 6:17, Joel 2:2–11; Dan. 10:20–21, 2 Macc. 5:2–4).

In one biblical story, the prophet Elisha is present at a battle between Israel and the Arameans. When his attendant expresses alarm at the Arameans' military, their horses and chariots, Elisha prays for his eyes to be opened. Suddenly, he sees that Israel's side is being fought with *invisible* angelic horses and chariots of fire, God's very presence (2 Kings 6:15–23).[18] Similarly, the Book of Revelation claims that Rome or Babylon may have amassed legions of "horses and chariots" (Rev. 18:13), but the side of God has angelic armies on horseback.

However, even if the armies are intended to be the martyrs who have taken on angelic attributes in heaven, The Apocalypse studiously avoids attributing any decisive action to them. There is no battle imagery of the conflict and no role for the heavenly army in the conflict, except to follow the Word of God out of heaven (Rev. 19:14, 19:19–20:4). The Word of God and God conquer the enemy, while an angel from heaven locks away

Satan (Rev. 19:20–21, 20:1–3).[19] Moreover, in a part of narrative that seems to be told sequentially, it is *after all of these events* that "the souls of those who had been beheaded for their testimony to Jesus … came to life and reigned with Christ a thousand years" (Rev. 20:4). Therefore, after divine forces have done the conquering, the martyred righteous will come to life again to rule in the millennial kingdom.

Actually, there is one more force that fights on God's side and, surprisingly, it's the birds:

> Then I saw an angel standing in the sun, and with a loud voice he called to all the birds that fly in midheaven, 'Come, gather for the great supper of God, to eat the flesh of kings, the flesh of captains, the flesh of the mighty, the flesh of horses and their riders – flesh of all, both free and slave, both small and great.'
>
> (Rev 19:17–18)

Since they fly "in midheaven," the birds are not considered to be earthly creatures in The Apocalypse, reinforcing the point that *nothing* from the earth participates in the killing.[20]

Again, I invite skeptical readers to go to the Book of Revelation itself and read chapter 19. Pay close attention to what actually kills all these enemies of God, who represent imperialism, military might and economic wealth. They are consumed by fire, the perennial biblical manifestation of God (Rev. 19:20), and killed by the heavenly avenging Word of God figure (Rev. 19:21), after which "all the birds were gorged with their flesh" (Rev. 19:21). To be sure, this is not how this battle is typically recalled, or all biblical literalists would become Audubon Society members.

The Battle of Gog and Magog, as recounted in The Apocalypse, similarly lacks any earthly armies fighting on God's behalf.[21] On the side of Satan, finally loosed from a thousand-year prison, are "the nations at the four corners of the earth" (Rev. 20:8). Again, this symbolizes earthly imperial powers and military forces. This time, in the final battle to end all cosmic Evil, the *only* thing that conquers them is fire: "And fire came down from heaven and consumed them. And the devil who had deceived them was thrown into the lake of fire and sulfur" (Rev. 20:9–10).

Throughout the entire Bible, both in the Hebrew Bible or Old Testament and in the New Testament, fire is the premiere theophany or manifestation of the presence of God or his supreme angels.[22] It appears in the burning bush, the pillar of fire that led Israel by night, the LORD's descent on Mount Sinai, the throne vision of Isaiah, and at the top of the chariot that Ezekiel saw (Exod. 3:2, 13:21–22, 19:18; Isa. 6:1–6; Ezek. 1:4).[23] According to Matthew, John the Baptist states that Jesus will baptize with the Holy Spirit and with fire (Matt. 3:11), which is fulfilled in Acts when the disciples experience flames of fire descending on their heads at Pentecost (Acts 2:3). In popular culture, we associate Satan with fire and sulfur, but this is unbiblical. According to The Apocalypse, the devil is consigned to fire and sulfur because that is the consuming presence and judgment of God. In fact, Death and Hades will be "thrown into the lake of fire" as punishment (Rev. 20:14).

In contrast to the Holy Wars of Armageddon and Gog and Magog, the four angelic horsemen release human wars as destructive forces into the world, alongside famines, pestilences, and deaths by wild animals (Rev. 6:3–8). These are ordinary wars, however, that function as generalized forces of suffering – like the famines and wild lions. They are not "Holy Wars," and the people in these wars do not fight on God's side (Ezek. 38:21). That only happens in the two Divine Wars, in which the appointed killers on God's side are only God and the Word of God.

This point is missed repeatedly in a myriad of contemporary and even scholarly readings of the Book of Revelation.[24] A long history of misinformed medieval interpretations erroneously *replaced* the divine forces in God's two Holy Wars with human agents of retribution. That is why today it is commonplace to equate the heavenly armies automatically with earthly human armies, in contradiction to The Apocalypse. However, this mistaken reading ignores not just the identity of the avengers, but also the book's original identification of the righteous as pacifistic martyrs.

The righteous are not fighters, rather they are precisely identified as those who did not fight back under oppression. Their souls hide under the altar in heaven and cry out for justice, saying: "Sovereign Lord, holy and true, how long will it be before YOU judge and avenge our blood?" (Rev. 6:9). The answer that a divine voice gives is totally unsatisfactory from a human, militaristic point of view: "rest a little longer, until the number would be complete ... of their brothers and sisters who were soon to be killed as they themselves had been killed" (ibid.). In other words, God's answer is that these passive resisters are only a fraction of the waves of innocents who will be killed by the persecution of the Roman Empire. It will go on and on until an indeterminate amount of unfair death occurs – and this requires patience and martyrdom. However, The Apocalypse promises that someday soon God will avenge them through angelic armies, the figure of the Word of God and through fire – God's own presence. Divinity will do the killing, at the end of time. This may be an ethically problematic vision for other reasons, but it is a grave mistake to assume that The Apocalypse calls humans to kill for God.

It is indeed ironic that a book that has become the hallmark of violent religious terrorism was, in its original reading, a call to pacifism. See how explicit the angel of Jesus Christ is about this in the Book of Revelation:

> Let anyone who has an ear listen: If you are to be taken captive, into captivity you go; if you kill with the sword, with the sword you must be killed. Here is a call for the endurance and faith of the saints.
>
> (Rev. 13:9)

In its original context, The Apocalypse calls its followers to one action: actively waging peace.[25] This book that is Scripture for so many Christians and Muslims ironically equates pacifism with the endurance of oppression and having faith that God will act to transform the world. This is the only form of resistance it envisions against a global imperialistic, militaristic, and economic Empire. The righteous are to follow the example of Christ on the Roman cross, an innocent Lamb who is slaughtered.

Sadly, then, the Apocalypse has been misremembered for millennia. According to the Book of Revelation itself, only divine beings can solve the problem of Evil in the world and God's army is not earthly.

So when and how did this message change?

## Notes

1 All Bible quotations follow the New Revised Standard Version, or NRSV (Attridge 2006).
2 There have been many scholarly definitions of the literary genre "apocalypse." The most influential of these has been the result of a collective scholarly endeavor preserved in the biblical journal *Semeia* Vol. 14. John J. Collins, editor, *Apocalypse: Morphology of a Genre*, in *Semeia* 14 (Missoula, MT: Scholars Press, 1979). That definition identifies an apocalypse in early Judaism and early Christianity as:

> a genre of revelatory literature with a narrative framework, in which a revelation is mediated by an otherworldly being to a human recipient, disclosing a transcendent reality which is both temporal, insofar as it envisages eschatological salvation, and spatial insofar as it involves another, supernatural world.
>
> (Collins 1979, 9)

3 David Hellholm proposes a correction to the *Semeia 14* definition of "apocalypse," which is that it should attend to the function of apocalypse: "intended for a group in crisis with the purpose of exhortation and/or consolation by means of divine authority," (Hellholm 1986, 27). Collins' agreed with the addendum (Collins 2001, 33).
4 Most biblical scholars agree that the earliest Jewish apocalypse that is extant is "The Book of The Watchers," chapters 1–36 of the collection called *1 Enoch*, from approximately 250–300 BCE (Nickelsburg 2004). Mark 13 may be the earliest Christian apocalypse, predating the Book of Revelation by around two decades.
5 For decades, biblical scholars disagreed on whether the visions in apocalyptic literature are strictly fictional, or whether any real experiences lay behind the visions, which in turn were stylized as compositions. Early on, Michael Stone and Daniel Merkur argued that real visionary experiences lay behind the apocalyptic visionary accounts (Stone 2003, 2011, especially 92–62, 104; Merkur 1989, 2004, 343). More recently, the tide has turned in favor of locating the religious experiences behind apocalyptic visionary accounts, which does not imply that Revelation is a strict "record" of what John experienced in his vision, but only that a genuine visionary experience in some way informed the narrative. For this reason, I change tenses depending on the point of view of John the character in Revelation, whom we presume to be an autobiographical representation of the author, to some degree. Apocalypses

pose a difficulty with respect to tense, however, because the overarching plot of the narrative is a sequence of future events that are often described in the past tense, i.e., "I saw," "I heard."

6  Note that in Revelation 4:1, the door to the heavenly Temple stands open and a divine voice says "Come up here, and I will show you what must take place after this." John is "present" there in the heavenly temple in this visionary state and, then in chapter 11, he is told to measure the temple of God and the altar in the priests' court, but not the "court outside the temple ... for it is given over to the nations" (Rev. 11:2, 21:15; cf. Ezek. 40:3, 43:10–17, 47:4–5). If this temple in Revelation 11 is still the heavenly one, then the "outer court" is earth, temporarily given over to the nations, and John's vantage point for his other heavenly visions makes more sense (e.g., Rev. 11:16).

7  Throughout the ancient Near East and Mediterranean, the sea was a symbol for primordial forces of chaos that usually gave birth to monsters. See Psalm 74 and the Babylonian epic *Enuma Elish.*

8  Scholars who study the Book of Revelation agree that John sees the world as controlled by Evil and as broken, but, depending on their focus, they stress the fundamental problem in different ways. Adela Yarbro Collins insightfully argued that John and his community felt "relative deprivation," a pervasive dissatisfaction with Rome that resulted in a feeling of oppression (Collins 1984). Drawing on the work of Peter Berger, Thompson argues that Christians possessed "deviant knowledge" of the world that excluded them from the majority worldview, so that they formed a "cognitive minority" that was derided and dismissed by the Roman "cognitive majority" (Thompson 1990, 191–97). Royalty highlights the crisis surrounding authority within the Church, a view that is buttressed by the early visions directed at "Jezebel" (Royalty 1998, 33–34). Bauckham warns against treating the audience as a persecuted whole, noting that the letter of Revelation is addressed to seven different churches, not all of which felt oppressed (Bauckham 1993b, 15–16). There is also evidence of physical persecution of Christians during the reign of Domitian (Aune 1997, lxvi–vii).

9  Other scholars, notably Paolo Sacchi and Paul D. Hanson, perceive the core of apocalyptic literature to be revelation about how God would ultimately conquer evil (Sacchi 1990; Hanson, P.D. 1975).

10  Schüssler Fiorenza notes that John bitterly polemicizes against Christians who "adapt and acquiesce to the political powers," and instead takes a stand of "no compromise," concluding that he himself seems to have experienced suffering and exile (Schüssler Fiorenza 1985, 194–99). Similarly, Pagels points out that John directed his anger at both the Romans and the accommodating members of the Church (Pagels 2012, 35).

11  Ironically, Bauckham, and more fully and quite convincingly, Frilingos, locate the vivid visual imagery of Revelation in a cultural representation of Roman spectacle, including circuses, monuments, rituals, festivals, and other displays of Roman imperial power (Bauckham 1993b, 17–18; Frilingos 2004).

12  Bauckham notes that the meaning and coherency of the symbols depends on the context of the specific social, political, cultural, and religious world of the original readers, so that "it would be a serious mistake to understand the images of Revelation as timeless symbols" (Bauckham 1993b, 13, 19).

13  Rowland returns to the earlier, nineteenth century dating of the book, beginning with Augustus and counting through Nero, with The Apocalypse being written in the chaos after Nero's death (Rowland 1982, 403, 406). Aune also maintains that it was composed in this reign of Nero, in the 60s CE "or even earlier," while adding that this "first edition" was updated into its present form in the reign of Domitian, c.95 CE (Aune 1997, lvii–iii). This brings it into accord

with the testimony of the Church Father Irenaeus, *c.*180 CE, who claims it was written in the latter part of Domitian's reign.

14 Although Domitian may not have systematically targeted Christians, Eusebius testifies to persecutions, exiles (such as that of John), and martyrdoms of Christians during his reign (Eusebius, *Ecclesiastical Histories* 3.17–20; Thompson 1990, 16–17).

15 Eusebius (*Ecclesiastical Histories* 4.26.9) also similarly attested in Philostratus (*Vita Apollonius* 8.5) and Tertullian (*Ad. Nat. 1.7.8–9; Apol. 5:3–4*) (Aune 1997, lxvii–viii; Millar 1977, 555).

16 Although there are various ways of transliterating the Greek into Hebrew and Aramaic, an Aramaic manuscript from Wadi Murabba`at confirms that this transliteration of "Neron Caesar" or *qsr nrwn* was used (Aune 1998a, 770).

17 Thompson, drawing on Peter Berger, contributes an important insight about the "cognitive minority" stance of the intended audience not only of Revelation, but of any apocalypse. Even when the audience constitutes a majority of the population, the feeling of a being a "cognitive minority" that is dismissed by the prevailing cultural cognitive worldview contributes to a feeling of "crisis," if that is the right word, that is not confined to class, social group, economic status or political status (Thompson 1990, 195–96; Berger and Luckmann 1967; Berger 1970).

18 Several biblical passages warn against placing hope for victory in earthly military forces, dubbed "horses and chariots," instead of God's spiritual forces. See e.g., Isa. 31:3. That is why the prophets Elijah and Elisha are called "Israel's [real] chariots and horsemen," (2 Kings 2:12, 13:14).

19 To be clear, even if one thinks that the heavenly army is made up of the martyred saints, they come from heaven and they do not kill. As Aune notes, "Like other battles in the narrative of Revelation, this one omits any reference to the conflict itself and emphasizes only the capture or decimation of the enemy.... The army accompanying the rider ... apparently plays no part in the conflict." (Aune 1998b, 1065).

20 Note that other biblical traditions associate birds and angels, e.g., Elijah is fed by ravens and by an angel (1 Kings 17:6, 19:5–7).

21 The book of Revelation draws on but alters the tradition of Gog and Magog in Ezekiel 38–39. Here, God defeats the kings who oppose him by using earthquakes, fire, pestilence, rain, hailstones, "swords of all against their comrades" (Ezek. 38:21), birds, and the wild animals of the earth (Ezek. 39:4, 17–19). Again, this is not a series of "Holy Wars" in which the righteous fight for God, but rather the armies of the wicked turning against one another as a generalized force of suffering, alongside meteorological phenomena and death by wild animals. In the depiction of the "supper of God" at Armageddon, Revelation omits the swords of comrades as well as the wild animals, probably to make a point about the battle being a cosmic one that pits heaven against earth.

22 A close second is wind (Gen. 3:8, 2 Kings 2:11–12, Job 38–42, Ezek. 37:9).

23 LORD here translates the divine name YHWH (except in Hebrew), and not "Lord" which is Adonai.

24 In this reading of Revelation, I profoundly disagree with a few biblical scholars who interpret the 144,000 martyrs of Revelation 7 to be an army that reappears in chapters 17 and 19. This includes the work of Bauckham, which I greatly respect. Intriguingly, he bases his interpretation on the *War Scroll* of the Dead Sea Scroll sect. (Bauckham 1993b, 78, 104–105; 1993a, 210–37). However, that sect was quite different than the audience of Revelation. The 144,000 martyrs, those who "washed their robes and made them white by the blood of the Lamb," and who as a result stay before God's throne in the heavenly temple (Rev. 7:14–15), are not vengeful figures. Instead, they are those who are

comforted after their unjust death, such that "God will wipe away every tear from their eyes" (Rev. 7:17). The "heavenly armies" of Revelation 19:14 are just that. In my view, Bauckham had it right when he noted, "John's message is not, 'Do not resist!' It is, 'Resist! – but by witness and martyrdom, not by violence" (Bauckham 1993b, 92).
25 The phrase "actively waging peace" is from a 1989 Christmas Day sermon by Father Gary L. Rowe, formerly of Grace Episcopal Church, Newport News, Virginia.

## Bibliography

Attridge, Harold, ed. 2006. *NRSV, The HarperCollins Study Bible.* New York: Harper-Collins.

Aune, David E. 1993. "Revelation: Introduction." In *HarperCollins Study Bible: New Revised Standard Version.* New York: HarperCollins.

Aune, David E. 1997. *Revelation 1–5.* Word Biblical Commentary 52A. Dallas, TX: Word Books.

Aune, David E. 1998a. *Revelation 6–16.* Word Biblical Commentary 52B. Dallas TX: Word Books.

Aune, David. 1998b. *Revelation 17–22.* Word Biblical Commentary 52C. Dallas, TX: Word Books.

Bauckham, Richard J. 1993a. *The Climax of Prophecy: Studies on the Book of Revelation.* Edinburgh: T&T Clark.

Bauckham, Richard J. 1993b. *The Theology of the Book of Revelation.* Cambridge: Cambridge University Press.

Beal, Timothy. 2002. *Religion and Its Monsters.* New York: Routledge.

Berger, Peter. 1970. *A Rumor of Angels.* Garden City: Anchor.

Berger, Peter and Luckmann, Thomas. 1967. *The Social Construction of Reality.* Garden City: Anchor.

Butler, Sally A.L. 1998. *Mesopotamian Conceptions of Dreams and Dream Rituals. AOAT.* Vol. 258. Münster: Ugarit Verlag.

Collins, Adela Yarbro. 1984. *Crisis and Catharsis: The Power of The Apocalypse* Philadelphia: Westminster.

Collins, John J. 1979. *Apocalypse: The Morphology of a Genre. Semeia 14.* Missoula, MT: Scholars Press.

Collins, John J. 2001. *Seers, Sibyls and Sages in Hellenistic-Roman Judaism.* Boston: Brill.

Flannery-Dailey, Frances. 2004. *Dreamers, Scribes and Priests: Jewish Dreams from the Hellenistic and Roman Periods.* Leiden: Brill; Atlanta: Society of Biblical Literature Press.

Frilingos, Christopher A. 2004. *Spectacles of Empire: Monsters, Martrys, and the Book of Revelation.* Philadelphia: University of Pennsylvania Press.

Hanson, John S. 1980. "Dreams and Visions in the Graeco-Roman World and Early Christianity." In *Aufstieg und Niedergang der römischen Welt,* edited by W. Haase, II, 23/2: 1395–1427, 1422. Berlin, New York: de Gruyter.

Hanson, Paul D. 1975. *The Dawn of Apocalyptic.* Philadelphia: Fortress Press.

Hellholm, David. 1986. "The Problem of Apocalyptic Genre and The Apocalypse of John." *Early Christian Apocalypticism: Genre and Social* Setting, edited by Adela Yarbro Collins, *Semeia 36,* 13–64. Atlanta: Society of Biblical Literature Press.

Himmelfarb, Martha. 1993. *Ascent to Heaven in Jewish and Christian Apocalypses.* Oxford: Oxford University Press.

Merkur, Daniel. 1989. "The Visionary Practices of Jewish Apocalyptists." In *Psychoanalytic Study of Society* 14, edited by L.B. Boyer and S.A. Grolnick, 118–48. Hillsdale, NJ: The Analytic Press.

Merkur, Daniel. 2004. "The Visionary Practices of Jewish Apocalyptists." In *Psychology and the Bible: A New Way to Read the Scriptures. Volume II: From Genesis to Apocalyptic Vision,* edited by J. Harold Ellens, 317–47. Westport, CT: Praeger.

Millar, Fergus. 1977. *The Emperor in the Roman Word (31 B.C.–A.D. 337).* Ithaca, NY: Cornell University Press.

Nickelsburg, George W.E. 2004. *1 Enoch: A New Translation.* Minneapolis, MN: Fortress Press.

Noegel, Scott. 2007. *Nocturnal Ciphers. The Allusive Language of Dreams in the Ancient Near East.* American Oriental Series 89. New Haven, CT: American Oriental Society.

Oppenheim, Leo A. 1956. *The Interpretation of Dreams in the Ancient Near East: With a Translation of an Assyrian Dream-Book.* TAPS 46, 3. Philadelphia: American Philosophical Society.

Pagels, Elaine. 2012. *Revelations: Visions, Prophecy and Politics in the Book of Revelation.* New York: Viking.

Rowland, Christopher. 1982. *The Open Heaven: A Study of Apocalyptic in Judaism and Early Christianity.* New York: Crossroad.

Royalty, Robert. 1998. *Streets of Heaven: The Ideology of Wealth in The Apocalypse of John.* Macon, GA: Mercer University Press.

Sacchi, Paolo. 1990. *L'apocalittica guidaice e la sua storie.* Brescia: Paideia. In English translation, 1997. *Jewish Apocalyptic and its History.* Sheffield: Sheffield Academic Press.

Schüssler Fiorenza, Elizabeth. 1985. *The Book of Revelation: Justice and Judgment.* Philadelphia: Fortress.

Scullard, H.H. 1976. *From the Gracchi to Nero.* 4th ed. London: Methuen.

Stauffer, Ethelbert. 1947. "666." *Coniectanea neotestamentica* 11: 237–44.

Stone, Michael. 2003. "A Reconsideration of Apocalyptic Visions." *Harvard Theological Review* 96, 2: 167–80.

Stone, Michael. 2011. *Ancient Judaism: New Visions and Views.* Grand Rapids, MI: Eerdmans.

Szpakowska, Kasia. 1999. *Behind Closed Eyes: Dreams and Nightmares in Ancient Egypt.* Swansea: Classical Press of Wales.

Thompson, Leonard. 1990. *The Book of Revelation: Apocalypse and Empire.* New York: Oxford University Press.

Trudinger, P. 1987. "The 'Nero Redivivus' Rumour and the Date of The Apocalypse of John." *St Mark's Review* 131: 43–44.

Zgoll, Annette. 2006. *Traum und Welterleben im antiken Mesopotamien Traumtherorie und Traumpraxis im 3.-1. Jahrtausend v. Chr. Als Horizont einer Kulturgeschichte des Träumens.* Münster: Ugarit-Verlag.

# 2 By this sign will you conquer

## Transformations of the Book of Revelation

During the fourth century CE, the Roman Emperor Constantine ruled. Christianity was just one of many small religions to which Romans could turn and, although it had been illegal, it had become the favorite religion of Constantine's mother, Helena. According to the ancient historians, Lactantius and Eusebius, in 312 CE Constantine had a dream or vision in which he saw a sign and heard "By this sign of Christ you will conquer." At the Battle of the Milvian Bridge in Rome, fighting against another Roman Emperor named Maxentius, Constantine put the sign on all of his soldiers' shields. Not only did he win, but Maxentius was drowned in the Tiber river, thereby securing Constantine's ascension as sole Emperor.

It was ironic for a pacifist religion to be interpreted thusly as a religion of power, but it helped Christianity become legalized and quickly grow in influence in the Imperial court. On his deathbed, Constantine's worried mother, Helena, convinced him to renounce the many gods that he had previously worshipped, except for the God of Christianity, which (having derived from Judaism) claimed that there should be worship of only the one, true God. By the time of the rule of Emperor Theodosius in 380 CE, Christianity had become the official religion of the Roman Empire.

This would have been ironic to the point of absurdity for John of Patmos, who had surmised three centuries earlier that *Rome was the great Beast controlled by Satan.* Yet, the new Christian Empire did carry out one of John's wishes. The Beast, now officially Christian, vigorously stamped out competing forms of Christianity of which it did not approve. Councils decided what was acceptable "orthodoxy" from "heresy" by remembering the history of Christianity in a way that privileged their position as speaking for orthodoxy (Bauer 1971).[1]

This new, official Roman religion was no longer the same religion of Jesus, nor of the first generation of Christians, who were Jews who believed that Jesus was the Messiah (Acts 2:5, 22–42; 5:31, 42). Many biblical scholars have argued that Jesus himself was a Jewish countercultural revolutionary, who was strongly opposed to the values of the Roman Empire that eventually killed him (Horsley 1997, 2002). Some Jews, including his disciples, had placed hopes in Jesus as their future King who would overthrow Rome. This acclamation peaked in the form of a public display honoring him at a festival time, a particularly dangerous time for revolution in the eyes of Rome. According to the Gospels, the crowds welcomed Jesus into Jerusalem by waving palm fronds, proclaiming: "Blessed is the coming Kingdom of our father [King] David! Hosanna [Praise!] in the highest!" (Mark 11:10; Luke 19:38; Matt. 21:9). Biblical scholars, such as Paula Fredricksen, conclude that Roman officials would have surmised from the incident that Jesus would lead a revolt, as had several other Judeans of the early first century. They imposed on him crucifixion, the penalty for crimes against the state. As she further points out, one of the only points on which all gospels, both canonical and non-canonical agree, is that above Jesus' cross was a sign that read "King of the Jews," the charge for which he was crucified (Fredricksen 2000).[2]

The Romans had misunderstood. Jesus had indeed expected a radical reversal of the status quo, claiming that the poor and hungry would inherit the Kingdom, while the wealthy and full would be excluded (Luke 6:20–25). However, Jesus appeared to have in mind the eschatological Kingdom of God, not a physical kingdom as some of his disciples seemed to have expected (Mark 1:14, 8:31–32, 9:34, 10:35–37). Certainly, the Gospels remember Jesus as a pacifist who refused to take up arms, even against those who came to arrest and kill him (Luke 22:51; Matt. 26:52; John 18:11).[3] The Book of Revelation thus correctly remembers him as a martyred Lamb, since he had preached that we should "turn the other cheek" when attacked (Matt. 5:39, Luke 6:29).

Though preserved in the Scriptures, these peaceful and anti-imperialistic elements of Jesus' message did not square well with the propaganda of the wealthiest military Empire on earth. That Empire did not see the advantage in overturning the status quo. After the fourth century, Roman Christianity identified the Evil Babylon of Revelation not with Rome but with "the Jews," despite the fact that Jesus and all the apostles had been Jews. As Constantine's vision at the Milvian bridge already shows, Christ increasingly became identified less with the slain Lamb of Revelation and more with the avenging figure of the Word of God who kills with a sword from his mouth (Rev. 9:11–16).

This powerful portrait of Christ required a New Testament that included the Book of Revelation. In the mid-fourth century, the list of sacred Scriptures making up a "canon" of the New Testament was still fluid and most clerics' lists did *not* include the Book of Revelation. It was Bishop Athanasius of Alexandria of the newly legalized Christian religion who made it his campaign to fight against heretics and to set forth, on Easter in 367 CE, his approved list of "canonical books."[4] As biblical scholar Elaine Pagels points out, the canonical lists from many earlier Church leaders, and the lists from all the surviving contemporaries of Athanasius, *all omit the Book of Revelation* – and often only this book (Pagels 2012, 161).

In fact, many early Christian critics did not mince words when it came to their dislike of The Revelation According to John. Bishop Dionysius of Alexandria had lamented that some Egyptian Christians misinterpreted the book by reading it literally in terms of a thousand-year reign of Christ on earth (which would come later to be called the "millennial kingdom"). He also repeated other Christian criticisms that the book was "unintelligible, irrational, and the title false ... it is not John's, and it is not a revelation at all" (ibid., 162).

Bishop Athanasius was not a literalist, but interpreted The Apocalypse symbolically, as had his predecessor Dionysius. Having worked closely with Emperor Constantine, Athanasius no longer interpreted the Beast as an Empire and certainly not as Rome. Now, the Beast represented Christians deceived by the Devil, Christians who war against Christ unwittingly. "The great whore," Babylon, was heresy itself, and the destruction of the damned into the lake of fire heralded the destruction of his heretical enemies (ibid., 165). As Pagels astutely points out, Bishop Athanasius' interpretation of Revelation reflected his own struggles against heretics, such as the priest Arius. That priest had been his enemy ever since Athanasius, at age eighteen, had helped draft the Nicene Creed, making Arius' view of Jesus' divinity an official heresy (ibid., 138, 143).

## Onward Christian soldiers! A role for the Emperor and the Antichrist

In time, Roman interpretations of the Book of Revelation overturned the identity of Christians as pacifistic martyrs. Roman interpretations of the Book of Revelation changed the angelic armies in the Holy Wars to the Emperor's armies composed of the righteous. Rome went from being the villain of The Apocalypse to being the hero.

This is clearly evident in the *Tiburtina*, one of the versions written shortly after the death of Constantine in the middle of the fourth century CE. The plot is an improvisation of Revelation that flatters the Roman Emperor (Cohn 1970). In fact, the new Emperor Constans, the son of Constantine, takes the place of the Word of God.

In the *Tiburtina*, motifs and images from Revelation are rearranged in a new, updated plot. As the *Tiburtina* unfolds, there is first an age of plenty under Constans for 120 years, suggesting the kind of long life that the biblical antediluvian heroes enjoyed. Constans defeats the heathen cities and temples, much as the Word of God defeats the kings of earth in the Battle of Armageddon (Rev. 19:11–21). Unlike the Book of Revelation, *those who refuse conversion to Christianity, who are therefore on the side of Evil, die by the swords of the human armies.* The Jews are converted, recalling the 144,000 Jews in the Book of Revelation who are sealed (Rev. 7:1–8). Then the "Holy Sepulchre" shines forth from its Church, much like the heavenly Temple does in Revelation (Rev. 1:19), after which twenty-two peoples of

Gog and Magog arise (Rev. 20:7–9; Cohn 1957). Whereas in the Book of Revelation this battle is the final eschatological conflict fought by the fire of God Himself (Rev. 20:10), in the *Tiburtina*, it is *the Emperor and his human army* who defeat the forces of Gog and Magog. Hence, the Emperor Constans replaces the role of the Word of God at Armageddon and he replaces the role of God at Gog and Magog.

However, the *Tiburtina* had not entirely forgotten how the plot of Revelation proceeds, so the endtime events continue to unfold. After winning against the forces of Gog and Magog, Constans rides to Jerusalem to hand the Kingdom over to God (Cohn 1970). This incorporates another hugely influential apocalyptic text, Daniel 7, in which the Ancient of Days, a symbol for God, hands all kingdoms and authority over to "one like a Son of Man," traditionally understood in Christian circles to be Christ (Dan. 7:13–14). In other words, here is another case in the *Tiburtina* in which the Roman Emperor appropriates a divine role, but now it is not God who hands the world over to Christ, but *the Emperor* who hands the kingdom over to *God.* In this interpretation, the military leader has become indispensable to God. In some ways, Constans takes on a greater role than God Himself.

As the Roman *Tiburtina* continues, it elaborates on a figure that would influence apocalyptic interpreters down to our present day: the Antichrist. To most people's surprise, this figure does not appear in the Book of Revelation! Try as one might to find him, the Antichrist isn't in there. The term "anti-christos" or "against Christ" does appear briefly in the New Testament in 1 and 2 John, in both the singular and the plural forms as "those who are against Christ." In the context of 1 and 2 John, the terms refer to those who oppose the doctrine that Christ came in the flesh, an ancient Christian interpretation called docetism (later deemed a heresy). In the letters of John, "anti-christos" is a Christian with the wrong theology. However, early Roman Christian interpretations applied it to the Book of Revelation and saw the Antichrist as whole triad of the Dragon, the Beast, and the second beast, since these symbols could no longer function as Satan, the Roman Empire, and the Roman governmental and priestly cultus.

In the *Tiburtina*, "anti-christos" thus becomes a larger than life eschatological figure who opposes God in a cosmic battle. The Antichrist appears in the Temple in Jerusalem and the Lord sends the angel Michael to defeat him. Only then does Christ come again – so he does at least appear somewhere in this retelling of Revelation!

## The emergence of Christendom and more changes to apocalyptic Christianity

The Roman Empire more or less persisted as "Byzantium" in the Greek-speaking part of the Empire, from Greece to the East, until 1453. However, the Latin speaking part of the Roman Empire, from Italy to the West, began to fall already by the fifth century. Instead of conquering the tribes of Gog and Magog, the Western Roman Empire was itself conquered by a host of different "barbarian" tribes, as they were called, which included the Anglo-Saxons and the Franks. After a short unification in the year 800 of France, Germany, Italy, and the Low Countries under the newly chris-tened "Holy Roman Emperor" Charlemagne and a few of his Carolingian successors, the Vikings of Scandinavia and the Magyars of Eastern Europe proved once more that barbarians could seriously trouble the Holy Roman Empire (Asbridge 2010, 6).

In exchange, the official religion of the once mighty Roman Empire absorbed the tribal religions of its conquerors. The new pagan inhabitants converted to Latin Christianity, merging with it ideals of warfare derived from tribal Germanic, Frankish, Anglo-Saxon, and Viking roots. When cul-tures collide, transmission always occurs in both directions, as coins from Viking York England well testify: the "I" of "Petri" for Saint Peter is made of Odin the Allfather's hammer, the weapon of the god of warfare (ibid., 15).

Beginning with the Carolingians, bishops began "sponsoring and even directing brutal campaigns of conquest and conversion [to Latin Christi-anity] against the pagans of eastern Europe," and, by the year 1000 CE, it was common for Western Christian clergy to bless the conquerors, their weapons and their armor (ibid., 15). This was not "Christianity" but rather the militant "Christendom," a civilization that selectively remembered its own history in such a way as to distance itself from the realities of its inter-connectedness with Asia and "Islamdom" (Hodgson 1993, 1977). And as Latin speaking Christendom spread, it tended to turn the religion of Jesus into a warrior culture even more than the Romans had.[5]

What began to emerge in Western Europe around the turn of the first millennium was not a unified Empire, but a highly localized series of feudal societies clustering around multiple centers of a military aristo-cracy, the noble knights. In retrospect, the knights were a curious fusion that cannot be described too simply, motivated by materialistic greed for land and wealth, a desire for power and romantic glory, ideals about chiv-alry reserved for their own aristocratic class and, to one degree or another, pious Christian obedience. That they were an in-fighting, dangerous, armed aristocratic class whose energies required channeling was, in no small part, one motivation for the First Crusade.

## Christendom and the Book of Revelation: Holy Wars, Jerusalem as paradise, and fighting the Antichrist

Rather than just being the "age of the Crusades," the unromanticized history of the Middle Ages is a complex portrait of both conflict and cooperation that is still being unearthed (Kostick 2011). This complex portrait is vital in correcting against the popularity of the over-simplified portrait of a "clash of civilizations" (Huntingdon 1996), which has a deleterious effect on understanding the causes of, and solutions to, terrorism today. The period of the Crusades by "the West" against "the Muslim world" also saw peace treaties, mutual trade and benefit, intermarriage, the transmission of medical and artistic knowledge, and even the occasional political alliance against common enemies (Asbridge 2010, 175–80; Frenkel 2011). Medieval persons lived the reality of history. Propagandistic history cannot adequately represent the messy and complicated nature of human interaction.

However, the apocalyptic worldview is much neater than real history. It conveniently (although falsely) divides the world into two simple sides, Good and Evil, with no neutral in between (Rev. 3:16). As Europe looked back, the medieval period tended to be remembered not for its complex social interactions between different kinds of Islam and different personalities from various areas of Christian Europe, but rather for an oversimplified apocalyptic scenario that proved to be extremely potent in the imagination until today.

The historian Thomas Asbridge notes that the conflict between Latin Christendom and the Muslim world was not inevitable and, in some ways, the choice of Muslims as the enemy was an incidental choice for Pope Urban II (Asbridge 2010, 37). The concept of a Christian Holy War was also at first counterintuitive. Tancred, one of the leaders of the First Crusade, "burned with anxiety because the warfare he engaged in as a knight seemed to be contrary to the Lord's commands."[6] When Pope Urban II gave a sermon at Clermont in 1096 to mobilize the knights for a "Holy War," he had to argue, as his predecessor Pope Gregory VII had done unsuccessfully, that Christians could engage in crusading and still be good Christians.

As Pope Urban explained at Clermont, the goal of this war was twofold: to help their Eastern Orthodox brethren (the same brethren whom they would target in the Fourth Crusade of 1204) and to take back Jerusalem, the Holy Land, from the Muslims.[7] Unabashedly, the Pope made it clear that there were both materialistic and religious goals behind the First Crusade, as this Holy War would later come to be known. In his sermon at Clermont, Pope Urban was blunt about both aspirations:

> O bravest knights.... Let no possessions keep you back, no solicitude for your property.... There is not much wealth here and the soil scarcely yields enough to support you. On this account you kill and devour each other, and carry on war and mutually destroy each other. Let your hatred and quarrels cease, your civil wars come to an end, and all your dissensions stop. Step out on the road to the holy sepulcher, take the land from that wicked people [the Saracens or Muslims] and make it your own. That land which, as the scripture says, is flowing with milk and honey, God gave to the children of Israel.

> Jerusalem is the best of all lands, more fruitful than all others ... a
> second paradise of delights (account by Robert the Monk).
>
> (Allen and Amt 2003, 41)

Instead of their own infertile land, Pope Urban promised the knights the
land of milk and honey, or perhaps he had in mind Revelation's wealthy
New Jerusalem.

The Pope also motivated his noble crowd by appealing to the apocalyptic sentiment that had peaked in the decades after the first millennium.
In another account of his sermon at Clermont, the Pope suggests that
other Eastern lands (known as "Outremer") could be conquered in addition to Jerusalem, since the endtime was coming soon. In addition to combating the Muslims to reclaim the Holy Sepulchre in Jerusalem, the Pope
urged the knights to consider preparations for battle against the Antichrist
soon rising in the East: "For it is clear that Antichrist is to do battle not
with the Jews, not with the Gentiles; but, according to the etymology of his
name, he will attack Christians" (account by Guibert of Nogent) (Allen
and Amt 2003, 46). The knights' military campaign was thereby firmly
endowed with a higher, salvific purpose.

Pope Urban II's apocalyptic argument for the First Crusade still paled
in comparison to that of Peter the Hermit, a wandering prophet who was
so well revered that followers collected the hairs of his donkey as religious
relics (Asbridge 2010, 41; Cohn 1957, 62). It was said that Christ had
appeared to him in the Church of the Holy Sepulchre on a pilgrimage
and had given him a Heavenly Letter. After a tour fueled by apocalyptically infused sermons inspired by this Letter, Peter set off for Jerusalem in
the spring of 1096 with his own army, a "People's Crusade" of 15,000,
made up mostly of the poor (Asbridge 2010, 41; Cohn 1957, 63). They
were also poor in weaponry and military training. Most of them, except for
Peter, were slain as soon as they crossed into Muslim lands.

Stoked with apocalyptic fervor, popular Crusades would occasionally
break out in widespread, frenzied hysteria throughout the Middle Ages. The
venerable historian Norman Cohn identifies a particular set of social and
economic factors that repeatedly preceded the outbreak of apocalyptic
fervor spurring popular armies to join the official Christian Holy Wars.
These factors included: rapid economic and social change, a breakdown in
traditional family ties, frequent famines, a steep rise in urbanization, and a
new class of urban poor who possessed a growing recognition of their own
economic deprivation relative to others (Cohn 1970, 62–63). The poor had
always been poor, but now they had a new consciousness of their poverty.
An apocalyptic myth let the urban and landless poor find meaning in taking
up arms and roaming to foreign lands for reasons of cosmic proportion.

Being starved as well as illiterate, the peasants who took part in the Crusades had confused the Muslim-ruled city of Jerusalem with the *eschatological* New Jerusalem from the Book of Revelation displaying golden streets

and gates of jewels and pearls (Cohn 1970, 65; Royalty 1998). As Cohn relates,

> no wonder that when the masses of the poor set off on their long pilgrimage the children cried out at every town and castle: 'Is that Jerusalem?' – while high in the heavens there was seen a mysterious city with vast multitudes hurrying towards it.
>
> (Cohn 1970, 65)

In the popular imagination, Jerusalem was God's promise of plenty for the righteous Christians who fought the Evil hordes of Gog and Magog. They had almost nothing and they were promised nearly everything: wealth, food, salvation, and, according to Urban II, entry into heaven and the complete remission of sins for whomever died fighting for the cause.[8]

From the outset of the First Crusade, the public response to apocalyptic rallies calling for Holy War was simply astounding. As one historian notes, "Not since the distant glories of Rome had military forces of this size been assembled" (Asbridge 2010, 42). While contemporaries exaggerate the numbers of troops up to half a million, at least 60,000–100,000 Western Christians set off for the Holy Land, a shockingly large group for the time. In addition to around 7,000–10,000 knights, another 35,000–50,000 infantry troops, tens of thousands of non-combatants, women and children all marched forth (ibid.). In the minds of many of these Crusaders, they were acting out the Book of Revelation, fighting against Evil, the Antichrist, and the hordes of Gog and Magog.

One semi-legendary figure, King Tafur, explicitly adopted a role from the Book of Revelation. Assuming the mantle and name of the angel of death, the knight exchanged his armor for black sackcloth and his horse in favor of walking with a giant sickle, which was useful for actual killing as well as for symbolism (Rev. 14:15–19). His army consisted of the barefoot, starving peasants who had survived the ill-fated People's Crusade led by Peter the Hermit. They reportedly ate anything they could find, including roots, grass, and the corpses of their enemies. When the Tafur army entered battle in Syria and Palestine, they gnashed and clattered their teeth indicating that they meant to eat their enemies alive. This inspired sheer terror in the Muslim armies, who fled from them and called them "No Franks, but living devils" (Cohn 1970, 65–66).

## Muslim responses and the development of *jihad*

Just as the motivations for the Crusades were more complicated than popular history represents, in reality there was no single "Muslim response," despite the simplified *jihadist* portrait that Islamist extremists today project onto the era. Rather, for centuries, there was a series of regional responses to the Crusades that had various mixtures of revenge, political calculations, greed, and degrees of genuine religious piety (just as on the Christian side).

Theologically, there was justification in Islam for fighting back against the Crusaders. The Qur'an prescribes *jihad*, or struggle, and sees internal *jihad* against temptation as being the "greater *jihad*," the more important struggle, whereas external *jihad* or warfare is the "lesser *jihad*." External *jihad* is warranted, according to the Qur'an, only when it is defensive: "Fight in the way of Allah against those who fight against you, but begin not hostilities. Allah loves not the aggressors" (Qur'an 2:190).

Yet at first, despite the existing theological basis for defensive *jihad*, medieval Muslims in the Near East did not possess a concept of waging total *jihad* against the Crusaders. The idea of *jihad* in this sense coalesced only gradually, as a response to the scale, frequency, and severity of the Crusades. At the beginning of the First Crusade, the local Muslim populations underestimated the troops and failed to appreciate that the apocalyptic tenor of the Christian war would fuel many more campaigns. After the massacre in Jerusalem, Muslims in the Levant and the Holy Land made a plea to those in Baghdad for help, which was not forthcoming for years. The Iraqi poet Abu l-Muzaffar al-Abiwardi, living at the time of the First Crusade, expressed his outrage at this situation:

> Sons of Islam, behind you are battles in which heads rolled at your feet.
> Dare you slumber in the blessed shade of safety, where life is as soft as an orchard flower? ...
> This is war ...
> I see my people slow to raise the lance against the enemy: I see the Faith resting on feeble pillars.[9]
>
> (Abu l-Muzaffar, end of the twelfth century)

For the first few decades after the fall of the Syrian coastal plain, Jerusalem and Galilee, Muslim leaders in Damascus saw the problem in political rather than religious terms. They contracted a series of ceasefire arrangements with the Franks, including *muwada`a* (reconciliation), *muhadana* (armistice), and *munasafa* (equal division) (Riley-Smith 1978; Frenkel 2011, 32). As rounds of fighting continued to break out in the Levant, some Muslim commanders started using the idea of defensive *jihad* to mobilize their retaliation, taking on military titles such as "the tamer of the infidels and polytheists" and "defender of the religion" (Frenkel 2011, 37).[10]

From 1127 to 1192, under the unification of Syria under Zengi, Nur al-Din, and then Saladin, the religious language finally consolidated into a notion of *jihad* as Holy War (Friedman, 2011, 233–234). Like the bishops and apocalyptic preachers on the Christian side, Nur al-Din put forward Jerusalem as the goal of the whole struggle. By taking the military title "marshal of the armies" and the religious title of "subduer of the heretics," he too turned the struggle into a religious one that aimed to fight Evil (Frenkel 2011, 40). By the end of the century, Saladin had fully cultivated the portrait of himself as the "defender of Islam" and the champion of *jihad*, especially when he managed to retake Jerusalem.

The truth of history is, of course, always complicated on the human level. Even the successful and piously zealous Saladin would fight intra-Muslim wars and make multiple truces with the Franks in between his battles (Friedman 2011, 234). However, this medieval period solidified a concept of *jihad* that would be selectively remembered thereafter to perpetuate the simple apocalyptic portrait of a cosmic war of Good versus Evil. In the twentieth and twenty-first centuries, apocalyptic radicals, both Muslim and Christian, would construct an over-simplified history of medieval *jihad* as a unified Holy War of the Muslim realm pitted against the similarly unified and religious "Crusaders" and they would use the Book of Revelation in order to do so.

## Christendom's demonization of the Muslims and Jews

Drawn along by their own desperation, the promised wealth of Jerusalem and the pious importance of their impending fight against the Antichrist, the first Crusaders set off to the Holy Land with one goal in mind: to kill Muslims for Christendom. Some popular preachers, like Peter the Hermit, added another goal along the way: to kill Jews, too.

In order to motivate their listeners to war, both Pope Urban II and Peter the Hermit resorted to the time-honored tradition of demonizing the enemy. Thus at Clermont, the Pope declared that the Muslims were "a despised and base race, which worships demons."[11] Shortly after calling Christians to win back the Outremer lands for Christendom to fight the coming Antichrist, the Pope whipped up emotions with graphic descriptions of the purported atrocities of Muslims, such as giving the Eastern Christian pilgrims drinks that caused their bowels to burst so that they could search their intestines for gold and silver that they might have swallowed.[12]

Many scholars argue that, before the waves of Crusaders invaded the Muslim Levant, they had not had any prior contact with living Muslims or "Saracens," the name applied by Christians to all Muslims regardless of region (Kangas, 2011, 152). Latin Christian descriptions of Saracens portrayed them as monsters, "the race of Cain" and "sons of whores." Abbot Suger slandered them as "inhuman, crude and homicidal barbarians with a striking bodily resemblance to wolves and ravens as a visible mark of their perpetual shame" (Kangas 2011, 139; Abbot Suger 1992, Cap. 21, Plate 186, Col. 1319B). The popular biographies of "Mathomus," or Muhammad, drew largely on the derogatory imagination of their authors to pervert whatever source material they did obtain. For instance, the ridiculous explanation of Guibert of Nogent for why Muslims do not eat pork was an appalling tale of Mathomus having an epileptic fit, falling down, and being devoured by pigs, which thereafter became forbidden food (Kangas 2011, 144; Guibert of Nogent 1996, 99–100).

Regardless of such libel, in the eyes of Anna Comnena (1083–1148), the daughter of the Byzantine Emperor Alexius I whose request for aid had first prompted Pope Urban II's call to Holy War, the Crusaders' treatment of the Muslims was no less than shocking. Writing in *The Alexiad*, a biography of her Emperor father, Anna describes how the Norman contingent of Peter the Hermit's army attacked the region around Nicaea in Asia Minor (modern Turkey). She depicts them as "rioting most cruelly in every way. For they tore some of the children apart limb from limb and, piercing others through with wooden stakes, roasted them in fire," in addition to "every kind of torture" (Allen and Amt 2003, 58).

Unfortunately, Anna's account is somewhat believable. When the First Crusade finally overtook Jerusalem, the Christian armies committed a wide-scale massacre numbering in the tens of thousands, slaughtering nearly every Muslim man, woman, and child. The testimony of a Christian eyewitness clearly frames it as the Book of Revelation's portrait of angelic justice, writing:

> the horses waded in blood up to their knees, nay up to the bridle. It is a just and wonderful judgment of God that the same place [the area around the Temple] should receive the blood of those whose blasphemies it had so long carried up to God.
> (Cohn 1970, 68; Raymond of Aguilers, 1844–1895, III, 300)

This was not the Gospels' "turn the other cheek" ethic; it was a dramatization of the Book of Revelation on a human scale.

In the attack, Jews were killed alongside Muslims. The Jews of Jerusalem hid themselves in the synagogue and begged for their lives, but the Crusaders set it on fire and burned them all alive. The Christians hated the Jews for being "Christ killers" or "those who murdered God." It was a tradition that would continue until modern times.

The slaughter of the Jews did not just occur at destination's end. Populist preachers taught that killing a Jew who had refused baptism meant the remission of the killer's sins. Throughout Western Europe, mobs arose that decided to inaugurate their own crusade by killing "the enemy of the Lord in our midst." A twelfth-century historical account by Albert of Aachen relates what occurred after Peter the Hermit's army set off for the Holy Land:

> a large and innumerable host of Christians from diverse kingdoms and lands; namely, from the realms of France, England, Flanders, and Lorraine ... they rose in a spirit of cruelty against the Jewish people

scattered throughout these cities and slaughtered them without mercy, especially in the kingdom of Lorraine, asserting it to be the beginning of their expedition and their duty against the enemies of the Christian faith.

(account by Albert of Aachen, twelfth century,
in Allen and Amt 2003, 49)

Official Church doctrine held that Jews had to be converted before the Second Coming. Thus, Christian attackers throughout Europe gave Jewish men, women, and children the choice to be baptized or die. In this era before the Nazis, identification as a "Jew" was based on religion, rather than on false racial characteristics, and Jews could theoretically escape murder by being baptized as Christian. Most of the time, the Jews did not convert to the religion of their attackers, preferring instead to die.

The Jews who were thronged by Crusaders at Mainz in 1096 chose mass suicide, rather than receiving baptism or letting the Christians kill them. As apocalyptic fervor spread amongst the Christians of the town, the Jews hid on the property of a sympathetic local bishop, discussed the options, and prayed. According to a Jewish account, they too were religiously motivated, saying amongst themselves,

After all it is not right to criticize the acts of God – blessed be he and blessed be his name – who has given to us his Torah and a command to put ourselves to death, to kill ourselves for the unity of his holy name. Happy is anyone who is killed or slaughtered, who dies for the unity of the name, so that he is ready to enter the world to come, to dwell in the heavenly camp with the righteous … he exchanges the world of darkness for the world of light, the world of trouble for the world of joy, and the world that passes away for the world that lasts for all eternity.

(Solomon bar Samson, twelfth century, in Allen and Amt, 2003, 55)

As their former neighbors, now Crusaders, charged the gates and flooded the courtyard, the 700 Jews of Mainz willingly slew their children and then themselves.

In just a few months of 1096, Christians who were part of the "People's Crusade" had slaughtered 12,000 Jews throughout Europe in what historian Norman Cohn chillingly calls "the beginning of a tradition" (Cohn 1970, 103). Crusaders continued to kill Jews throughout France and Germany at the start of the Second Crusade in 1146 and in every crusade thereafter, both populist and official.

Some church officials, such as the abbot Bernard of Clairvaux who called for the Second Crusade, urged the Crusaders not to kill the Jews. His argument for leaving the "Christ killers" alive was because "they are living signs to us," existing to remind Christians constantly of the punishment due to evil people (dispersal out of their nation), which serves the purpose of saving more Gentiles. After the full number of Gentiles was saved, then "all Israel will be saved" (Rom. 11:25–26).[13] As future eschatological Christians, they were worthy of life.

## Apocalypse as genocidal reality

The Apocalypse has already been acted out time and again in history as genocide, since fantasy often frames and supports experiences of reality (Žižek 1997, 60, 66). From 1095 onward, the story was retold over and over throughout Christendom: fear and fight all of the Saracens and the Jews, for they are on the side of Satan and the Antichrist, whom they worship. Jews and Muslims were demonized in sermons and throughout medieval Christian art, in the psalters, sculptures, stained glass windows, and illuminated manuscripts of the Bible. Not infrequently, Christian art depicted Jews alongside Saracens and monsters, since all were the "Other" (Strickland 2003).

The message was impossible to escape anywhere in Christendom, creating a pervasive atmosphere of fear towards Jews and Muslims that would color any individual interfaith interactions. A medieval Christian pilgrim coming into Frankfurt in the fifteenth century would first pass through a fresco inside the northern tower of the Alte Brücke, the old bridge, depicting an imaginative warning of how the Jews' maliciously tortured Christian children. At the top, it showed a child being dismembered with tools as part of the "blood libel charge," the myth that Jews used the blood of Christian children in their Passover bread. The main part of the fresco showed Jews cavorting with the Devil, drinking pig excrement, and suckling from a pig, which they must love since they refuse to eat it (Jüedisches Museum 2015). These images of murdered Christian children, Jews associating with devils, and the "Judensau" or Jew pig, appeared in iconography throughout Europe.

At last, the hordes of "Gog and Magog" had an identity that would stick until the present day.

## Creating the Jewish scapegoat

The view that Jews deserved the punishment they received has had a long legacy. It certainly did not die out with Protestant Reformation of the sixteenth century. The Reformer Martin Luther demonized Jews perhaps even more than had the leaders of the Crusades:

> I have read and heard many stories about the Jews which agree with this judgment of Christ, namely, how they have poisoned wells, made assassinations, kidnapped children, as related before…. There are many other similar stories. For their kidnapping of children they have

often been burned at the stake or banished (as we already heard). I am well aware that they deny all of this. However, it all coincides with the judgment of Christ which declares that they are venomous, bitter, vindictive, tricky serpents, assassins, and children of the devil who sting and work harm stealthily wherever they cannot do it openly.

(Luther 1971 [1543])

Luther advocated "sharp mercy" for the Jews, which he likened to acting "like a good physician who, when gangrene has set proceeds without mercy to cut, saw, and burn flesh, veins, bone, and marrow" (Luther 1971 [1543]). As 3,000 in Israel were slain to save the rest of the people, Luther reasoned that the Jews should be beaten, put to work and their synagogues burned for the benefit of Christians.

Even today, the medieval fabrication of the blood libel charge still circulates amongst the extremist media of radical Islamists, who do not represent the vast majority of Islam, and in propaganda by white racist members of various Christian Identity hate groups, who do not represent most of Christianity. As the reader of this book will see, it is a curious fact that most of the diverse varieties of violent terrorists who adopt the Book of Revelation as prophecy for themselves – no matter what their country of origin or religion – share in demonizing Jews as the enemy.

The thoughtful reader who has followed this book from the beginning will certainly ask, "How did the villains of the Book of Revelation change from being identified as the Emperors of Rome to being cast as the Jewish people, when Jesus and his disciples were all Jews?"

The historical answer to why the Jews became the marginalized scapegoat of "Western" society concerns politics, economics, and religion. From late antiquity until the late eighteenth century, when the First Amendment of the American Bill of Rights in 1789 called for the separation of Church and state in America and the French Constitution did the same in 1791 in France, citizenship had always been tied to religion. Throughout the Middle Ages into the modern era, one needed to be either a Christian or a Muslim living in the correct Empire to have full citizenship. Thus, until the nineteenth century, Jews were always the disenfranchised minority, lacking the same legal protection as the majority.

No matter how much Jews might have contributed to their societies, this was their plight regarding citizenship. This political situation of European Jews left them unprotected, making them easy targets to blame when economic insecurities plagued the masses. As is the case for most minority populations, when economic times were good, Jews were accepted or even cherished for the gifts they brought to society. In fact, since Christians were not permitted to lend to other Christians with interest because of interpretations of Old Testament laws against usury, Jews were the only ones allowed to be in the banking industry. Other Jews lent their talents to crafts, medicine, and scholarship. When economic times were harsh, as they frequently were, the population's anger mounted and searched for a scapegoat among the non-citizens in their midst.

Kings, church officials, and others in charge recognized the value of this convenient outlet for the violent frustrations of the masses. Repeatedly, they banished all the Jews from European nations unless they submitted to Christian conversion: from England in 1290 (though they were later readmitted in 1656), from France in 1306, from Warsaw, Sicily, Lithuania and Portugal in 1483, and from Brandenburg, Germany, in 1510. "In 1492 Columbus sailed the ocean blue" ... and the Jews were evicted from the nation of Spain. Time and time again, those in charge of the Christian Empires realized that mass killings of Jews or mass expulsions of Jews had the same result: the Jews left behind homes, goods, and money, which could be distributed to exert a calming effect on non-Jewish populations. Consider the example of Philip II, who came to the throne of France in 1182, kicked out the Jews, and pacified the aristocracy with their lands and goods. Needing a solution to the Church's ban on Christian money-lenders, King Philip recalled the Jews to France in 1198 and placed them in banking positions as serfs specially appointed to the King (Cohn 1970).

This pattern of forced exile and attack created a long historical memory of propaganda against Jewish peoples, justified through rumor and slander. The phenomenon of societies scapegoating minorities in times of economic trouble is, sadly, axiomatic for the human species. More complicated to explain, is how the religion of a Jewish Messiah could change into the very ideology that justifies the oppression of the Jews, especially in an apocalyptic framework.

## Religious scapegoating: "the Jews killed Jesus"

For the remainder of this book, the apocalyptic theme of a Jewish conspiracy and the demonization of Jews will crop up again and again. It is important to backtrack historically for a moment in order to explore how the idea of Jews as "killers of Christ" finds its roots in the earliest days of the Church. Otherwise, it is too easy to forget that Jesus himself was a Jew, as were the disciples, and that crucifixion was a Roman punishment for treason.

Unlike today, the burning question for the first generation of Gentile converts to Christianity was "How *Jewish* do we need to be in order to be Christian?" Paul's exasperation with his converted Gentile churches in Galatia and Philippi was centered on their desire to be *devoutly Jewish* by keeping key points of the Jewish law, such as the kosher food system, keeping the Jewish festivals and undergoing circumcision (Gal. 2:11–14, 4:8–11, 5:11–12; Phil. 3:2–6). Particularly in the case of circumcision, Paul saw this as an obstacle that would deter conversion of the Gentiles and argued that they did not need to keep the Jewish law (Stendahl 1973).[14]

However, the portrait of the early Church that emerges in the New Testament is inconsistent with whether Christians should keep the Jewish law. The Book of Acts records that a great debate on this topic arose in the Jerusalem Church. They sent a letter with Paul and Barnabas to Antioch and other Gentiles in the Levant agreeing on a few "necessary rules" for being a Christian: to keep kosher and refrain from sexual immorality (e.g., Acts 15:1–35). Yet in Paul's letters, he claims that the church of Jerusalem had only asked one thing of his ministry, that they remember the poor. He also states that he opposed Peter "to his face" on the issue of keeping kosher (Gal. 2:6–13, 2:10, 6:12–13).

In the Gospel of Matthew, Jesus is pretty clear that the Jewish law should be kept strictly:

> Do not think that I have come to abolish the Law of Moses and the teachings of the prophets ... until heaven and earth pass away, not one stroke, not one letter will pass away from the law until all is accomplished. Therefore, whoever breaks one of the least of these commandments, and teaches others to do the same, will be called least in the kingdom of heaven; but whoever does them and teaches them will be called great in the kingdom of heaven. For I tell you, unless your righteousness *exceeds* that of the scribes and Pharisees, you will never enter the kingdom of heaven.[15]
>
> (Matt. 5:17–20)

However, Paul took a different view by maintaining that Gentiles did not need to keep the Jewish law (Gal. 3). Still, Paul was not "anti-Jewish," but rather saw Jewish law as an obstacle to Gentile conversion (Stendahl 1973). He believed that God had not rejected the Jewish people (Rom. 11:1–2) and he viewed Christians as grafted onto the first covenant (Rom. 9:24–26; 11:19–26).

Thus, it seems quite surprising that a religion that had grown out of Judaism came to assign blame for Jesus' death on all Jews for all time. Perhaps the most powerful impetus for the idea accidentally comes from the Gospels themselves. The earliest canonical Gospel, Mark, written *c.*70 CE, tells of the fickleness of "the crowd" who followed Jesus' ministry but then turned on him. Building on Mark's account, the author of the Gospel of Matthew portrays "the crowd" at Jesus' trial as yelling, "His death be on us and upon our children!" (Matt. 27:25). Of course, the crowd is Jewish, as is everyone in the story except for the Roman officials, including Jesus and his Jewish disciples. For Matthew, a Jewish Christian, this addition to the story appears to chronicle his deep emotion regarding the death of Jesus and perhaps an intra-religious fight with the Jews who rejected Jesus as the Jewish Messiah. It may even refer to the historical involvement of some Jewish Temple clergy who apparently did incite Rome to arrest Jesus (Fredricksen 2000). It was not, however, to place the blame for his death on all Jews for all time, especially when read in the light of the whole Gospel. Just a bit earlier, Jesus blessed the Jewish children, placing his hands on them and saying "the Kingdom of heaven belongs to such as these" (Matt. 19:14). There is no reason to think Jesus' blessing was revoked!

However, by the Middle Ages it had become commonplace to assert that "The Jews," all of them, were to be held responsible in perpetuity for killing Jesus. This was the reason used to justify the slaughter of countless Jews across Europe and the Holy Land during the Crusades. It is as ludicrous as saying that all Italians, the descendants of the Romans, are responsible for the death of Christ. The charge of "deicide" – that "the Jews" killed God – was not revoked formally by the Catholic Church until the *Nostra Aetate* document during the Second Vatican Council in 1965. To date, the fringe Catholic Traditionalist movement has not accepted Vatican II.

## The Middle Ages live again

The changes that the Middle Ages wrought on the Book of Revelation profoundly transformed how The Apocalypse would be remembered. From that point onward, the apocalyptic scenario would include a set of ideas not in the original text, including: Holy Wars fought by human armies, the legend of the Antichrist, the identification of the hordes of Gog and Magog as Jews and Muslims, a role for political leadership in exacting God's revenge on the wicked, the idea of a glorified Jerusalem as a war prize and the substitution of humans for the avenging angels of God's armies.

For some terrorists, it is still the Middle Ages.

### Anders Behring Breivik

On July 22, 2011 in two places in Norway, Anders Behring Breivik acted out a medieval fantasy by killing seventy-seven people, mostly children. His target was the liberal Norwegian establishment that advances multicultural tolerance, which worked against what Breivik believed to be his mission: to act as a member of the reconstituted Knights Templar to rid Europe of the Muslims. Court psychiatrists debated whether Breivik was insane at the time of the murders and therefore not capable of standing trial. Part of the controversy was the inability for most people to imagine that a man who systematically gunned down sixty-nine children could possibly be sane. The eventual court decision that he was sane, and therefore culpable, moved the world closer to recognizing that horrendous atrocities can be committed by otherwise reasonable people acting out an apocalyptic fantasy.

By his own account, Breivik spent nine years writing his 1,518 page "compendium" or manifesto, *2083: A European Declaration of Independence.*

Published online in 2011 just before the murders, he signs its Foreword with his alias, Andrew Berwick, as follows:

> Sincere and patriotic regards,
> Andrew Berwick, London, England – 2011
> Justiciar Knight Commander for Knights Templar Europe and one of several leaders of the National and pan-European Patriotic Resistance Movement/With the assistance from brothers and sisters in England, France, Germany, Sweden, Austria, Italy, Spain, Finland, Belgium, the Netherlands, Denmark, the US etc.
>
> (Breivik 2011, 17)

The cover is emblazoned with a red cross on a white background, costume of the medieval crusading Knights Templar. In the self-aggrandizing Appendix, Breivik includes photos of himself clothed in various regalia emblazoned with the Crusader cross, including a military uniform, hazmat suit, and military special operations clothing (Breivik 2011, 1511–1513).

The Knights Templar was a medieval military order founded in the early twelfth century, shortly after the victorious conquest of Jerusalem in the First Crusade, and charged by the Roman Catholic Church with the protection of Latin Christian pilgrims traveling to the Holy Land. Purportedly, the Knights set up headquarters in the "Temple of Solomon," the captured Al-Aqsa Mosque in Jerusalem. The monastic order grew until it had a fairly large membership that included many highly skilled Crusader knights. Breivik claimed that the order had been reconstituted in London in 2002 with twelve members, representing various Western European countries and the Balkans (Breivik 2011, 827). Section 1.11 of his compendium is entitled "What the Crusades Were Really Like" and Breivik defends the legitimacy of the Crusades in the face of a perceived Muslim onslaught, which he sees as occurring now in the form of multiculturalism and liberal humanism.

It is unclear whether there really is a reconstituted Knights Templar of a few radical persons or if it just exists in Breivik's own mind. Regardless, the stated mission reveals this terrorist's goals: including a "100 year plan to contribute to seize political power in Western European countries currently controlled by anti-nationalists [cultural Marxist/multiculturalist regimes]," to "service and protect the indigenous people of Europe" and to "stop the ongoing European cultural and demographical genocide facilitated by the cultural Marxists/multiculturalists, suicidal humanists, and capitalist globalist elites." As for all apocalyptic believers, in Breivik's mind, the goal to "disallow the Muslim invasion/colonization of Europe" is defensive. As a member of an "international Christian military order," Breivik believes that, like the medieval knights of the Crusades, he represents a beleaguered European population under attack from outside forces, resulting in what he calls the "Islamisation of Europe."

Breivik's own words demonstrate how the Book of Revelation, which was used in the Middle Ages to justify killing Muslims, still spawns the same hatred today:

> We need to bring back a crystal clear vision and goal for our [European] existence whether it is a formal embracing of research and development, nationalist principles or the former [referent unclear] intertwined with spirituality under a permanent Christian cultural framework. "And I looked, and behold a pale horse: and his name that sat on him was death, and Hell followed with him." Revelations 6:8.
>
> (Breivik 2011, 1223)

For Breivik, the Crusades are repeating themselves, and he is engaged in a holy struggle against Evil.

And unfortunately, he is not the only terrorist who believes this to be the case.

### Al Qaeda and the Crusaders

Al Qaeda, the most well-known Islamist terrorist group, is actually a network of affiliated radical Islamists who believe that they are fighting in a Crusade-like period. They too believe that a giant battle between "the West" and "the Muslim world" rages on, with the difference that they are fighting on the other side. Like Breivik, they believe they are being persecuted by the encroachment of another cultural and political system, only for them it is "Western." Like Breivik, Al Qaeda feels that its terrorist actions are defensive, despite the terrorism that both commit, because the threat of multiculturalism and interreligious dialogue is so grave. And also like Breivik, they do not know the actual classical medieval scriptures of their tradition well, but rather a selectively constructed, censored history of their own tradition, drawn in broad apocalyptic strokes.[16]

In 1998, a number of radical Islamists and future terrorists, including Osama bin Laden and Ayman al-Zawahiri, Al Qaeda's number one and two at the time, were signatories to an article entitled "The World Islamic Front's Declaration to wage *Jihad* Against the Jews and Crusaders," published in the Arabic newspaper *Al-Quds Al-Arabi*. In this document, they explained that we are living in a unique age: "Never since Allah made the Arabian Peninsula flat, created its desert, and encircled it with seas has it been stormed by any force like the Crusader hordes that have spread in it like locusts" (February 23, 1998).[17]

For the signatories, the "Crusader hordes" are still at it.[18]

To apocalypticists, the goal of bringing about God's Kingdom is more important than anything or anyone existing here and now. In the case of militant apocalypticism, this means that you kill in order to fight Evil. This turns the original Book of Revelation, with its pacifist martyrs awaiting divine intervention, completely upside down. Even more surprisingly, it turns upside down the Qur'an's proscription against aggressing in warfare. Nevertheless, in the minds of the members of Al Qaeda, they are the right-eous ones, seeking to live under true Islamic law and to bring about a pan-Islamic state in which everyone will live in this way. By their horrible actions, including 9/11, they believe that they are acting out God's plan, since they are convinced that the West is wicked and controlled by Satan.

In fact, the only thing that Al Qaeda hates more than the West is moderate Islam, which is why it has murdered eight times more Muslims than non-Muslims to date. In 2002, Osama bin Laden addressed a letter, "Moderate Islam is a Prostration to the West," to moderate Muslim leaders in Saudi Arabia who had sought multicultural discussions and interfaith dialogue with Americans. In this letter, not intended for Western eyes, he identified the real core of what motivated his external *jihad*, the violent struggle against those whom he considered to be "the infidels." As he iden-tified this center of "what the debate truly revolves around," and by this he meant the debate between radical and moderate Islam, he put warfare in an apocalyptic framework:

> But what's more important, and what the debate truly revolves around, and what the [moderate Muslims] shy away from mentioning, is the word of the Messenger [Muhammad] as has been relayed by Ahmad and others from Ibn Omar: "I have been sent *in the final hours with the sword*, so that none is worshipped but Allah alone, partnerless. My pro-vision has been provided under the shadow of my spear, and humili-ation and contempt is upon whoever opposes my command."[19]

In other words, like the medieval Crusaders whom he loathed, bin Laden believed that we are living in the endtimes and that he was engaged in a Holy War.

In such a militant apocalyptic scenario, there are only two sides: Good (God) and Evil (Satan). The belief that anyone against them must be on the side of Evil is what drove both Osama bin Laden and Anders Breivik to commit mass murder. In the next chapter, I outline the contemporary translation of the apocalyptic worldview that motivated them and still motivates legions of other terrorists, from ISIL/ISIS to armed Christian anti-federalists in America. I also explain how to tell a peaceful apocalypti-cist from a violent one.

## Notes

1 The many authors in Kirk and Thatcher's landmark volume introduced social memory theory broadly to biblical studies. Social memory theory points out that all collective memories are constructed in ways that reflect the impinging concerns of the present and that often reinforce contested social areas of power (Kirk and Thatcher, 2005). The early fourth century Church councils,

for instance, labeled as heretics numerous groups who considered themselves to be true Christians, such as various gnostics, Valentinians, Sabians, Arians, docetics, Jewish Christians, and so forth.

2  Paula Fredricksen examines the Christian tradition that blames "Jews" in general for Jesus' death, and she carefully lays out the canonical evidence that Romans killed Jesus, with the support of the few ruling Jewish Temple elite (Fredricksen 2000).

3  According to Matthew, Jesus did claim that he did not "come to bring peace to the world ... but a sword" (Matt. 10:34), but he appears to refer to the division in families and society that would occur in light of the proclamation of the coming eschatological Kingdom of God.

4  No "New Testament" was canonized until the Church finally accepted the official list at the Synod of Hippo Regius in 393 CE.

5  Jesus' vision of poverty, equal distribution of wealth, simplicity, celibacy, and pacifism was not forgotten, however. It was taken up by the monastic orders, such as the Franciscans and Dominicans, who were idealized as imitating the life of Christ, while the majority of Christians were not expected to live as strictly.

6  Ralph of Caen, *Gesta Tancredi* (Riley-Smith 1986, 36).

7  In Christianity, Augustine had first laid the foundation for the idea of a "just" war, waged under precise conditions, which was compatible with the Christian faith. Pope Gregory VII had tried unsuccessfully to mobilize the "Knights of St. Peter" to fight the Muslims on behalf of the Greek church, but his campaign was twenty years too early to gain support.

8  From the account of Urban II's call for the crusade at Clermont, according to Fulcher of Chartes (Allen and Amt 2003, 40).

9  Abu l-Muzaffar al-Abiwardi on the Fall of Jerusalem (Allen and Amt 2003, 79–80).

10  Frenkel cites inscriptions from *Repertoire Chronologique d'Epigraphie Arabe* VIII.236 (##3122).

11  Fulcher of Chartes (Allen and Amt 2003, 40).

12  Ibid.

13  Bernard of Clairvaux (Allen and Amt 2003, 137).

14  The best articulation of this is still by Stendahl 1973, who argues that Paul, like other people in his time period, was concerned with the salvation of groups of people, not individuals, as in how to get the Gentiles into the Jewish covenant.

15  In this Gospel Jesus is sometimes shown tightening the observance of the Law, contrary to the popular portrait of Jesus that rather has Paul in mind! See Matt. 5:21–32. In this Gospel, when Jesus does appear to contravene the Law, it is only because he interprets the Law through his thorough knowledge of it in a way that fulfills the intent of it (Matt. 12:3–8).

16  Qureshi and Sells make the point that contemporary Islamic militants do not know the classical Muslim traditions, but, like Fundamentalists in other religions, they reconstruct the tradition without knowledge of history or scholarship (Qureshi and Sells, 2003), 1–48.

17  Signatories, "Al-Qaeda's Declaration of War Against Americans" (Ibrahim 2007, 11–16).

18  Does the imagery of swarms of locusts also recall the fifth angel who blew his trumpet in Revelation, bringing up soldier locusts from the pit of hell? (Rev. 9:1–11.)

19  Osama bin Laden, "Moderate Islam is a Prostration to the West" (Ibrahim 2007, 17–62, italics added for emphasis).

# Bibliography

Abbot Suger of Saint Denis. 1992. *The Deeds of Louis the Fat*, translated by Richard Cusimano and John Moorhead. Washington: Catholic University of America Press.

Allen, S.J. and Amt, Emilie, eds. 2003. *The Crusades: A Reader*. Ontario: Broadview Press.

Asbridge, Thomas. 2010. *The Crusades: The Authoritative History of the War for the Holy Land*. New York: HarperCollins.

Bauer, Walter. 1971 [1934]. *Orthodoxy and Heresy in Earliest Christianity*, edited and translated by Robert Kraft and Gerhard Krodel. Philadelphia: Fortress.

Breivik, Anders. 2011. *2083: A European Declaration of Independence*.

Cohn, Norman. 1970 [1957]. *The Pursuit of the Millennium*, Revised and expanded edition. New York: Oxford University Press.

Fredricksen, Paula. 2000. *Jesus of Nazareth, King of the Jews: A Jewish Life and the Emergence of Christianity*. New York: Vintage Books.

Friedman, Yvonne. 2011. "Peacemaking: Perceptions and Practices in the Medieval Latin East." In *The Crusades and the Near East: Cultural Histories*, edited by Conor Kostick, 131–160. New York: Routledge.

Frenkel, Yehoshua. 2011. "Muslim Responses to the Frankish Dominion in the Near East, 1098–1291." In *The Crusades and the Near East: Cultural Histories*, edited by Conor Kostick, 27–54. New York: Routledge.

Guibert of Nogent. 1996. *Dei Gesta per Francos*, edited and translated by R.B.C. Huygens. *Corpus Christianorum Continuatio Medievalis* 77a. Turnhout: Brepols.

Hodgson, Marshall G.S. 1993. *Rethinking World History: Essays on Europe, Islam, and World History*. Cambridge: Cambridge University Press.

Hodgson, Marshall G.S. 1997. *Venture of Islam*. Vols 1–3. Chicago: University of Chicago Press.

Horsley, Richard. 1997. *Paul and Empire: Religion and Power in Roman Imperial Society*. London: T&T Clark.

Horsley, Richard. 2002. *Jesus and Empire: The Kingdom of God and the New World Disorder*. Minneapolis: Fortress Press.

Huntingdon, Samuel P. 1996. *The Clash of Civilizations and the Remaking of World Order*. New York: Touchstone.

Ibrahim, Raymond, ed. 1007. *The Al Qaeda Reader*. New York: Broadway.

Jüedisches Museum Frankfurt Main. 2015. "Permanent Exhibitions." Accessed February 2, 2015, http://juedischesmuseum.de/127.html?&L=1.

Kangas, Sini. 2011. "*Inimicus Dei et Sanctae Christianitatis?* Saracens and their Prophet in Twelfth-century Crusade Propaganda and Western Travesties of Muhammad's Life." In *The Crusades and the Near East: Cultural Histories*, edited by Conor Kostick, 131–160. New York: Routledge.

Kirk, Alan and Thatcher, Tom (eds.). 2005. *Memory, Tradition, and Text: Uses of the Past in Early Christianity*. Atlanta: Society of Biblical Literature.

Kostick, Conor, ed. 2011. *The Crusades and the Near East: Cultural Histories*. New York: Routledge.

Luther, Martin. 1971 [1543]. "On the Jews and Their Lies." In *Luther's Works*, translated by Martin H. Bertram. Vol. 47. Minneapolis, MN: Augsburg Fortress.

Pagels, Elaine. 2012. *Revelations: Visions, Prophecy and Politics in the Book of Revelation*. New York: Viking.

Pippen, Tina. 1999. *Apocalyptic Bodies: The Biblical End of the World in Text and Image*. London: Routledge.

Qureshi, Emran and Sells, Michael A. 2003. "Introduction: Constructing the Muslim Enemy." In *The New Crusades: Constructing the Muslim Enemy*, edited by Emran Qureshi and Michael A. Sells. New York: Columbia University Press.

Raymond of Aguilers. 1844–1895. *Historia Francorum qui ceperunt Iherusalem*. In *Recueil des Historiens des Croisades, Historiens Occidentaux*. Vol. III. Paris: Académie des Inscriptions et Belles-Lettres.

Raymond of Aguilers. 1968. *Historia Francorum qui ceperunt Iherusalem*, translated by John Hugh Hill and Laurita L. Hill. *Memoirs of the American Philosophy Society*. Vol. 71. Philadephia: American Philosophical Society.

Riley-Smith, Jonathan. 1978. "Peace Never Established: The Case of the Kingdom of Jerusalem." *Transactions of the Royal Historical Society*, 28: 99–101.

Riley-Smith, Jonathan. 1986. *The First Crusade and the Idea of Crusading*. Philadelphia: University of Pennsylvania Press.

Royalty, Robert M. *The Streets of Heaven: The Theology of Wealth in the Apocalypse of John*. Mercer University Press, 1998.

Stendahl, Krister. 1973. *Paul Among the Jews and Gentiles*. Philadelphia: Fortress Press.

Strickland, Debra Higgs. 2003. *Saracens, Demons, and Jews: Making Monsters in Medieval Art*. Princeton, NJ: Princeton University Press.

Žižek, Slavoj. 1997. *The Plague of Fantasies*. New York: Verso.

# Part II

# The apocalyptic formula and terrorism

# 3   How not to make a terrorist

## Peaceful vs. radical apocalypticism

If a suspected terrorist is deemed to be mentally sound, as is most often the case (Post 2007), then the common starting point for counter-terrorism experts is to assume that he or she thinks in a rational manner. Too often, this unconsciously means "acting as we would act." We recognize that a suspected terrorist might not value human life in the same way as we do, have the same ethics regarding the harming of innocents, or even have the desire to preserve his/her own life. However, we still assume that there are certain core goals that any rational player should share, such as the preservation of his/her own group, nation or members of his/her religion. In the case of a militant apocalyptic believer, however, this analytic assumption could be dead wrong. That is because radical apocalypticism works according to its own brand of rationality.

Most people holding apocalyptic beliefs are not violent. It is the case that a sizeable number of Americans maintain some apocalyptic beliefs to varying degrees. If we use the expectation of Jesus' imminent return by 2050 as a measure of apocalyptic fervor, 41 percent of Americans say this will "probably" occur and up to 79 percent believe that Jesus will return "someday" (Pew 2010, 2009). The US is an apocalyptic nation, but the vast majority of Americans would not employ violence in conjunction with these beliefs. There is no inherent relationship between apocalypticism of this variety and violence.

On the other hand, many terrorists are not only apocalyptic, they commit acts of terrorism *due to* their apocalyptic beliefs. And while there are very few terrorists in the world, they can cause significant loss of life and property and generate much psychological fear.

Hence, we must be able to distinguish between peaceful apocalyptic frameworks and militant ones, and identify the factors that drive peaceful apocalyptic believers to commit violence.

### The need for a new understanding of the role of religion

Most scholars, policy makers, intelligence analysts, and journalists vastly underestimated the power of religion as a motivating force in the 1979

Iranian Islamic Revolution and the 2010–11 wave of Arab Spring revolts, all of which took the non-Islamic "West" by surprise.[1] In part, this is due to a tendency for many in "Western" regions, such as America, Canada, Europe, Australia, and New Zealand, to underestimate the power of religion to spur broad social change. This was the conclusion of intelligence specialist Robert Jervis when speaking of the 1979 Islamic Revolution:

> The main difficulty was that [intelligence] analysts, like everyone else at the time, underestimated the potential if not existing role of religion in many societies ... *it still seemed inconceivable that anything as retrograde as religion, especially fundamentalist religion could be crucial* ... it is difficult for most people living in a secular culture to empathize with and fully understand religious beliefs – especially when the religion is foreign to them.
>
> (Jervis 2010, 25, 39)

As the children of democracies founded on the separation of Church and state, particularly in America, political religion can be a kind of blind spot for us.

In Europe, Canada, Australia, and New Zealand, there is a tendency for the intelligence community to discuss religion as an isolated system of "beliefs and practices," divorced from political and material interests. This makes it particularly difficult to understand the worldview underlying theocracies, Islamist democracies, or, as in the case of Iran, an Islamic Republic (Flannery *et al.* 2013). Definitions of terrorism often stress political motivations, but typically distinguish this from religious goals (Hoffman 2006, 34, 40; 22 US Code, Sec. 2656 f(d)).

Decades ago, sociologist Clifford Geertz put forward a helpful definition of religion of religion as *a cultural system.* He defined religion as a set of symbols that creates an overarching construction of reality. As a way of conceiving of the general order of existence itself, a religion tends to appear to be *uniquely realistic* to its adherents as the only possible explanation of reality. Hence, religion can powerfully motivate its adherents to act in certain ways that are coherent within that worldview (Geertz 1973, 5).[2]

This starting point for defining "religion" is especially helpful in the case of apocalyptic religion. Perhaps even more so than other religious systems, the apocalyptic revelation appears to be uniquely realistic to its adherents. As a way of organizing reality, the revelation is usually all encompassing, including morality, economics, views on the environment, social relations, law, cultural histories, the ethics of violence, gender roles, food preparation and consumption, dress, and even the weather. *As a matter of course, it envisions the imminent arrival of a new political system,* and thus cannot be separated neatly from politics. Without a thorough understanding of religion, we miss the entire conceptual framework within which an apocalyptic group, leader or nation might operate. Additionally, we miss that their "religious" goals may also impact their views of politics, society, gender, violence, economics, law, and so forth.

## Religion as the context for "rational" action

Immediately after 9/11, a question was repeated in the media: "Why are they attacking us?" or, in other words, "Why do they hate us?" (Zakaria 2001). In fact, Al Qaeda had explained in print (albeit in Arabic) three years earlier why they believe that they are at war with America and why they feel that America started it.

Five radical Islamist signatories, including Sheikh Osama bin Muhammad bin Laden and Ayman al-Zawahiri, signed "The World Islamic Front's Declaration to wage *Jihad* Against the Jews and Crusaders," issued February 23, 1998 in the Arabic newspaper *Al-Quds Al-Arabi*. Bin Laden and al-Zawahiri would go on to become the number one and two leaders of Al Qaeda. In the article, they specifically list their grievances against the "Jews and Crusaders" – that is, Israel and America and their allies – whom they believe are assaulting Islam. The *jihadists*'[3] list of grievances against America at first appears to be political: America's military occupation of the Arabian peninsula, over one million deaths in the Iraq (Persian Gulf) war, our allegiance with Israel and what the signatories claim is our goal to fragment the remaining Muslim states of the Middle East and Africa. However, the *jihadists* clearly cast the grievances in religious terms, stating, "All these crimes and sins committed by the Americans are a clear declaration of war on Allah, His Messenger, and the Muslims" (Ibrahim 2007, 11).[4]

This is why Al Qaeda would later claim, against the view of the vast majority of Muslims, that the heinous terrorism of 9/11 was a *defensive* act against American aggression. To Americans, this reasoning is mind-boggling, an utterly ridiculous statement. Yet from Al Qaeda's point of view, they were the victims. This claim is not a deception, it is an apocalyptic claim. In 2002, Osama bin Laden published an open letter to the American people titled "Why We are Fighting You." In part it reads: "Why are we fighting and opposing you? The answer is very simple. 1. Because you attacked us and continue to attack us" (Bin Laden 2002).

In the "Buckle of the Bible Belt" in Arkansas where I was living at the time of the 9/11 attacks, people wondered out loud and in print what Osama bin Laden *really wanted*. Was it political power, money, or increased status and influence? Perhaps, most surmised, he was just crazy. Behind this idea is the assumption that religions promote non-violence or at least respect for all human life. These expectations are entirely understandable from a non-apocalyptic or a peaceful apocalyptic context, such as is the case with most of Islam. Almost all of the world's 1.7 billion Muslims firmly reject the terrorism of Al Qaeda. In part, this is because the Qur'an forbids both suicide and violence against innocents, especially children and women, and it arguably does so more clearly than the Bible.

However, religion in general also has a violence-producing side (Rapoport 1992, 118). Militant Islamists, like those in Al Qaeda and ISIL/ISIS, interpret the religion of Islam quite differently than do 95–99 percent of the world's Muslims. While the *jihadists* might claim to value human life, they rationalize acts of violence by deeming their enemies to be subhuman or by deciding that human life is of a lesser concern than their greater cause. They interpret their own aggression and violence as defensive action. They strive to *upset* the status quo of society and to work for goals that often compete with the welfare of their national interests. And, yet, by psychological standards, they are normally not mentally ill, as despicable as their acts may be (Post 2007; Weatherston and Moran 2003). As one terrorism expert concludes, "the outstanding common characteristic of terrorists is their normality" (Crenshaw 1981).

This is an important point to reiterate, because many older discussions of terrorism, including academic ones, connect it automatically with mental illness. This is especially easy to do when emotions flare up, such as when the world witnesses videos of members of ISIL/ISIS beheading innocents or using children as assassins. We conclude, in terrible shock and dismay, that those people must be crazy.

The influence of this pathology model of terrorism was rampant in scholarship in the 1970s and 1980s (Weatherston and Moran 2003). For instance, in his book on terrorism, Parry confidently asserts, "most political terrorists have not been normal" and "not all political terrorists are insane or mentally disturbed, but most are" (Parry 1976). In a later article, he wrote, "most terrorists are crazy, they have to be crazy" (Parry 1977). Similarly, Pearce advises his intended audience of police negotiators to treat the terrorist as "an aggressive psychopath, who has espoused some particular cause because extremist causes can provide an external focal point for all the things that have gone wrong in his life" (Pearce 1977).

Truly, the reality is much more complicated. Victoroff concluded that only rudimentary psychological assessments of terrorists had been conducted as of 2005. He warned that: "Terrorist behavior is probably always determined by a combination of innate factors, biological factors, early developmental factors, cognitive factors, temperament, environmental influences, and group dynamics" (Victoroff 2005, 34). Weatherston and Moran add that distinctions must be made between those with mental health problems who become terrorists and those who develop problems due to the stress of "the terrorist lifestyle" (Weatherston and Moran 2003, 708).

The reader may be getting angry that I am asking us to consider that some terrorists may be rational. However, we will *never* be able to combat terrorism effectively if we end up with the frustrated conclusion: "Well, they're just crazy!" Instead, we must grasp the apocalyptic logic by which their rationality operates. In order to conduct effective analysis, and to end terrorism in the long term, we *must* consider the goals, worldview, motivations, and ethics of the terrorists themselves.

Geertz' definition of religion as a cultural system highlights the fact that actions based on religious motivations *can very well seem irrational to out-siders, while at the same time being rational and reasonable within a given religious framework*. This is the irony of cultural counter-terrorism – we have to learn to have cultural sensitivity and empathy (though not sympathy) with people who hate us and often want to kill us, in order to stop them. It isn't easy at all.

But there is a lot at stake. As we move forward with foreign policy and counter-terrorism actions, Americans and Europeans still often have a tough time recognizing that terrorists do not share our assumptions. However, rational views in non-apocalyptic thinking are irrational from an apocalyptic viewpoint and vice versa.

## The long reach of apocalypticism

The apocalyptic traditions of early Judaism and early Christianity have become a worldwide phenomenon lasting for millennia. "Apocalypticism" is a scholarly term for a thought system that exists across many religions as well as in secular variations. Apocalypticism is totalistic in scope, ordering all societal relationships, providing key aspects of self-identity and inform-ing an adherent's view of reality itself. For a person who has a mild affinity for apocalypticism, this worldview may compete with their other concep-tual systems, including political and social concerns. However, the dedic-ated apocalyptic believer understands all aspects of reality in terms of how they fit into an overarching apocalyptic framework.

It is important to note that the term "apocalyptic" is an *etic* one. It derives from outside of the religious or secular tradition under study, from scholars like me who wish to highlight certain features in the worldview under examination. Oftentimes apocalyptic believers themselves might not characterize their beliefs as "apocalyptic." This is especially true for secular variations of the system and some may bristle at my use of the term to apply to their particular religion or tradition, which they view as unique. I well understand this. Each contemporary apocalyptic culture adapts an inherited apocalyptic framework in particular ways that make it unique in some respects and any full analysis of a particular group should examine its historical context and the nuances of its belief system.

However, hundreds of very distinct groups still share certain features of an "apocalyptic thought system" that remains remarkably similar across cultures. Just as in the original Book of Revelation, the primary supposi-tion of an apocalyptic worldview is that the mundane world is profoundly influenced by Evil (Sacchi 1990; Hanson 1975). From group to group, Evil is viewed as embodying different forms: Satan, capitalism, humanity, tech-nology, other races, evil aliens. Whatever the form, the belief that the world is broken and ruled by Evil remains potent for adherents of the tradition.

In the apocalyptic worldview, a revelation, disclosing that the way things seem to be is not the ultimate reality, ensues from the divine realm to a human recipient through various means (Collins 1979). Rather, there is a transcendent realm, in which God or higher beings rule, with the promise that this better realm will someday dramatically replace ordinary reality. In the groups that we will examine in this book, this transcendent realm takes on different forms. It could be variously conceived of as heaven, the Kingdom of God, the Mahdi's kingdom on earth, the rule of pure white people in America, the rule of pure black people in America, the comeback of Nature after the annihilation of humankind or another planet to which the righteous will be transported. Whatever form it takes, this utopia is coming soon.

In other words, the overarching structure of Abrahamic apocalypticism remains the same, but, like a rendition of "Twinkle, Twinkle, Little Star" played in different jazz renditions, the melody remains while being significantly tweaked. If you didn't know "Twinkle Twinkle," you'd probably miss it because the renditions sound so different. Yet, once you know the original tune, it is recognizable in a hundred different forms.

So it is with the apocalyptic worldview.

## Formula for apocalypticism

A peaceful apocalyptic believer accepts the following three "reality propositions":[5]

1  *A secret about the nature of this world*: The ordinary, mundane world is broken and unduly influenced by evil of some kind, locked in a struggle with goodness.
2  *A secret about the state of the righteous*: The righteous are oppressed, while the wicked flourish, although appearances may be to the contrary.
3a *A secret about another higher or future world*: There is a transcendent world in which justice, peace and happiness reign. It is either a place somewhere out there that the righteous will go to someday, or it is a world that will someday come to the righteous.
3b *A secret about the future*: At a special time, the gap between the mundane world and the transcendent one will be closed. A higher power from that transcendent world will intervene through some figures of divine deliverance, acting as intermediaries between ordinary humans and the transcendent world (e.g., Christ, the Jewish Messiah, the Muslim Mahdi, angels, good aliens or ascended Masters). Through this endtime intervention, the righteous will be rewarded and they will partake of the divine realm. History, as we know it, will be transformed and Evil will come to an end.

The basic outlook of this peaceful version of apocalyptic thought is pretty simple. It affirms that there is deep pain about the way this world runs.

This view hopes for a divine, perfect world and a better, utopian time when good people finally get what they deserve. It's easy to see why this thought system has had such broad appeal.

Since this thought system assumes that human effort does not ultimately transform our world, the apocalyptic worldview leads to different social ethics than do non-apocalyptic ones. Generally, if one fervently believed that a divinely-led end to history would unfold very soon, there would be less reason to invest in long-term efforts regarding better health care, the environment, pollution, sustainable energy, or the restructuring of social inequality or income disparity. In apocalyptic logic, the divine realm is going to change it all anyway. Apocalyptic believers can be compassionate – they might engage in feeding the poor, for instance, to alleviate suffering right now. However such temporary measures are different than having a long-term, future-oriented vision, such as fighting climate change or investing in our grandchildren's futures through sustainable eco-cities. This is because fervent apocalyptic believers genuinely believe that this earth is passing away.[6]

Apocalyptic believers tend to divide the world's inhabitants into two groups: those who know and abide by the revelations and those who don't and fight them. Apocalyptic believers regard those in their own camp who are not strict enough as hypocrites, essentially "out-group" members who are not righteous/saved/enlightened.

Moreover, believers in the apocalyptic thought system take comfort in knowing the world is not as it appears and another realm will restore justice. Like John of Patmos, the cosmic secrets revealed to them completely change the way they look at this mundane world. They are convinced that they know about matters such as the identity of the real rulers of the earth, unknown events coming in time, hidden spatial locations, secrets regarding human identity or the real nature and significance of worldly events and conflicts (Rowland 1982, 9, 14–17; Flannery-Dailey 2006, 231–248). Apocalyptic leaders who continue to receive revelations from the otherworldly realm, as well as apocalyptic *interpreters* of the original revelations (such as the Book of Revelation or the Qur'an), can gain tremendous authority in their communities.

People who share an apocalyptic worldview want above all to bridge the gap between this mundane world and the transcendent realm. In peaceful versions of the apocalyptic system, they believe that they have no influence over the timing of when these two become one, when "the Kingdom of God is on earth as it is in heaven."[7] They can only patiently wait for the divine deliverance to come, perhaps striving to be as holy as possible in the meantime and to alleviate the present suffering of others. Only rarely do they accept the message in the original Book of Revelation, that enduring suffering is their form of peaceful resistance in this world.

The scholarly term for "beliefs about the endtime" is "eschatology." I call this outlook, waiting for an endtime without influencing when it will occur, "*passive eschatology*." Of the 41 percent of Americans who believe that Jesus will return by 2050, most have a *passive eschatology*, patiently waiting for the endtime as they live their faith as well as they can. They aren't passive Christians – they might try to alleviate the suffering of others or strive to save others through conversion – but they believe that the timing of Jesus' Second Coming is out of their hands. They don't believe they can speed it up or slow it down; it just isn't up to them. With such a major part of their worldview being out of their control, Christians with a *passive eschatology* often quote Jesus' statement that "No one knows about that day or hour, not even the angels in heaven, nor the Son, but only the Father" (Matt. 24:36; Mark 13:32; Acts 1:7).

Depending on the variety of this apocalyptic system, the agents of deliverance can take different forms. They could be as diverse as angels, Christ, a female Christ, the Jewish Messiah, the Muslim Mahdi, a benevolent race of aliens or even sentient artificial intelligence. The agents relay a revelation to the representative(s) of the elect, perhaps in the form of visions, new interpretations of revelations or insights that reveal the world is not as it seems. The expectation is that these agents will conquer evil and/or usher in the new age of goodness in a utopian, fair, and happy world.

It should be noted that the utopia may not be the *ultimate* end to history. Instead, there may be a new, "divinely" ordered society that is so different from what came before that it qualifies as eschatology. Drawing on the influence of the Book of Revelation, the pure era is often expected to arrive after the battle at Armageddon. That era may be as short as a few years long, a thousand years long as stated in Revelation, or as long as 10,000 years. It is characterized as a period of purity unlike any other, led by an enlightened or perfected being or group. Eventually, the era ends with the final climatic battle against the kings of Gog and Magog, paving the way for God's permanent rescue of the world.

## Formula for radical apocalypticism

By examining hundreds of violent examples of apocalyptic groups, I have identified four additional reality propositions that, when taken altogether, typically characterize apocalyptic groups with violent tendencies. These features have a propensity to belong to a thought system of radical apocalypticism, with leanings toward violent behavior, rather than peaceful forms of apocalypticism, maintaining belief in the reality propositions discussed earlier.

Radical apocalyptic believers accept all of the reality propositions just mentioned (a secret about the world, the righteous, and a higher future world), but they hold them to a more extreme degree. If a peaceful believer in apocalypticism experiences good and evil as an explanation of the world, the radical apocalyptic believer experiences ultimate Good and ultimate Evil. If a peaceful believer in apocalypticism sometimes feels that the righteous are oppressed, the radical apocalyptic believer feels persecuted to a greater degree and can name the enemy clearly as a concrete, real foe.

The fourth proposition is the belief that only the radical apocalyptic group knows the truth, the real interpretations and revelations secret from or misunderstood by others:

4    *Authoritative Revelation/Interpretation:* Divine revelation or the authoritative interpretation of original revelation (e.g., the Bible, the Qur'an or hadith, the US Constitution) is ongoing to our group's leaders.

Alone, this belief does not lead to violence by itself, although it may lead to exclusivist attitudes and social tensions with those outside the group. However, combined with the next three reality propositions, violence becomes more likely:

5    *Active Eschatology:* Our actions are key to ushering in the new stage of the coming Good world. I, as a righteous person, can trigger the end of the Evil age through my actions, especially through eliminating Evil on earth. (Note: this involves the presumption that "I am Good" or at least acting on the behalf of the Good.) This will bring about divine intervention and the age of God/Goodness.

In contrast to *passive eschatology, active eschatology* holds that the actions of the righteous can trigger the imminent intervention of the endtime. The cosmic role that an active eschatologist believes that he or she plays elevates his or her own importance to national, global or even universal proportions. This alone provides the apocalyptic believer with a kind of unparalleled power, such that their actions lie outside the scope of normal human judgment. In addition, the lofty goal – the capacity to bring about divine intervention and an era of Goodness through eliminating Evil – might justify the means that he or she uses to eliminate Evil. In other words, for an active eschatologist, the fate of the world is at stake and he or she can play the key role in ending the current corrupt system.

With just two more propositions, the ideology of radical apocalypticism is complete:

6    *"Othering"/Concretized Evil:* Those who are not with us are against us and belong to "Evil." The revelation that we have received allows us to identify this enemy. They are irredeemable, while we represent the side of God/the Good.

The sixth reality proposition goes further than just recognizing that people do evil things. Clearly, that is the case. Peaceful apocalyptic believers would readily acknowledge that there are evil people who make bad choices and harm others. Rather, this radical apocalyptic proposition involves a level of deep hatred directed at those who are understood as being totally "Other" and totally "Evil." The Evil is a concrete enemy, someone real and identifiable.

Typically, the process of "Othering" contributes to the radical apocalyptic group's collective identity and solidarity. When there is a "them," there is more easily an "us." The strong communal bond that members experience can be one of the greatest motivations for adhering to the radical apocalyptic view or justifying acts of violence:

7   *Redemptive Violence/Revenge.* Violence is somehow redemptive, whether self-martyrdom or the killing of others. We know when and how the Good world emerges and our violence is necessary to bring this Good world into existence. Our enemies have wronged us and our revenge is God's will (or at least in the interests of the transcendent world). Our vengeance serves a higher purpose.

The scriptural basis of many religions, including all of the Abrahamic traditions, may be interpreted as validating the idea of righteous, redemptive violence (Juergensmeyer 2003). The Torah in Judaism has examples of *herem*, or the wholesale slaughter of every man, woman, and child, found in the accounts of the conquest of Canaan by Israel (Deut. 20:16). In a historical-critical reading, this story may be told in the context of a retrojected war fantasy (Collins 2004, 159–82).[8] However, for radical apocalypticists, the story justifies slaughtering God's enemies over land. For example, although rabbinic law places the greatest value on human life in too many examples to enumerate, the Jewish extremist Yigal Amir killed Israeli Prime Minister Yitzhak Rabin for reaching political comprises with the Palestinians. In his preliminary court hearing, when asked if he acted alone, Amir answered, "It was God" (*CNN* 1995; Karpin and Friedman 1998).

Redemptive violence appears in Christianity, as the Book of Revelation's destructive interpretation has led to more wars and genocides than any other single book. Additionally, in Luke, Jesus seems to tell his disciples to arm themselves: "And the one who has no sword must sell his cloak and buy one" (Luke 22:35–38). This odd verse conflicts with the messages of Jesus to "turn the other cheek" and "love your enemies." Hence, New Testament scholars believe the passage appears either as irony, an interpolation by a later editor, a potential path that Jesus subsequently discards or as a one-time event. As we will see in Chapter 6, militant Christians see the verse as a justification for taking up arms against their enemies.

In the case of Islam, violence is allowed under certain conditions. Influenced by the media, many non-Muslims mistakenly assume there is much more inherent violence in the Qur'an than in the Jewish and Christian

Bible. The Qur'an contains the apocalyptic worldview, as I will discuss in the next chapter, but it is framed in terms of God's future judgment, not humankind's. The name Islam means "peace" and the Qur'an strongly forbids offensive *jihad* or the struggle against evil, stating: "Aggress not, for Allah [God] loves not the aggressors" (2:190–193).

Although forbidding offensive *jihad*, the Qur'an does mandate violence in the case of defensive *jihad*:

> And fight in the way of God with those
> Who fight with you, but aggress not: God loves not the aggressors.
> ... [but] slay them [the aggressors] wherever you come upon them,
> And expel them from where they expelled you;
> [Their] Persecution [of you, of Islam] is more grievous than [your]
>     slaying [them].
> But fight them not by the Holy Mosque
> Until they should fight you there;
> Then, if they fight you, slay them-
> Such is the recompense of unbelievers –
> But if they give over, surely God is
> All-forgiving, All-compassionate.
> Fight them, till there is no persecution
> And the religion is God's.
>
> (2:190–193; Arberry 1955, 53–54)

Most Muslims interpret this excerpt from the sura called "The Cow" as mandating peace, except in the gravest cases of self-defense where the existence of Islam is at stake. In radical Islamist readings, by contrast, the same passage is used to justify attacking enemies wherever they may be, as we will see in Chapter 4.

Even Buddhism, which is often rightly thought of as a supremely peaceful religion, may be construed as having a theology of redemptive violence, as I show in Chapter 8 for the group Aum Shinrikyo. The guru of this dangerous group selected elements of Buddhism and fused them with apocalyptic Christianity, resulting in an *Active Eschatology* that sought to trigger Armageddon for the sake of eliminating the world's bad karma.[9]

Thus, many religions contain theologies that may be interpreted by radical apocalypticists in a violent manner. Feeding the idea of redemptive violence is the conviction of radical apocalyptic terrorists that violence is justified for wrongs that they or others have experienced. The scholar Louise Richardson has wisely stated, "The most powerful theme in any conversation with terrorists past or present, leader or follower, religious or secular, left wing or right wing, male or female, young or old, is revenge" (Richardson 2006). When a group deeply feels the need for revenge over some real or imagined wrongs, religion not only justifies acts of revenge, it also imbues them with divine authority.

Vengeance thus becomes an act of piety. This is aptly captured in the words of Suhail al-Hindi in a martyr book that he compiled after the death of his younger brother, the Palestinian *shahid* or suicide bomber Abu-Surur:

> That day he was born for revenge … revenge for me and for my country and my people and the honor of the umma. Revenge for Majdal from which my parents were forced to flee, despite their passionate love of their soil, despite their sweat and blood, despite their huge love of its soil. Yes he will take revenge, he will take revenge, he will take revenge, Allah permitting.
>
> (Oliver and Steinberg 2005, 148)

Radical apocalyptic thinking turns revenge into a divine calling.

## Casting conflict as a cosmic war

In addition to my formula for radical apocalypticism, another helpful tool for understanding when a religious group will be violent stems from the work of religion and sociology scholar, Mark Juergensmeyer. He found that when religious groups envision conflict as a scenario of "cosmic war," they are likely to become violent (Juergensmeyer 2003, 148–66). Cosmic wars, according to Juergensmeyer,

> are larger than life … evoke great battles of the legendary past … relate to metaphysical conflicts between good and evil … are intimately personal but can also be translated to the social plane," and ultimately "transcend human experience.
>
> (Ibid., 149)

In other words, an ordinary human conflict takes on cosmic dimensions of divine forces in struggle.

According to Juergensmeyer, a real-time worldly conflict exhibiting the following characteristics is likely to be cast as a cosmic war:

1    Perceiving the struggle as a defense of basic identity and dignity (i.e., it is "… of ultimate significance – a defense not only of lives but of entire cultures").
2    Losing the struggle would be unthinkable (… "beyond human construction, … taking place on a transhistorical plane").
3    Blocking the struggle which cannot be won in real time or in real terms (… "hopeless in human terms… the possibilities of victory are in God's hands).

(Ibid., 164–66)

The grandiosity and ultimate importance of the end, cosmic war, justifies the means, violence.

Juergensmeyer's work is extremely clarifying and influential for those examining religious violence and terrorism (Stern 2003; Aslan 2009). For the present study, it sheds enormous light on the moods that radical apocalypticists exhibit in relation to the first and second reality propositions, *a secret about the world and about the righteous.* Juergensmeyer's framework explains why radical apocalypticists envision a battle between ultimate divine Good, on whose side they are fighting, and cosmic Evil, against which they are locked in an intractable struggle. The scenario of cosmic war also illustrates why there can be no compromise for radical apocalypticists and why they view moderate members of their own religious traditions as traitors who are Evil.

Juergensmeyer's attention to the framework of cosmic war clearly shows the highly problematic nature of labeling our past counter-terrorism efforts as "the Global War on Terror." The name legitimizes the terrorists' framework of cosmic war by implying that the combat zone encompasses all lands and people. However, the present nomenclature substitute, "Overseas Contingency Operation," has never caught on in the imagination of the general public.

## The relationship of "Othering" and redemptive violence in radical apocalypticism

As I show in Chapter 1, in the original Book of Revelation, only divine actors commit violence, which is pushed off into a mythical, symbolic, eschatological sphere. Not only do humans *not* mete out violent punishment, the righteous are the martyrs, the pacifists. In the end, God defeats Satan, Death, and Hades itself. Evil is a divine problem that requires a divine solution.

However, the world has inherited, practically fully intact, the medieval framing of apocalypticism (as I argue in Chapter 2): the ideas that our enemies are Evil itself and they should be killed by those acting for God. The stark identification of the peoples of Gog and Magog with the perceived enemies of Christendom, especially Jews and Muslims, has resulted in memorable portraits of demonization that continue to today. Radical Islamist and right-wing Christian Identity propaganda against Jews still contains the same medieval blood libel charge. Media in numerous Muslim countries, such as in the Syrian television series *Ash-Shatat* that ran on state sponsored Lebanese Al-Manar, continues to propagate the image of Jews killing Christian children to use their blood in the Passover matzah bread (ADL 2005). Similarly, there is no shortage of demonization of Christians by radical Islamists and of Muslims by radical Christians, as we will see in subsequent chapters.

It is a natural evolutionary strategy for humans to be aware of threats against their own groups, label other groups as dangerous and engage in intra-group violence. However, ensconced within the apocalyptic framework, any human inclination toward intra-communal violence takes on mythic proportions of *divine Right vs. demonic Wrong*. Radical apocalyptic adherents, more often than peaceful apocalyptic believers, describe themselves by using language connoting piety, moral certitude, and especially purity. They are genuinely certain that they themselves are the good guys, the earthly representatives of divinity and the sole stewards of the divine will.

It is a dangerous step when an apocalyptic group begins to strongly cast as "Other" those who do not agree with them. This "Othering" is a conceptual process whereby the "in-group" (the radical apocalyptic group) ceases to be able to identify in any empathetic fashion with "out-group" members (everyone else). The boundaries that separate the in-group become harder to cross, whether one is trying to join or to leave. The in-group members increasingly cast the world as being either "with us or against us." The apocalyptic adherents describe the out-group members by using terms that convey varying degrees of impurity: stating that they are dirty, filthy, stained, etc.

Depending on the apocalyptic system, groups that are frequently equated with Evil include: Jews, Muslims, liberals, humanists, communists, Zionists, Americans, the federal and state government, bankers, academics, Freemasons, the Illuminati, the United Nations, the Council on Foreign Relations, and persons of particular ethnic or racial categories. Radical apocalyptic believers often describe out-group members with dehumanizing language: dogs, bacteria, a plague, a virus, a cancer, pigs, apes, vermin, snakes, and so forth. They may also employ demonizing language: devils, demons, minions of Satan, pawns of the devil, antichrists, "the Great Satan" or "the Little Satan."

Not just colorful language, those words dehumanizing and demonizing "the enemy" express a deeper conviction. That conviction was one that the Nazis held of the Jews: they are less than human and they do not belong in our society. Once a committed radical apocalyptic believer accepts that some out-group is truly Evil and that the in-group should play a part in eradicating that Evil to trigger and hasten the coming utopia, carrying out that action becomes a matter of commitment to the faith. Thus, the process of "Othering" and the idea of concretized evil can actually lead to the final proposition of redemptive violence.

The apocalyptic believer who accepts propositions one through seven, sees violence as a matter of self-sacrifice on behalf of the cosmos, the world, and the greater Good. Hence, the violent radical apocalyptic terrorist believes that he or she is pious.

## Stages of violent group formation

As many psychologists have noted, terrorism is more of a group psychological phenomenon than an individual one (Post 1986). Anthony Stahelski has laid out a helpful schema for the stages of social psychological conditioning in violent group formation. According to Stahelski, the completion of all five stages of conditioning makes a terrorist (Stahelski 2004). Recognizing these stages in a radical apocalyptic group that maintains all seven reality propositions in the formula given above can shed additional light on whether the group will turn from violent ideology to violent action. This could contribute significantly to the most difficult part of prediction in counter-terrorism: ascertaining when a group will act violently or when a "lone wolf" will reach out with violence.

In Stahelski's schema, Stage 1 consists of "depluralization," in which a person's membership from other groups is stripped away, resulting in isolation of the person. This could involve a person leaving the dominant culture for a sub-culture, but in some cases the culture itself isolates a person. As one member of Hamas described the childhood culture that paved the way for his joining: "My entire spiritual, cultural, and social world revolved around the movement, and it was natural for me to join Hamas.... All the religious men in the area joined Hamas" (Stern 2003, 47).

Stage 2 in Stahelski's schema is "self-deindividuation." In this stage, an individual ceases to be self-identified as an individual as personal identity is gradually destroyed. This occurs in a variety of manners, including but not limited to: giving up personal objects, money or activities that are distinctive to the individual or lessening relationship ties to those outside the group. It would certainly involve giving up personal autonomy in favor of the ideas promoted through the group-think. A member of a radical apocalyptic group would view him/herself as essentially the same as the other members and perhaps describe all the members with the metaphor of one body, organism or being. Dissent would become difficult.

In Stage 3 – "Other-deindividuation" – radical apocalyptic group members view non-group members increasingly as non-individuals. This establishes a mood that "They are all the same," which is the same as saying that *they* (members of the out-group) are Evil and no longer recognizable as individuals.

The depth of this cultural conditioning is profound and often underestimated. It can become a kind of self-reinforcing social cycle, a dynamic that feeds upon itself with ever-increasing intensity. A striking instance of this was uncovered in the 1980s by the psychologist Yoram Bilu and his team, who collected over 2,000 written dream accounts of Jewish and Palestinian children living within and beyond the Green Line (Bilu 1994). These fifth to seventh graders on both sides of the Israeli–Palestinian conflict had similar dreams that showed the cultural process of "Other-deindividuation" already occurring at their young ages. In the dreams in which the child dreamer encountered another person, over 90 percent were violent and the dreamer often partook of the aggression. As Bilu notes,

Jews and Arabs appeared in each other's dreams stripped of any personal characterization that would depict them as distinctive individuals. Dream characters were never nominally identified [i.e., they lack individual names]. Rather they were accorded collective designations, often with strong depreciatory connotations: Arab terrorists, Arab criminals, Jewish oppressors, Zionist usurpers. Grim, tough, frightening facial expressions and the color black completed the stereotypical view of the enemy.

(Bilu 1994)

In the children's dreams, this collective face of the enemy harassed, beat, expelled, and killed innocent victims. The Jewish children's dreams tended to end with retaliation against the aggressors that spelled some sense of relief, while the Palestinian children's dreams did not (Bilu 1994).

Positive personal interactions with non-group members, especially at a young age, can be a mitigating influence against future violence. Bilu notes with measured hope that a few of the children's dreams, on both the Israeli and Palestinian sides, showed some ambivalence toward the enemy and even the ability to express the other side's point of view in a dream. One young Palestinian child dreamt of being arrested and beaten by the collective image of Israeli soldiers, only to have a kind Israeli officer put a stop to it and send the child home. This kind of *individuation* of the enemy – recognizing that they are not all bad – is indeed a "[crack] in the wall of hatred" (Bilu 1994). Individuation, as the term implies, can occur through person-to-person kindness.

Failing such intervention, Stahelski's Stages 4 and 5 describe the social-psychological processes of "dehumanization" and "demonization" that occur as a group becomes increasingly prone to violence. By "dehumanization," Stahelski refers to cases in which a group uses non-human language to describe non-group members, i.e., rats, pigs, dogs, roaches, bacteria, viruses or mud-people. By "demonization," Stahelski means that a group casts its enemies as forces of Evil by using language such as devils, demons or infidels (Stahelski 2004).

While Stahelski ranks demonization as worse than dehumanization, I find that these two stages are often not very discrete. Unfortunately, when the Iranian Supreme Leader Khamenei refers to Israel as "a cancerous tumor that must be cut off," this is not necessarily of less concern than referring to Israel as "the Little Satan" (Erdbrink 2012).

## Case study for the formula for radical apocalyptic terrorism: the Covenant, Sword, and the Arm of the Lord (CSA)

On April 19, 1985, 200 federal and state law enforcement officers surrounded a farm in Elijah, Arkansas, that housed the community and military compound of the group called the Covenant, Sword, and the Arm of the Lord (CSA). The main leaders of the CSA were James Ellison and Kerry Noble. After tense negotiations resulting in a peaceful surrender, the authorities found fifty hand grenades, 1.5 lbs of C4 explosives, a home-made tank, 155 gold coins, one M72 antitank rocket, ninety-four long arms, thirty handguns, thirty-five sawed-off shotguns and machine guns, one heavy machine gun, and, perhaps most frightening, a large thirty gallon drum of potassium cyanide (worth about $567,000 on today's market) (Stern 2003, 10–11).

This group initiated the plan to bomb the Alfred P. Murrah Federal Building in Oklahoma City. Ten years later to the day of the siege, on April 19, 1995, Timothy McVeigh and Terry Nichols eventually carried out that plan. As the single worst act of domestic terrorism before 9/11, the Oklahoma City bombing killed 168 people, including nineteen children under age six, and wounded over 680. Surprisingly, the group began as a utopian community that intended to share God's love.

Led by James Ellison and influenced by the Reverend Robert Millar and Kerry Noble, the group began as "Zarephath-Horeb," a community of like-minded Christians who wanted to live in remote simplicity with a feeling of holiness, belonging, and safety. In Stahelski's terms, at this early stage they exhibited "depluralization" by moving away from society to a rural area in Arkansas, near Missouri. In Noble's words, they aimed to be a reli-gious fellowship of "clean living," language that associates the righteous with purity (Bartlett 2013). As an apocalyptic movement with a *passive eschatology*, they preached a strict form of Christianity and waited for the endtime.

However, as the group's self-identity grew in its cohesion, it entered a phase of "self-deindividuation." Each night the congregation would gather, with Kerry as the main teacher. As happens during other charis-matic Christian liturgies, the Holy Spirit would begin to enter the various congregants. Sometimes a person would receive the "spirit of prophecy," prompting him to point to a dissenting member who had doubts by point-ing out the person's "pride." Then that person would sit in a special chair and confess all of his sins, while others with the gifts of the Holy Spirit would lay hands on him and speak in tongues to cure him.

This is more than social shaming. It is a form of personal sacrifice that results in enormous social pressure to conform to "group-think," effecting the phase of self-deindividuation by rooting out any individuality. As a Prophetess named Donna said: "we would have to be willing to sacri-fice much for the good of the group, that *only by our fusing together in one body* could He accomplish His will in us" (Stern 2003, 15). In Chapter 8, we will see the ultimate example of this identity fusion of group members in Aum Shinrikyo, when the members believed themselves to be actual "clones" of their guru through sharing his DNA, brainwaves, and spiritual energy.

What followed next in the history of CSA further advanced the process of self-deindividuation. Jim Ellison became more militant in his preparation for the endtimes that the group believed were coming. Instinctually, he instituted behaviors that stripped each member of his/her self-identity in favor of conformity to the group. The men were required to shave all beards, cut their hair, and wear military fatigues as if in the army. The congregants pooled all of their money and burned their memorabilia from the days before joining the group, including photos and sentimental objects. In an effort to further cut themselves off from the outside world and to make the boundaries around the group even tighter, they burned their televisions and radios and sold their wedding rings, advancing self-deindividuation even more.[10]

At this point in the history of the group, Ellison introduced them to *Christian Identity* teaching. Many groups of the radical Christian Right in America share a racist ideology, Christian Identity, which I discuss at length in Chapter 6. This teaching proclaims that Anglo-Saxons are the true Israel and America is the sacred land, given as a God-inspired Christian inheritance. For the CSA, this doctrine facilitated the third phase in Stahelski's schema of social psychological conditioning, Other-deindividuation. All non-whites were considered to be "mud-people" who are less than fully human. Once CSA incorporated this theology, all individuals not in the CSA or in like-minded Christian groups were cast as the Enemy and lumped together: Satan, Satanists, witches, humanists, communists, socialists, Zionists, the US government, Jews, the Antichrist, the United Nations, the International Monetary Fund, the Council on Foreign Relations, the mythical Illuminati, and the "One Worldless" ZOG, or Zionist-operated government supposedly conspiring to take over the world. The association of Satan and the Antichrist with all these groups "demonized" them, Stahelski's final stage of violent social psychological group conditioning.

Stahelski's schema enables us to recognize the stages of violent group formation, but it also charts a progression in ideology. Early on, CSA began as a group that held the first three reality propositions of the apocalyptic formula:

1  *A secret about the nature of this world* (unduly influenced by Evil of some kind, locked in a struggle with ultimate Good);
2  *A secret about the state of the righteous* (who are currently oppressed by the wicked, who flourish);
3a *A secret about another higher or future world in a future time …* (in which the Kingdom of God, coming soon, will set all right again).

Waiting for the endtime, they simply withdrew in order to live a communal life in Christian fellowship, attempting to be more pure than a society they thought would negatively influence their kids.

As time went on, Ellison adopted Christian Identity teaching. He began to accrue more and more interpretative authority through ongoing visions from the Holy Spirit as well as the new Christian Identity teaching. In other words, CSA was adding a layer of *Authoritative Interpretation/Revelation*, which only other Christian Identity-related groups understood. The core revelation of Identity teaching was accepting the "*Othering*" of non-whites, who were considered to be *Concretized Evil*, the literal descendents of the devil.

As various dates for the endtime predicted by Ellison came and went, the group began to embrace a theology of *Redemptive Violence/Revenge*. With complete interpretive authority, Ellison directed the group to spend all that they could buying guns and ammunition in preparation for Armageddon. He taught that it was a holy cause for their people to defend themselves and their food stocks in the tribulations to come. Influenced by Christian Identity preaching and a racist fictional book called *The Turner Diaries*, Ellison thought a race war that was coming to the US would be the tribulation preceding the Second Coming of Jesus to earth.

Eventually, the group set up "Silhouette City," a mock training ground with fake buildings and targets designed as Jews, gays, blacks, and other enemies. Male CSA members trained with paramilitary-style exercises in rigorous and demanding preparation for the endtime. They believed the endtime would pit Evil, the government, and non-whites, against them, the righteous. The most dangerous element of Silhouette City was the "Endtime Overcomer Survival Training School," in which the CSA group trained around 1,500 like-minded Christian Identity adherents as militants (Juergensmeyer 2003, 34). After they trained, they left to start or join other apocalyptic militias around America. We are still feeling the reverberations of this training today.

Eventually the group settled into belief in full-blown *Active Eschatology*. Several CSA members believed that God would use them to bring about Armageddon. This *Active Eschatology* is clearest in the statement of one CSA military commander, Randall Rader, who warned that things were getting so bad, "if God doesn't start Armageddon soon, I will."[11] Rader would eventually split off from CSA, joining the white supremacist group, The Order, in Idaho, to act out this *Active Eschatology*.

With all of the reality propositions of radical apoclaypticism in place, CSA became a violent terrorist organization. Under Ellison's guidance, the group planned a variety of terrorist acts and attempted to carry them out, albeit unsuccessfully: assassinating the families of federal judges on Christmas Day (thwarted by a car wreck on the way there), poisoning the Chicago or DC water supply, attacking major metropolitan power supplies, bombing a "gay" church in St Louis, assassinating people in a "gay" park in St Louis, bombing power grids and blowing up the Alfred P. Murrah Federal Building in Oklahoma City.[12] In their thinking, each of these acts would inflame the societal tensions that would instigate the race war that would bring about the Second Coming. Hence, they considered their actions to be pious and good.

On April 19, 1985, 200 federal and state law enforcement officers surrounded the CSA farm. Given all the arms that were stockpiled, combined with the members' paramilitary training and hatred of government officials, the standoff should have ended in a bloody firefight. After all, Ellison, Rader, and Noble had been training their men for months for this very moment.

However, Noble had recently had a change of heart. Just prior to the siege in April 1985, Noble and another CSA member had traveled to a St Louis church congregation known to be welcoming to gays. He had a suitcase bomb with a timed detonator with which he planned to blow up the church. It would have been the largest act of domestic terrorism to date. However, sitting through the liturgy with the first gay people he had ever actually met, he said in an interview that he first noticed they looked "normal," which was not at all what he had expected (Bartlett 2013). He had demonized them in his mind, but in reality they were just people. When the music began, some of the congregants raised their hands up to God. This was the practice of his own church at the CSA compound and, if anyone has ever seen it or done it, this hand raising can be a vulnerable and intimate reaching out to the divine. Seeing this ritual touched Noble deeply and, in his own words, he recalled, "The Lord said if you draw nigh unto me I will draw nigh unto you. He didn't say, 'if you aren't gay ...' and these people were drawing nigh unto him" (Wilson 2008). For Noble, it was a dramatic turning point. In his own words, he realized that the gay people in the congregation didn't fit into society, just like he didn't fit (Bartlett 2013).

What happened to Kerry Noble? Through person-to-person contact, Noble began to reverse the process of *"Othering"/Concretized Evil* by recognizing that the gay congregants were just people like him, outsiders and Christians searching for intimacy with God. Against his apocalyptic reality framework, Noble connected with these individuals. To analyze it in Stahelski's terms, Noble reversed the processes of Other-deindividuation and demonization. To his surprise, he saw particular individuals with whom he could identify, not just "gay people" or "devils."

The perceptual shift dissolved his hatred and broke down his resolve to do violence. Noble not only diffused the bomb and walked out of the church, but on April 19 he helped negotiate the peaceful surrender of the Covenant, Sword, and the Arm of the Lord group to the state and federal law enforcement. He received five years on weapons charges and, since then, has worked to shed light on his change from an intended terrorist to someone promoting a peaceful Christian theology. Ellison received a sentence of twenty years, but got out in 1987 after turning in leaders of the Aryan Nations.

## De-radicalization, not aggression

As the example of the CSA indicates, if all seven of the belief propositions that I sketched above are held deeply, then the apocalyptic group will likely be violent if provided with material means. Of course, a constant focus on counter-terrorism should be reducing the means with which terrorists carry out violence, e.g., keeping suitcase nukes or missiles away from dangerous people. However, given that humans can kill with a bomb, a gun, our hands, a car or by shoving someone into harm's way, completely eliminating the means for a violent apocalyptic believer to carry out terrorism is simply impossible. Rather, we must begin to transform *the ideology* of marginal members of terrorist organizations, potential recruits, and the surrounding culture on all sides. Kerry Noble's case shows the power of individual encounters to touch and transform the human heart in surprising ways.

While changing culture and ideology is a long-term, collective task, we can at least start by understanding radical apocalyptic ideology so that we don't take actions as a society that increase the chances of apocalyptic believers committing violence.

All apocalyptic believers, whether peaceful or violent, see themselves as oppressed. At the very least, they feel themselves to be part of a marginal group, at odds with the dominant culture, as Noble expressed. Their persecution may in fact be real, since they may be attacked physically, oppressed economically, denied rights that others possess, or publicly mocked or humiliated. The oppression may also just be perceptual, such as cultural oppression through the overwhelming presence of a countervailing culture. Either way, persecution is the real and potent experience of apocalyptic believers and the foundation of their self-identity.

Thus, an operative dynamic is woven into the very fabric of the apocalyptic system, whether in its peaceful or violent forms. Simply put: increasing the sense of oppression of any apocalyptic group only validates and deepens their apocalyptic worldview. In the case of those with *Active Eschatology*, oppression only deepens their motivation and sense of urgency to actively bring about the endtime sooner. If the actions of the active eschatologist include *violence or terrorism*, oppressing them further – or contributing in any way to their sense of oppression – only deepens the conviction that they are locked in a struggle with Evil and that the fate of the world depends on their loyalty.

This dynamic is completely counterintuitive without a deep understanding of the radical apocalyptic framework. In the case of apocalyptic terrorism, any attack on individuals or their group, including arrests, torture or mockery, only deepens their original convictions. In the case of true adherents of radical apocalypticism, such actions will never serve as a deterrent. This realization might well frustrate our country, policy makers and intelligence analysts to no end. Yet aggressive military action and anger that violently stems terrorism in the short-run often feeds the terrorist cycle in the long-run.

## So now what?

In this book, I do not take a pacifist path, as much as I wish that I could. I well understand the necessity for certain kinds of military engagement and recognize that there are no easy solutions to the problem of terrorism. After all, terrorists are often highly suspicious of outsiders' ideas and view negotiation as a capitulation to Evil. Of course, they also want to kill innocent people.

However, when it comes to countering radical apocalypticism, if war is our dominant counter-terrorism framework, we tend to entrench *both* sides and feed a violent, dynamic cycle in which one step leads to the next:

- Our aggression and disrespectful characterization of the enemy feeds social grievances in a marginalized community susceptible to radicalization.
- This mood fuels radical apocalyptic terrorist convictions and spurs recruitment.
- This results in more terrorism.
- This results in more aggression from our side.
- This further entrenches terrorists and feeds more terrorist recruitment.

And so on (Flannery *et al.* 2013). The cycle has been repeating for decades in multiple networks of terrorism, including both domestic and transnational terrorism. The manner in which we conduct short-term counter-terrorism efforts can unintentionally create second-, third-, and fourth-order effects that generate more terrorism in the long-run.

If we desire to stop the cycle someday, we must begin to understand the appeal of the radical apocalyptic worldview and engage in a multifaceted *cultural counter-terrorism* that transforms the very situation in which terrorism arises and continues. Humanizing ourselves, showing respect for the casualties of "the other side," expressing our individual dissent with group-think, facilitating the freedom of dissent and individual expression in other cultures, encouraging grass-roots engagement across the group divide, promoting interreligious dialogue, refusing to imbibe a fear culture propagated by the media in the wake of terrorist events, having realistic public risk assessment of terrorism and working to alleviate oppressive social situations of poverty, discrimination, and human devaluation are successful, long-term strategies for combating terrorism.

## Notes

1 "The West" is a convenient term for designating a certain group of relatively culturally similar countries (those in Europe, America, Canada, Australia, and New Zealand) with a significant population that has historically identified with a Western European heritage. However, it is a culturally constructed term that is changing and that is therefore often inaccurate. Moreover, the term plays

into the simple bifurcation of the world that some terrorists propagate. Also, as we become a more connected planet, and the cultural make-up of individual countries changes, the term may obscure the complexity of the cultural influences on which our countries draw. In the absence of a more precise but not cumbersome term, I retain occasional use of the term but use quotes, i.e., "West" and "Western," to indicate the problematic nature of the terms (Qureshi and Sells 2003, 1–48).

2  More exactly, Geertz' definition of religion reads as follows: Religion is

> a set of symbols [expressed in myths, rituals and practices] that acts to establish powerful, pervasive, and long-lasting moods and motivations [ethics and attitudes] in [humans] by formulating conceptions of a general order of existence [worldview] and clothing these conceptions with such an aura of factuality [through myths, social expectations, and the practice of rituals] that the moods and motivations seem uniquely realistic.
>
> (Geertz 1973, 5)

3  Since, at the time, they had not all committed acts of terrorism, I use the signatories' own self-identifier, *jihadists* or *mujahideen*, to signify a radical branch of Islamists willing to use violence to achieve their political and religious aims.

4  Unless otherwise noted, all translations of Al Qaeda's literature are from Ibrahim 2007.

5  I owe this helpful phrase to my colleague Mike Deaton.

6  There are certainly exceptions, such as the Creation Care movement in the Christian evangelical community in America and the recent open letter by 200 evangelical ministers calling on the US Congress to act on climate change. This is still probably a minority movement opposed by many evangelicals, who see environmental care as either a waste of time, or even as a sin because it denies belief in God's power. Compare these contrasting views found in statements by evangelical Christian groups: the Evangelical Environmental Network 2011. Accessed February 2, 2013, www.creationcare.org/index.php; and The Cornwall Alliance for the Stewardship of Creation. Spring 2000. Accessed February 2, 2013, www.cornwallalliance.org/articles/read/an-evangelical-declaration-on-global-warming/.

7  The sentiment only appears in Matthew's version of the Lord's Prayer, however. Compare Matt. 6:9–13 and Luke 11:2–4.

8  An excellent collection of essays by biblical scholars on the varied concept of war in the Hebrew Bible is Kelle and Ames (2008).

9  The violent potential of Buddhism (well known to Buddhism scholars) recently came to light with a controversial *Time Magazine* cover featuring Myanmar monk Wirathu with the caption, "The Face of Buddhist Terror." He has taken the name the "Buddhist bin Laden" to capture the idea that his actions are against Muslims. Hannah Beech, "The Face of Buddhist Terror," *Time Magazine* (July 1, 2013). www.time.com/time/magazine/article/0,9171, 2146000,00.html. Accessed July 12, 2013.

10  Eventually, Ellison received a revelation that God told him to take a second wife, a dangerous development indicating that the group was solidifying its identity even more around Ellison himself as the exception.

11  From original footage of Randall Rader at the CSA compound in *Silhouette City* (Wilson 2008).

12  From Kerry Noble's interview in *Dangerous Persuasions* (Bartlett 2013).

## Bibliography

22 US Code, Section 2656 f(d). Legal Information Institute, Cornell University Law School. Accessed October 10, 2010, www.law.cornell.edu/uscode/text/22/2656f.

ADL – Anti-Defamation League. January 9, 2004. "Satellite Network Recycles The Protocols of the Elders of Zion." Accessed July 11, 2013, http://archive.adl.org/special_reports/protocols/protocols_recycled.asp.

Arberry, A.J., trans. 1955. *The Koran Interpreted*. New York: Simon & Schuster.

Aslan, Reza. 2009. *How to Win a Cosmic War: God, Globalization, and the End of the War on Terror*. New York: Random House.

Bartlett, David, director. 2013. *Dangerous Persuasions*. "Brainwashed – Covenant of Hate," Season 1, episode 5. Aired February 15, 2013 on Investigation Discovery.

Beech, Hannah. July 2013. "The Face of Buddhist Terror." *Time Magazine*. Accessed July 12, 2013, www.time.com/time/magazine/article/0,9171,2146000,00.html.

Bilu, Yoram. 1994. "The Image of the Enemy: Cracks in the Wall of Hatred." *Palestine-Israel Journal* 1, 4. Accessed May 7, 2012, www.pij.org/details.php?id=694#.

Bin Laden, Osama. November 24, 2002 "Why We Are Fighting You." *Guardian*. Accessed January 20, 2013, http://observer.guardian.co.uk/worldview/story/0,11581,845725,00.html.

*CNN*. November 7, 1995. "Rabin's Alleged Killer Appears in Court." *CNN* website. Accessed January 15, 2015, www.cnn.com/WORLD/9511/rabin/amir/11-06/.

Collins, John J. 1979. "Introduction." In *Apocalypse: Morphology of a Genre. Semeia* 14, edited by John J. Collins, 5–49. Missoula, MT: Scholars Press.

Collins, John J. 2004. *An Introduction to the Hebrew Bible*. Minneapolis, MN: Fortress Press.

Crenshaw, Martha. 1981. "The Causes of Terrorism," *Comparative Politics* 13, 4: 379–399.

Erdbrink, Thomas. February 3, 2012. "Khamenei: Iran Will Back 'Any Nations, Any Groups' Fighting Israel." *Washington Post*. Accessed February 10, 2013, http://articles.washingtonpost.com/2012-02-03/world/35445760_1_supreme-leader-resumption-of-nuclear-talks-nuclear-facilities.

Flannery-Dailey, Frances. 2006. "Lessons on Early Jewish Apocalypticism and Mysticism from Dream Literature." In *Paradise Now: Essays on Early Jewish and Christian Mysticism*, edited by April Deconick, 231–48. Leiden: Brill; Atlanta: SBL Press.

Flannery, Frances, Deaton, Michael L. and Walton, Timothy R. 2013. "Radical Apocalypticism and Iranian Nuclear Proliferation: A Systems Oriented Analysis." *International Journal of Intelligence and Counter-intelligence*. 26, 4.

Geertz, Clifford. 1973. *The Interpretation of Cultures*. NY: Basic Books.

Hanson. Paul D. 1975. *The Dawn of Apocalyptic*. Philadelphia: Fortress Press.

Hoffman, Bruce. 2006. *Inside Terrorism*. Revised and expanded edition. New York: Columbia University Press.

Ibrahim, Raymond, trans. 2007. *The Al Qaeda Reader*. New York: Broadway Books.

Jervis, Robert. 2010. *Why Intelligence Fails: Lessons from the Iranian Revolution and the Iraq War*. Ithaca, NY: Cornell University Press.

Juergensmeyer, Mark. 2003 [2000]. *Terror in the Mind of God: The Global Rise of Religious Violence*. Revised edition. Berkeley: University of California Press.

Karpin, Michael and Friedman, Ina. 1998. *Murder in the Name of God: The Plot to Kill Yitzhak Rabin*. New York: Henry Holt and Co.

Kelle Brad E. and Ames, Frank R., eds. 2008. *Reading and Writing War: Rhetoric, Gender, and Ethics in Biblical and Modern Contexts.* Atlanta: SBL Press.

Oliver, Anne Marie and Steinberg, Paul. 2005. *The Road to Martyrs' Square.* Oxford: Oxford University Press.

Parry, Albert. 1976. *Terrorism: From Robespierre to Arafat.* New York: Vanguard Press.

Parry. Albert. January 12, 1977. "Terrorism, its problems, solutions," *Washington Star.*

Pearce, K.I. 1977. "Police negotiations," *Canadian Psychiatric Association Journal* 22, 4:171–175.

Pew Forum on Religion and Public Life. April 9, 2009. *Christians' Views on the Return of Christ.* Accessed January 20, 2013. www.pewforum.org/Christians-Views-on-the-Return-of-Christ.aspx.

Pew Research Center for the People and the Press. June 22, 2010. *Life in 2050: Amazing Science, Familiar Threats.* Accessed January 20, 2013, www.people-press.org/2010/06/22/section-3-war-terrorism-and-global-trends/.

Post, Jerrold M. 1986. "Hostilité, conformité, fraternité: The Group Dynamics of Terrorist Behavior." *International Journal of Group Psychotherapy* 36: 211–224.

Post, Jerrold M. 2007. *The Mind of the Terrorist.* New York: Palgrave Macmillan.

Qureshi, Emran and Sells Michael A. (eds.). 2003. *The New Crusades: Constructing the Muslim Enemy.* New York: Columbia University Press.

Rapoport, David C. 1980. "Messianic Sanctions for Terror." *Comparative Politics* 20, 2: 195–213.

Rapoport, David C. 1984. "Fear and Trembling: Terrorism in Three Religious Traditions." *American Political Science Review* 78: 658–677.

Rapoport, David C. 1992. "Some General Observations on Religion and Violence." In *Violence and the Sacred in the Modern World*, edited by Mark Juergensmeyer, 118–40. London: Frank Cass.

Rapoport, David C. and Alexander, Yonah, eds. 1982. *The Rationalisation of Terrorism.* New York: University Publications of America.

Richardson, Louise. 2006. *What Terrorists Want.* New York: Random House.

Rowland, Christopher. 1982. *The Open Heaven: A Study of Apocalyptic in Judaism and Early Christianity.* New York: Crossroad.

Sacchi, Paolo. 1990. *L'apocalittica giudaica e la sua storia.* Paideia: Brescia. Idem, 1997. *Jewish Apocalyptic and Its History*, translated by W.E. Short. JSPSup, 20. Sheffield: Sheffield Academic Press.

Stahelski, Anthony. March 2004. "Terrorists Are Made, Not Born: Creating Terrorists Using Social Psychological Conditioning" *Journal of Homeland Security.*

Stern, Jessica. 2003. *Terror in the Name of God.* New York: Ecco.

Victoroff, Jeff. February 2005. "The Mind of the Terrorist: A Review and Critique of the Approaches." *Journal of Conflict Resolution* 49, 1: 3–42. Accessed January 14, 2015, http://dx.doi.org/10.1177/0022002704272040.

Weatherston D. and Moran, J. 2003. "Terrorism and Mental Illness: Is there a Relationship?" *International Journal of Offender Therapy and Comparative Criminology* 47, 6: 698–713.

Wilson, Michael, Director. 2008. *Silhouette City.* Social Satisfaction Media.

Zakaria, Fareed. October 14, 2001. "The Politics of Rage: Why Do They Hate Us." Accessed January 20, 2013, www.thedailybeast.com/newsweek/2001/10/14/the-politics-of-rage-why-do-they-hate-us.html.

# 4 *"One who swims in the sea does not fear rain"*

## Al Qaeda and Sunni radical apocalypticism

We learned about an enemy who is sophisticated, patient, disciplined, and lethal. The enemy rallies broad support in the Arab and Muslim world by demanding redress of political grievances, but its hostility toward us and our values is limitless. Its purpose is to rid the world of religious and political pluralism, the plebiscite, and equal rights for women. It makes no distinction between military and civilian targets.

(Preface to The 9/11 Commission Report, by Thomas H. Kean, Chair and Lee H. Hamilton, Vice Chair, 9/11 Commission, 2004)

The days and nights will not pass until we avenge ourselves as on September 11. Your minds will be troubled, your lives embittered, and the course of events will lead to that which is hateful to you. As for us, we have nothing to lose. One who swims in the sea does not fear rain.

(Osama bin Laden, truce offer to the Americans, audio-taped message dated January 2006, Ibrahim 2007, 221–225)

In February 1998, five radical Islamist signatories published a page long announcement in an Arabic language newspaper in London. Sometimes called "The World Islamic Front's Declaration," it was a declaration of war on America nearly three years before 9/11 (Bin Laden *et al.* 1998). The signatories included Sheikh Osama bin Laden, the leader of Al Qaeda, and Ayman al-Zawahiri, leader of the Egyptian Islamic Group and second in command in Al Qaeda, who would later replace bin Laden as leader upon his death on May 2, 2011 (US Indictment S (10) 98). After listing what they considered to be the atrocities of America and Israel, the signatories of the declaration make the following proclamation:

in compliance with Allah's order, we hereby issue the following decree to all Muslims: The ruling to kill the Americans and their allies – civilians and military – is an individual obligation incumbent upon every Muslim who can do it and in any country.

(Ibrahim 2007, 13)

It was a command that multiple members of Al Qaeda would seek to fulfill across the globe, in Yemen, Somalia, the Sudan, Afghanistan, Pakistan, Kenya, Morocco, Saudi Arabia, Jordan, London, Iraq, the Philippines, Indonesia, Madrid, Los Angeles and, most terribly and famously, on 9/11 in New York and Washington DC.

It goes without saying that the command to kill civilians indiscriminately is shocking in any major religion. However, from the point of view of Islam, the declaration is especially disturbing for its lack of humanity and its untraditional interpretation of Islamic law.

The pronouncement enshrines a particular radical Islamist interpretation of the notion of *jihad* in a fashion that the vast majority of Muslims heartily reject. The Qur'an is the supreme judicial authority in Islam,[1] and the sura called "The Cow" discusses the permitted role of violence in Islam:

> And fight in the way of God with those
> Who fight with you, but aggress not: God loves not the aggressors.
> … [but] slay them [the aggressors] wherever you come upon them,
> And expel them from where they expelled you;
> [Their] Persecution [of you, of Islam] is more grievous than
> [your] slaying [them].
> But fight them not by the Holy Mosque
> Until they should fight you there;
> Then, if they fight you, slay them-
> Such is the recompense of unbelievers –
> But if they give over, surely God is
> All-forgiving, All-compassionate.
> Fight them, till there is no persecution
> And the religion is God's.
>
> (2:190–93)[2]

For the vast majority of the world's Muslims, this sura means that they cannot aggress, cannot kill innocents, should only fight defensively and should leave off defending themselves once those aggressing against them cease. That is why so many Muslim leaders around the globe have publicly and vehemently denounced the terrorism of 9/11 as heinous and anti-Islamic, including: President Khatami of Iran, Shaykh Muhammed Sayyid al-Tantawi, the Imam of al-Azhar mosque in Cairo, 'Abdulaziz bin 'Abdallah Al-Ashaykh, chief mufti of Saudi Arabia, the League of Arab States, and the Fiqh Council of America (see Kurzman 2002).

Indeed, Islam calls internal *jihad*, or the struggle against temptation, "the greater *jihad*." Islam relegates external *jihad*, or fighting against physical enemies, to the status of "the lesser *jihad*."[3] Within that lesser *jihad*, Islam only permits defensive *jihad*, strictly forbidding offensive *jihad*. This is why Abdel-Mo'tei Bayyoumi, of the al-Azhar Islamic Research Academy, in Cairo, Egypt could proclaim confidently a week after 9/11: "There is no terrorism or a threat to civilians in *jihad*," since he defines *jihad* as true religious struggle, which by its very nature would have to be defensive and protective of the innocent (Bayyoumi 2001).

However, the extremist Islamist signatories of the 1998 declaration follow a different interpretation of *jihad*. By starting with the list of griev-ances against the US and its allies, or what the document calls the "Crusader-Jewish alliance," they claim that the US and its allies have aggressed against the whole Muslim community or *ummah*. The declara-tion names three offenses: the American troop presence in Saudi Arabia, the holiest of Muslim lands; aggressions against Iraq by the Crusader-Jewish alliance, including massacres of over one million Iraqis and devast-ating sanctions; and the occupation of Jerusalem by Israel.

It refers to these as "crimes and sins committed by the Americans," but more importantly, it also asserts that these actions are "a clear declaration of war on Allah, His Messenger, and the Muslims" (Ibrahim 2007, 12). In other words, the 1998 declaration claims that America had already aggressed against all of Islam and God, implying that the declaration's command to Muslims to kill Americans qualifies as defensive *jihad* under Islamic jurisprudence and theology. However, later writings by al-Zawahiri and bin Laden would go even further than this, clearly contravening the Qur'an by arguing that offensive *jihad* is now obligatory for faithful Muslims (ibid., 18–62).

When viewed within a Muslim context, the 1998 declaration that announced Al Qaeda's declaration of war on Americans is even more radical than it first appears to the non-Muslim world. The theology bla-tantly contradicts the positions held by the overwhelming majority of the world's 1.7 billion Muslims, who maintain that the Qur'an forbids the murder of innocents (5:32) as well as suicide (4:26). They see Al Qaeda's radical terrorism not only as immoral, but also as un-Islamic.

Islamic law divides every action into one of five categories: obligatory, recommended, neutral, disliked or forbidden. Most Muslims would inter-pret the Qur'an to mean that the killing of innocents is *haraam* (5:32), completely forbidden. By definition, terrorist actions would be *haraam*. The radical signatories of the World Islamic Front's Declaration try to argue around this by claiming that *there are no innocents in America*. Therefore, the 1998 declaration is making an argument on the basis of radical Islamic jur-isprudence: killing Americans is neither forbidden nor disliked, nor merely a neutral act or even an approved act, it is now "obligatory." In fact, the World Islamic Front's Declaration commands each and every Muslim to kill Americans, another extreme position in Islamic *sharia* law: it isn't just a *fard kifaya*, a duty maintained as long as someone in the community fulfills it, it is a *fard ayn*, a duty that each faithful Muslim must perform.

Although it is a difficult number to gauge precisely, only about 7 percent of the world's Muslims are Islamists, those who desire to live under an Islamic government run by religious law (Esposito n.d.). Only a minority of those Islamists is violent, willing to use force to achieve this goal (perhaps less than 1 percent). Since mainstream Muslims reject these interpretations as representing Islam, the term "radical Islamist" is controversial, as is "militant Islamist," since both suggest that the problem is specific to Islam. Better nomenclature would be helpful.

The vast majority of Muslims reject extremist Islamist interpretations of Islam. Just before the death of bin Laden, the core membership of Al Qaeda was most likely only around 500–1,000. Unfortunately, a very small number of people can do an enormous amount of damage. Too often that minority group earns a bad reputation for the parent religion, despite the interpretation's fringe status.

Amongst extremist Islamists, I must make another differentiation. Around the world, there are other Islamist extremist groups classified as terrorists, such as Hamas, the Algerian Islamic Front, Lashkar-e-Taiba, and the Taliban. As terrible as they are, the majority of the groups' members do not genuinely share Al Qaeda's global ambitions for its *jihad*. Some Islamist extremists have regional goals that are really geared for political autonomy or power, while others have global *jihadist* goals in service of a theological agenda.

Oftentimes global *jihadists* are referred to as "Al Qaeda-inspired." The original Al Qaeda, "The Base," has spawned multiple offshoot groups, including Al Qaeda in the Islamic Magreb (AQIM), Al Qaeda in Iraq (AQI), Al Qaeda in the Arabian Peninsula (AQAP), Al Qaeda in Pakistan, Al Qaeda in Yemen, Al Qaeda in the Land between Two Rivers (in Iraq), and ISIS/ISIL, now "the Islamic State." However, the tension between local and global ambitions caused some groups to break away or form independently, such as Al Shabaab in Somalia, Ansar-al-Din in Mali, Egyptian Islamic Jihad, MUJAO the Movement for Unity and Jihad in West Africa, and Boko Haram and its offshoot, Ansaru, in Nigeria. The proliferation of the "Al Qaeda network" is certainly worrying, but the lack of unity here reflects an inherent tension in the groups' political and theological framing of conflict: the local groups may not privilege the original Al Qaeda's narrative of global *jihad* and are not necessarily puppets to al-Zawahiri's dictates. However, the case of ISIS/ISIL demonstrates one instance in which the breakaway group is even more extreme than Al Qaeda, which is the topic of the next chapter.

There have been many excellent scholarly studies of Al Qaeda's history, formation, and present activities (see, for example, Johnsen 2013). Reiterating these is not my goal. Instead, I wish to show how Osama bin Laden and Dr. Ayman al-Zawahiri shaped a radical new apocalyptic vision. This theology set them apart from many other leaders of the *mujahideen*, the fighters in the way of *jihad*. Framing the goal apocalyptically justified their violence and paved the way for rise of the self-declared "Islamic State."

## Parameters of this analysis

Muslims would not typically call their religion "apocalyptic." "Apocalypticism" and "radical apocalypticism" are etic (external) categories derived from overarching patterns found in thousands of examples drawn from contemporary groups and texts, as I discuss in the Introduction. The analysis that follows, which applies the formula for "radical apocalypticism" to the actions and writings of Al Qaeda, applies only to extremist Sunni Islamist theology and not to mainstream Sunni Islam. Shi'ism and other forms of Islam also demand a separate analysis, since they are distinctively different from Sunni Islam, for example, in the understanding of the role of the authoritative interpreter and in eschatology involving the Mahdi.

Despite these caveats, there are benefits to using this reductionist lens of "radical apocalypticism." Viewing Al Qaeda as a radical apocalyptic group clarifies connections to other forms of ideological and religious terrorism, lending clarity to what seems at first to be a bewildering array of terrorist groups. The formula can also help distinguish the goals of regional Islamists, who are often unfortunately lumped together in the "Al Qaeda network," from those with global *jihadist* ambitions. Finally, understanding the theological and social trajectory of radical apocalyptic beliefs that began with Al Qaeda may shed light on the motives of offshoot groups such as ISIS/ISIL. From this, we may glean more effective and more comprehensive counter-terrorism strategies.

## Al Qaeda's radical apocalyptic worldview

Post 9/11, both bin Laden and al-Zawahiri continued to urge Americans to convert to Islam. For instance, in September 2005, four years after the 9/11 tragedy, al-Sahab interviewed Ayman al-Zawahiri in an piece called "Four Years after the New York and Washington Raids." Al-Zawahiri invited Americans to convert to (their version of) Islam:

> We call upon Americans to be honest with themselves and to realize that their current creed – which is composed of materialistic secularism, the distorted Christianity that has nothing to do with Jesus Christ, the hereditary Crusader hatred, and their submission to Zionist hegemony over money and politics – this creed, this mixture, will only lead them to destruction in their world, and torments in the Hereafter.
>
> (Ibrahim 2007, 187–188)

To me, as an American, his assumption that the terrorism of 9/11 would motivate us to convert is stunning. It so boggles the mind that it rings as insincere.

But there is a different logic at work here, an apocalyptic logic. To me, as a scholar of radical apocalypticism, al-Zawahiri's hope that he could "help" us come to a clearer realization of our sinful path through attacking us rings as sincere. Understanding the self-identity, short-term goals, and long-term ambitions of Al Qaeda's leaders allows us to fight the network more effectively. The formula for radical apocalypticism illuminates their thought system in ways that can also help us better predict the scope and nature of their future actions.

## 1 A secret about the nature of this world

Like other apocalyptic believers, bin Laden believed that this world is ruled by Evil, a stance that his successor Dr. Ayman al-Zawahiri still maintains. In an open letter to the American people posted on the internet in October, 2002, bin Laden tried to link his letter with the Qur'an, first by beginning with the phrase that starts each chapter of the Qur'an, "In the Name of Allah, the Compassionate, the Merciful." He then includes two Quranic verses by way of an introduction (Bin Laden 2002):

> Permission to fight is given to those who are attacked, for they have been wronged and surely Allah is able to give them victory.
>
> (22:39)

> Those who believe, fight in the cause of Allah, and those who disbelieve, fight in the cause of [against] evil. So fight you against the friends of Satan; ever feeble indeed is the plot of Satan.
>
> (4:76)

By appealing first to the authority of the revealed Qur'an, the word of Allah in Islam, bin Laden suggests that the views in the letter are holy and in accordance with Islam. Together the quotes sum up the secrets of the world that bin Laden wished to convey: Allah is commissioning Al Qaeda's *jihad* because it is fighting evil, friends of Satan who rule the world.[4]

Osama bin Laden was a radical apocalypticist, a "true believer" who fervently believed that his acts of violence were in the service of Allah. He viewed Al Qaeda's attacks on 9/11 as a *defensive action* against what they perceived to be our evil offenses. Stating "one who swims in the sea does not fear rain," bin Laden scoffed at the impact of the 2003 war in Iraq in comparison to the past treatment of Muslims at the hands of the Western "Crusaders."

In numerous original writings directed at both fellow Muslims and (non-Muslim) Americans, Al Qaeda's leaders clearly and frequently listed what they deemed to be America's atrocities. Both bin Laden and al-Zawahiri maintained that America and its allies, known as the "Crusader-Zionist alliance" or "the Crusader West," rule the world and oppress it. They and the other signatories of the 1998 declaration listed the following offenses by the Crusaders: the "occupation" of Saudi Arabia by American troop bases, the "occupation" of Palestine by Israel and sanctions and wars against Iraq (preceding the American war of 2003–2010).

To bin Laden and al-Zawahiri, the (modern) Crusaders make up the cruelest force in human history, "sacrificing 300 million lives in all its wars," i.e., including Europe and America's role in World War I and World War II (Ibrahim 2007, 33). Bin Laden believed that Americans have been especially cruel to Muslims: "You have starved the Muslims of Iraq, where children die every day. More than 1.5 million Iraqi children have died as a result of your sanctions, and you amazingly did not show concern" (Bin Laden 2002).

He also rejected our democracy for its separation of religion and politics, which in his eyes meant we reject the "absolute authority of the Lord your Creator" (Bin Laden 2002). Similarly, al-Zawahiri wrote a treatise against the Egyptian Muslim Brotherhood condemning their participation in the democratic process because the resulting human laws weaken *sharia* law (Ibrahim 2007, 116–36).

For bin Laden, our depraved character was evident in a lengthy list of sins: the legalization of homosexual marriage, secularism, materialism, and colonialism (ibid., 61). He claimed that we alone permit usury and "the Jews have taken control of your economy, thereby taking control of your media, and now control all aspects of your life" (Bin Laden 2002). In general, he considered us to be the supreme example of debauchery, which, he noted, we mistakenly label as "personal freedom." To him, our depravity was made clear in immoral acts of fornication, homosexuality, intoxicants, drugs, gambling, the sex trade, and usury resulting in "the Satanic-American invention of AIDS" (Bin Laden 2002).

The idea that any hint of truth tinges some of his accusations may make us uncomfortable, especially considering the source. But not all his allegations are outlandish. Bin Laden stated that Americans let the rich have an inordinate sway over our elections, favor whites over other races in the justice system, exploit women as sexual objects, and pollute the planet. He thought our contribution to greenhouse gases was a sin, saying: "You have destroyed nature with your industrial waste and gases more than any other nation in history. Despite this, you refuse to sign the Kyoto agreement so that you can secure the profit of your greedy companies and industries" (Ibrahim 2007, 204).[5]

Certainly, these last few charges could be and have been leveled against the US by Americans. However, while we sometimes debate and discuss some of those items while trying to improve our country, for bin Laden and al-Zawahiri, *these points are marshaled as atrocities that provide evidence of our evil nature.* This key shift in perspective is crucial for understanding the leadership of Al Qaeda. These accusations are not mere slander of our way of life. Rather, bin Laden is convinced that we are ignorant of the extent of our own evil. Like John of Patmos who saw that "Babylon" or Rome was actually fueled by the power of the Dragon, bin Laden was certain that America fulfills that same role. Bin Laden put it simply in his open letter to America: "It is saddening to tell you that you are the worst civilization witnessed in the history of mankind" (Ibrahim 2007, 202).

The extent to which bin Laden believed that we Crusaders embody evil should not be underestimated. In writing to the Saudi government to chastise them for dialogue with the "Crusading West," bin Laden made several claims: "The *sharia* provides a true and just path, securing Muslims, and providing *peace to the world*. The West of a surety knows the path *and battles us because of it*" (ibid., 31). Overall, he claimed that America and its allies intentionally set out to destroy world peace and we oppose him *because* we know he is on the side of Allah.

## 2 *A secret about the state of the righteous*

As a dedicated believer in a radical apocalyptic system of thought, Osama bin Laden considered the suffering of oppressed Muslims in Palestine, Iraq, Somalia, Afghanistan, and elsewhere to be evidence that the evil Crusading West rules the world. On al-Jazeera a few days before the American 2004 presidential elections, bin Laden spoke dramatically of how he had conceived of the plans for 9/11 after seeing the Israeli bombardment of Lebanon in 1982, which was accomplished with the aid of the American Sixth Fleet:

> I still recall those distressing scenes – blood, severed limbs; women and children massacred. Everywhere there were homes being destroyed and high-rises collapsing over their residents, while bombs ruthlessly rained down on our homes. It was just like a crocodile devouring a child who could do nothing but scream!
>
> (Ibid., 215)[6]

Apparently, bin Laden did not care that he was addressing some Americans upon whom he had recently visited the same fate. Instead, he used these terrible memories to justify Al Qaeda's actions as the only possible course of action, adding, "And does a crocodile understand any language other than that of arms?" (ibid., 215).

In the radical apocalyptic worldview, it is a given that the wicked oppress the righteous and flourish until such time as the divine/God dramatically enters history. The stronger this experience of oppression, the more entrenched the apocalyptic thought system becomes. Throughout bin Laden's writings, we find repeated mentioning of the suffering of Muslims and incredulous remarks that Americans did nothing to stop the deaths of 1.5 million Iraqi children (ibid., 193, 199).[7]

By now it should be evident that opposing Al Qaeda's core membership with force inevitably fails to de-motivate them. It actually *strengthens their dedication to their cause* by feeding into their radical apocalyptic sense of oppression by an Evil enemy. This religious worldview does not allow room for negotiation or compromise, complicating the determination of appropriate action. Al Qaeda will not consider the US and its European allies to be *Good* unless we convert to their form of Islam or, at least, consent to live under their form of *sharia* law and pay a 10 percent tax to our rulers.

Bin Laden seemed to hope that some Americans might find the truth in his religion because of (not in spite of) 9/11 and come over to the side of the righteous. In his letter to Americans, "Why We are Fighting You," he declared: "The first thing that we are calling you to is Islam" (ibid., 201). This "offer" was a hope that we would turn away from Evil, which was why the invitation to radical Islam was accompanied by the threat of vengeance: "We desire for you goodness, guidance, and righteousness, so do not force us to send you back as cargo in coffins" (ibid., 206–207). To bin Laden and to all radical apocalypticists, the world is simple: we are Good when we side with him, we are Evil when we don't.

Like the seer in the Book of Revelation, Al Qaeda first directs its angry message against co-religionists considered to be hypocrites. However, unlike John of Patmos, its vision includes the faithful acting out of violent terrorism against its enemies. And for this reason, Al Qaeda has been responsible for at least eight times as many Muslim deaths as non-Muslim deaths, even counting the casualties of 9/11 (Al-Obadi 2009).

To bin Laden and al-Zawahiri, *jahiliyya* or utter ignorance envelops the whole world, a term that conjures up the time before conversion of the Arabians from paganism to Islam. Bin Laden and al-Zawahiri fault their Muslim brothers and sisters for sharing "Western" values: interreligious dialogue, cultural discussions instead of external *jihad* and belief in democracy that is not wholly based on *sharia* law. In fact, many Muslims would argue that democracy and Islam are compatible. Arguably, the Prophet Muhammad created the first multi-cultural democracy in Medina, with the first democratic constitution, the Medina Document (Bhutto 2008, 33–34).

By contrast, al-Zawahiri warned the Egyptian Muslim Brotherhood, saying, "democracy is a man-made infidel religion, devised to give the right to legislate to the masses – as opposed to Islam" (Ibrahim 2007, 122). He condemned them for trying to fit democracy and *sharia* law together, which he deems impossible. Thus he pronounced: "The current rulers of Muslim countries who govern without the *sharia* of Allah are apostate infidels. It is obligatory to overthrow them, to wage *jihad* against them ..." (ibid., 122).[8] This idea appears in an Al Qaeda sponsored letter to the Saudi government that condemns moderate Muslims and refers to their "satanic manner" in showing willingness to cooperate with democracies to achieve "universal peace, security and natural relations" (ibid., 31). Peace is not Al Qaeda's goal.

To Al Qaeda, the secret of the world is that Satan and his friends, the US and its allies, are running it. The secret of the righteous is that Al Qaeda and the Islamist extremists who agree with them are being oppressed and are commanded to fight back.

### 3 *A secret about another future world*

Despite their doctrinal irregularity, members of Al Qaeda also believe in many of the central tenets of Islam: the Qur'an reveals that Allah rules from heaven and after death the observant will go to a heavenly Paradise, while the wicked will burn in Jahim, the fires of hell. Like other Muslims, they await the coming of the Day of Judgment, in which Allah's rule will reward all of the righteous and punish all of the wicked. However, for Al Qaeda, this time is coming very soon. They can trace its signs in present political and social developments.

On March 1, 2002, Osama bin Laden penned a letter to the Saudi government condemning them for responding to an American letter that asked for friendship in the wake of 9/11. He rejected the Saudis' attempt to co-exist peacefully with the US, since bin Laden outlined what he saw as the "West's" only options: "Either submit [convert], or live under suzerainty of Islam [under Muslim rule and sharia law], or die" (Ibrahim 2007, 42).[9]

Bin Laden discloses the core motivation driving his *jihad* and the rationale for the stark options in a crucial part of his letter to the Saudis. By citing a *hadith*, a saying attributed to a chain of authorities stretching back to the Prophet Muhammad, bin Laden reveals:

> But what's more important, and *what the debate truly revolves around*, and what the signatories [of the moderate Saudi letter] shy away from mentioning, is the word of the Messenger as has been relayed by Ahmad and others from Ibn Omar: "*I have been sent in the final hours with the sword*, so that none is worshipped but Allah alone, partnerless."
>
> (Ibid., 41)[10]

Bin Laden believed that we are living in the final hours. As he wrote already by October 2001, the Day of Judgment had already come, since 9/11 and the response of the US and its allies in attacking the Taliban in Afghanistan had "divided the entire world into two separate camps – one of faith, where there is no hypocrisy, and one of infidelity" (ibid., 194).

### Adding radical ingredients to the apocalyptic mix

The majority of all apocalyptically minded believers are non-violent. The majority of the world's 1.7 billion Muslims shape their lives into peaceful examples of Allah's will, patiently waiting and hoping for the Day of Judgment. As I discussed in Chapter 3, the addition of a few reality propositions distinguishes the thought system of radical apocalypticism from peaceful apocalypticism. Al Qaeda holds them all: believing that it has the exclusive, authoritative interpretation of truth, upholding an *active eschatology*, "othering" and demonizing the enemy, and perpetuating a theology of martyrdom and murder that it deems to be in pious accordance with Allah's will.

## 4 *Authoritative Revelation/Interpretation*

One hallmark of radical apocalyptic believers is the conviction that only the righteous group has the correct interpretation of the major scriptures. For Al Qaeda, their Islam is the only Islam (sometimes, even over and against ISIS/ISIL).

Although lacking clerical credentials and proper training in Quranic studies, Bin Laden drew his interpretation of radical Sunni Islam and world events mainly from two prior interpreters: the Egyptian Sunni writer Sayyid Qutb and the Palestinian Sunni theologian Abdullah 'Azzam.

Before his execution in 1966, the influential literary expert, Sayyid Qutb, argued that the immorality and colonialism of the Western powers constitutes aggression against the Muslim world. Futhermore, he stated, there is no difference between defensive *jihad* and offensive *jihad*. Qutb had spent two years in the US in 1949–1951. The excesses and consumerism of the country had disgusted him, turning this marginally religious Muslim into an ardent religious and political activist against the West and secularism. After his return to Egypt, Qutb eventually became a leading member and the chief intellectual figure of the Muslim Brotherhood. Arrested in 1954, he endured poor conditions in prison, where he wrote several works, including a vast Quranic commentary. He was released from prison in 1965 only to be rearrested and executed after publishing his most famous work, *Ma'alim fi al-tariq* or *Milestones along the Way* (1981). Although many older Islamist writers also contributed to the idea of offensive *jihad*, Qutb's works had a profound impact on shaping contemporary radical Islam. This notoriety was secured by Qutb's martyrdom at the hands of the Egyptian government (Cook 2005b, 102–106).

Qutb argued that Islam was living again in a time of ignorance akin to the period before the advent of Islam and that without *jihad* Muslims could not practice Islam freely, a position that drew on his own sense of persecution. According to Qutb, Muslims needed to rise up against their secular leaders in Muslim lands and against any Western powers that oppress them, since Muslims must recreate Allah's divinely ordained civilization. This *jihad* against the godless West and hypocritical Muslim leaders would aid the world, for only under Muslim rule could humankind hear the truth about Islam to accept or reject it (Qutb 1981).

Qutb's writings strongly shaped the influential Palestinian cleric, Abdullah 'Azzam. He crafted his theology of *jihad* in a living laboratory, the war in Afghanistan against the mighty Soviet Union from 1979–1992. Throughout the 1970s, the secular regimes that had replaced monarchies in Egypt, Libya, Syria, Iraq, and Yemen were increasingly transforming into autocratic, nationalist governments. The other models available in Muslim lands were the remaining monarchies in Saudi Arabia, Morocco, and Jordan. Beginning in 1979, an Islamist experiment began to compete with these secular and royal states.

The Shi'ite Islamist Ayatollah Ruhollah Khomeini led a revolution that transformed the US-backed secular regime of the Shah Reza Pahlavi. It became the new Islamic Republic of Iran, a theocratic republic governed partly by a clerical system and adherence to belief in Twelver Shi'ism (Kurzman 2004). While Sunnis like 'Azzam and bin Laden would reject many important tenets of Shi'ite Islam, such as what constitutes the legitimate line of successors to Muhammad, the Iranian model showed the Sunni radicals that an Islamist challenge to secularism and Western influence could succeed. In response, and perhaps partly to compete with Iran, the Saudis began to favor the strict Islamist school of Wahhabist thought that had influenced the early Egyptian Muslim Brotherhood and Sayyid Qutb.

In 1984, Abdullah 'Azzam created MAK – *Mektab al Khidamat* – the "Services Bureau," an organization intended to bring *mujahideen* from all over the world to fight in Afghanistan against the Soviets. It was the precursor to Al Qaeda and remarkably successful, in large part due to financing and operational organization by the Saudi Osama Bin Laden. He conducted fundraising through non-governmental networks and Muslim charities involving financial backers from Saudi Arabia, the US (through the Alkifah Refugee Center in Brooklyn, NY), and the Persian Gulf states, the so-called "Golden Chain" (9/11 Commission 2004, 55, 66). While bin Laden provided a worldwide organizational and financial network, 'Azzam, the scholar and theologian, helped provide a global jihadist theology that reinterpreted classical Muslim positions on *jihad* ('Azzam 1985).

The same year that he created MAK, the theologically trained 'Azzam issued a *fatwa* or religious ruling called "Defense of Muslim Lands." The Wahhabist thought of Qutb, as well as the medieval writer Ibn Tamiyya, greatly influenced 'Azzam (d.1328). Like Qutb, 'Azzam argued that it is time for faithful Muslims to wage external *jihad* in protection of Muslims who have been aggressed against. He placed the greatest importance on Palestine and Afghanistan (ibid., 22–25). But like bin Laden would after him, 'Azzam also demanded the withdrawal of all Jews and Westerners from Saudi Arabia. This *fatwa* widened the scope of *jihad* globally through a religious edict that authoritatively interpreted prior traditions (ibid., 26–31).

By quoting various *hadith*, 'Azzam clearly casts as *fard ayn*, or an individual duty incumbent on each Muslim, the obligation to fight to protect other Muslims wherever they are. In his introduction to the *fatwa*, 'Azzam summarizes the conclusions that he later presented in a speech to 100 Islamic scholars:[11]

That if a piece of Muslim land the size of a hand span is infringed upon, then *jihad* becomes *fard ayn* on every Muslim male and female, where the child shall march forward without the permission of its parents and the wife without the permission of the husband.

(Ibid., 5, 22, 44, 45)

Having argued theologically on behalf of external, defensive *jihad*, he insisted that the welfare of the *ummah*, or worldwide community of Muslims, must supercede national interests, saying: "Unfortunately, when we think about Islam we think nationalistically. We fail to let our vision pass beyond geographic borders that have been drawn up for us by the Kuffar [heretics or infidels, the Western powers]" (ibid., 35). Using the image of concentric circles, he claimed that if Muslims anywhere have been aggressed against, for example in Afghanistan, then it becomes the *fard ayn* of the rest of Muslims to help. This would continue in ever expanding circles of effectiveness until it encompassed the whole world (ibid., 8, 14). His theology thus elevates what most Muslims consider to be the "lesser *jihad*" to a higher level, as he argues: "One of the most important obligations is the forgotten obligation of fighting" (ibid., 12). In 'Azzam's view, fighting is an "obligation," not just recommended or optional. His interpretation was highly influential for Al Qaeda and both bin Laden and al-Zawahiri later quoted from his writings extensively.[12]

Through his charismatic presence and his clerical interpretation of *hadith* and the events of the Afghan war, 'Azzam acquired the authority to claim that *jihad* is even superior to the act of supporting the *hajj*, the once in a lifetime pilgrimage to Mecca that every able-bodied Muslim is obligated to make as one of the five major pillars or duties of Islam. Speaking of the observance of this supremely holy ritual in Islam, 'Azzam said to other Muslims: "You are jesting with your worship, while you worshippers offer your worship, *mujahideen* offer their blood and person" (ibid., 10). He thereby suggested that *jihad* is a sixth major pillar of the faith that is as just as obligatory as the five pillars, including prayer and undertaking the *hajj* pilgrimage to Mecca (ibid., 12, 14).

In 'Azzam's plan, once Afghanistan was secured with an Islamist government, this political step would facilitate the liberation of Jerusalem from Israel, the real enemy (Aboul-Enein 2008a; Cook 2005b, 128–131). The liberation of Jerusalem has always held messianic implications in the Abrahamic traditions and this resonance may also be felt in 'Azzam's writings.

The "Last Day" is important in all of Islam, but 'Azzam links belief in it to willingness to fight external *jihad*. His quotations of the following one *hadith*, citing Tabarani, have been extremely influential: "I have been raised between the hands of the Hour with the sword, until Allah the Exalted is worshipped alone ..." ('Azzam 1985, 3, 10). This verse about "the Hour" imparts an eschatological coloring to 'Azzam's calls to liberate Afghanistan and Palestine. This verse is similar to a famous collection of *hadith* cited by Bukhari that claims in the last Hour *jahilliyya,* or general ignorance, will spread and there will be "al-Harj" in abundance, which Abu Musa explains means "killing" in the Ethiopian language.

For 'Azzam, the Afghan war was a decisive moment in history. He claimed that Allah acted in such a miraculous fashion that it could be called "eschatological," sending the following signs:

- a flock of birds that would take flight just before a Soviet airstrike,
- scorpions that do not sting the *mujahideen,*
- sweet smells coming from the bodies of the slain *mujahideen,*
- corpses of the slain mujahideen that do not decay [at a regular rate],
- fog that shields the Islamist fighters from the Soviets,
- enemy rounds that not explode,
- a bullet that hit the Afghan leader Haqqani's belt and did not injure him,
- and martyrs smiling in death.

(Aboul-Enein 2008a, 5)

He further claimed that angels fought alongside the *mujahideen,* the same angels who had fought alongside the Prophet, which suggested that these were eschatological times that could recapture that early glory of Islam in a new age ('Azzam 1990; Aboul-Enein, 2008b). In fact, 'Azzam's writing on this concept led to the very name for Al Qaeda: "This deen [religion] will triumph and must burst forth from a *qaeda al-sulba* [a firm foundation] … Will the triumph over the Soviets be the seeds from *where an Islamic empire that will alter world history will emerge?*" (Aboul-Enein 2008b, 4, 8). As we continue to trace the growth of Al Qaeda and later *jihadist* movements, we must recognize 'Azzam's influence and the reach of this vision that informs the idea of the "Caliphate," which the self-declared "Islamic State" claims to have reestablished.

## 5a *Active Eschatology*

'Azzam and the Taliban benefited enormously from funding from the US and Saudi Arabia, who contributed billions of dollars to the rebel forces. In time there would be Alkifah Services Bureaus in Brooklyn, Atlanta, Boston, Chicago, Pittsburgh, and Tucson, bringing in additional funding (9/11 Commission 2004, 58; Emerson 2002, 129–137). But this was more than a political fight. It was a religious struggle.

When bin Laden arrived in Afghanistan at the age of twenty-three, he fully accepted the theological interpretations of Abdullah 'Azzam. He could envision the liberation of Afghanistan through the worldwide support of the Islamic *ummah.* Through MAK, bin Laden gained the operations experience to make that a reality. By late 1988, bin Laden, along with Muhammad Atef of the Egyptian Islamic Jihad and Abu Ubaidah al Banshiri, created Al Qaeda, "The Foundation" or "The Base," which operated out of Afghanistan and Peshawar, Pakistan (US Indictment S (10) 98, 4). As *mujahideen* from all over the world arrived to fight the infidels, bin Laden also began to believe in a pan-Islamic vision that would recreate the glory of the original Arab Muslim Empire of the Sunnis in the time of the Prophet's Companions.

The Afghanistan conflict was the crucible that formed Al Qaeda, because it was eschatology in action, both operationally and theologically. The far-reaching religious goal envisioned by 'Azzam, that the whole Muslim world could retake Afghanistan and then Palestine and Saudi Arabia for Islam, seemed to be becoming a reality. In 1986, bin Laden set up a training camp for *mujahideen* in Pakistan. Eventually his sponsored camps would train between 10,000–20,000 *mujahideen* (9/11 Commission 2004, 67). Trained in combat, *mujahideen* also learned new *jihadist* theology from bin Laden that motivated others to action.[13]

During the Afghan conflict, bin Laden also cemented theological and operational ties with other key figures of Al Qaeda, pre-eminently Dr. Ayman al-Zawahiri, the prominent leader of the Egyptian Islamic Jihad (US Indictment S (10) 98, 5–6; 9/11 Commission Report, 2004, 57).[14] Due in part to their similar theological views of global *jihad*, al-Zawahiri merged his group with Al Qaeda and placed himself under the authority of bin Laden, later becoming the leader of Al Qaeda upon bin Laden's death. In this *jihad* in Afghanistan, bin Laden also formed close associations with other critical figures who would later work with the Al Qaeda network: the so called "Blind Sheik" Abdel Rahman from Egypt, of the Islamic Group, who would move to Jersey City, New Jersey to preach radical *jihad* from the Brooklyn Farouq mosque; Wali Khan, or Osama Asmurai, who would cooperate with the bin Laden network in the Philippines and Tajikistan; Abu Zubaydah, who would help operate a terrorist training camp near the Pakistan border with Afghanistan; Ramzi Yousef, who would help plan the 1993 World Trade Center bombing and a foiled Manila air plot to put bombs on a dozen airplanes; and Khalid Sheikh Mohammed, who would also help plan the foiled Manila air plot and mastermind the 2001 attacks of 9/11 (9/11 Commission 2004, 145–150). As the US contemplates fighting Al Qaeda and ISIS/ISIL through other wars, it is important to appreciate that the ties in the Al Qaeda network were formed in just this way.

When 'Azzam and his two sons were killed by a remotely detonated car bomb on November 24, 1989,[15] perhaps by rival Islamists, it changed the focus of the theological energies of many of the radical Islamists involved in the Afghanistan conflict. For 'Azzam, the *jihad* was global, but global in the sense that the concentric circles of the *ummah* that he envisioned in his *fatwa* would extend to include the whole world. The primary focus was on liberating Afghanistan, then Palestine, and also Saudi Arabia from Western influence. With his death, bin Laden ascended to leadership and his theological focus replaced that of 'Azzam and his supporters. For 'Azzam, the center of the circle of the *ummah* was movable to different regions that he wanted to see liberated. For bin Laden, the emphasis changed to the outermost global circle that eliminates Western hegemony everywhere: the whole world would be the center of the circle.

By the fall of 1989, bin Laden was held in high enough esteem amongst radical Islamists to receive an invitation to set up a base in Sudan by Hassan al-Turabi. The fact that the Sudan became the base of bin Laden's operations from about 1991–1996[16] speaks to his early pan-Islamic theological vision for Al Qaeda. Ten years before the horrible events of 9/11, the Al Qaeda network that bin Laden based in the Sudan was already global in scope, combining terrorist actions and training with construction and business operations all over the world. The group had interests and activities in: Germany, China, Malaysia, the Philippines, the former Soviet states of Ukraine, Belarus, Cyprus, Croatia (Zagreb), Bosnia (Sarajevo), Azerbaijan (Baku), Vienna, Budapest, Nairobi, Tanzania, and the Sudan. Its terrorist military wing, bin Laden's "Islamic Army Shura," enlisted volunteers from Saudi Arabia, Egypt, Jordan, Lebanon, Iraq, Oman, Algeria, Libya, Tunisia, Morocco, Somalia, and Eritrea, and established cooperative relationships with extremists from Chad, Mali, Niger, Nigeria, Uganda, Burma, Thailand, Malaysia, Indonesia, and Bosnia (9/11 Commission 2004, 58). As time went on, the list of *jihadi*-affiliated groups grew to include presence in London, Yemen, Djibouti, Albania, Algeria, Tunisia, Lebanon, Tajikistan, and Chechnya, and key al Qaeda operatives could be also be found in Orlando, Florida, California, Virginia, Texas, and Oregon (US Indictment S (10) 98, 6, 27).

Well before 9/11, bin Laden's Sudanese base provided assistance to a number of other terrorist groups across the globe, including: the Moro Islamic Liberation Front in the Philippines, the Abu Sayyaf Brigade in the Philippines, Jemaah Islamiya (JI) in Indonesia, Malaysia, Singapore, and the Philippines, a Pakistani group of insurrectionists in Kashmir and Tajik Islamists in the Afghanistan northern border. He also kept up contacts during the Bosnian conflicts, reached out to Iran and Hezbollah, and had close ties with Alkifah Muslim organizations in Brooklyn, Atlanta, Boston, Chicago, Pittsburgh, and Tucson (ibid., 6, 27). Bin Laden was trying to create global change based on a global vision.

As his theological voice grew throughout his career as leader of Al Qaeda, bin Laden offered up his own interpretations of *jihad* as authoritative, despite the fact that he was not a trained theologian like 'Azzam. In 1996, bin Laden, who lacked the theological credentials to do so, issued a *fatwa* entitled "Message from Osamah Bin-Muammad Bin-Laden to His Muslim Brothers in the Whole World and Especially in the Arabian Peninsula: Declaration of *Jihad* Against the Americans …" (ibid., 25; Bin Laden, 1996). After this, bin Laden regularly issued his own *fatwas*, putting forth his theological opinions on the need for a worldwide *jihad* against the "Crusaders," especially America. These *fatwas* were later cited in the United States Indictment against him and other members of Al Qaeda as evidence of his conspiracy to murder US nationals (US Indictment S (10) 98, 15, 16, 20). Feeding the apocalyptic fantasy of radical Islamists around the globe, in April of 1988, Soviet army forces actually did begin to leave Afghanistan. For a decade, this acted as proof to radical Islamists of the imminent victory of the *mujahideen* over the large secular nations, as bin Laden argued in his 1996 *fatwa*. From 1996 to 2001, the Taliban and bin Laden came together to create what religion scholar David Cook has called "a contemporary radical Muslim messianic kingdom" in Afghanistan (Cook 2005a, 172). The Taliban was known for its strict interpretation of *sharia* law and its harsh enforcement of punishments. This included maiming and death, as well as its severe control over lifestyles – in particular the extreme curtailment of rights for girls and women.

For extremist Sunni Islamists, this regime served as a realized eschatological vision of a pure Islamic regime. In March 2001, the Taliban dynamited the giant, serene Buddhas of Bamiyan that had been built directly into the sandstone cliffs. The act earned condemnation from most of the world, including the majority of Muslims, who saw it as a demonstration of the Taliban's intolerance. However, for Islamist extremists, the act of destroying these "idols" proved the Taliban's total fidelity to a literal interpretation of *sharia* law on a level unprecedented anywhere else in the world (ibid., 175–176).

At first, the various Islamist factions in Afghanistan, especially the Northern Alliance and the Taliban, fought bitterly amongst themselves. Even after the Taliban secured power, most of them disagreed with bin Laden over his "global apocalyptic vision" (ibid., 175). Despite this, under Muhammad `Umar the Taliban harbored bin Laden after he left the Sudan in 1996. From 1998 to 2001, the Taliban and Al Qaeda allied against a new common enemy, the United States. In time, some members of the Taliban would become "radicalized" into bin Laden's point of view, while the majority kept their focus on regional aspirations.

Bin Laden's thought system operated on a global and eschatological level. He told the Saudis in a letter that it was a Muslim destiny to "battle a great nation" (the US) since only three options are available for all of humankind: "The matter is summed up *for every person alive*. Either submit [embrace Islam], or live under the suzerainty of Islam, or die." (Ibrahim 2007, 42). This vision goes far beyond a regional or political battle with limited aims. This scope is wide enough, and the divine calling palpable enough, to rightly be considered *Active Eschatology* – the apocalyptic belief that the effort of the righteous believers will change the world and inaugurate a unique new era ruled by God/Allah.[17] The Islamist rule of the Taliban was a taste of that.

Thus, Afghanistan was much more than just the military training ground for a global influx of *mujahideen*. It was also the crucible of radical

Sunni Islamist theology, a place to act out concepts of an unfolding escha-tological war. By 2005, this *Active Eschatology* was still prominent in the mind of Ayman al-Zawahiri, as is evident in a letter he sent to the leader of Al Qaeda in Iraq, Abu Musab al-Zarqawi. In this letter he unfolds a larger vision:

> It has always been my belief that *the victory of Islam* will never take place until a Muslim state is established in the manner of the Prophet in the heart of the Islamic world, specifically in the Levant, Egypt, and the neighboring states of the Peninsula and Iraq; however, the center would be in the Levant and Egypt.... As for the battles that are going on in the far-flung regions of the Islamic world, such as Chechnya, Afghanistan, Kashmir, and Bosnia, they are just the groundwork and the vanguard for the major battles which have begun in the heart of the Islamic world.
>
> (al-Zawahiri 2005)

In his view, the eventual victory of Islam over the world would begin with a purified Caliphate in the Levant, Egypt, the Arabian Peninsula and Iraq. As Al Qaeda in Iraq gradually transformed into ISIS/ISIL, this *Active Eschatology* would inspire that group's strategy of conquering broad swaths of that geographic area for the Caliphate.

## 5b *Active Eschatology* in other Islamist apocalyptic interpretations

Al Qaeda is not alone amongst Islamist extremists in conceiving of a global eschatological vision. Since 1990, a host of Muslim apocalyptic writers have emerged to offer new eschatological interpretations of Islam. Like bin Laden, many of these writers lack the requisite clerical qualifications for authoritative theological exposition of the Qur'an and *hadith*, but they are still influential on a popular level. Their interpretations and knowledge of the original texts is often inaccurate, but they claim a divine inspiration that bears a particular hallmark: fitting modern events – wars, national conflicts, environmental developments, socio-economic changes, and political movements – into carefully sequenced apocalyptic predictions from the Qur'an or *hadith*.

This is the radical Muslim version of the Christian *Left Behind* series: wildly inaccurate regarding the source texts, but vastly influential on a popular level. These writers fit all the major political conflicts between any Muslim nation and "the West" into their interpretations of the Qur'an. They rely on medieval *hadith*, often of an unreliable quality, or the Bible, including evangelical Protestant interpretations of the Book of Revelation. Since the use of the Bible as a source of apocalyptic authority has been frowned on throughout the history of Islam, their methods as well as their eschatological interpretations and predictions often earn the condemna-tion of mainstream Muslim clerics. This has not dimmed their popularity much.

As David Cook argues, the writings of the apocalyptic interpreter Bashir Muhammad 'Abdallah illustrate the eclectic method employed to map today's events onto scriptures. 'Abdallah draws on Quranic passages, Isa. 9:1, Dan. 7, Rev. 12–13, and Ezek. 22 in an effort to establish a one-to-one correlation between the textual symbols, contemporary events, and nations to yield prophecies that fit onto present-day political events. For example, 'Abdallah identifies the beast of Revelation 12–13 as the Antichrist and its seven heads as the UN Security Council (America, Russia, England, France, Germany, Japan, and China). He further explains that the "begin-ning of the first appearance of the beast" is the war led by America against Iraq and the Dragon is the Zionist conspiracy (Cook 2005a, 44, 185–189). This style of prophecy is remarkably similar to that of Hal Lindsey, who frightened and intrigued millions of Americans in the 1980s with his orac-ular mapping of contemporary politics onto the Book of Revelation in *The Late Great Planet Earth* (Lindsey 1970).

Other Muslim writers have focused on interpreting the 1979–1991 Afghanistan conflict and 9/11 as the fulfillment of apocalyptic prophecy. In a book entitled *Harmajjadun*, or Armageddon, the Egyptian writer, Amin Jamal al-Din, identifies America's post 9/11 attack on Afghanistan as the precursor to the battle of Armageddon (Cook 2005a, 180–183). Using classical Muslim sources from the eighth century prophesying various con-flicts between the Muslims and the Byzantines, Jamal al-Din predicts that the West will finish with Afghanistan and thereafter attack Egypt. Follow-ing this, the eschatological figure, the Mahdi, will unite the Muslim world to destroy the Western armies at Armageddon. Finally, the Mahdi will conquer Constantinople and Rome, destroying the Vatican (ibid., 180–183).

Other interpreters have interpreted 9/11 and bin Laden himself as the fulfillment of prophecies. However, unlike other apocalyptic leaders we will encounter in this book, bin Laden did not seem interested in claiming any divine titles for himself in his eschatological scenarios.[18] Some writers on propagandist websites, however, portrayed bin Laden with messianic imagery before his death. They suggested that he might have been the Mahdi who would unite the Muslim world in the endtime or that he is the *mujaddid* or the renewer that Allah sends once a century (ibid., 179).[19] The Palestinian Salah al-Din Abu 'Arafa interprets Exodus apocalyptically to present bin Laden as an eschatological Moses who will liberate Muslims against Pharaoh, the United States (ibid., 181).[20]

The cultural lesson for policy makers and intelligence analysts is that there is no difference between politics and religion for apocalyptic believers. Radical apocalyptic believers with an *Active Eschatology* will some-times act out their apocalyptic fantasies in the political realm.

## 6 *"Othering"/Concretized Evil*

Of course, it is extremely easy for Al Qaeda to locate evil enemies: they have only to look outside of the radical Islamist community. Bin Laden and al-Zawahiri both divide the world firmly into "us vs. them" or "Good vs. Evil." For the leaders of Al Qaeda, the process of "Othering" is universal: everyone who is not firmly in their own camp is viewed as Evil itself. In Stahelski's social psychological framework, the whole world outside of radical Islam is Other-deindividuated as infidels (Western) or as apostate infidels (Muslims). By calling America "the head of the snake," bin Laden effectively dehumanized and demonized the "Other" as well.

On October 7, 2001, the day that the US launched its military campaign against Al Qaeda and the Taliban in Afghanistan, al-Jazeera released a pre-taped message by bin Laden. After praising Allah for 9/11 and attributing the results to a divine hand, bin Laden recounts America's atrocities: killing one million Iraqi children, havoc in Palestine, atomic bombings on Japan in WWII and the American wars in Iraq and Afghanistan. According to him, "America and her supporters" are "the head of global infidelity." He continued: "I say to you that these events have *divided the entire world into two separate camps* – one of faith where there is no hypocrisy, and one of infidelity ..." (Ibrahim 2007, 191–195). The two camps deserve either *wala'* (loyalty/love) or *bara'* (enmity/hate) (Ibrahim 2007, 63–115).

Al Qaeda illustrates how far the concept of "concretized Evil" can extend, generating moods of hatred and vengeance. For bin Laden, it is one's religious duty to hate the infidels, since they are opposed to God. He stated, "So there is an enmity, evidenced by fierce hostility, and an internal hate for the heart" that only ends if the infidel converts or agrees to live under the *sharia* law accepted by Al Qaeda. He added further:

> But if the hate at any time extinguishes from the heart, this is great apostasy; the one who does this will stand excuseless before Allah....
> Battle, animosity, and hatred – directed from the Muslim to the infidel
> – is the foundation of our religion. And we consider this a justice and a kindness.
>
> (Ibrahim 2007, 43)

For bin Laden, such battle and hatred are justified because the infidels oppose "our Creator", Allah. He construed it as a kindness because through fighting us, we might just see the error of our ways and convert and submit to radical Islam.

It is difficult to say which group Al Qaeda hates the most: moderate Muslims, Jews or Americans/Europeans. Al Qaeda has killed at least eight times more Muslims than non-Muslims (Al-Obaidi *et al.*, 2009). Bin Laden and al-Zawahiri lumped together the rest (Other-deindividuation) by using the combined title the "Crusader-Zionists." Like the radical Christian

Identity apocalypticists whom I examine in Chapter 6, bin Laden believed that a "Zionist lobby" controlled the American government and motivated President Bush to attack Iraq for oil (Ibrahim 2007, 210–212).

## 7   *Redemptive Violence/Revenge*

Even when the members of an apocalyptic group despise the enemy, believe they know the truth, and trust that they can inaugurate the blissful rule of God on earth, they still will not habitually perpetuate violence without a theology that supports this brutality as something positive and redemptive. Shockingly, Al Qaeda believes they are the good guys.

Terrorism specialists often mention the facts that the violence is symbolic and the victims of terrorism are not the intended audience (Richardson 2006; Hoffman 2006, 34). Terrorists attack innocents to get the attention of the president, the media, or the European public. However, it is also important to note that radical apocalyptic terrorists, including Al Qaeda, subscribe to theologies that eliminate the concept of the innocent bystander as well as the idea of the audience. Sometimes, in this thought system, no one is considered to be innocent and the intended audience is God.

As we have seen, bin Laden and al-Zawahiri's *fatwas* mandated the obligation to battle the enemy based on interpretations of *hadith* and other sacred texts. But the "enemy" encompasses practically the whole world, since al Qaeda divides the world into only two camps deserving of either love or enmity. Al Qaeda's theology eliminates the idea that there are any non-combatants, viewing all Americans, Canadians, and Europeans as legitimate targets. Bin Laden repeatedly stressed that due to the nature of our democracy, the American people voted for their president and our taxes support the US military (Ibrahim 2007, 200, 280–282). Therefore, according to him, every American was responsible for the military atrocities in Iraq, Somalia, Afghanistan, and Palestine (through American's support of Israel). Bin Laden explained: "This is why the American people are not innocent of the innumerable crimes committed by the Americans and Jews against us. Allah Most High legislated the permission and option to take revenge" (ibid., 201). In bin Laden's view, violence is the just response: "You have occupied our lands, transgressed against our manhood and dignity, spilled our blood, plundered our wealth, destroyed our homes, dislocated us, and played with our security – *and we will give you the same treatment*" (ibid., 224).

Intent on revenge and suffused with theology that frames murder as "a noble death" apocalyptic believers such as the members of Al Qaeda turn to terrorism (ibid., 224). However, it is important to note that bin Laden, like other terrorists we will encounter in this book, bristled at the label "terrorist," except when he applied it to President Bush. In a taped appearance on al-Jazeera in October 2004, he admitted his role in 9/11 for the first time. He deflected responsibility onto America by asking rhetorically, "Shall a man be blamed for protecting his own? Self-defense [by Al Qaeda] and punishing the wicked in kind – are these shameful acts of 'terrorism'?" (ibid., 216). Only in this one rare instance did bin Laden seem to show the most infinitesimal spark of recognition of his crimes. He continued, "... *And even if it is [terrorism], we have no other option*" (ibid., 216). To bin Laden, 9/11 was redemptive, sacred violence.

Psychological analyses of terrorists show that they are not mentally ill as a group (Crenshaw 1981). Many other factors motivate terrorists, such as group dynamics and cultural, social, and political circumstances of discontent (Victoroff 2005). Islamist extremists repeatedly cite regional conflicts as evidence of Muslim oppression, including those in Palestine, Iraq, Afghanistan, Algeria, Somalia, Chechnya, and Bosnia. This sense of vast suffering apparently feeds the decision to lash out in violent and symbolic retaliation, which is viewed as a morally correct form of violence.

Al Qaeda-style terrorism requires suicide terrorism operations, which it is at great pains to cast as "redemptive violence," since the Qur'an prohibits both suicide and the murder of innocents. The specific justifications for 9/11 style of terrorism came from another non-theologian, Dr. Ayman al-Zawahiri, the current leader of Al Qaeda. He makes a few feeble arguments, both in terms of Islamic jurisprudence and plain logic. It would be laborious to provide a comprehensive refutation of his argument here. However, pointing out some obvious misinterpretations illustrates how difficult it is for radical Islam to make a theological case for terrorism in terms that other Muslims would consider to be Islamic.

In Part 1 of a treatise attempting to justify suicide terrorism, al-Zawahiri must first establish the permissibility of suicide according to Islamic law (Ibrahim 2007, 137–171). Since there is no passage in the Qur'an that al-Zawahiri can marshal in his argument, he must turn to a rather obscure *hadith* unknown to most, "the boy and the king," in which an evil king wants to kill a boy who will not renounce Islam. The king cannot succeed because on each attempt the boy calls to Allah, who saves him through a miracle, such as an earthquake or the capsizing of his captors' boat. Under pressure, the boy finally reveals to the king that there is one way to kill him, which is to hang him on a tree, use his own arrow, invoke the name of Allah and the fire the arrow. Hearing this, the king kills the boy in this manner, but the death unintentionally inspires others to affirm their faith in Islam. Like the boy, they refuse to renounce their religion and the king forces them to jump into a fire.

This ill-fitting story is some of the best evidence that al-Zawahiri can muster in support of suicide terrorism. It is indeed an emotional story about a boy who could only be slain with Allah's permission and who empowered others to heed the call to Islam. However, it is emphatically *not* proof that suicide martyrdom is permissible in Islam. The boy did not kill himself. None of the people killed themselves willingly, except by jumping into a fire under duress. And none of the Muslims in the *hadith* killed anyone else. In fact, the *hadith* could be interpreted to indicate that the king was evil because he oppressed others for their religion and that pacifistic martyrdom in the face of oppression can inspire others to be loyal to Islam.

Al-Zawahiri then makes four other arguments regarding suicide: it is "permissible" for one to charge a superior enemy even if it is relatively certain that one will be killed (as long as one expects to do some damage), it is "superior" to be steadfast against the enemy and refuse to surrender even to the point of death, it is "superior" to be steadfast to the point of death instead of renouncing one's faith, and it is "permissible" to kill oneself to guard against revealing secrets under torture (Ibrahim 2007, 157–160). Like the story of the boy and the king, these situations bear little resemblance to the kind of suicide terrorism in which Al Qaeda has engaged. Instead, each case portrays a faithful Muslim who is actively aggressed upon in his person militarily by a foe, which has no parallel to Al Qaeda's suicide terrorism of 9/11. Since in the other examples the enemy kills the Muslim, only the last case of the captured Muslim prisoner may even be considered a suicide and it bears no similarity to Al Qaeda's terrorism.

In Part 2 of the treatise, al-Zawahiri attempts to circumvent the Quranic prohibition on the killing of innocents. He strains to ask the question, betraying his knowledge of the quranic injunction against harming inno-cent life:

> [Often] mixed among the infidels, whom the *mujahidin* target in warfare, are those *whom it is not permitted to kill – such as Muslims, dhimmis* [Jews and Christians pledged to live under the rule of Islam], *women and children, and so forth … is killing ones such as these – acciden-tally, not on purpose – forgiven* in face of the highest goods that would be realized from waging jihad against the infidels, the enemies of Allah Supreme?
>
> (Ibrahim 2007, 162)

Given that his argument specifies that the killing occurs "accidentally, not on purpose," it cannot apply to the indiscriminate suicide terrorism of 9/11 in which the twin towers and Pentagon contained women and Muslims!

Ignoring this, al-Zawahiri must consider three theological positions held by learned clerics: total prohibition of killing innocents (one extreme), total legitimacy to bombard the infidels even if there are Muslims or their children amongst them (the other extreme), or permissi-bility to bombard only under specific conditions (the middle position). By stating that Al Qaeda takes the third view, he tries to portray Al Qaeda as moderate and reasonable (Ibrahim 2007, 168).

Al-Zawahiri ends his treatise by claiming that there is simply no other way to fight America than to engage in terrorism. This definitely gives the impression that the treatise is less a theological proof than an exercise in circular reasoning with an a priori conclusion.

Al Qaeda's theological reasoning to justify 9/11 and its other terrorist operations is thus wholly unconvincing in an Islamic context. What is especially noteworthy is that al-Zawahiri, who is not credentialed in Islamic theology, would deign to write a theological treatise drawing on Islamic jurisprudence in an attempt to persuade Muslims of a fundamental change in the Qur'anic position on violence and suicide. However, Al-Zawahiri is not alone in his approach. Holbrook shows that other radical Islamists selectively use thirty Quranic texts out of context to justify violence, overlooking the literal interpretation of the verses (Holbrook 2010).

## Lessons for counter-terrorism

After 9/11, President George W. Bush and the US Congress established by law the bipartisan, independent National Commission on Terrorist Attacks Upon the United States, known as the 9/11 Commission. It issued its findings as the *9/11 Commission Report*, a governmental report of impressive sweep and detail published in 2004.

The *Report* concluded its mammoth collection of data with analysis, including new appraisals of the threat of global terrorism. In 2004 the 9/11 Commission understood the threat far better than the government had just after September 11, 2001: "In the post 9/11 world, threats are defined more by the fault lines within societies than by the territorial boundaries between them" (9/11 Commission 2004, 361). The *Report* goes on to explain that Osama bin Laden draws on a stream of radical Islamist theology extending from Ibn Taimiyyah to Sayyid Qutb, noting:

> that stream is *motivated by religion and does not distinguish politics from religion* thus distorting both. It is further fed by *grievances* ... Bin Ladin and Islamist terrorists mean exactly what they say: to them America is the font of all evil, the "head of the snake," and it must be converted or destroyed.
>
> (9/11 Commission 2004, 362, italics added for emphasis)

The 9/11 Commission identifies a religious framework and grievances as the basis for Al Qaeda's terrorism. Other extremist groups holding similar religious thought systems nurse similar grievances today. In the chapters that follow, I apply the formula for radical apocalypticism to a range of challenging groups, including ISIS/ISIL, domestic Christian Identity groups in the US, eco-terrorists, and Asian new religious movements. Perhaps the most important insight that derives from the analysis is that terrorism arises out of discontent; thus, combative actions rarely put an end to terrorist ideology.

This point was not well understood before and just after 9/11, because Al Qaeda's religious framework was not well understood. To arrive at a new, far-sighted analytic and policy narrative, we must first look back at errors that were made. My purpose is not to retread any criticisms already dealt with by the 9/11 Commission regarding intelligence flaws or to single out a particular partisan approach for critique. While I will point out far-reaching mistakes by the Bush administration in addressing terrorism, mistakes that are still reverberating today, I will also note miscalculations that I believe the Obama administration is currently making and suggest directions for changing course.

## A failure to comprehend radical apocalyptic terrorism

When the governing framework of radical apocalyptic terrorism is not well understood, we can take policy steps that actually worsen the situation and create unintended consequences. This is how the executive branch responded after 9/11. To be fair, our country had never faced such an unprecedented act of terrorism on our own soil or this kind of Islamist terrorism. Many complicated geo-political and social issues complicated the decisions in how to move forward. I have the benefit of hindsight and this is in no way a smug academic critique of what the intelligence, executive or legislative branches should have known. I do, however, maintain that understanding religion per se should have been a top priority for the intelligence community and policy makers after the 1979 Islamic Revolution in Iran. Arguably, it still is not.

Yet the lesson of the response to 9/11 is that when religious and cultural dimensions of terrorism are not *at the forefront* of intelligence collection and analysis and when that information is subsequently not well understood by the executive and legislative branches, the most well-intentioned policy initiatives and strategic responses can have disastrous effects.

### *Unintended consequences*

The official *9/11 Commission Report* documents multiple mistakes made when dealing with the threat from Al Qaeda before 9/11. Chief among these errors was the lack of any National Intelligence Estimate on terrorism from 1997 to 2001, the Bush White House's disregard of the Presidential Daily Briefs that dramatically highlighted the danger of bin Laden and the failure to take Al Qaeda seriously as the top threat to the US. This occurred despite repeated warnings from the outgoing Clinton administration and multiple intelligence agencies and experts in the summer and early fall of 2001. These included CIA, FBI, Director of Central Intelligence (DCI) George Tenet, and Richard Clarke, the national counterterrorism coordinator and the only expert on terrorism with a continuous perspective gained from advising four presidential administrations. Regardless of his credentials, Richard Clarke was functionally demoted at the suggestion of National Security Advisor Condoleezza Rice during re-organization (9/11 Commission 2004, 98, 200, 212, 260–262, 342–343).

Clearly, President Bush and his top advisors did not fully appreciate the scope of the threat facing America from bin Laden and Al Qaeda until the events of 9/11 unfolded. This attack did not fit the pattern of past terrorist incidents in America, in which terrorists with some limited political objective attacked a target linked to their grievances. However, amongst the data collected by intelligence agencies and presented to the executive branch, the evidence was there for an indiscriminate, large-scale attack on average Americans within our border. According to the 9/11 Commission (2004, 262–263):

- Al Qaeda had already issued multiple writings and *fatwas* on its theology of offensive *jihad* against America as well as several declarations of war.
- Al Qaeda had already been linked to transnational terrorist bombings: US Embassies in Nairobi, Kenya, and Dar es Salaam, Tanzania on August 7, 1998, the bombing of the USS *Cole* on October 12, 2000, and the attempted "millennium" bombing of the Los Angeles Airport by Ahmed Ressam on December 14, 1999.
- Both President Clinton and President Bush knew that Al Qaeda and bin Laden were threats.
- During the summer of 2001, the FBI Counter-terrorism Division, CIA, DIA, NSA, FAA, and Counter-terrorism Security Group headed by Clarke all reported an uptick in threat alerts, generating warnings such as a June 30 briefing entitled "Bin Ladin Planning High-Profile Attacks" (9/11 Commission 2004, 258–260).
- Some excellent Senior Executive Intelligence Briefs (SEIB) and Presidential Daily Briefings (PDB) highlighted the threat clearly. On June 30, 2001, the SEIB contained an article titled "Bin Ladin Threats are Real," but Deputy Secretary of Defense Paul Wolfowitz questioned the reporting (9/11 Commission 2004, 258–260).
- As late as August 6, 2001, the PDB was entitled, "Bin Ladin Determined to Strike in US." It noted Al Qaeda had members who had resided in the US for years, including an active recruiting cell in New York. It also related "sensational threat reporting" that bin Laden wanted to hijack a US aircraft, although this could not be corroborated.
- The same PDB included this observation:
  "Clandestine, foreign government, and media reports indicate Bin Ladin since 1997 has wanted to conduct terrorist attacks in the U.S. Bin Ladin implied during US television interviews in 1997 and 1998 that his followers would follow the example of World Trade Center bomber Ramzi Yousef and 'bring the fighting to America".

Despite mounting evidence, competing priorities overshadowed these warnings.

The *9/11 Commission Report* attributes many organizational and practical reasons for not addressing the threat more directly. However, I want to ask, why did government officials personally and collectively underestimate the threat of Al Qaeda? More recently, as Kroft (2014) highlights, why did the intelligence community under James Clapper again underestimate the rise of ISIS/ISIL, as President Obama admits? I suggest that the blind spot both times partly stemmed from an inability to understand the religious worldview of the enemy.

In the US, we did not fully appreciate how profoundly a theology of cosmic war could translate into actual attempts at a global *jihad*, even though calls to rally support for that cause had been openly published since at least 1998. In a speech to the troops in Alaska, President Bush revealed his confusion: "It's hard for me to figure out what was going through the minds of those who planned and attacked America. They must have thought we were soft" (Bush 2002). The basic premise that Al Qaeda believes that we are powerful because we are Evil is often difficult for us to grasp.

It is sometimes necessary to look backwards in order to go forward. If a focus on understanding religion had been a priority in intelligence collection and policy formation before and after 9/11, the threats could have been more recognizable. Using open source accounts of Al Qaeda's beliefs to understand their religious worldview would have shed light on a number of important points:

- Osama bin Laden accrued authority and power through his role as a theological interpreter and made unusual claims for himself as a non-theologian issuing *fatwas*.
- The many *fatwas* from Al Qaeda served to radicalize geographically disparate communities of radical Islamists, giving voice to their discontent and filling their lives with a goal and purpose.
- Bin Laden's theology of global *jihad*, appreciated within an Islamic context, represents a significant departure from past understandings of *jihad*.
- The battlegrounds in Afghanistan served as a space to act out eschatological and theological dreams. Fighters expressed extreme motivation and purpose regardless of the outcome of the battles.
- Al Qaeda did not consider anyone in the US or allied nations to be innocent.

Grasping these points could have alerted intelligence to the global nature of Al Qaeda's new kind of *jihad*. Recognizing the scope and depth of their ambition would have, in turn, shed light on their connections to many transnational terrorist incidents in the 1990s. (Indeed, recognizing the scope of their vision should impress upon us today that they could choose to operate anywhere.) A focus on understanding their religious worldview would have allowed analysts to appreciate the extreme dedication that bin Laden's ideology could engender and the reach of the Al Qaeda network. This would have illuminated bin Laden's actual role much earlier. Instead, early reports focus mainly on his role as a financier.

In addition, an understanding of radical apocalypticism would have nuanced the portrait even more, in the following ways:

- Al Qaeda's *active eschatology* might have conveyed the urgency with which radical Islamists would want to strike, as well as the extent of their dedication and persistence.
- Al-Zawahiri's *theology of redemptive violence*, in the form of his justification of suicide terrorism and the killing of innocents, might have shed light on the range of methods that Al Qaeda could employ and the targets they would choose.
- Al Qaeda's view of *concretized Evil* could have conveyed the potential large scope and indiscriminate nature of the intended victims. It could also have suggested the potential that they would attack the top symbolic targets that they associated with Evil. In their original plans, these included the White House and Capitol building, CIA and FBI headquarters, and nuclear power plants (9/11 Commission 2004, 154).

If the administration had been focused on understanding religion and radical apocalypticism, perhaps 9/11 would even have been preventable. However, failing this understanding, several of the responses of the Bush administration after 9/11 actually exacerbated the problem of radical Islamist terrorism in a way that still affects the world today.

## "The War on Terror"

At 8:46 a.m., American Airlines Flight 11 crashed into the North World Trade Center; at 9:03 a.m., United Airlines Flight 175 crashed into the South Tower; and at 9:37 a.m., American Airlines Flight 77 crashed into the Pentagon. At 9:45 a.m., President Bush spoke on the phone to Vice President Cheney and said, "I heard about the Pentagon. We're at war ... somebody's going to pay" (9/11 Commission 2004, 39).[21] His immediate sentiment makes sense as an immediate reaction by a president whose instinct was fight and not flight, a quality that we tend to admire in American presidents. However, as a long-term narrative to guide strategic response, characterizing the conflict as a war only established the playing field on Al Qaeda's terms.

In his comments during the week that followed 9/11, President Bush often made this pledge: "My administration has a job to do and we're going to do it. We will rid the world of the evil-doers" (Perez-Rivas 2001). Upon arriving on the South Lawn on September 16, 2001 after meetings with his principals at Camp David, the president gave a short speech and then took questions from reporters. In thirteen minutes total, the president used the term "evil" or "evil-doers" nine times, including saying "we've never seen this kind of evil before." In these famous, unscripted remarks, he also stated, "This crusade, this war on terrorism, is going to take awhile" (Bush 2001). The frequent references to evil and President Bush's use of "crusade" evoked significant worry amongst European allies (Ford 2001).

The same day, the French foreign minister Hubert Vedrine made this prescient statement: "We have to avoid a clash of civilizations at all costs. One has to avoid falling into this huge trap, this monstrous trap conceived by the instigators of the assault" (ibid.).

He may not have known how tempting it would be for Americans to frame the conflict as a "clash of civilizations." The Presidential Cabinet was familiar with apocalyptic speech, since President Bush and some of his aides professed to be dedicated, born-again evangelical Christians. According to some journalistic sources, the president tried to urge French President Jacques Chirac to join the war in Iraq on the basis of fighting "Gog and Magog" to fulfill biblical prophecy, although the authenticity of this story has recently been challenged.[22] In his autobiography, Chirac referred to Bush's "quasi-mystical mission" (Chirac 2012, 276).

In my position as an academic, I would never presume to have access to President Bush's inner religious thoughts. I can only judge how he framed the Iraq conflict in his speeches as a war between Good and Evil. As early as 1998, the World Islamic Front had issued a "declaration of war" that painted the world in the same terms. The president's public comments simply swapped the sides of Good vs. Evil in a cosmic war.

Just one day after 9/11, President Bush announced, "This will be a monumental struggle of good versus evil, but good will prevail" (Gore 2007, 54). According to former Vice-President Al Gore, two days after that announcement, Bush gave a speech in the National Cathedral in which he stated that his "responsibility to history" was to "rid the world of evil" (Gore 2007, 54). Furthermore, he appeared to subscribe to the idea of a divinely ordained victory when he addressed a joint session of Congress later in the week. He asserted that "freedom and fear, justice and cruelty, have always been at war, and we know that God is not neutral between them" (ibid., 55).

This is "cosmic dualism" in the full apocalyptic sense: the world is divided into Good and Evil, and God is only on the side of the Good. Surprisingly, this was the leader of the United States making political speeches and forming public policy actions based on these assertions. In his speech to Congress on September 20, 2001, the president clearly spoke of a divided world: "Every nation, in every region, now has a decision to make:

Either you are with us, or you are with the terrorists" (9/11 Commission 2004, 337).[23] This kind of dualism leaves little room for complexity or nuance. One way or the other, it also reinforces the apocalyptic worldview.

In the presidential address on September 20, 2001, Bush publicly coined the term "War on Terror" that he had already used for days. It would remain in political and media usage for the foreseeable future, even after the Obama administration officially discontinued its use in favor of the far less memorable "Overseas Contingency Operation."[24] Bush saw the efforts to counter terrorism as a war against Evil itself. Lest this seem like an exaggeration, consider this quote from President Bush's address to rally the troops in 2002 in Alaska:

> Either you're with us or you're against us. Either you stand for freedom, or you stand with tyranny.... As you probably figured out by now, *I view this current conflict as either us versus them, and evil versus good. And there's no in between. There's no hedging. And if you want to join the war against evil, do some good.*
> 
> (Bush 2002, italics added for emphasis)

In calling this a war, dividing all possible participants into two sides, identifying those two sides with Good and Evil and claiming that God would bring victory to only his side, President Bush supported – whether intentionally or unintentionally – much of the apocalyptic worldview that we needed to nuance and combat.

Worse yet, President Bush repeated the term "crusade" in a *scripted* speech, not just in the unscripted remarks earlier on the White House lawn. When referring to the Canadians, he complimented them by saying, "They stand with us in this incredibly important *crusade* to defend freedom" (Bush 2002). While "crusade" was perhaps meant as an innocent turn of phrase to mean "a collective striving," Al Qaeda had lobbed the insulting title of "Crusaders" at us for almost a decade. Bush's embracing of the term inescapably evoked the battle of Good versus Evil. The name that Al Qaeda had given us became part of our own self–identity as a nation.

If Bush didn't mean to refer to the medieval "Crusade" of Christians against Muslims, other US officials did. Lt. General William G. Boykin, a general in charge of war policy, spoke from an Oregon church pulpit in uniform. He stated that we were in a Holy War as a "Christian nation battling Satan" (Gore 2007, 58–59).[25] Despite the ensuing controversy, he was never forced to resign and was defended by Donald Rumsfeld, Bush's Secretary of Defense (*CNN* 2003). Former Vice-President Gore notes that Boykin felt fine "using the language of the Crusades – even though the United States was desperately seeking Muslim allies at the time – because his commander in chief had repeatedly used religious language and symbols in his presentation of his policy" (ibid., 58). People surrounding Bush definitely believed in the apocalyptic worldview and whether or not

Bush agreed, he employed its language. As Gore states: "with the radical Right, we have a political faction disguised as a religious sect, and the president of the United States is *heading* it" (ibid., 61).

Extremist Islamist interpreters took President Bush's use of the term "crusade" as proof positive that Americans were in fact what they had alleged: Crusaders. The medieval period was never conceptually distant for Qutb, 'Azzam, and bin Laden. They drew repeatedly on the medieval interpreter, Ibn Tamiyya, to create a social memory that reduces history to Crusaders warring against true Islam. Al Qaeda now saw this narrative of history affirmed, as bin Laden explained:

> Our goal is for our nation to unite in the face of the Christian Crusade. This is the fiercest battle. *Muslims have never faced anything bigger than this* [eschatological language of a singular moment in history]. *Bush said it in his own words: "crusade."* ... *He said "crusade." Bush divided the world into two: "either with us or with terrorism."* Bush is the leader; he carries the big cross [of crusading Christendom] and walks.... *Those who follow Bush in his crusade against Muslims have denounced Allah.* ... This is a recurring war. *The original crusade brought Richard from Britain, Louis from France, and Barbarus from Germany. Today the crusading countries rushed as soon as Bush raised the cross.*
>
> (CNN 2002, italics added for emphasis)

At the time, the executive and legislative branches failed to grasp fully that we were fighting an ideology rather than an army or group that could be attacked and defeated. President Bush stated, "Our war on terror begins with al Qaeda, but it does not end there. It will not end until every terrorist group of global reach has been found, stopped, and defeated" (Gore 2007, 337). He also promised to "hunt down" every last terrorist "no matter where they hide" (Bush 2002). Such comments give the clear impression of vanquishing a conventional, limited enemy.

To his great credit, President Bush clearly stated in his joint speech to Congress and the American public on September 20 that, "The enemy of America is not our many Muslim friends; it is not our many Arab friends. Our enemy is a radical network of terrorists, and every government that supports them" (Gore 2007, 337). Had he not said this, the backlash against American Muslims might have been even greater. However, these comments do not recognize Al Qaeda's brand of terrorism as an ideology that revives and spreads when we confront terrorist groups in the wrong manner. It does not recognize that *we unintentionally spread the ideology when we subscribe to the same narrative ourselves*, albeit with different characters in play. Instead, we should be engaged in changing the apocalyptic narrative entirely and avoiding its framing language.

The effort to track down the 9/11 terrorists at first meant an attack on Al Qaeda and the Taliban in Afghanistan. This offensive was eerily reminiscent of the context that had spawned Al Qaeda and MAK in the first place, fighting the *mujahideen* in Afghanistan. As it had for the Soviets, the battle in that terrain and against that style of fighting proved to be harder than expected. However, by spring of 2003, a new conflict involved the US that diverted most of our military resources away from Afghanistan and from actually finding and combating Al Qaeda. The new battleground was Iraq, which had not attacked us on 9/11 and which contained no weapons of mass destruction.

### The axis of evil and the doctrine of pre-emptive strike

In his State of the Union address on January 29, 2002, President Bush named Iraq as part of the "Axis of Evil," along with Iran and North Korea. As historical hindsight has proven, Iraq had nothing to do with 9/11, nor was it home to Al Qaeda. (The "Axis of Evil" phrase was also *highly* unfortunate for our geo-political relationships with Iran. At the time Iran was led by a moderate President Khatami, who had just aided us in the fight against the Taliban and Al Qaeda in Afghanistan.) By March 19, 2003, the US had invaded Iraq, but many questioned whether the administration had planned this before 9/11.

There is evidence that several members of the administration were predisposed to attacking Iraq immediately as the aftermath of 9/11 unfolded. Secretary of Defense Donald Rumsfeld admits that he considered striking Iraq on that very afternoon.[26] National Security Advisor Condoleezza Rice testified that during the week after 9/11 in the first session at Camp David chaired by the president, Rumsfeld asked what should be done about Iraq and Deputy Secretary Paul Wolfowitz made a case for striking Iraq during "this round" of the war on terrorism.[27] In his testimony to the 9/11 Commission, General Tommy Franks noted that planning for an invasion of Iraq had already occurred in Central Command or CENTCOM in the summer of 2001, before 9/11. Immediately after 9/11, Tommy Franks requested that they resume planning for the action.[28] According to General Colin Powell, during those first days after 9/11, Wolfowitz pushed for the invasion of Iraq. The president resisted, making Afghanistan his first priority.[29]

On March 19, 2003, the US did finally strike Iraq. The war has been criticized on a number of fronts, including the diversion of severely needed troops and resources from the attempt to find Osama bin Laden and Al Qaeda in Afghanistan. Additionally, Saddam Hussein had nothing to do with 9/11, as the president himself admitted six months after the invasion.[30]

From a humanitarian standpoint, the invasion was devastating (Tapp *et al.* 2008). While the US did not target innocent persons in Iraq, the conflict from 2003 to 2011 resulted in civil war, casualties, and disruptions far more severe than most Americans realize. Estimates for the numbers of dead range from 130,000 to one million, with most studies settling on about 500,000 Iraqi civilians dead and millions displaced (Vergano 2013). This US-led conflict and the aftermath of its civil war also left approximately five million child orphans in Iraq, including one half million orphaned children living on the street (UN HRC, 2012). In addition to the threats on their physical safety, these children grew up disconnected from family structures, adequate shelter, hopes of future employment, positive self-identities, and meaningful social networks. Unsurprisingly, extremist groups have arisen to fill these gaps.

In the context of counter-terrorism aimed at extremist Islam, the war in Iraq carried with it a particularly negative theological implication. The invasion of coalition forces led by General Franks was a "pre-emptive strike" against a country that had not directly attacked us, signaling a departure from normal US foreign policy (Gupta 2009). In the "National Security Strategy of the United States of America," the so-called "Bush doctrine" laid out the foreign policy guidelines that formed the basis of the plan to invade Iraq. In the Preface to the strategic policy, President Bush writes: "As a matter of common sense and self-defense, America will act against such emerging threats before they are fully formed" (National Security Strategy 2002). The policy goes on to state:

> We will disrupt and destroy terrorist organizations by ... defending the United States, the American people, and our interests at home and abroad by identifying and destroying the threat before it reaches our borders. While the United States will constantly strive to enlist the support of the international community, *we will not hesitate to act alone, if necessary, to exercise our right of self-defense by acting pre-emptively against such terrorists ... we recognize that our best defense is a good offense ...*
>
> (Ibid., 6, italics added for emphasis)

The reasoning of the document is that *this is a time unlike any other.* "Given the goals of rogue states and terrorists, the United States can no longer solely rely on a reactive posture as we have in the past.... We cannot let our enemies strike first" (ibid., 15).

However, if a reason for the pre-emptive strike was also to deter terrorists and send a message to radical Islamists, it had the opposite effect. From the point of view of moderate as well as radical Islam, the "Bush doctrine" legitimizes a pre-emptive strike on a Muslim nation. That places the US in the Quran's category of an aggressor on the Islamic *ummah*. As stipulated in suras such as The Cow, in this case faithful Muslims are called to defend themselves in *jihad* "until the religion is Allah's" (2:190–193). Some Muslims who had been previously appalled by the terrorism of 9/11 began to look at America in a new light: as an aggressor against whom they needed to fight. The result was that whereas Al Qaeda did not have a significant presence in Iraq before the 2003 Iraq war, the American war led to the formation of Al Qaeda in Iraq (AQI), as Iraqi insurgents joined the cause of bin Laden. And as we will see in the next chapter, AQI helped give rise to ISIS/ISIL.

When the US is under attack, many of us have a tendency to retreat to the position that it is not a time for self-critique. Yet in order to move forward wisely, we have to look backward and learn from our mistakes. The Bush doctrine of a pre-emptive strike in Iraq and the war in Iraq from 2003 to 2011 are directly connected to a resurgent Al Qaeda network. This is not just my opinion. It is the conclusion of the 2007 National Intelligence Estimate on Terrorism that sums up the combined findings of sixteen intelligence agencies:

> We assess that al-Qa'ida will continue to enhance its capabilities to attack the Homeland [America] through greater cooperation with regional terrorist groups. Of note, we assess that al-Qa'ida will probably seek to leverage the contacts and capabilities of al-Qa'ida in Iraq (AQI), its most visible and capable affiliate and the only one known to have expressed a desire to attack the Homeland. In addition, *we assess that its association with AQI helps al-Qa'ida to energize the broader Sunni extremist community*, raise resources, and to recruit and *indoctrinate operatives, including for Homeland attacks.*
>
> (NIE 2007, italics added for emphasis)

In 2007, the general intelligence consensus was that America still faced "a persistent and evolving terrorist threat over the next three years." The main threat came from "Islamist terrorist groups and cells, especially Al Qaeda, driven by their *undiminished intent to attack the homeland* and a continued effort ... to adapt and improve their capabilities" (NIE 2007, italics added for emphasis). The war in Iraq had not deterred the terrorists, it had energized them.

In sum, President Bush and his cabinet framed the pre-emptive strike on Iraq in apocalyptic language. Whipped up by rhetoric of Good versus Evil, and driven by fear after 9/11, the US attacked a country that had not attacked us and that was not responsible for 9/11. We diverted troops and intelligence away from chasing those responsible for 9/11, including Osama bin Laden in Afghanistan, in order to wage a war in Iraq that was costly, in lives, dollars, and reputation. Our attack on Iraq not only failed to diminish the motivation of Al Qaeda (since it wasn't located there), it facilitated the creation of Al Qaeda in Iraq. This network energized Sunni insurgent groups, leading to the formation of ISIS.

### Creating terrorists out of oppression

Terrorism expert Louise Richardson argues perceptively that revenge for perceived grievances is the most constant theme that emerges in conversations with terrorists. She relates a story about Hesmat Abdul Rahman, a Jordanian mother, whose twenty-five-year-old son Zaid Horani watched the American invasion of Iraq on television (Richardson 2007). Out of anger, he became a *jihadist* who recruited other Jordanian *jihadists* (Richardson 2007). Horani's story may be expanded to millions, some of whom will become sympathetic to extremism.

The ongoing devastation resulting from the Iraqi war continues to generate broad resentment, contributing to radicalization in Iraq. There have been many studies trying to estimate the mortality rate for the Iraqi war. All agree that it is high, but estimates vary widely depending on the method of collection of data. In 2008, researchers from top universities in the US and Canada assessed the methodologies of thirteen of these studies (Tapp *et al.* 2008). Including government studies, the researchers assessed the most rigorous and reliable methodologies to be used by Roberts, *et al.*, and Burnham, *et al.*, both of which were published in the British medical journal *The Lancet*. The Roberts study gathered evidence from March 20 to September 15, 2004 and found 98,000 excess deaths[31] in the first six months of the invasion (Roberts 2004). The Burnham study gathered data from March 20, 2003 to July 15, 2006 and estimated 654,965 excess deaths, 601,027 of which were attributable to violent causes, for an average of 540 deaths per day as a result of the war (Burnham 2006).[32]

These statistics do not take into account other human costs of the war in Iraq: 2.5 million civilians displaced by the war, at least 4.5 million orphans (out of a total national population of thirty million), 600,000 orphans living on the street, and 740,000 war widows (one out of every eleven women between the ages of fifteen and eighty) (MIT 2013). The young age of the population in Iraq, and in the Middle East generally, compounds the gravity of the civilian deaths (Webster 2013).[33] In 2003, approximately half of the population of Iraq comprised children, with 45 percent of the population being under the age of fourteen (UNICEF 2003). Is this catastrophic situation resulting after our military engagement in Iraq a proportional response to the loss of life on 9/11?

The radical apocalyptic worldview thrives on perceived oppression. Any American actions oppressing Muslim civilians or insulting the dignity of human life or Islam strengthens the explanatory power of radical apocalyptic ideology. Aside from the incalculable human cost, policy makers should also pragmatically take into account the physical, psychological, and social impact on children. They are part of an up and coming generation that could desire revenge. An Iraqi eight- year-old who survived the invasion of Iraq in 2003 would be twenty in 2015. What is that twenty-year-old's inclination towards radicalization going to be, if his/her memories are of the devastation of the American invasion, abundant personal losses, displacement, civil war, injury illness, and poverty?[34]

In addition, the scandal at Abu Ghraib prison, in which American military prison guards photographed their abuse and mockery of inmates, not only incensed the radical Islamist community, but also received the condemnation of the whole world. Al-Zawahiri has mentioned the incidents numerous times, along with abuses at other problematic prisons like Guantanamo (Ibrahim 2007, 178). Al Qaeda in Iraq (AQI) recently orchestrated the escape of several hundred prisoners from the Abu Ghraib and Taji prisons (Al Jazeera 2013). Al Qaeda also participated in almost a dozen other recent jailbreaks, including in Libya and Pakistan. Al-Zawahiri has vowed to do the same at Guantanamo Bay (*ABC News* 2013; Starr and Cohen 2013; Newsmilitary 2013). Many believe that the orange jumpsuit in which ISIS clothes their victims in their gruesome videos may well be a symbol of the same uniform at Guantanamo.

## Challenges and opportunities after Bin Laden's death: conceptual re-focusing

The death of Osama bin Laden under President Obama's administration on May 2, 2011 certainly removed the most iconic figure of Al Qaeda as well as an operational and ideological leader. The Obama administration tried to minimize casualties in the special operations attack and provided his body with full Muslim rites and a burial at sea. By doing so, the administration attempted to balance the practical necessity of eliminating key terrorist leaders with the understanding that the manner in which this is conducted will determine whether the ideology of radical Islamist terrorism spreads.

Without a doubt, killing bin Laden and other leaders has lessened the operational capability of the core of Al Qaeda. According to Robert Cardillo, Deputy Director of National Intelligence for Intelligence Integration, as of April 2012 Al Qaeda had a reduced operational capacity and greatly reduced size. Apparently, al-Zawahiri does not appear to inspire loyalty in his followers to the same degree as did bin Laden (Cardillo 2012). Al Qaeda regional affiliates remain, including Al Qaeda in Iraq (AQI), Al Qaeda in the Arabian Peninsula (AQAP), Al Qaida in the Islamic Magreb (AQIM), and Al-Shabaab, but the core organization of Al Qaeda is weaker overall. An unnamed Senior US Counter-terrorism Official in the same briefing added, "some could argue that the [original] organization that brought us 9/11 is essentially gone" (ibid.).

Perceptively, though, the same Senior Official added the following remarks that pertain to religion:

> I think we divide al-Qaeda into two segments, one, the organization against which we've made significant progress.... But the

movement.... The movement certainly survives. The ideology of the global jihad, bin Laden's philosophy, that survives in a variety of places outside of Pakistan. And I think it's also important to note that al-Qaida is a resilient organization. It's faced incredible, diverse difficulties in the past after leaving Afghanistan. It was patient. It managed to wait us out.

(Ibid.)

Unfortunately, the *Charlie Hebdo* attacks in Paris on January 8, 2015 showed that they did wait us out.

## Notes

1 The generally accepted sources of legal authority in Muslim jurisprudence are, in descending order: (1) Qur'an, (2) *sunna*, the example of the Prophet – including the *hadith* or the deeds and sayings attributed to him by other sources, (3) argument by analogy, (4) the consensus of the *ummah* or world-wide community of Muslims, often represented by the *ulema*, the learned scholars who are the interpreters and developers of *sharia* law, which is local law based on all of the above, and (5) independent reasoning.
2 All translations of the Qur'an by Arberry (1996).
3 The expressions "greater *jihad*" and "lesser *jihad*" are widely known in Islam, but are not based on Qur'anic usage or on a secure *hadith*. This is a disputed *hadith*, appearing in the sayings of a medieval commentator, Ibrahim ibn Abi Ablah.
4 Near the end of 2002, Bin Laden quoted the same passage as the most important point for Muslims in Iraq to remember, as war with the US appeared imminent. Osama bin Laden, "To The Muslims of Iraq" (Ibrahim 2007, 243–249).
5 In February 2002, sixty American thinkers wrote the letter "What We're Fighting For" against terrorism. The response came from 153 Saudi scholars, who wrote the letter "How We Can Coexist" in May 2002. Osama bin Laden then posted the open letters "Why We are Fighting You," directed to Americans, as well as an open letter to the Saudi signatories entitled "Moderate Islam Is a Prostration to the West" (Ibrahim 2007, 197–208).
6 Osama bin Laden, "Your Fate is in Your Hands Alone" (Ibrahim 2007, 214–219).
7 In a taped message timed to coincide with the bombing of Taliban forces in October 2001 following the events of 9/11, bin Laden mentioned "one million innocent children" killed in Iraq, in "Osama bin Laden's Oath to America" (ibid., 193–195). In "Why We are Fighting You," published in February 2002, he states that "more than 1.5 million" Iraqi children have died from American sanctions (ibid., 197–208).
8 Curiously, al-Zawahiri's letter was written before President Morsi became the democratically elected leader in Egypt. Morsi represented the Muslim Brotherhood and some observance of *sharia* law, but the army and masses forcibly threw him out of that role, partly in the name of liberal change.
9 Osama bin Laden, "Moderate Islam is a Prostration to the West" (Ibrahim 2007, 22–62).
10 Bin Laden is quoting the same hadith as "Defense of the Muslim Lands" ('Azzam 1985).
11 'Azzam is renown amongst radical Islamists. According to Oliver and Steinberg,

"for many Hamas activists, the words of Dr. Abdullah 'Azzam constitute almost holy writ" (see Oliver and Steinberg, 2005, photo 12 caption).

12  Osama bin Laden, "Moderate Islam is a Prostration to the West," and Ayman al-Zawahiri, "Sharia and Democracy," in Ibrahim (2007), pp. 120–136, quoting an excerpt from 'Azzam's 1991 work *The Bitter Harvest: The [Muslim] Brotherhood in Sixty Years.*

13  In Al Qaeda camps, a dozen men who heard bin Laden's speeches came forward to volunteer, becoming the "muscle" terrorists in 9/11 (*9/11 Commission Report* 2007, 233).

14  By contrast, Cook names the group as Gama`at al-Islamiyya, the "Islamic Group," which US government documents name instead as a separate organization led by Sheikh Omar Abdel Rahman and then by Ahmed Refari Taha a.k.a. Abu Yasser al Masri. (US Indictment S (10) 98, 6; US Treasury, 2004, 1114 and 1129; Cook 2005b, 133).

15  It was rumored that musk (a good smell) emanated from his body even after death.

16  Dates for the Sudan base vary, but I here follow the findings of the US Indictment S (10) 98, 4.

17  Note that as of 2005 David Cook notes that "Materials concerning Bin Ladin's personal apocalyptic thought are weak, to date," although he affirms Bin Ladin's connections between the Hour of Judgment and militant Jihad (Cook, 2005a, 174, note 4). Since I greatly respect Cook's work and rely on his interpretations of contemporary Muslim apocalyptic writers below, it seems appropriate to explain that this is in part due to our differing contexts as scholars of religion. By "apocalyptic," Cook probably has in mind *eschatology* alone, and he is correct that there is not a heavy emphasis on the Day of Judgment in bin Laden's theology. However, I mean "apocalyptic" in terms of an entire revelatory system of thought, and I do find ample evidence of a belief in *active eschatology* in bin Laden's thinking.

18  Bin Laden did demand an oath of loyalty from martyrs and key players in Al Qaeda, but "many, including [Abd al Rahim al] Nashiri, found the notion distasteful and refused" (*9/11 Commission Report* 2004, 152), citing Intelligence report, interrogation of KSM, November 21, 2003.

19  Cook cites that the writers are Louis 'Atiyatallah and Husayn bin Mahmud. Accessed January 22, 2003 and January 27, 2003, www.jehad.net.

20  Cook cites Salah al-Din Abu 'Arafa. 2001. *Al-Qur'an al-`azim yunabbi bi-damar al-Wilayat al-Muttahida wa-gharq al-jaysh al-Amriki.* Jerusalem: n.p.

21  Citing White House notes and Ari Fleischer notes, September 11, 2001 and a Fleischer interview with the 9/11 Commission on April 22, 2004.

22  Several scholars have explored whether President Bush's own thinking was apocalyptic (Selvidge 2008; Northcott 2004). According to a French journalist, Chirac stated that Bush used the "Gog and Magog" argument to try to persuade him to join forces in the 2003 invasion of Iraq, whereupon he consulted the theologian Thomas Römer at the University of Lausanne (Maurice 2009; Potter 2009). A recent essay, however, argues that Römer, not Bush, used the language of "Gog and Magog" in explaining how Bush argued for the Iraq invasion to Chirac (Spector 2013).

23  Citing the White House transcript, President Bush's Address to a Joint Session of Congress and the American People, September 20, 2001.

24  The phrase "War against Terrorism" framed the principals' discussion at least as early as September 17, 2001 (9/11 Commission 2004, 333, 337).

25  Gore also notes that Boykin "helped organize the use of abusive treatment of prisoners in Iraq" and he connects this to Boykin's disdain for Islam (Gore 2007, 59).

26  (9/11 Commission 2004, 335), citing DOD notes, Victoria Clarke notes, September 11, 2001; DOD notes, Stephen Cambone notes, September 11, 2001; interview with Steven Cambone July 15, 2004.
27  (9/11 Commission 2004, 335), citing Condoleezza Rice meeting February 7, 2004 and Woodward 2002, 83–84.
28  (9/11 Commission 2004, 336), citing interview with Tommy Franks on April 9, 2004.
29  (9/11 Commission 2004, 335), citing interview with Colin Powell on January 21, 2004.
30  The president stated on September 17, 2003 that there was no evidence that Saddam Hussein was involved with 9/11 but that "There's no question that Saddam Hussein had Al Qaeda ties," which turns out to be erroneous (Bush 2003; Richardson 2006, Chapter 7).
31  "Excess" meaning above the normal death rate for the period.
32  Subsequent to the publication of the studies in *The Lancet*, a British medical journal, the figures were judged to be too high by the Bush administration in the US, the Blair administration in the UK, and by other studies. However, the peer-reviewed article by Tapp, *et al.*, judged Roberts' and Burnham's methodologies to be the most rigorous amongst all available mortality studies for the Iraqi war, including governmental studies. (Tapp *et al.* 2008).
33  For the "youth bulge" in the Middle East, see Fuller 2003.
34  Maternal and child health conditions are appallingly bad in Iraq at present. See Webster (2004).

## Bibliography

9/11 Commission. 2004. *The 9/11 Commission Report: Final Report of the National Commission on Terrorist Attacks Upon the United States, Authorized Edition.* New York: W.W. Norton & Co.

*ABC News* "Interpol: Warning Linked to Prison Breaks," aired August 3, 2013. Accessed August 3, 2013, http://abcnews.go.com/International/wireStory/interpol-makes-warning-linked-prison-breaks-19860820.

Aboul-Enein, Youssef. LCDR MSC, USN. 2008a. *The Late Sheikh Abdullah Azzam's Books. Part I: Strategic Leverage of the Soviet-Afghan War to Undertake Perpetual Jihad.* West Point, NY: Combating Terrorism Center. Accessed May 1, 2013. www.ctc.usma.edu/wp-content/uploads/2010/06/`Azzam_part_1.

Aboul-Enein, Youssef, LCDR MSC, USN. 2008b. *The Late Sheikh Abdullah `Azzam's Books. Part II, Remedy for Muslim Victimization.* West Point, NY: Combating Terrorism Center. Accessed August 8, 2013, www.ctc.usma.edu/posts/the-late-sheikh-abdullah-`Azzams-books-part-ii-remedy-for-muslim-victimization.

*Al Jazeera*, "Al-Qaeda claims attacks on Iraqi prisons," aired 23 July 2013. Accessed July 24, 2013, www.aljazeera.com/news/middleeast/2013/07/20137221126181914.html.

Al-Obaidi, Muhammad, Abdullah, Nasir and Helfstein, Scott. December 1, 2009. *Deadly Vanguards: A Study of al-Qa'ida's Violence Against Muslims.* In *Combating Terrorism Center at West Point Occasional Papers.* Accessed December 10, 2009, www.ctc.usma.edu/posts/deadly-vanguards-a-study-of-al-qaidas-violence-against-muslims.

Al-Zawahiri, Ayman. July 9, 2005. "Letter to Abu Musab al-Zarqawi." October 11, 2005. Office of the Director of National Intelligence. Accessed May 29, 2015, www.odni.gov/index.php/newsroom/press-releases/184-press-releases-2005.

Arberry, A.J. 1996. *The Koran Interpreted.* New York: Touchstone.

'Azzam, Abdullah. 1985. "Brothers of Ribatt to Brothers of Ribatt," translated by the Brothers of Ribat. Accessed August 10, 2013, http://archive.org/stream/Defense_of_the_Muslim_Lands/Defense_of_the_Muslim_Lands_djvu.txt.

'Azzam, Abdullah. 1990. *Jihad Shaab Muslim.* Yemen: Maktabah Jeel al-Jadid and Beirut: Dar Ibn Hazm Press.

Bayyoumi, Abdel-Mo'tei. September 20–26 , 2001. *Al-Ahram Weekly Online.* Accessed August 5, 2013, http://web.archive.org/web/20010924102356/www.ahram.org.eg/weekly/2001/552/p4fall3.htm.

Bhutto, Benazir. 2008. *Reconciliation: Islam, Democracy, and the West.* New York: HarperCollins.

Bin Laden, Osama. August 23, 1996. "Declaration of War against the Americans Occupying the Land of the Two Holy Places."

Bin Laden, Osama. February 23, 1998. "Declaration of War" (Arabic). *Al-Quds al-Arabi*: 3. Accessed August 4, 2013, www.library.cornell.edu/colldev/mideast/fatw2.htm. Accessed 8 August 2013, www.pbs.org/newshour/updates/military/july-dec96/fatwa_1996.htmlBin Laden, Osama. February 23, 1998. "Truce Offer to the Americans" (Arabic). Accessed August 4, 2013, www.library.cornell.edu/colldev/mideast/fatw2.htm.

Bin Laden, Osama. October 2002. "Why We Are Fighting You." *Guardian.* Accessed March 20, 2012, http://observer.guardian.co.uk/worldview/story/0,11581,845725,00.html.

Buhari, Sahih. n.d. *Afflictions and the End of the World,* translated by M. Musin Khan. Vol. 9, Book 88, No. 187. Center for Muslim-Jewish Engagement. Accessed May 29, 2015, www.usc.edu/org/cmje/religious-texts/hadith/bukhari/088-sbt.php.

Burnham G., Lafta R., Doocy S. and Roberts L. 2006. "Mortality after the 2003 Invasion Of Iraq: A Cross-Sectional Cluster Sample Survey." *The Lancet* 368:1421–28.

Bush, George W. September 16, 2001. "Remarks by the President Upon Arrival, The South Lawn." Accessed August 13, 2013, http://georgewbush-whitehouse.archives.gov/news/releases/2001/09/20010916-2.html.

Bush, George W. February 16, 2002. "President Rallies the Troops in Alaska." Accessed August 13, 2013, http://votesmart.org/public-statement/3963/#.Ugpu9VNdobs.

Bush, George W. September 17, 2003. "Bush: No Link between Iraq, Sept 11 Attacks." Interview on *Fox News Sunday.* Accessed March 20, 2010, www.foxnews.com/story/0,2933,97527,00.html.

Cardillo, Robert. April 27, 2012. Office of the Director of National Intelligence. "Media Conference Call: Background Briefing on the State of Al-Qaida." Accessed August 12, 2013, www.odni.gov/index.php/newsroom/speeches-and-interviews/99-speeches-interviews-2012/563-background-briefing-on-the-state-of-al-qaida-media-conference-call?tmpl=component&format=pdf.

*Chicago Tribune.* January 11, 2015. "'Unprecedented' Rally is Largest in France's History, Officials Say." *Chicago Tribune.* Accessed January 11, 2015, www.chicagotribune.com/news/nationworld/chi-france-rally-20150111-story.html#page=1.

Chirac, Jacques. 2012. *My Life in Politics.* New York: Palgrave Macmillan.

Cook, David. 2005a. *Contemporary Muslim Apocalyptic Literature.* Syracuse, NY: Syracuse University Press.

Cook, David. 2005b. *Understanding Jihad.* Berkeley: University of California Press.

CNN World, "Transcript of Bin Laden's October Interview," aired February 5, 2002, on CNN. Accessed January 15, 2015, http://archives.cnn.com/2002/WORLD/asispcf/south/02/05/binladen.transcript/index.html.

CNN US, "Rumsfeld defends General who commented on war and Satan," aired October 16, 2003, on CNN. Accessed August 13, 2012, http://web.archive.org/web/20080510143721/www.cnn.com/2003/US/10/16/rumsfeld.boykin.ap/index.html.

Crenshaw, Martha. 1981. "The Causes of Terrorism." *Comparative Politics* 13, 4: 379–399.

Emerson, Steven. 2002. *American Jihad: The Terrorists Living Among Us*. New York: Free Press.

Esposito, John. n.d. "It's the Policy Stupid. Political Islam and US Foreign Policy." Prince Alwaleed bin Talal Center for Muslim–Christian Understanding, Georgetown University. Accessed August 10, 2003, http://acmcu.georgetown.edu/135400.html.

Ford, Peter. September 19, 2001. "Europe Cringes at Bush 'Crusade' Against Terrorists," *Christian Science Monitor*. Accessed August 10, 2013, www.csmonitor.com/2001/0919/p12s2-woeu.html.

Fuller, Graham E. 2003. "The Youth Factor: The New Demographics of the Middle East and the Implications for U.S. Policy," Brookings Institute. Accessed June 12, 2013, www.brookings.edu/~/media/research/files/papers/2003/6/middleeast%20fuller/fuller20030601.pdf.

Geertz, Clifford. 1973. *The Interpretation of Cultures*. NY: Basic Books.

Gore, Al. 2007. *The Assault on Reason*. New York: Penguin Press.

Gupta, Sanjay. 2009. "Administration of President George W. Bush, The Doctrine of Pre-emptive Strike" *International Political Science Review* 29, 2: 181–96.

Hoffman, Bruce. 2006. *Inside Terrorism*. New York: Columbia University Press.

Holbrook, Donald. 2010. "Using the Qur'an to Justify Terrorist Violence: Analysing Selective Application of the Qur'an in English- Language Militant Islamist Discourse." *Perspectives on Terrorism* 4, 3. Accessed July 15, 2013, www.terrorismanalysts.com/pt/index.php/pot/article/view/104/html.

Ibrahim, Raymond, ed. and trans. 2007. *The Al Qaeda Reader*. New York: Broadway Books.

Imtiaz, Huma. June 10, 2012. "Drone Program is Counterproductive for Pakistan's Goals: Rehman." *Express Tribune*. Accessed July 20, 2012, http://tribune.com.pk/story/406195/concerns-over-drone-strikes-cannot-be-brushed-aside-sherry-rehman/.

Johnsen, Gregory D. 2013. *The Last Refuge: Yemen, Al Qaida American's War in Arabia*. New York: W.W. Norton & Co.

Khatab, Sayed and Bouma, Gary D. 2007. *Democracy in Islam*. New York: Routledge, 2007.

Kilcullen, David and McDonald Exum, Andrew. May 16, 2009. "Death From Above, Outrage Down Below" *New York Times*. Accessed September 11, 2011, www.nytimes.com/2009/05/17/opinion/17exum.html?pagewanted=all.

Kroft, Steve. September 28, 2014. Interview with President Barack Obama, *60 Minutes*. Accessed September 30, 2014, www.cbsnews.com/news/president-obama-60-minutes/.

Kurzman, Charles. March 15, 2002. "Islamic Statements Against Terrorism." Accessed August 5, 2013, http://kurzman.unc.edu/islamic-statements-against-terrorism.

Kurzman, Charles. 2004. *The Unthinkable Revolution in Iran.* Cambridge, MA: Harvard University Press.

Lindsey, Hal with Carson, Carole C. 1970. *The Late, Great Planet Earth.* Grand Rapids, MI: Zondervan Publishing House.

Maurice, Jean-Claude. 2009. *Si vous le répétez, je démentirai . . .* Paris: Plon.

MIT Center for International Studies. 2013. "Iraq: the Human Cost," by the MIT http://web.mit.edu/humancostiraq/. Accessed August 10–14, 2013.

National Security Strategy of the United States of America. September 2002. Accessed August 14, 2013, www.state.gov/documents/organization/63562.pdf.

*Newsmilitary.* August 1, 2013. "Al-Qaida leader vows to free Muslims from U.S. Prisons." stripes.com. Accessed August 14, 2013, http://newsmilitary.com/pages/15985618-al-qaida-leader-vows-to-free-muslims-from-us-prisons.

Northcott, Michael. 2004. *An Angel Directs the Storm: Apocalyptic Religion and American Empire.* London: I.B. Tauris.

Oliver, Anne Marie and Steinberg, Paul. 2005. *The Road to Martyrs' Square: A Journey into the World of the Suicide Bomber.* New York: Oxford University Press.

Perez-Rivas, Manuel. September 16, 2001. "Bush Vows to Rid the World of 'Evil-doers'." CNN Washington Bureau. Accessed June 15, 2013, http://edition.cnn.com/2001/US/09/16/gen.bush.terrorism/

Potter, Mitch. May 29, 2009. "Was Bush on a Mission from God?" *Toronto Star.* Accessed August 1, 2010, www.thestar.com/news/2009/05/29/was_bush_on_a_mission_from_god.html.

Qutb, Sayyid. 1981. *Milestones,* translated by S. Badrul Hasan. Karachi: International Islamic Publishers.

Roberts, L., Lafta, R., Garfield, R., Khudhairi, J. and Burnham, G. 2004. "Mortality before and after the 2003 invasion of Iraq: cluster sample survey." *The Lancet* 364: 1857–1864.

Richardson, Louise. 2006. *What Terrorists Want.* New York: Random House.

Sanchez, Ray, Smith-Sparks, Laura and Mullen, Jethro. Updated January 17, 2015. "Terror Cell Warning as Europe Scrambles to Handle Threats." CNN. Accessed January 17, 2015, http://edition.cnn.com/2015/01/16/europe/europe-terrorism-threat/index.html.

Schmitt, Eric, Mazetti, Mark and Callimachi, Rukmini. January 14, 2015. "Disputed Claims over Qaeda Role in Paris Attacks." *The New York Times.* Print, January 15, 2015, A1.

Schone, Mark and El-Buri, Rehab. December 23, 2009. "Fort Hood: Hasan Asked Awlaki If It Was Okay to Kill American Soldiers." Accessed August 8, 2013, http://abcnews.go.com/Blotter/FtHoodInvestigation/fort-hood-hasan-asked-awlaki-kill-american-soldiers/story?id=9410718.

Selvidge, Marla J. 2008. "The New World Order: Messianic Rhetoric and Dreams of the Senior Bush Administration." *Political Theology* 9, 1: 61–78.

Spector, Stephen. March 28, 2013. "Gog and Magog in the White House: Did Biblical Prophecy Inspire the Invasion of Iraq?" *Journal of Church and State.* Accessed October 8, 2014, http://jcs.oxfordjournals.org/content/early/2013/03/27/jcs.cst003.full.pdf+html.

Starr, Barbara and Cohen, Tom. August 6, 2013. "Prison Breaks are Among Reasons for Heightened Security." CNN. Accessed August 6, 2013, www.cnn.com/2013/08/05/politics/us-embassies-close.

Tapp, Christine, Burkle, Frederick M., Wilson, Kumanan, Takaro, Tim, Guyatt, Gordon H., Amad, Hani and Mills, Edward J. March 7, 2008. "Iraq War Mortality Estimates: A Systematic Review." *Conflict and Health* 2, 1: 1–13. Accessed May 29, 2015, http://dx.doi.org/10.1186/1752-1505-2-1.

UN Human Rights Council, 19th Session. February 22, 2012. Document A/HRC/19/NGO/143. "Joint Written Statement by the International Youth and Student Movement for the United Nations." Accessed May 29, 2015, http://daccess-dds-ny.un.org/doc/UNDOC/GEN/G12/109/51/PDF/G1210951.pdf?OpenElement.

UNICEF Evaluation Database. July 2003. "2003 IRQ: Iraq Watching Briefs – Overview Report, July 2003." Accessed August 14, 2013, www.unicef.org/evaldatabase/index_29697.html.

US Army (FM 3–24). 2014. *Army Field Manual 3–24*, Marine Corps Warfighting Publication 3–33.5, "Counterinsurgency." December 15.

US Indictment S (10) 98 Cr. 1029 (LBS) against Osama bin Laden, Muhammad Atef, Ayman al Zawahiri, Saif al Adel, Mamdouh Mahmud Salim, Abdullah Ahmed Abdullah, Muhsin Musa Matwalli Atwah, Khalid al Fawwar, Wadih El Hage, Anas al Liby, Ibrahim Eidarous, Adel Abdel Bary, Fazul Abdullah Mohammed, Ahmed Mohamed Hamed Ali, Mohamed Sadeek Odeh, Mohamed Suleiman al Nalfi, Mohamed Rashed Daoud al-`Owhali, Mustafa Mohamed Fadhil, Khalfan Khamis Mohamed, Ahmed Khalfan Ghailani, Fahid Mohammed Ally Msalam and Sheikh Ahmed Salim Sedan.

US National Intelligence Estimate (NIE). July 2007. "The Terrorist Threat to the National Homeland." Accessed August 10, 2013, www.dni.gov/files/documents/NIE_terrorist%20threat%202007.pdf.

US Treasury. Revised July 1, 2004. *Code of Federal Regulations: Money and Finance* 31:200-End. Washington, DC: Office of the Federal Register, National Archives and Records Administration.

Vergano, Dan. October 2013. "Half-Million Iraqis Died in the War, New Study Says." *National Geographic.* Accessed September 10, 2014, http://news.nationalgeographic.com/news/2013/10/131015-iraq-war-deaths-survey-2013/.

Victoroff, Jeff. February 2005. "The Mind of the Terrorist: A Review and Critique of the Approaches." *Journal of Conflict Resolution* 49, 1: 3–42. Accessed January 14, 2015, http://dx.doi.org/10.1177/0022002704272040.

Webster, Paul C. March 16, 2013. "Roots of Iraq's Maternal and Child Health Crisis Run Deep." *The Lancet* 381, 9870: 891–894.

Woodward, Bob. 2002. *Bush at War.* Simon & Schuster.

# 5 The case of the self-declared "Islamic State"

## ISIS/ISIL

> It seems to me that the action of the terrorists ... does not seek the impersonal elimination of the other. Everything lies in the challenge and the duel – that is to say, everything still lies in a dual, personal relation with the opposing power. It is a power which humiliated you, so it too must be humiliated. And not merely exterminated. It has to be made to lose face.
>
> (Jean Baudrillard, "The Spirit of Terrorism" 2001)

Since 9/11 and Al Qaeda's rise to international prominence, no terrorist group has gained as much media attention as this group known variously in the media as ISIS/ISIL. Arguably, no group has provoked more fear.

The group has had numerous changes in leadership and name changes that reflect different stages of growth. The roots of the self-declared "Islamic State" group began under Abu Musab al-Zarqawi, who led fighters in Afghanistan before moving to Iraq in 2001. There he joined with Ansar al-Islam, "Partisans of Islam," a militant Kurdish movement that aims to establish an Islamic state in Iraq. Al-Zarqawi's followers grew during the 2003–2011 US-led war in Iraq in the very contexts of discontent discussed in Chapter 4, including the creation of almost five million orphans (UN HRC 2012).

In October 2004, al-Zarqawi vowed obedience to Osama bin Laden, after which the US State Department designated the group a foreign terrorist organization called AQI, "Al Qaeda in Iraq." A rift soon grew between AQI and the core organization of Al Qaeda. Al-Zawahiri and bin Laden felt that the extreme violence used by AQI and attacks against Shi'a Muslims would cause them to lose popularity amongst Muslims (Laub and Masters 2014).

In 2006, AQI grew as it merged with new insurgent groups, prompting the US to target al-Zarqawi. His death on June 7, 2006 in a US sponsored strike slowed the group down, but not for long. Instead, AQI found greater resolve as it merged with other Iraqi Sunni extremist groups, announcing the formation of the ISI or "Islamic State of Iraq" on October 13, 2006. ISI formed under the leadership of Abu Ayyub al-Masri, who stepped up violence against Shi'a Muslims even further. A joint US–Iraqi operation killed al-Masri in April 2010, leaving the way open for the current leader, Abu Bakr al-Baghdadi, to assume leadership. Al-Baghdadi, above all, shaped the group's current direction by means of gruesome methods of execution, torture, and a fairly savvy social media campaign. The strike on al-Masri may have actually opened the way for Abu Bakr al-Baghdadi to radicalize the group even further. He has extended the reach of the group beyond the borders of Iraq not just to Syria, but also potentially to Lebanon, Jordan, France, the US, other European countries, Canada, and Australia (ibid.).

In April 2013, the group changed its name to "Islamic State of Iraq and the Levant," or ISIL, signaling its plans to range beyond Iraq geographically. Under Abu Bakr al-Baghdadi, whose first name recalls the first caliph or successor to the Prophet Muhammad in Sunni Islam, ISIL affiliates began fighting on the side of the rebels against Syrian dictator Bashar al-Assad. This conflict has generated a documented death toll of over 191,000 and millions of refugees, including 1.1 million children and thousands of orphans (Human Rights 2014; UNHCR 2013).

As they had in Afghanistan under MAK and Al Qaeda, *mujahideen* have streamed from around the globe to aid in the fight. However, under al-Baghdadi's leadership, the group that became ISIL acted with extreme violence. Fighting against other Muslims and Christians, they have murdered children, beheaded victims (allegedly including children) (Mann 2014), raped and enslaved women, engaged in mass executions, crucified their victims or "traitors" and displayed their heads on pikes as warnings. These actions complicated possible responses for the US in the Syrian conflict. Condemning the barbarity of Bashar al-Assad, the US tried to avoid unintentionally arming extremists while defending the innocent. As ISIL employed gruesome and cruel tactics, al-Zawahiri called on the group to leave the Syrian conflict. In his opinion, their violence would backfire in the struggle against Bashar al-Assad and hurt the wider cause. Put bluntly, ISIL or ISIS – Islamic State in Iraq and Syria – went too far even for Al Qaeda.

When al-Baghdadi ignored Zawahiri's command, he showed just how far ISIS/ISIL would go. With a growing army of fighters, they stormed across Syria and Iraq. Having acquired significant financial assets from the capture of oilfields in Syria, a bank that they robbed and donations, ISIS/ISIL continued to arm itself and draw recruits from all over the world (Laub and Masters 2014). They have utilized social media and created a host of slick videos. These include propaganda videos of *mujahideen* recruits explaining their motivations and a series of "Episodes" with a "long-term hostage," British journalist John Cantlie, propagandizing for the group (presumably against his will). On June 29, 2014, the group declared themselves to be "al-Dawlah al-Islamiyah," the "Islamic State." They claim it is a reinstatement of the Sunni Caliphate that most other Muslims believe ended in 1924, with the demise of the Ottoman Empire.

Abu Bakr al-Baghdadi named himself Amir al-Mu'minin (Leader of the Faithful) Caliph Ibrahim. Religious members envision the Caliphate to be a pure religious Muslim state run by sharia law, uniting the true believers in the Sunni world. Instead, the vast majority of Sunni Muslims refuse to call that terrorist group by its self-designated title or pejoratively refer to it as the Un-Islamic State.

Distinguishing the leaders of ISIS/ISIL from those of Al Qaeda is the former's peculiar fascination with using gruesome violence. ISIS/ISIL also employs a social media campaign that attempts to gain recruits and widen its sphere of actions globally. Beginning with the release of a video on 19 August 2014 showing a masked ISIS member beheading US journalist James Foley, ISIS has continued to release a series of infamous videos showing the beheadings of their captives and the murder of a Jordanian pilot by burning.[1] Inspired rather than repelled by the videos, the CIA estimates that by September 11, 2014 about 20,000–31,500 fighters in Syria and Iraq joined ISIS. However, months of bombing killed 6,000 fighters by January 2015 (Starr 2015). Authorities thwarted alleged terrorist plots, plans consisting of random public beheadings, in Australia, the Netherlands, and London. Law enforcement analysts, and policy makers in the US, Europe, Australia, Canada, and moderate Muslim nations, such as Kosovo, worry greatly about the hundreds of their citizens joining ISIS/ISIL. These countries fear those citizens could return to wreak havoc at home. Fueling this fear, Amedy Coulibaly held sixteen hostages and killed four in the Hyper Cacher kosher grocery store in Paris on January 8, 2015 out of support for ISIS.

Beginning in September 2014, ISIS/ISIL leaders stepped up internet calls for random violence and the killing of US, French, Australian, and Canadian citizens in "lone-wolf attacks." They urged their followers to kill any disbelievers, "whether civilian or military," saying specifically:

> Rig the roads with explosives for them. Attack their bases. Raid their homes. Cut off their heads. Do not let them feel secure. Hunt them wherever they may be. Turn their worldly life into fear and fire. Remove their families from their homes and thereafter blow up their homes.
>
> (Levs and Yans 2014)

Since these horrific calls to violence began to be issued in the autumn of 2014, law enforcement and intelligence specialists now must consider this possible motive when encountering a range of crimes. These include shootings by Michael Zehab-Bibeau, who killed a solider guarding the Canadian War Memorial and fired shots in the Canadian Parliament building, to Zale Thompson's axe attack on New York city police officers.

ISIS/ISIL is one of the most theatrically violent radical apocalyptic groups in the modern world. Their dramatic enactments well illustrate

Baudrillard's claim that terrorists are interested in the symbolic struggle above all else, even more than in actually defeating their enemies and winning their aims. As Baudrillard states: "Everything lies in the challenge and the duel – that is to say, everything still lies in a dual, personal relation with the opposing power" (Baudrillard 2001). In the case of ISIS/ISIL, the antagonism toward the "Other" defines the self-identity of its members, who are deemed pure *in contrast to others*. Moreover, without drawing its adversaries to battle, ISIS cannot fulfill its apocalyptic destiny.

As the US, Canada, Europe and a host of Muslim nations rally to fight this new threat, understanding the worldview and motivations of ISIS/ISIL is of paramount importance. Although first-hand theological statements are limited, ISIS/ISIL appears to subscribe to each tenet of the radical apocalyptic formula. Given the global nature and potential involvement of lone wolves in the ISIS/ISIL onslaught, only a strategy that addresses the appeal of its ideology can be successful in preventing future radicalization.

## Analyzing ISIS/ISIL through the radical apocalyptic formula

1   *A secret about the nature of this world*: The ordinary, mundane world is broken and unduly influenced by evil of some kind, locked in a struggle with ultimate good.

and

2   *A secret about the state of the righteous*: The righteous are oppressed, while the wicked flourish, although appearances may be to the contrary.

The motivations of those who join ISIS/ISIL differ. As US Field Manual 3–24 recommends, states should carefully discriminate between leadership, combatants, auxiliary, and passive bystanders (US Army, FM 3–24 2014). Some "join" because they effectively have little choice, some reluctantly go along with those who rule locally, some are misled as to the true activities of the group, and some genuinely subscribe to the extremist ideology. For the most committed *mujahideen* of the ISIS/ISIL group who have spoken publicly, the struggle is clear: the whole non-Muslim world is oppressing Muslims.

In response to oppression, Al Hayat Media Center released an ISIS propaganda video entitled *There is No Life Without Jihad*. The video aimed at an English speaking audience to recruit *jihadists*. Anthropologists distinguish between the "great tradition," the authoritative or elite articulations of a culture often contained in textual sources, and the "little tradition," the experiences of common "folk society," which may be communicated orally (Redfield 1960). Without first-hand contact with active terrorists, it is often difficult to gain access to the "little traditions" in a group.

However, the little traditions are vital for understanding the motivations of fighters on the ground. Videos published by the Al Hayat Media Center for ISIS/ISIL on social media can offer invaluable insights into the beliefs of the rank-and-file group members.

The professional looking video shows several young, English speaking *mujahideen* sitting in a circle on the ground in front of the black and white flag of ISIS (Al Hayat 2014). A young man, a fighter with the new name of "Brother Abu Yahya ash Shami – from Australia" begins by providing evidence to fellow Muslims in Australia for why this *jihad* is necessary. His de facto starting point is that "Palestine, a long time it's been gone, it's been pounded, the Jews have taken it. Our sisters in Fallujah, day after day, they give birth to deformed babies" (ibid.). He suggests that somehow "the Jews" are responsible for injuring the unborn babies of Palestinian Muslims. The young man is not very articulate about actual grievances, but he obviously feels oppressed on behalf of other Sunni Muslims. He speaks with great emotion on his face, saying: "Look at the … [inaudible] … disgrace this *ummah* is going through. Look and see and wake up and understand why this is happening" (ibid.). Another fighter, "Brother Abu Dujana al Hindi – from Britain," whom the video poster identifies as Cardiff student Reyaad Khan, states, "the more enmity shown to us, we're just getting stronger" (ibid.). The belief that theirs is a *defensive* struggle is clear. The personal experiences and motivations that these fighters articulate are tinged with humiliation, disgrace, and oppression.

Similarly, "Brother Abu Yahya ash Shami of Australia" provides insight into what he claims are the motivations of some 2,000 or so "Westerners" from America, Canada, Australia, the UK, and other allied nations who have joined ISIS/ISIL. He pleads:

> Oh my brothers, living in the West … I know how you feel in your heart, you feel depressed. The cure for the depression is *jihad*.… You feel like you have no honor. Oh my brothers, come to *jihad* and feel the honor we are feeling. Come to *jihad* and feel the happiness we are feeling.
>
> (Ibid.)

His comments show ISIS tapping into a sense of meaninglessness and depression that some people experience before radicalization. Numerous studies on the psychology of terrorism conclude that terrorists are psychologically normal but motivated by cultural, social, and political circumstances (Crenshaw 1981, Victoroff 2005). Feeling like the righteous people living in a broken world, they search for a framework that lends coherent meaning to their struggle and makes suffering *matter*.

3   *A secret about another higher or future world* …: There is a transcendent world in which justice, peace, and happiness reign.

The fighters gain hope by the expectation of Paradise. Several mention Paradise in *There is No Life Without Jihad*, along with the coming resurrection when each person will be judged. The fighters believe, as all Muslims do, that Allah mercifully rewards those who righteously act. They differ from mainstream Muslims, however, in believing that their violence is righteous and will secure them a place in Paradise.

A perception that their enemies are overwhelming motivates these fighters. They lump all enemies into one: the Syrian dictator Bashar al-Assad (who is an Alawite, a sect formerly recognized by Shi'ite Islam as a variant of Shi'ism), America, America's European and Canadian allies, Jews everywhere, moderate Sunni Muslims and Shi'ite rule, especially in Iraq.

A young ISIS fighter, newly named "Brother Abu Dujana al Hindi – from Britain," uses fear of Allah's judgment day to motivate future *mujahideen*. He aims his message at fellow Muslims who haven't decided to fight in the way of *jihad*, reminding them of the *yawm ad-din*, the Day of Judgment. As they are resurrected with "[their] sins around [their] neck," they will be shown "the sister who was violated by the Shabiha" (the armies of Bashar al-Assad). He claims that his fellow Muslims will also see "the child that got beheaded for being Muslim. And Allah will ask you 'Where were you'? And [I promise] you won't be able to speak"(Al Hayat 2014). Ironically, these are precisely the crimes that ISIS/ISIL has perpetrated against Muslims.

4    *Authoritative Revelation/Interpretation:* Divine revelation or the authoritative interpretation of original texts is ongoing to the group's leaders.

Something that separates Abu Bakr al-Baghdadi from either Osama bin Laden or Ayman al-Zawahiri and that makes him even more dangerous is that he has a Ph.D. in Islamic studies from the Islamic University in Baghdad. He comes from a family of "preachers" and "professors of Arabic language, rhetoric, and logic" (McCoy 2014). Moreover, he also claims to be descended from Muhammad through Hussein.

His intellectual background potentially gives him greater authority in asserting interpretations of Islam. However, emphasizing a connection to the Prophet's family is odd. Shi'a Islam, and not Sunni Islam, holds that the legitimate successors to Muhammad must be blood relatives of the Prophet. The historical Sunni and Shi'a divide is that Shi'ites follow a line of Imams from the Prophet's family, while Sunnis follow a line of caliphs through Abu Bakr, a friend of the Prophet.

However, Sunni law does stress familial descent in one special case: the coming Mahdi, a figure associated with the endtime. The expectations surrounding this figure differ greatly between Sunni and Shi'a Islam, as well as amongst different groups of Shi'ites. However, in general Sunni Islam expects that the Mahdi will fulfill three conditions: he will be an adult

Muslim male descended from the Quraysh tribe, to which the Prophet Muhammad belonged; he will exhibit mental probity and physical and mental integrity; and he will have leadership and authority over a land (Wood 2015). Under Baghdadi, ISIS/ISIL has fulfilled the third requirement by conquering a wide territory that they proclaim to be the new *khalifa* or Caliphate. He has attempted to show that he fulfills the second by leading ISIS/ISIL in strict, brutal implementation of *sharia* law in its "pure," medieval glory, with beheadings and slavery.

Al-Baghdadi also claims to fulfill the first requirement of familial descent. In a documentary showing events at the Al-Fordo Mosque in Raqqa, a speaker stresses to those Sunni Muslims assembled, "Your leader is a descendant of Hussein and the tribe of the Prophet. We ought to love the family of the Prophet. You have to support him by paying your money, sacrificing your life, anything you can do" (Vice News 2014). The crowd, which includes children, responds in unison, "We swear allegiance to the Prince of the Faithful." They call him "Al-Baghdadi al-Qurashi," al-Baghdadi of the tribe of Muhuammad, or "Al-Baghdadi al-Husseini al-Qurashi," that is, al-Baghdadi of the family of Hussein of the Quraysh tribe (Vice News 2014).

Hence, in al-Baghdadi, ISIS/ISIL is proclaiming the fulfillment of the arrival of the Mahdi, the endtime figure who will unite all true Muslims.[2] This claim demands unparalleled devotion to al-Baghdadi, far exceeding that afforded to bin Laden and earlier leaders of ISIS/ISIL and AQI. It imparts him with the authority to rule the Caliphate and provide authoritative interpretations of law.

5   *Active Eschatology*: Our actions are key to ushering in the new stage of the coming Good world. I, as a righteous person, can trigger the end of the Evil age through my actions, especially through eliminating Evil on earth.

The presence of an *Active Eschatology* is one of the clearest indicators that a group will be violent. In the case of ISIS/ISIL, the group is already known to be violent, but recognizing this reality proposition in their thought system can shed further light on their motivations and suggest appropriate and effective courses of action.

We do not yet have any lengthy theological treatise by al-Baghdadi himself, although he made one public appearance in which he spoke from the minbar (pulpit) of a mosque (ibid.). However, the centrality of Dabiq, Syria in the eschatology of the group is clear. It is not only the name of ISIS/ISIL's main publication, it was also the site of their murder of US aid worker Peter Kassig. In that video, the ISIS/ISIL assassin explains: ""Here we are, burying the first American crusader in Dabiq, eagerly waiting for the remainder of your armies to arrive" (Wood 2015). According to a prime spokesperson known to be an ISIS/ISIL recruiter, Musa Ceratonio,

ISIS/ISIL believes that the "armies of Rome," which could be interpreted as the US, or Turkey or another entity, will battle the remnant of the faithful at Dabiq. After that the Caliphate will expand widely, creating a pure society under *sharia* law. This society is akin to Revelation's millennial kingdom. The Antichrist, the *dajjal*, will then appear. Talking to a reporter, Cerantonio explained that the *dajjal* will come from Khorasan, eastern Iran, and kill the members of ISIS/ISIL until only 5,000 remain. They will be cornered in Jerusalem. At the last minute, Jesus will come again, kill the *dajjal*, and rescue the true Muslims (Wood 2015).

We can glean additional details of the eschatology of ISIS/ISIL in a letter procured in a counter-terrorism strike in June 2005. The letter, which US Intelligence considers to be authentic, outlines Ayman al-Zawahiri's eschatological plan to al-Zarqawi, the leader of AQI, the precursor to ISIS/ISIL (al-Zawahiri 2005). The core elements of the eschatological plan appear to be shared by the leadership of Al Qaeda, AQI and, later, ISIS/ISIL.[3]

In the letter, al-Zawahiri reveals what he believes was prophesied in *hadiths*. His plan for "Jihad in Iraq" outlines several stages. The first stage is to rid Iraq of the Americans by expelling them. The second stage is to "establish an Islamic authority or [e]mirate, then develop it and support it until it achieves the level of a Caliphate over as much territory as you can...." The letter then explains that the emirate is destined to struggle with the foreign (infidel) forces and the traitorous locals, who will try to prevent the emirate from becoming "a stable state which could proclaim a Caliphate." Hence, al-Zawahiri expects opposition, conflict, and war to unfold at this stage. The third stage is to "Extend the jihad wave to the secular countries neighboring Iraq." The fourth stage expects a "clash with Israel," although the letter explains this stage may occur earlier or concurrently with other stages (ibid.).

Al-Zawahiri stresses that the mission should not end when American forces leave Iraq, but "Instead, their ongoing mission is to *establish an Islamic state, and defend it, and for every generation to hand over the banner to the one after it until the Hour of Resurrection*" (ibid., italics added for emphasis). The mission for the "Islamic state," centered in Iraq, is to serve as a pure government that lasts until the Day of Judgment, the equivalent of the Christian millennial kingdom. The letter conveys a sense of an unfolding eschatological destiny that includes events both within and outside of the group's control. While not claiming infallibility, the letter reads like *ex eventu* prophecy that predicts the future in progressive stages culminating in Allah's Day of Judgment.

It appears that al-Baghdadi is familiar with al-Zawahiri's plan, since ISIS/ISIL has already acted out several of the stages. These include waiting for America to withdraw from Iraq, establishing an Islamic State, expanding to neighboring states, and drawing the United States into the conflict. If he is following the plan like a script, a "clash with Israel" would be next.

To understand the power of ISIS/ISIL to radicalize new recruits, the starting point must be to appreciate fully that the "Islamic State" claims to be the final Caliphate leading to the "Hour of Resurrection." The *mujahideen* in the video *There is No Life Without Jihad* refer to the imminence of the Caliphate by saying "The din [judgment]... of Allah is being established" (Al Hayat 2014). The fighter "Brother Abu Muthanna al Yemeni – from Britain" states repeatedly and passionately to his "sheik" that the "khalifa [Caliphate]" is "imminent." He begs "send us, we are your sharp arrows, throw us at your enemies, wherever they may be ... we will return the borders which goes all the way to [inaudible, possibly 'Los Angeles']"(ibid.). For the *mujahideen*, the Caliphate has global, eschatological implications of cosmic importance. This means that, for the leadership with an *Active Eschatology*, calculations made on behalf of the Caliphate are not political in the sense of upholding national interests above all. Rather, these actions uphold transcendent interests, maintaining the purity of the so-called Caliphate at all costs, even at the expense of their own people on the ground.

6   *Othering/Concretized Evil*: Those who are not with us are against us. Our group knows the identity of the people that are "Evil" vs. "Good," and those not in our group belong to "Evil."

The letter to al-Zarqawi also mentions that the "Muslim masses" will rally against an enemy: first, the Jews, and second, America (al-Zawahiri 2005). At the time of this writing, ISIS/ISIL has not directly threatened Israel. However, Coulibaly's pledge of allegiance to ISIS/ISIL should signal that his act of targeting the Jewish clientele of a kosher grocery store may be the beginning of a wider campaign.

In his Presidential address the night before the thirteenth anniversary of 9/11, President Obama took on ISIL by saying: "ISIL is not 'Islamic.' No religion condones the killing of innocents, and the vast majority of ISIL's victims have been Muslim" (Obama September 10, 2014). The president certainly articulated the viewpoint of the vast majority of faithful Muslims in the world and staked out important ground to try to prevent Islamophobia from spreading.

However, radical apocalyptic groups consider their actions to be pious, despite the violence. Their most hated target is always members of the parent religion who do not accept their radical interpretations. Hence, ISIS/ISIL directly addressed President Obama's statement in a video. British journalist James Cantlie calmly responds in English with some "facts" on behalf of the terrorist group. Reading from a script, he retorts that in Mosul and Sinjar the Islamic State did not kill Christian and Yazidi children. This is a claim that the US and allies would reject. James Cantlie then adds: "And they [ISIS/ISIL] do not regard the Shi'a as Muslims at all. In fact according to them the Shi'a are considered worse than Americans, as they are apostates, claiming to be Muslims while worshipping the dead" (ISIS 2014). As he mentions the Shi'a, the visual image switches from Cantlie in his orange hostage jumpsuit to an image of Shi'ites carrying caskets draped in bloody coverings. Apparently, ISIS demonizes the Shi'a even more than they do Americans, which makes perfect sense in a radical apocalyptic framework.[4]

Differing opinions on violence against the Shi'a caused a rift between al-Zawahiri and al-Zarqawi, leader of AQI, forerunner to ISIS. While they agreed that the Shi'a are apostates, al-Zawahiri felt violence against them would create negative publicity in the *ummah*:

> the majority of Muslims don't comprehend this and possibly could not even imagine it. For that reason, *many of your Muslim admirers amongst the common folk are wondering about your attacks on the Shia.* The sharpness of this questioning increases when the attacks are on one of their mosques, and it increases more when the attacks are on the mausoleum of Imam Ali Bin Abi Talib, may God honor him. *My opinion is that this matter won't be acceptable to the Muslim populace however much you have tried to explain it, and aversion to this will continue.*
>
> (al-Zawahiri 2005, italics added for emphasis)

Hence, for pragmatic reasons, Al Qaeda began to distance itself already from AQI in 2005 on account of aggression towards the Shi'a. As AQI gave rise to ISIS/ISIL and committed increasingly violent acts against fellow Muslims in 2013–2014, Al Qaeda appears to have formally cut ties to the group. This rift does not, however, preclude future cooperation between the ISIS and Al Qaeda.

This brings us to the final reality proposition readily apparent in the ideology of ISIS/ISIL:

7   *Redemptive Violence/Revenge.* Violence is somehow redemptive, whether it be self-martyrdom or the killing of others. We know when and how the Good world is going to come about and our violence is necessary for bringing this about. Our enemies have wronged us and our revenge is God's will.

Beginning with its roots in AQI, the "Islamic State" exhibits greater brutality than even Al Qaeda. In his lengthy letter to al-Zarqawi, al-Zawahiri pragmatically criticized their degree of violence, which most Muslims would despise. He wrote:

> (5) Scenes of slaughter:
> Among the things which the feelings of the Muslim populace who love and support you will never find palatable – also – are the scenes of slaughtering the hostages. You shouldn't be deceived by the praise of

some of the zealous young men and their description of you as the shaykh of the slaughterers, etc. They do not express the general view of the admirer and the supporter of the resistance in Iraq ...

(al- Zawahiri 2005)

Now that AQI has become the self-declared "Islamic State," they have significantly amplified their "scenes of slaughtering the hostages" with their infamous videos beheading "Westerners" and burning a Jordanian pilot alive. Al-Zawahiri believed this unchecked violence would turn popular Muslim opinion against them and it has. This is likely to be all the more the case as findings from the United Nations Committee on the Rights of the Child emerge. A team of eighteen independent experts found that ISIS/ISIL routinely murders, rapes, and tortures children, using them as human shields. They also sell some into sexual slavery and use mentally challenged children as suicide bombers (AFP 2015). The sense of *Redemptive Violence* and *"Othering"* is so strong with ISIS/ISIL, that some fighters somehow consider such aggression to be pious, especially when the atrocities are directed at children of minorities.

Some jihadists revel in violence and in martyrdom. As "Brother Abu Bara al Hindi – from Britain" says in *There is No Life Without Jihad*: "We just want to meet our Lord. We just want to give our blood and use our bodies as a bridge from the Caliphate, the Caliphate is close" (Al Hayat 2014). He puts the matter clearly to other Muslims, asking:

What prevents you from attaining martyrdom and the pleasure of your Lord? Look around you while you sit your comfort, and ask yourself "Is this how you want to die?".... Do you wish to be resurrected with the dust from the ... *kuffar* [heretics] still in your lungs? Or do you wish to be resurrected showing your wounds and what you sacrificed for Allah?

(Ibid.)

As Juergensmeyer points out for other conflicts cast as cosmic wars, the *mujahideen* of ISIS/ISIL believe fighting is more important than any other priority, including self-preservation (Juergensmeyer 2003, 164–165). Thus, an ISIS/ISIL fighter states: "Know that if it's your family, your wife, these people whom you claim to love, if you really love them then martyrdom is what you do for them" (Al Hayat 2014).

## From the "great tradition" to little ones

In the experience of actual communities, radical apocalypticism does not unfold as a formula. There is no conscious effort to impart this particular set of reality propositions from one member to another. Rather, there is a potent theology, coherent and absorbent, that instills this orientation to reality deeply into each member of the group as it is passed along fluidly. One documentary on ISIS/ISIL records a simple conversation that illustrates many of the points in the radical apocalyptic framework described above. The documentary shows how the "great tradition," the official theology of ISIS/ISIL created by its leaders, is transmitted in the "little tradition," the everyday experience of average community members (Vice News 2014, Redfield 1960).

In the video, the man who operates the "preaching van" speaks to his small son, aged six or seven. Thus, the "great tradition" is speaking to the "little tradition." Getting down on his knees, a smiling and obviously proud father named "Abdullah of Belgium" asks his young son whether he is from Belgium or the Islamic State. He prompts the child to answer "Islamic State," and follows the point up by asking the boy what is in Belgium. The child gives a scripted answer: "infidels." As in the radical apocalyptic framework described earlier, the father clearly teaches his son to divide the world into Good and Evil persons. Since in reality Belgium is a diverse place, the conversation also gives insight into the way that members of ISIS/ISIL uncritically lump whole populations outside of the group together into one Evil mass. In Stahelski's terms, this is the process of "Other deindividuation" and "demonization" (Stahelski 2005).

The father then asks the child whether he wants to be a *mujahid*, a jihadist, or to execute a martyrdom operation. The child answers that he prefers to be a *mujahid*, to kill for redemptive violence rather than to die for redemptive violence. As the father puts it, these seem to be the child's only two choices, clearly illustrating that violence is core to the ISIS/ISIL culture. Next, the father asks, on camera, "Why do we kill the infidels (*kuffar*)? What have the infidels done?" Repeating an obviously rehearsed answer, the boy smiles and beams the answer, "They kill Muslims." He is delighted with himself for getting the answer right and pleasing his father. It is not clear if the child understands the content of his answer. But, over time, his ability to get the message "right" will instill a clear sense of oppression key to forming both self-identity and in-group identity. The father continues, asking, "All the infidels? Like the infidels of Europe?" The son agrees, "The infidels of Europe, all the infidels" (Vice News 2014). In this worldview, seamlessly passed to the next generation, there are only two sides to reality and the boy will grow up believing that he is on the side of Good.

What comes through most vividly in the "little traditions" captured in this documentary is the restoration of pride, positive self-identity, and sense of empowerment that Abdullah and the other *muhajideen* exhibit. They refer to the humiliation that they have experienced, but maintain that *jihad* has restored their self-pride, calling Syria "the land of honor" (ibid.). As Richardson has pointed out, revenge is often the key motivation for terrorism (Richardson 2006), but it is even more potent when revenge leads to a feeling of honor.

Although ISIS/ISIL has employed some women as terrorists, the video called "There is No Life without Jihad" clearly conveys a feeling of male intimacy and inclusion, a band of brothers acting together in virtue. Juergensmeyer has made incisive observations about religious violence lending empowerment to marginalized men, linking the act of terrorism to a construction of masculinity (Juergensmeyer 2003, 190–218). This linkage between violent piety and masculinity is highly intoxicating when imparted to the young as they form their very notions of self worth.

Clearly, the appeal of this extremist apocalyptic theology can be lessened when an alternate positive self-identity and sense of empowerment is fostered in these children and young men. Unfortunately, under President Obama the U.S. has bombed seven predominantly Muslim countries, including Syria, Iraq, Afghanistan, Pakistan, Yemen, Somalia, and Libya. He is the fourth US President to have bombed Iraq. For both ethical and pragmatic reasons, we must think about the message we send as a nation. If we traumatize or make enemies of the children today, they are more likely to be our adversaries tomorrow.

In the case of ISIS/ISIL, tomorrow may come sooner rather than later. The group not only uses child soldiers (as has Boko Haram and the Lord's Resistance Army, amongst other terror groups), but also wants to communicate that fact to the world proudly. A photo from the autumn shows the child of a jihadist father smiling and holding a severed head. A recent ISIS video shows a boy of about ten years old appearing to execute two Russian hostages with a pistol (Martinez 2015). Movingly, Zarine Khan, the mother of a young man recruited through social media by the terrorists, appeared on television to plead, "We have a message for ISIS.... Leave our children alone" (ibid.).

But ISIS and Al Qaeda are not likely to do that. Both organizations have realized that radicalization is a long game. In 2003, the population of Pakistan alone included seventy-three million children under eighteen years of age, out of a total population of 176 million (UNICEF 2003). Those children are mostly grown now. Too many of them grew up in the shadow of US drone strikes, thinking of the US as an oppressor.

An effective long-term counter-terrorism strategy targeting Islamist extremism *must* be part of a larger, inclusive foreign policy identifying and allying with predominantly Muslim populations. In fact, the US has led NATO in intervening on behalf of majority Muslim populations in both Kosovo and Bosnia-Herzegovina. However, that narrative is not as well-known as scenarios of US-led conflicts in Muslim nations (Flannery 2014). The positive history must be remembered in order to counter the explanatory power of radical apocalyptic Islamist ideology, which tries to perpetuate a dualistic notion that the "West" is opposed to the Muslim world.

US and allied nations must commit to diplomacy and extreme efforts at preventing further military conflicts, wherever this is possible. Foreign policy initiatives that support social justice programs in populations susceptible to extremism must be a key component of a comprehensive counter-terrorism strategy. The effort to create thriving societies in which the next generation can find stable self-meaning must be broad based. Such programs need not all come from governments; to be most effective, they should primarily include local organizations. In addition to US AID, UNICEF, or other UN related programs, there should be much greater support for grass-roots organizations, NGOs, and faith based organizations that improve the life of marginalized populations. Happy people just don't become radical apocalyptic terrorists.

The last two decades have taught us that apocalyptic terrorism is nurtured in the most distressed areas of the globe. America and her allies cannot afford to ignore any region needing social justice initiatives to aid the life and welfare of its persons. This absolutely includes issues of social inequity within the US itself, in which a shocking *one-third of children* live in poverty (UNICEF 2014).

In the last chapter of this volume, I argue that US counter-terrorism strategy is facing two different philosophies striving to be heard. One believes that it is possible to stem terrorism by eliminating terrorists. The other, which this book advocates, maintains that it only possible to end terrorism by addressing the ideology that makes terrorism attractive in the first place. This applies to both transnational terrorism, such as ISIS and Al Qaeda, and domestic terrorism, to which I turn in the next chapter.

## Notes

1 By the time of the writing of this section in mid autumn 2014, those beheaded on video include James Foley, Steven Sotloff, Ali al-Sayyed, Abbas Medlej, several Kurdish and Syrian soldiers, David Haines, Peter Kassig, Alan Henning, Hervé Gourdel, Kenji Goto Jogo, and Haruna Yukawa. They also burned alive a Jordanian pilot, Muath al-Kasabeh, to which Jordan responded with heavy airstrikes.
2 While we do not possess the source information on this yet, a claim that al-Baghdadi is the eschatological Mahdi could be at play. While traditions differ regarding the Mahdi, in general he is expected to unite the Muslim world.
3 This is in contradistinction to the conclusions of Wood, who sees Al Qaeda as non-apocalyptic and more practical, whereas ISIS is definitely apocalyptic (Wood 2015). I would say that both are radical apocalyptic groups, but ISIS is more theatrical and gruesome and more efficient at raising an army. It is possible that the leaders of ISIS are drawing on more details from contemporary Muslim apocalyptic interpreters that spur them to more activity.
4 Ironically, the second ISIS video *Lend Me Your Ears*, featuring British hostage James Cantlie, criticized the speech of President Obama on September 11, 2014 for being "disappointing" and "simplistic" in maintaining "America is good, the Islamic state is bad…." (ISIS 2014).

# Bibliography

9/11 Commission. 2004. *The 9/11 Commission Report: Final Report of the National Commission on Terrorist Attacks Upon the United States, Authorized Edition.* New York: W.W. Norton & Co.

AFP – Agence France Presse. February 4, 2015. "UN Warns of 'Systematic' Abuse against Children in Iraq."

Alexander, Peter. September 12, 2014. "Obama Administration: Yes, We are at 'War' with ISIS." Accessed October 15, 2014, www.nbcnews.com/watch/nightly-news/obama-administration-yes-we-are-at-war-with-isis-328718915879.

Al Hayat Media Center. June 21, 2014. "There is No Life Without Jihad." Vice News. Accessed October 10, 2014, https://news.vice.com/article/pro-isis-recruitment-video-encourages-foreign-fighters-to-join-jihad. Also published by "Conflict Studies." August 30, 2014. Accessed October 10, 2014, www.youtube.com/watch?v=Iv2Pr99cQ0M&bpctr=1412877073.

Al-Zawahiri, Ayman. October 2005. "Letter to Abu Musab al-Zarqawi, dated 9 July 2005." Office of the Director of National Intelligence. Accessed October 9, 2014, www.odni.gov/index.php/newsroom/press-releases/184-press-releases-2005.

Baudrillard, Jean. November 2, 2001. "The Spirit of Terrorism," translated by Rachael Bloul. *Le Monde.* Accessed February 2, 2015, www.egs.edu/faculty/jean-baudrillard/articles/the-spirit-of-terrorism/.

Crenshaw, Martha. 1981. "The Causes of Terrorism." *Comparative Politics* 13, 4: 379–399.

Flannery, Frances. 2014. "Towards a New Social Memory of the Bosnian Genocide: Countering Al-Qaeda's Radicalization Myth with the CIA 'Bosnia, Intelligence, and Clinton Presidency' Archive." In *The Role of Intelligence in Ending the War in Bosnia in 1995*, edited by Timothy R. Walton, 111–132. Lanham: Lexington Press.

Human Rights Data Analysis Group (Commissioned by the Office of the UN High Commissioner for Human Rights, UNHCR). August 2014. "Updated Statistical Analysis of Documentation of Killings in the Syrian Arab Republic." Accessed August 30, 2014, www.ohchr.org/Documents/Countries/SY/HRDAGUpdatedReportAug2014.pdf.

ISIS. n.d. *Lend me your Ears*, Episode 2. Accessed October 10, 2014, www.youtube.com/watch?v=_wzGnQIhLhc.

Juergensmeyer, Mark. 2000. *Terror in the Mind of God.* Berkeley: University of California.

Juergensmeyer, Mark and Kitts, Margo, eds. 2011. *Princeton Readings in Religion and Violence.* Princeton, NJ: Princeton University Press.

Laub, Zachary and Masters, Jonathan. Updated August 8, 2014. "Backgrounders: Islamic State in Iraq and Syria." Council on Foreign Relations. Accessed on August 10, 2014, www.cfr.org/iraq/islamic-state-iraq-syria/p14811.

Levs, Josh and Yans, Holly. September 22, 2014. "Western Allies Reject ISIS Leader's Threats against Their Civilians." Accessed October 15, 2014, www.cnn.com/2014/09/22/world/meast/isis-threatens-west/.

McCoy, Terrence. June 11, 2014. "How ISIS Leader Abu Bakr al-Baghdadi Became the World's Most Powerful Jihadist Leader." *Washington Post.* Accessed June 17, 2014, www.washingtonpost.com/news/morning-mix/wp/2014/06/11/how-isis-leader-abu-bakr-al-baghdadi-became-the-worlds-most-powerful-jihadi-leader/.

Mann, Jonathan. August 6, 2014. "Christian Leader: ISIS Beheading Children."

CNN. Accessed August 7, 2014, http://edition.cnn.com/video/data/2.0/video/world/2014/08/06/idesk-iraq-christians-persecuted-mark-arabo-intv.cnn.html.

Martinez, Michael. January 15, 2015. "ISIS Video Claims to Show Boy Executing Two Men Accused of Being Russian Spies." CNN. Accessed January 20, 2015, www.cnn.com/2015/01/14/middleeast/isis-video-boy-execution-russian-spies/index.html.

Obama, Barack. August 20, 2014. "Statement by the President." The White House, Office of the Press Secretary. Accessed August 21, 2014, www.whitehouse.gov/the-press-office/2014/08/20/statement-president.

Obama, Barack. September 10, 2014. "Statement by the President on ISIL." White House. Accessed on September 10, 2014, www.whitehouse.gov/the-press-office/2014/09/10/statement-president-isil-1.

Prokupecz, Simon. October 21, 2014. "Denver Teens Set Out for Syria; parents, F.B.I. Bring Them Back." Accessed October 21, 2014, www.cnn.com/2014/10/21/us/colorado-teens-syria-odyssey/.

Ramsay, Gilbert. Spring 2009. "Relocating the Virtual War," *Defence Against Terrorism Review* 2, 1: 31–50.

Redfield, Robert. 1960. *The Little Community and Peasant Society and Culture.* Chicago: The University of Chicago Press.

Richardson, Louise. 2006. *What Terrorists Want.* New York: Random House.

Stahelski, Anthony. 2005. "Terrorists Are Made, Not Born: Creating Terrorists Using Social Psychological Conditioning." *Cultic Studies Review* 4, 1: 1–10.

Starr, Barbara. January 22, 2015. "U.S. Officials Say 6,000 ISIS Fighters Killed in Battles." CNN. Accessed January 22, 2015. www.cnn.com/2015/01/22/politics/us-officials-say-6000-isis-fighters-killed-in-battles/index.html.

UN Human Rights Council. n.d. "The Future of Syria: Refugee Children in Crisis," Accessed August 20, 2013. http://unhcr.org/FutureOfSyria/.

UN Human Rights Council. 19th Session, February 22, 2012. Document A/HRC/19/NGO/143. "Joint Written Statement by the International Youth and Student Movement for the United Nations." Accessed on March 10, 2012, http://daccess-dds-ny.un.org/doc/UNDOC/GEN/G12/109/51/PDF/G1210951.pdf?OpenElement.

UNICEF. February 24, 2003. Pakistan: Statistics. Accessed August 14, 2013, www.unicef.org/infobycountry/pakistan_pakistan_statistics.html.

UNICEF. 2014. Fanjul, Gonzalo. "Children of the Recession: The Impact of the Economic Crisis on Child Well-Being in Rich Countries." Accessed February 5, 2015, www.unicef-irc.org/publications/733.

US Department of the Army, Headquarters, Marine Corps Combat Development Command, Headquarters, Department of the Navy, Headquarters, United States Marine Corps. May 2014. FM 3–24/MCWP 3–33.5. Washington, DC Accessed June 20, 2014, http://armypubs.army.mil/doctrine/DR_pubs/dr_a/pdf/fm3_24.pdf.

Vice News. August 13, 2014. *The Islamic State: Part I.* Accessed August 15, 2014, https://news.vice.com/video/the-islamic-state-part-1.

Victoroff, Jeff. February 2005. "The Mind of the Terrorist: A Review and Critique of the Approaches." *Journal of Conflict Resolution* 49, 1: 3–42. Accessed January 14, 2015, http://dx.doi.org/10.1177/0022002704272040.

Wood, Graeme. March 2015. "What ISIS Really Wants." *The Atlantic.* Accessed February 10, 2015, www.theatlantic.com/features/archive/2015/02/what-isis-really-wants/384980/.

# 6 *"The Lord God is a Man of War"*

## Christian Identity teaching and radical apocalyptic terrorism

WE BELIEVE the White, Anglo-Saxon, Germanic and kindred people to be God's true, literal children of Israel.

(Doctrinal Statement of Kingdom Identity Ministries, capitalization original)

The servant of God will find as we continue in our searching of the scriptures that every book of the Bible meets and ends in the book of Revelation.

(David Koresh, Exposition of the First Seal)

On April 19, 1995, Timothy McVeigh drove a Ryder rental truck up to the side of the Alfred P. Murrah Federal Building in Oklahoma City, Oklahoma. The truck held over 6,000 lbs of ammonium nitrate mixed with nitromethane, a racing fuel. The events were unfolding just as the Christian Identity affiliated Covenant, Arm, and the Sword (CSA) militia had planned a decade earlier while training 1,200 recruits in the Endtime Overcomer Survival Training School. McVeigh had possibly developed the plan with close associates at Elohim City, a Christian Identity encampment to which some CSA members had withdrawn, including Rev. Robert Millar and James Ellison.[1] He had also drawn inspiration from a similar account in William Pierce's fictional *Turner Diaries*, a virtual Bible of the radical Right in America. The *Turner Diaries* depicts the revolt of a white race Organization, the good guys, against the System, the oppressive federal government.[2] For years, McVeigh had zealously printed, sold or given away the book at gun shows.

This time the fictional plan was executed for real, injuring over 600 and killing 168 people, including nineteen children under age six, since McVeigh had parked the truck next to the building's daycare center. As a sixteen-month-old boy lay dying, McVeigh fled in a get away car with clippings from the *Turner Diaries*, including one that read "The real value of our attacks today lies in the psychological impact, not in the immediate casualties" (Hartzler 1997).

The date of the largest domestic terror attack on US soil was no accident. Along with Terry Nichols and Michael Fortier, McVeigh had planned the bombing to protest the tragedy at the Branch Davidian compound in Waco, Texas, that had occurred two years earlier on April 19, 1993. That disaster began as a shootout and fifty-one-day siege that ended in a fire that burned the whole compound, killing seventy-four people, including twenty-three children. Ten years earlier, the date of April 19, 1985 had also been the scene of an eerily similar standoff between the CSA and the FBI.[3] This standoff had ended peacefully thanks in part to the negotiations of a transformed Kerry Noble, who now speaks out against extremism. April 19, 1995 also coincided with the execution of the white supremacist Richard Wayne Snell, a familiar presence at the CSA compound who had been convicted of shooting an African American Arkansas State Trooper and a pawn store owner whom he mistakenly believed to be Jewish.

Coincidentally, April 19, 1775 was also the date of the Battles of Lexington and Concord, which opened the American Revolution. Pierce, McVeigh, Nichols, Snell, Millar, Ellison, and a host of other members of the radical Right subscribed to the idea that a new revolution will someday unfold against the unjust federal government. Like thousands of others in the US today, they fused this political worldview with an apocalyptic interpretation of Christianity that identifies the Babylon of the Book of Revelation to be the US government. They believed that the US government operates in collaboration with an Evil assortment of oppressors, including Jews, gays, liberals, pedophiles, University professors, anti-gun advocates, feminists, and people of color.

Thus, April 19 has come to resonate throughout a constructed history of the radical Right as a day of patriotic resistance. It echoes the start of the American Revolution, the fight against the federal government at the CSA compound, the siege at Waco and the government's execution of Richard Snell. As remembered by some, it also marks the day in 1992 of the FBI's first siege on the Weaver family at Ruby Ridge, Idaho.

The groups that this chapter surveys differ in their constituencies and geographical scope. Members often float from group to group or join multiple organizations. Tying many together is a shared ideology of radical apocalyptic Christianity known as "Christian Identity teaching." This doctrine fuses an expectation of the imminent return of Christ with a belief in a coming time of Tribulation for whites, who are believed to suffer persecution from non-whites and the federal government. Much like the extremist forms of Sunni Islam that we have examined, this extremist of Christianity displays characteristics of the radical apocalyptic formula, translated into another cultural context. And just as radical Islam has little to do with mainstream Islam, this interpretation of radical apocalyptic Christianity bears little resemblance to mainstream versions of Christianity.

## Christian Identity teaching: its roots and present influence

Apocalypticism is alive and well in America. According to a 2010 Pew Research Center finding, 41 percent of Americans expect that Jesus Christ will definitely (23 percent) or probably (18 percent) return to earth by 2050 (Pew 2010). Another study, Portraits of American Life, found that 67 percent believe in the Devil or demons, 47 percent of Americans report that an angel has helped them directly, and 55 percent report that they have experienced a supernatural miracle (PALS 2006). A survey given in Roman Palestine at the time of the Book of Revelation would have scored much lower in apocalyptic beliefs.

It is not surprising that apocalyptic groups flourish throughout the US. Despite our separation of Church and state, regional climates permit exceptions. One moment occurred when presidential candidate and Texas Governor Rick Perry promoted and spoke at a giant evangelical prayer rally led by a group that believes that they expel demons.[4] Especially in some areas of the country, apocalyptic thinking has become relatively mainstream.

Some strains of apocalypticism are not well accepted, however. Christian Identity teaching is a virulently racist and often militant interpretation of apocalyptic Christianity that is not considered to be "politically correct" in the US. One rarely ever sees it openly preached by any church leaders and many Americans are unaware it exists. Yet, Identity teaching circulates as a well-practiced "little tradition" throughout certain regions of the US (Redfield 1960). Many of the 500 white supremacist hate groups that proliferate in the US draw on Christian Identity teaching, including those associated with the KKK and Aryan Nations. Over thirty hate groups are explicitly "Christian Identity" organizations.[5] The actual influence of Christian Identity teaching is probably even broader. Various small Protestant and non-denominational congregations across America, and some of the hundreds of US-based Christian militias, such as those in the "Patriot movement" often embrace Christian Identity teaching.

## British-Israelism

There is no central leader or church that propagates Christian Identity teaching, but, wherever taught, it encompasses certain standard beliefs. As early as the seventeenth century an idea emerged in sermons that the British are the true inheritors of Israel, an idea that influenced the Puritans in America. From the late eighteenth century into the mid nineteenth century, millennial sermons took hold from time to time in Britain as well as America. This theory of "British-Israelism" or "Anglo-Israelism" first gained popularity in the lectures of Richard Brothers. He was a retired naval officer who received visions and who was eventually institutionalized for insanity. Later, John Wilson lectured on British- Israelism in

Ireland and England. He taught that the English were the true Israel, or the "ten lost tribes," as opposed to the Jews, who were "Judea" (Barkun 1997, 5–7). His lectures were published posthumously as *Lectures on Our Israelitish Origin* at a time when the British Empire extended its powerful reach around the turn of the twentieth century. This lent colonial power to this belief in God's special covenant with the Anglo-Saxons. In Wilson's version, an element of anti-Semitism crept in. He alleges that the Jews were a contaminated people through intermarriage, a view finding ready support in the Bible in a different context (Ezra 9–10). From the 1870s onward, various British-Israelite associations sprang up in Britain. Some favored a theory that the descendants of the Israelites are the British and others identified the Israelites as the Anglo-Saxons and Germanic peoples (Barkun 1997, 9–11).

At the end of the nineteenth and early twentieth century, this historical revisionism gained additional supporters in America by some who traced their ancestry to Anglo-Saxon, Scandinavian, Celtic, and Germanic roots (ibid., 18–22). Some of the main preachers of the philosophy were Edward Hine, Charles Totten, Charles Fox Parham, who founded the Pentecostalist movement, and J.H. Allen, one of the founders of the Holiness church movement (Church of God). Thus, the ideas took hold in early versions of the Christian denominations that are amongst the fastest growing segments of global Christianity today (Pew 2006).

The inheritors of the teaching did not all view Jews negatively. In the versions of British-Israelism influenced by Hine, Jews had a special pride of place as the House of Judah, which would be united someday with the House of Israel (the Anglo-Saxon, Scandinavian, Germanic peoples). Together they would make up "All-Israel," with Jews holding a somewhat lower standing than the ten lost tribes.[6] By contrast, in other versions of the teaching, the Jews were displaced as the inheritors of the covenantal promises. They were also considered to be the errant or evil ones, the perpetual enemies of the Anglo-Saxons and their kindred.

Among the adherents of the anti-Semitic strain of British-Israelism was the automaker Henry Ford. He published and circulated the fictional *Protocols of the Elders of Zion*, a revision of an older fictional satire about Napoleon's plans to take over the world. The *Protocols* is presented straightforwardly as a real account revealing a transcript of a cabal of Jews who secretly run the world. It still circulates as an "authentic" text amongst Christian Identity and racist Right groups. Even more than Ford, a spokesperson for the motor company, William J. Cameron, was a virulent anti-Semite and British-Israelite. As editor of the *Dearborn Independent*, Cameron ran weekly anti-Semitic articles for a year and half in the early 1920s. He eventually published them in four volumes entitled *The International Jew*, which focused on a secret Jewish conspiracy to take over the world (Barkun 1997, 31–40). A libel suit against Ford and the *Independent* ended in mistrial and the publicity enhanced the stature of Cameron as an anti-Semite. He parlayed this reputation into becoming a leader of the British–Israel organization titled the Anglo-Saxon Federation (active 1928–1945).

Another important influence for spreading the doctrine of British-Israelism in the US was Herbert W. Armstrong. He founded the World-wide Church of God and, after his death in 1986, the church changed its name to Grace Communion International. Armstrong was a millennialist who taught that the Great Tribulation would begin imminently; in fact, he predicted that it would come during each decade of his sixty years of ministry. Armstrong believed this event would inaugurate the 1,000-year-long reign of Christ, who favored the Anglo-Saxon race. This influenced his interpretation of political events. Since he maintained the idea that the Jews were only Judah and not the people Israel, he was against the establishment of the nation of Israel. He felt the land was supposed to go eventually to the true Israel, the white Anglo-Saxons.[7]

The Grace Communion International church leadership, including many of the ministers alive during Armstrong's ministry, now disavows what it calls his "unusual ideas about prophecy" that had "a lot of doctrinal errors." Asking for forgiveness for believing and teaching "these erroneous doctrines," they state: "He taught that the United States and Britain are modern descendants of the northern ten tribes of Israel, and that many biblical prophecies therefore apply to the Anglo-Saxon peoples. He saw himself as an endtime fulfillment of prophecy …" (GCI 2015). As the church sought to correct its doctrinal positions, it had a huge momentum to reverse. When Armstrong died in 1986, his congregation had reached 120,000 each week, with an annual income of $200 million. Armstrong's TV ministry and *Plain Truth* magazine reached millions.

As the Grace Communion International church eventually realized, not only are these beliefs unbiblical, they are unkind and divisive. They now state with remorse: "We have criticized other Christians as false, deceived, children of the devil. We have much to apologize for. We are profoundly sorry …" (GCI 2015). Since the doctrine usurps the covenantal position of the Jewish people in favor of Anglo-Saxons, it can also foster anti-Semitic and racist tendencies in those who are so inclined. Worse yet, when British-Israelism combines with even more racist interpretations of Christianity, Christian Identity teaching emerges.

## Christian Identity teaching

British-Israelism began to morph into Christian Identity teaching between the early 1930s until shortly after World War II (Barkun 1997, xiii). Beginning in the 1960s, the writings of the apocalyptic lecturers/preachers Bertrand Comparet (d. 1983) and Wesley Swift (d. 1970) formed an Identity "canon" outlining foundational beliefs for the movement. It is not only traditional Scripture, such as the Bible, that functions as a canon, but any text afforded social authority such that its teachings or outlook becomes binding for life and practice in a group.

Both Comparet and Swift claimed interpretive authority over biblical Scriptures, such as the Book of Revelation, which they read through an apocalyptic and racist lens. They both postulated that the end was near. They also believed that white Christians would wage a great battle on the side of God against Satan, the Jews, and people of color. Those good, white people who survive will reign for a thousand years with Christ. Thus Comparet and Swift were "millennialists" in the true sense of the term. To be precise in the language of religious scholarship, they were "premillennialists," who expect the return of Christ to happen *before* the millennial kingdom. Both expected Jesus to return to earth physically, followed by a time of Tribulation and testing of the faithful, followed by the thousand-year reign of Christ and the victorious, white righteous.[8] This is all based on a somewhat literal interpretation of the apocalyptic eschatology of Revelation 20:1–6. However, it is sifted through racial revelations and fused with medieval concepts of the (white) people of God who fight in a literal army at the endtime.

Today, Christian Identity has no central home or single leader, but proliferates as a doctrine amongst the racist Right in numerous locations. There are a few churches that openly identify as Christian Identity churches per se, including Kingdom Identity Ministries (KIM) in Harrison, Arkansas. Harrison is also the location of Pastor Thomas Robb, the national director/Grand Wizard of the KKK and pastor of the Christian Revival Center. KIM, founded by Mike Hallimore, spreads its message beyond Arkansas through sharing or selling radio broadcasts, tapes, videotapes, CDs, numerous publications on race and the American Institute of Theology online Bible course. It also has a Children's Catalog, with items ranging from children's literature on the doctrine to a wooden Rod of Correction, i.e., a "Speak Softly Spanking Stick" to teach children "good old-fashioned discipline" (KIM 2014).

Christian Identity teaching has also influenced numerous racist hate groups, including: Wesley Swift and Richard Butler's Church of Jesus-Christ-Christian, affiliated with the KKK and the Aryan Nations; William Gale's Christian Defense League, which also has ties with the Aryan Nations; the Covenant, Sword, and Arm of the Lord; Elohim City; the terrorist Eric Rudolph, who was responsible for the 1998 and 1999 Atlanta bombings; Robert Miles' prison ministry associated with the Aryan Brotherhood; the Christian Patriot Defense, and Randall Rader, a CSA member who joined the anti-federalist group The Order. Other anti-federalist numerous militias, including the Posse Comitatus and Montana Freemen, also seem to have been influenced by certain aspects of Christian Identity teaching.

Other Christian denominations share many of the Christian Identity teaching elements. As in Christian Fundamentalism, Identity teaching

Christian Identity teaching 149

believes that the Bible is inerrant and should be interpreted literally, Christ will return to earth imminently, the endtime is near, and salvation entails a spiritual rebirth through the redemption offered by Jesus Christ. Identity teaching also accepts the pre-destination of the elect, a belief accepted in Reformed Protestantism since the time of John Calvin. Christian Identity churches practice baptism by immersion, a ritual shared by American Baptists everywhere. Like some small Protestant groups (usually non-denominational in affiliation), Identity teaching calls Jesus by a variant of his Hebrew name, Yahshua, and believes that Christians should honor the Jewish law as the inheritors of the New Covenant and as the true Israel.

However, two distinctive beliefs separate Christian Identity preaching from other denominations, including Fundamentalism, with which it is sometimes inappropriately lumped because of the other similarities. First, as Barkun has astutely noted, Christian Identity strongly rejects the Christian Fundamentalist doctrine of a rapture or rescue of Christians before the time of tribulation. While various Identity groups differ in their accounts of what will precisely occur in the endtime, Barkun writes, "Identity's hostility to the [theology of the] rapture is unwavering and cuts across organizational lines" (Barkun 2007, 103–106).[9]

Second, as its name suggests, Christian Identity teaching involves a central revelation about the true identity of the righteous and the wicked. The revelation is a racial one, namely that "the White, Anglo-Saxon, Germanic and kindred people [are] God's true, *literal* Children of Israel" (KIM 2014). Since they also believe that these are the last days and that only the white race inherits the blessings of the biblical covenants promised to Israel, the pressure is on. They believe they must keep the white race pure, separate from the world, and empowered to win the battles that will ensue in the time of tribulation. This expectation accounts for their rejection of the rapture doctrine, since Christians need to be around to fight their enemies in the endtime. Thus, it is pre-millenialist with a violent *Active Eschatology*. This racial revelation is easily woven into an anti-Semitic, apocalyptic worldview of reality that leans heavily towards radical apocalypticism; in fact they often believe that the Antichrist is Jewish. By contrast, many Fundamentalists have a positive attitude towards Jews and acknowledge that Jesus was a Jew. They hold out hope that a remnant of Jews will convert in the last days (Rom. 9:11).

## Christian Identity as radical apocalypticism

The Identity preacher Pastor Comparet, among others, locates the central revelation about race in an interpretation of the Garden of Eden story (Gen. 2:3) that believes there are two "seedlines." One seedline refers to those descended from Adam, a white man but not necessarily the first human, whose progeny make up the Christian white nations. Thus, in

these sermons "Adam" is equivalent to "white man." Identity adherents
believe that the white nations are the true Israel and, though dispersed,
they create the only civil governments based on biblical Law. The other
seedline stems from the devil's *literal* offspring or seed that was conceived
when he mated with Eve and she gave birth to Cain. Cain's descendents,
that is, Satan's descendants, are the Jews, who naturally hate and oppose
the true Israel, the white race. This seedline doctrine, which influenced
Identity teaching in its full-blown form after about 1960 (Barkun 1997,
150), goes far beyond the anti-Semitism of any British-Israelism. White
people and non-whites are considered to be biologically different species
with cosmic implications. This interpretation exceeds even the worst
depictions of Jews concocted in the Middle Ages.

The "seedline" teaching fulfills the sixth reality proposition in our
formula of radical apocalypticism, *Othering/Concretization of Evil.* Jews are
considered to be biologically Evil, demonic, and inferior to the white race,
which they oppose. This depiction of the Jews is the central point in Identity teaching from which all other propositions of the radical apocalyptic
worldview emanate, including:

> *A secret about the nature of this world*: The ordinary, mundane world is
> broken and unduly influenced by Evil of some kind, locked in a
> struggle with ultimate Good.

and

> *A secret about the state of the righteous*: The righteous are oppressed, while
> the wicked flourish, although appearances may be to the contrary.

and

> *A secret about another higher or future world … and a secret about the future*:
> A time is coming when God's kingdom will reign and defeat the rule
> of evil on the earth.

To adherents of Christian Identity teaching, there is a cosmic struggle
going on between the races, especially between whites of European
descent and the Jews. While the whites are Good, the Jews are the children
of the Devil, "the Satanic Anti-Christ forces of this world" (KIM 2014).
Kingdom Identity Ministries' website symbolizes these "children of Satan"
with a caricature of a big-nosed, curly-haired head of a Jew atop a Serpent's body bedecked with stars of David, with a tail culminating in a
larger star of David ("Seedline and Race," KIM 2014). Clearly, the image is
meant to convey that Jews are the embodiment of the Serpent Satan. The
"secret about the world" thus entails a secret about the past derivation of
the races.

This revelation about primordial "history" and racial identity informs Identity's interpretation of their present plight. Like many other radical apocalypticists, adherents of Christian Identity teaching feel persecuted and weak in the world as it is now. The doctrinal statement of Kingdom Identity Ministries states that the children of Satan are a "curse to the true Israel" and that there is a natural hatred between the white race and the children of Satan ("Doctrinal Statement," KIM 2014). Race mixing is viewed as Satan's plan to destroy the white race. The feeling of disempowerment is palpable. Some versions of Identity teaching display a paranoid fear that the white race will end if Christians do not take up adequate arms in the time of eschatological tribulation.

The KKK's public positions consistently relate a similar strong feeling of persecution and oppression, envisioning that a race war is being perpetrated against white people. The National Director of The Knights, Pastor Thomas Robb, writes:

> There is a race war against whites. But our people – my white brothers and sisters – will stay committed to a non-violent resolution ... [consisting] of solidarity in white communities around the world. The hatred for our children and their future is growing and is being fueled every single day.
>
> (KKK 2015)

Such language of a world-wide war fills the doctrinal statements and motivational speeches of the KKK and similar groups of the Christian racist Right, including the Aryan Nations, Aryan Brotherhood, and the appropriately named Christian Defense League.

In some groups on the racist Right, this sense of persecution can expand into elaborate conspiracy theories. Theories about secret, powerful, Jewish conspiracies abound amongst those on the racist Right, sometimes finding their way into fairly mainstream culture. For instance, as late as 2004, Wal-Mart sold *The Protocols of the Elders of Zion* with the suggestion that it may be "genuine," which might "cause some of us to keep a wary eye on world affairs" (ADL 2004; SPLC 2004). The chain pulled the book from the shelves and yanked the quote from its website only after the Anti-Defamation League and Simon Wiesenthal Center shed light on the book's racist history, requesting that, if sold, it include the disclaimer that it is a proven forgery.

This book and other conspiracy-laden texts feed the deep paranoia of the racist Right, including the racist Christian Right. Group solidarity is achieved through active "Othering" or creating a sense that the out-group is so distinctively different from the in-group that the two have nothing whatsoever in common. While Identity adherents view many groups with suspicion, including Catholics, Illuminati, Freemason, and non-white persons of color, Jews hold a special place of prominence as the targets of hate. Jews are portrayed as sub-human, the children of Satan, another species or collaborators with space aliens.

While speculations about UFOology and space aliens smack of the fantastic, alien conspiracy stories permeate the racist Right. They appeared in the thought of Timothy McVeigh, who believed that Jews and alien beings were working together with the federal government. In fact, McVeigh trespassed at Area 51, site of the supposed federal government cover-up of an alien spaceship landing. With a gun and a camera, he attempted to document the presence of UFOs and take a stand against governmental regulations (Michel and Herbeck 2001, 155–157). On death row, he was obsessed with the film *Contact*, which is about a scientist who connects with alien life (Barkun 2003, ix; Michel and Herbeck 2001, 156; Linder n.d.). As Michael Barkun has carefully shown, beliefs in UFOlogy, alien abduction, and government/Jewish conspiracy interweave throughout the beliefs of the racist Right in America, including groups both affiliated with and unassociated with Christianity Identity teaching.[10]

A book that has inspired many of these beliefs is Milton William Cooper's 1991 novel *Behold a Pale Horse*. Although it eschews the overt racism of Christian Identity teaching, this text is a favorite amongst conspiracy theorists on the radical Right, especially those whom Barkun dubs "New World Order conspiracists."[11] Along with the *Turner Diaries* and the *Protocols*, Cooper's book helps form the canon of some strains of the radical Right. Cooper writes *Behold a Pale Horse* in a pseudo-realistic style that purports to uncover numerous secret government documents and testimonies from his time in the Navy. Some of the documents or news stories are real, but Cooper pieces them together with an apocalyptic meta-narrative that reveals a supposed declaration of war by the elite Illuminati, i.e., the Jews and descendants of the Knights Templar. According to Cooper, they are part of a Luciferian plot to take over the world through controlling social and financial institutions, rewriting past social history, and exercising mind control. The elite conspirators include: the mysterious "Bilderbergers," a term drawn from an actual conference of European and American politicians and financiers held annually in the Netherlands, the Vatican, the CIA, the Prieure de Sion (which founded the Knights Templar), the Council on Foreign Relations, top Freemasons (since the lower eschelons are shielded from the truth), the Trilateral Commission, Jesuits, Knights of Columbus, the Brotherhood of the Dragon, Qabbalists, the Nazi Party, the Skull and Bones society at Yale, the Skull and Key society at Harvard, a secret Order of the Quest/JASON society, and FEMA, which runs secret concentration camps in which members of the Right are imprisoned (Cooper 1991, 82–85). To Cooper, behind all of these secretive or secret groups are space aliens who are duping all of the people who mistakenly believe they are friendly (Barkun 2003, 59–65). Cooper further claims that the *Protocols of the Elders of Zion* are real Illuminati transcripts and that AIDS/HIV is a conspiracy meant to decrease the population of blacks, Hispanics, and homosexuals.

Ultimately, Cooper's scheme is a "superconspiracy"[12] based on paranoid apocalyptic eschatology. He believed that, in 2000, the Galileo spacecraft would detonate a bomb within Jupiter, causing the birth of the Lucifer star, the onset of the millennium, and a global ice age (Cooper 1991, 77–78).

Such a cataclysmic change constitutes an endtime, or *eschaton*, similar to the kingdom of God in the Book of Revelation, from which Cooper's book derives its title. Accordingly, a drawing of the scene from Rev. 6:8 graces the book's cover and the third page features this quote:

> Behold, I looked and saw a pale horse, and his name that sat on him was Death, and Hell followed with him. And power was given unto them over the fourth part of the earth, to kill with the sword, and with hunger, and with the beasts of the earth.
>
> (Rev. 6:8)

This kind of esoteric, generally discredited "knowledge" appeals to those who hold the fourth reality proposition in the formula of radical apocalypticism, *Authoritative Revelation/Interpretation*. Identity preachers often claim to receive or understand a special revelation that other Christians do not. For instance, the Kingdom Identity Ministries website is one of the largest sources of Christian Identity teaching in America. It distributes an online Bible course called the "American Institute of Theology," the total collection of writings by Comparet, and texts associated with Swift's Church of Jesus Christ-Christian (KKK). While the website states that they are not in complete agreement with every point by these other authors, it assures the audience that the materials will provide "enlightenment through which the Holy Spirit will bring the reader or listener into knowledge of the truth with wisdom and understanding" (KIM 2014). Essentially, the church maintains that even if a small mistake in theology creeps in here or there, it is the authoritative conduit to the truth. Other Christian Identity venues display similar confidence in their revelations, which they believe are known only to a few. Barkun points out that "stigmatized knowledge" has tremendous appeal for those on the racist Right. This includes "forgotten knowledge," such as the origins of the races, "rejected knowledge," such as the role of space aliens, and "suppressed knowledge," such as that involved in the conspiracies of the ZOG, the Zionist Organized Government.[13]

Given the presupposition that a nefarious set of enemies are plotting a global takeover leading to the demise of humans, some Christian Identity groups could quite easily become radicalized. Some seek political change through electing like-minded officials. For instance, former KKK Grand Wizard David Duke, well acquainted with Identity teaching, successfully won the Republican nomination for the House of Representations in Louisiana in 1989 (Barkun 2003, 210–212). Others, such as the Covenant, Sword, and Arm of the Lord, advocate completely withdrawing from society to prepare for the time of Tribulation.

A group maintaining Christian Identity teachings is likely to be violent if it also believes in the two remaining reality propositions in our formula of radical apocalypticism:

> *Active Eschatology:* Our actions are key to ushering in the new stage of the coming Good world. I, as a righteous person, can trigger the end of the Evil age through my actions, especially through eliminating Evil on earth.

Members of the Christian Identity movement are consoled by the conviction that their present state of oppression will end when they are finally able to fight in the eschatological Tribulation. This will trigger God's Judgment and spell "the ultimate end of this evil race [Jews] whose hands bear the blood of our Savior (Matt. 27:25)." Unlike Fundamentalist Christians who look forward to the rapture, the Christian Identity members welcome the time of Tribulation "like no other" because it is their chance to right the wrong direction of the world. This is not *passive eschatology*, because they do not believe that God is completing this by Himself. Rather, Identity teaches that its armies are indispensible to God's success. This is a violent, *active eschatology*.

With such an important "end" in mind, the "means" will likely be violent if an Identity group holds a theology of *Redemptive Violence/Revenge.* This can take the form of self-martyrdom or the killing of others. Identity terrorism has favored the latter, embracing idea that "Our vengeance is God's vengeance." The Covenant, Sword, and Arm of the Lord (CSA) is a good example of a group that flipped from a passive to an *active eschatology* with a change in violence to match.

CSA began as a community of Fundamentalist Christians desiring to live a simple, pure Christian life in preparation for the endtime. Even when they began to stockpile guns and weapons, they were preparing for the time of Tribulation, just as they stockpiled food and other supplies. This marks a phase of *passive eschatology* in the group. However, the key members of CSA then began to accept a new teaching of Christian Identity preaching through James Ellison. He maintained that their actions would hasten the end through participating in the armed Tribulation, since "the Lord God is a man of War." At this point they switched to an *active eschatology*, hoping to start a race war like that depicted in the *Turner Diaries*.

On their land, the CSA set up a mock urban setting called *Silhouette City* and proceeded to train approximately 1,200–1,500 extremists from all over the country. They acted as a Christian militia preparing for the coming race war, training white participants to attack targets that included police officers and persons of color. The race war, which they would wage themselves, would be the time of Tribulation that triggered the arrival of Armageddon. One military leader was Randall Rader, who would later go on to join The Order militia responsible for the murder of talk show host Alan Berg. On film, he stated that he was getting impatient because of how bad things were getting in the world. He finally added that if the Lord didn't hurry up and start Armageddon, he was determined to start it himself.[14] This is precisely what the group tried to do when it prepared to poison the water supply of Chicago or Washington DC, bring down the power grid in Arkansas and Oklahoma, and blow up a bomb outside the Murrah Federal Building in Oklahoma City (Noble 2003, 134–135).

The impact of Christian Identity teaching amongst groups and individuals on the racist Right has been profound. The *CSA Journal*, a monthly newsletter disseminated to 2,000 subscribers on the racist Christian Right, published the idea that "the coming war is a step toward God's government." (Noble 1998, 87, 101, 135). When McVeigh killed 168 people in the Oklahoma City bombing, he did so as a radical apocalyptic terrorist who believed the innocent victims he killed were necessary collateral damage. He believed he was fighting a vast conspiratorial war waged by the government and evil Jews in the ZOG, or Zionist Organized Government. Fantasy informed his reality. He imagined himself fighting the Empire's Stormtroopers as well as their clerical workers in order to bring down the Evil Empire, as in one of his favorite films, *Star Wars*. He also drew on historical revisionism, believing that he was starting the Second American Revolution, a divine pursuit (Noble 1998, 135; Michel and Herbeck, 2001, 224–228).

McVeigh saw the evidence for the government's aggression and evil as manifested in at least three incidents that have resonated throughout the radical Right. The first incident was the 1983 killing of Posse Comitatus member Gordon Kahl, who had earlier murdered two federal marshals in North Dakota (Barkun 2003, 265–266). The other two events are referred to mythologically by their place names: Ruby Ridge and Waco. McVeigh was so invested in the siege at Waco that he visited during the standoff and stayed for days, handing out anti-federal government materials. He purposely timed his bombing for the anniversary of the fire at Waco, on April 19.

The Weaver family at Ruby Ridge followed the Christian Identity teaching in which McVeigh was steeped, but the community at Waco did not share the theology. Overall, in my assessment, both the Weavers and the Branch Davidians were fervently committed apocalypticists, but not yet radical apocalypticists who posed a threat, like McVeigh or the CSA.[15]

In part, I am writing this book to help avoid another needless tragedy like Ruby Ridge or Waco. Understanding the dynamics of the radical apocalyptic worldview that informs such situations can help prevent unintentional escalations of conflict. A genuine apocalypticist, like Vicki Weaver or David Koresh, will never be talked into backing down through threats, violence, and intimidation, which only exaggerate feelings of persecution and deepen the commitment to possibly die as a martyr.[16]

## Ruby Ridge

On Friday, August 21, 1992, a bright, sunny day in Ruby Ridge, Idaho, Special Operations forces fanned throughout the woods surrounding the cabin home of the Weaver family. The family dog began barking frantically. In response, Randy Weaver, his fourteen-year-old son, Sam, and a family friend, Kevin Harris, grabbed their guns. They ran through the woods to investigate the sounds, which they thought might be coyotes or bears (Weaver 2012).

Randy returned home first, followed by Kevin, who broke the terrible news that Sam was dead. At this point they still didn't know who was shooting at them. Sobbing, Randy, Sam's mom, Vicki, and Kevin, ran back down the driveway to retrieve Sam's body and bring it back to the house. Randy reports that he was so overcome with grief that he didn't care if they got shot, too.

Talking as a family, they tried to come to grips with the situation. They decided that if the shooters were with law enforcement, the authorities would surely contact the family the next day after realizing they had killed a child. There is no indication that the family expected an escalation at this point (Weaver 2012, loc. 829). At this point, Kevin indicated he had shot back, but he may not have known that he, or friendly fire, also killed US Marshal Bill Degan.[17] Later, Kevin would be acquitted on charges of manslaughter. If these recollections are accurate, even after Sam's death and the firefight, the Weavers and Kevin hadn't fully realized they were under siege. They wrapped the boy's body, grieved as a family, and woke up the next day numbed and saddened. They went about their basic chores in the yard and waited for contact from the authorities.

Things would get even worse over the next day. Randy decided to go see Sam's body one more time, which was placed in a shed in the yard. But as he approached it, he was shot through the back (Weaver 1998, 39–41). He ran towards the house past his teenage daughter, Sara, who was out in the yard with the chickens. Vicki, still grieving the loss of her son, Sam, stood behind the screen doorway watching them. Suddenly, she was shot through the door. The bullet went through her head as she held her ten-month-old baby, Elisheba, killing her in front of ten-year-old Rachel. The same bullet that tore through Vicki lodged in Kevin's chest and almost killed him too. For another nine days, law enforcement surrounded the house. Through a bullhorn and several negotiators, they tried to persuade the family to come out, assuring them of their safety. However, as Randy Weaver saw it, the dog, his son, Sam, and he himself were all shot in the back, and Vicki was shot in the head while holding their baby girl. The family now concluded that law enforcement wanted them all dead (Weaver 1998, 40–41).

When the authorities sent a robot armed with a shotgun onto the porch, this reinforced their fears. The robot taunted them by saying things like "We are having blueberry pancakes for breakfast. What are you fixing for your family Mrs. Weaver?" (Weaver 1998, xii).[18] This mockery felt especially cruel to the girls, who were barricaded with their mother's dead body. For nine days, the two wounded men continued to hide out with the two girls and baby, mistrustful of the authorities. Finally, on Monday, August 31, the besieged finally trusted one of the negotiators, former decorated Green Beret Bo Gritz. They linked hands and left the cabin.

What had prompted the US Marshals and FBI to surround, besiege, and fire on a family, including small children? Why was the mountain covered with heavily armed troops, including Delta Force trained Special Ops, tanks, helicopters, a guarded command post, large tents, mess facilities, and a communications center (Weaver 1998, xii)? It seems that the myth of Randy and Vicki Weaver was much larger than their actual life. It was the myth that prompted the response, rather than any actual crimes.

Indeed, the crimes with which Randy Weaver was initially charged hardly warrant the level of siege that the Weavers experienced, as later Senate hearings point out (US Senate Committee 1995, 14, 16). The first charges stemmed from associations that Randy Weaver had with two undercover agents, Frank and Gus, who befriended him for three years. They asked Randy to alter two shotguns for them by sawing them off. Randy was comfortable with guns, since he was a former Green Beret and homesteader in the wilderness. He altered the guns and sold them to Frank and Gus. If he had a $200.00 permit, it would have been legal. Randy reports disliking Frank and Gus at times, thinking that they were too extreme. Frank took Randy to the Aryan Nations World Congress,[19] but Randy felt uncomfortable and wrote: "I can understand hating someone because they hurt you or your family, but to hate someone just because they're of another race, is sheer ignorance" (Weaver 1998, 26–27).

After revealing that they were agents, Frank and Gus told him that if Randy agreed to work as an undercover informant for BATF (the Bureau of Alcohol, Tobacco and Firearms), they would drop the firearms charges against him. He laughed it off and refused. Eventually, after about six months, Randy was arrested and spent a night in jail. As told by both Randy and Sara Weaver, the authorities sent a letter with the wrong court date of March 20. The result was that Randy did not show up on the correct date of his actual hearing, February 20. As told by the Justice Department, the letter had indicated the court date was February 20 (DOJ Ruby Ridge1993). Either way, the failure to show up in court led to a bench warrant for Randy's arrest.

As the Senate hearing report on Ruby Ridge confirms, selling two sawed off shotguns is not a serious firearms violation. Randy Weaver was acquitted in his trial of that charge by using the defense of entrapment (US Senate Committee 1995, 14, 16). While Randy Weaver alleged that he was targeted due to religious and political beliefs, the Senate hearing did not conclude that BATF had done so (ibid., 12–16). Since something must account for the overinflated response of law enforcement during the siege, I suggest that while the BATF may not have consciously targeted the family due to religious beliefs, their ignorance of the meaning of their Christian Identity beliefs contributed to an inappropriate threat assessment of the family.

It appears that both law enforcement and the media had a view of the family they had pieced together from a number of suspicious elements. These included the family's Christian Identity-style beliefs, associations with racist groups such as the Aryan Brotherhood (to which they were introduced through the BATF undercover agents), anti-government political beliefs, and an alternative, homesteader lifestyle.

Randy Weaver, writing after the events at Ruby Ridge, has clarified some of their racist beliefs, although these may show some tactful editing done in hindsight. According to him, they did not consider themselves "white supremacists," since they do not accept that the white race is superior. This would indicate some divergence from Christian Identity teaching. Instead, he makes the distinction that they were "white separatists," against race mingling of any kind. Sara Weaver, in her writing, appears as an adult to reject racism.[20] Randy also adds that they were not "anti-government," but rather "anti-bad government," such as the kind of abuse that occurred at Ruby Ridge (Weaver 1998).

Politically, the Weavers would probably be called Libertarians today. Randy himself was a former Green Beret who had run for Sheriff of Boundary County in 1980 (Weaver 2012, loc. 478). Hence, the idea that he was anti-government or anti-law enforcement does not seem to square. Rather, the Weavers favored local government over federal government, which they saw as intruding into private and familial rights.[21] Although Randy's expertise as a former Green Beret certainly gave him a level of skill that was formidable as an opponent, it is not clear that he aimed to target authorities except in cases of self-defense.

Their lifestyle of self-sufficient homesteading was quite alternative at the time and engendered suspicion. Nowadays it is more common, not only amongst the radical Right, but amongst environmentally friendly homesteaders as well (Gould 2005).

All these impressions combined to form an atmosphere of mistrust by the authorities. Another possible factor contributing to the siege was that, according to Randy Weaver, he had slighted one "Herb B.," a law enforcement official. Thus, Randy wondered if the initial siege was partly driven by a personal grudge on the part of the authorities (Weaver 1998, 31).

However, even Randy Weaver admitted in the Senate hearings that he should have come off the mountain to avoid an escalation (US Senate Committee 1995, 6). The Weavers were highly wary of governmental authority and due legal process. When the bench warrant was issued, Randy and Sara both relate that the family stayed at home to try to straighten out the issue of the incorrect court date. In the meantime, they just ignored it. To make matters worse, the press fanned the flames by reporting that Randy Weaver was like "a wild animal up in the mountains," feeding the federal authorities' impressions of a dangerous situation brewing (Weaver 1998, loc. 631).

When telling the story, Randy Weaver typically leaves out of his account one of the biggest reasons the Weavers stayed on the mountain: Christian Identity teaching and conviction.[22] In a letter dated March 5, 1991, which Vicki wrote and both of them signed, their resolve not to come down based on religious reasons is clear. They would remain on the mountain because of divine revelation:

> We, the Weaver family, have been shown by our Savior and King, Yahshua the Messiah of Saxon Israel, that we are to stay separated on this mountain and not leave.... Whether we live or whether we die, we will not obey your lawless government.
>
> (US Senate Committee on the Judiciary 1995)

Between the two of them, Vicki was the true apocalypticist. She could never have been deterred through aggression from the authorities. Instead, the way to deescalate would have been to communicate a message to Vicki and Randy that made sense within the context of the Weavers' religious framework of Christian Identity teaching.

Vicki was extremely religious by any account. It was her reading of Hal Lindsey's *Late Great Planet Earth*, followed by her own visions and interpretation of Scripture, that first led the family from Iowa to Caribou Ridge and Ruby Drainage in Idaho, later nicknamed by the press "Ruby Ridge."[23] There they would live separate from society in preparation for the coming endtime. Vicki's reference to "Saxon Israel" is a clear allusion to Christian Identity teaching, derived from British-Israelism. From this, we can construe that the family expected that a time of testing, trial, and Tribulation would someday ensue. In this religious context, it would be unadvisable for law enforcement to create the appearance of such a time of Tribulation, if the goal is decreasing tension leading to an arrest rather than death.

The lack of understanding went in both directions. Vicki significantly worsened the authorities' views of the family by penning two letters to the US Attorney's Office in Boise. She wrote the letters in a Christian Identity framework, which she believed (in the Geertzian sense) to be "uniquely realistic," but which the authorities did not understand. Parts of the letters may be read in a heavily redacted US Department of Justice Report of the Ruby Ridge Task Force (hereafter DOJ Ruby Ridge). According to that report, on February 7, 1991, the US Attorney's Office received two letters signed by Vicki Weaver. The first was dated January 22, 1991 and was addressed to "The Queen of Babylon." This was a clear reference to the

Book of Revelation and a claim that the government was unjust and evil. She also wrote that the Weavers would only serve one master, "Yahweh Yahshua Messiah, the anointed One of Saxon Israel ... our law giver and our King." She then wrote out a quote: "a long forgotten wind is starting to blow. Do you hear the approaching thunder? It is that of the awakened Saxon. War is upon the land. The tyrants' blood will flow" (DOJ Ruby Ridge 1994, 40).

The quote is taken from a *Declaration of War*, a text distributed by thirteen men of the militant white separatist group The Order to newspaper outlets on November 25, 1984.[24] Members of the Order were responsible for murder. One member, Robert Jay Mathews, had died in a firefight with seventy plus members of law enforcement surrounding his house on Whidbey Island, Washington. Vicki may have furnished this quote to evoke the idea that, although the government is unjust, eventually the forces of good would triumph. However, the authorities would certainly have read the quote as expressing sympathy with the violence of The Order.

Her second letter, dated February 3, 1991, was addressed to the "Servant of the Queen of Babylon, Maurice O. Ellsworth, US Attny." It similarly stated: "Yah-Yahshua the Messiah of Saxon Israel is our Advocate and our Judge. The *stink of your Lawless government has reached Heaven* ..." (ibid., 40–41). Again, this reference from the Book of Revelation implies that the government's sinfulness is displeasing to God. The US Attorney's Office concluded that "the language in the letters appeared somewhat threatening." Thus, they requested a threat assessment by the US Marshal in Boise (ibid.).

The assessment results are heavily redacted in the Department of Justice report. However, one remark stands out: the Weavers "felt as though the end is near" (ibid., 42). While I cannot be certain without seeing the entire report, the ensuing conduct by the US Marshals strongly suggests that they did not fully understand the remarks within a Christian Identity context. They may only have picked up on some of the apocalyptic ideology contained in Vicki's letters. Without the Identity context, Vicki's comments seem odd, apocalyptic, and downright menacing. The letters use strange (Hebrew) names for Jesus, speak of a war in the land, and mention that the tyrants' blood will flow. The letters also convey that the Weavers, or at least Vicki, did not respect the authority of this government.

However, within a Christian Identity context, the letters are not necessarily menacing. They speak to standard beliefs in a coming time of Tribulation, eschatological victory for the Saxons (white Christians), and a new government of God to replace the current government. While reprehensible in its racism, the beliefs do not necessarily imply that the Weavers themselves intended to battle with the authorities at the present time. The letters indicate that they felt persecuted and believed eventually the forces of good would triumph.

I am not privy to the whole content of Vicki Weaver's letters. However inflammatory, racist, and subject to misunderstanding, the letters appear to lack two crucial elements of the formula for radical apocalypticism. First, in what is available, the Weavers' writings do not display full characteristics of *Active Eschatology*. Vicki had visions and believed that the end was coming. Even though they were willing to die for their beliefs, the family seemed to be preparing for the time of tribulation, rather than trying to trigger it. As Randy states:

> Our goal and our dream as we left [Iowa for Ruby Ridge], was to move into the mountains to be free. Free to worship the Creator in our own way, to build a home and live as self-sufficient as possible. We were not looking to do *battle with anyone*. We did *not* hate anyone. *We wanted to be left alone.*
>
> (Weaver 1998, 16, italics his)

If the recollection is accurate, theirs was a *passive eschatology* and not a threat.

Second, as far as I can tell from the Weavers' first-hand accounts, they lacked a clear theology of *Redemptive Violence* and did not seem to intend to kill anyone on behalf of the radical Right or Christian Identity movement. A mood of revenge or redemptive violence may be palpable in the quote from The Order that Vicki wrote. However, the quote is ambiguous regarding whether she intended for her family to wage violence.

A better understanding of the Weavers' religious worldview might have led authorities to take a less combative approach in arresting Randy after his failure to appear in court. As a precursor to the siege, they might have tried non-combative measures for much longer, including sending many letters back and forth, visiting and talking, and showing an effort to compromise and to work with him on setting a new court date. After Sam Weaver was killed, there could have been an apology leading to détente. Instead there was a "shoot to kill" order and a mindset amongst some of the leaders of the armed forces that no one should leave the cabin alive. Inadvertently, this only reinforced the radical apocalyptic beliefs that the family already held.

The tragic events of Ruby Ridge reverberate still throughout the radical Right as an example of the government's aggression and tyranny against its citizens.[25] The memory of Ruby Ridge has inspired acts of violence, including the Oklahoma City bombing. The Senate hearings held later on Ruby Ridge concluded: "while Randy Weaver made mistakes, so did every federal law enforcement agency involved in the Ruby Ridge incident … needlessly result[ing] in human tragedy" (US Senate Committee 1995, 6). Eventually, the Department of Justice awarded the three Weaver daughters $3.2 million dollars for the wrongful death of Vicki Weaver. Kevin Harris was awarded $380,000. Years later, FBI agents showed sensitivity to Sara Weaver when they returned the family's belongings from the siege.[26]

Although internal inquiries and disciplinary recommendations were made against the agents involved in the Ruby Ridge incident, in the end they received little discipline for their actions. In fact, several received bonuses and, in one case, a top promotion to the position of Deputy Director of the FBI (DOJ Review 2002, 40–41, 65). Several of the same agents involved would reappear in the disastrous siege and fire at Waco.

## Waco

The Branch Davidians, although problematic in other ways, were not racists. They also did not possess the characteristics that, according to our formula of radical apocalypticism, would indicate that they posed a threat to the greater community at the time of the standoff.[27] Comprehending the difference between peaceful and radical forms of apocalyptic Christianity may have prevented the tragedy at Waco, since law enforcement would have had a better understanding of the Branch Davidians' actual goals. Instead, Waco has become a key rallying point amongst members of the racist Right.

On February 28, 1993, heavily armed BATF agents made a "dynamic entry" into the Mt. Carmel center, a cluster of buildings in Waco, Texas. It housed some 130 people, including forty-three children, in Waco, Texas. The affidavit that led to the warrants contained several charges against the Branch Davidians, members of a religious sect living in the compound. Amongst the charges were converting weapons without a permit to do so (somewhat similar to the charge against Randy Weaver) and the existence of a methamphetamine lab on the premises. A 1996 House of Representatives majority report concluded that the BATF knowingly lied about the drug lab. This fabrication allowed them to attain additional heavy military assistance, including the use of National Guard helicopters and special operations training (Wessinger 2000, 63–64; US House of Representatives 1996, 30–55). Although child abuse lay outside the jurisdiction of the BATF, the affidavit also claimed that a "power-mad, manipulative cult leader" who spanked children and raped girls led the group (Tabor and Gallagher 1995, 102; Wessinger 2000, 62).

Prior to the confrontation, the leader of the group, David Koresh, invited the BATF to Mt. Carmel and volunteered to fax a copy of all gun receipts (Tabor and Gallagher 1995, loc. 167; Wessinger 2000, 60). However, on this day the BATF showed up with helicopters and seventy-six heavily armed agents. A gunfight quickly ensued.

There are conflicting accounts of how the violence began. The Davidians assert that BATF officers shot from helicopters and killed the group's pet dogs. The BATF claims that the Davidians shot first (Wessinger 2000, 66). After the first few minutes of the gunfight, the Davidians inside called 911 and asked for help, requesting that the agents stop firing. This not only indicates they felt aggressed upon and defensive rather than

aggressive and combative, it also suggests that there was still room to negotiate, since they had turned to some authorities for help.

Within minutes six Branch Davidians were dead,[28] as well as four BATF
agents. The media cast the incident as the Davidians' attempt at an inevitable apocalyptic showdown with the government. Yet, in a radio interview
later that day, Koresh called the deaths of the agents "unnecessary" (Tabor
and Gallager 1995, locs 165, 858, 1015).

An aggressive siege followed, lasting fifty-one days. A total of 668 agents
were involved from a variety of agencies: the FBI, BATF, Texas Rangers,
Waco police, McLennan County Sheriff's Office, US Customs, Texas
National Guard, Texas Department of Public Safety, and US Army (Wessinger 2000, 71; DOJ Waco 1993). The authorities' tactics vacillated
between negotiation and threats and intimidation. Tanks drove around
the yard. To keep the inhabitants from sleeping, authorities shone bright
spotlights all night at the dwelling. Loudspeakers continuously blared
derogatory statements, rock music, sirens, dentists' drills, babies crying,
the Muslim call to prayer and Tibetan chants (which they meant to be irri-
tating), and the sound of rabbits being slaughtered (Wessinger 2000, 74).
Later, the FBI came to the position that these psychological warfare tactics
worked against the goal of negotiating a peaceful surrender (DOJ Waco
1993, 139–140). The standoff ended on April 19, 1993 in a fire of a debat-
able cause[29] that took the lives of seventy-four Branch Davidians, including
twenty-three children. That brought the total number of casualties to
eighty-four. On both sides, the whole affair was clearly tragic.

In part, the initial "dynamic entry" may have been a media stunt to
enhance the reputation of the BATF, the existence and funding of which
were up for re-evaluation by the Senate Appropriations Committee on
March 10 (Wessinger 2000, 61). In fact, media frenzy was a factor from the
beginning, attracting attention nationwide and bringing onlookers from
the area and from other states.[30] The sympathizers included Timothy
McVeigh, who hung out at the siege for several days and distributed anti-
government bumper stickers, saying: "FEAR THE GOVERNMENT THAT
FEARS YOUR GUN," and "A MAN WITH A GUN IS A CITIZEN, A MAN
WITHOUT A GUN IS A SUBJECT."[31]

Early on, the authorities relied for information on members who had
left the group and on "anti-cult" activists who cast the Davidians as a
Jonestown-like cult.[32] This image prevailed in the media coverage, shaping
both public opinion and the views of authorities. The Davidians made videotapes for the press explaining their position, but the FBI withheld them.
Feeling they were being misrepresented and dehumanized in the media,
on March 9 they hung a banner outside their windows saying "God Help
Us We Want The Press" (Wessinger 2000, 72; Gazecki 1997).

The militarization of the siege exceeded Ruby Ridge. Indeed, some of
the same law enforcement agents were present at both.[33] The Hostage
Rescue Team (HRT) was called in, even though this was not a typical

hostage situation. Before the siege, others, including Koresh's own mother, had freely left the community for a variety of reasons (Haldeman 2007, 67). Throughout the siege, twenty-one children and fourteen adults also left. Those who remained inside (except for the children) were apparently free to make that decision, yet chose to stay.

Transcripts of Koresh's last conversation with an FBI negotiator on the phone on April 18, the day before the fire, show that until the very end the negotiator believed that Koresh psychologically controlled those inside. Koresh strenuously maintained that the Davidians were unique, intelligent people who made up their own minds. He explained that "Whoever wants to go out, can go out," but that the Davidians were mad because "A lot of the things the FBI, or these generals, are doing is just kind of way beyond the scope of reason" (Wessinger 2000, 106, 110). The Davidians were upset over the handling of the situation. In addition to the aggressiveness of the initial BATF raid, their grievances included law enforcement leaving the corpse of Michael Schroeder in the yard, tanks running over their cars and property, removing evidence, and using tactics of psychological warfare with children present.[34] In general, the Branch Davidians felt aggressed upon and disrespected. The negotiator asked Koresh to request that fifty volunteers come out. Koresh talked to them and then stated to the negotiator: "They're saying that because of these things, they want to stay the more" (Wessinger 2000, 112).

The Department of Justice report six months later concludes, "The abiding impression is not a bunch of 'lunatics,' but rather of a group of people who, for whatever reason, believed so strongly in Koresh that the notion of leaving the squalid compound was unthinkable" (DOJ Waco 1993, 205). These were not the hostages of a madman. These were fervent apocalyptic believers. They chose to follow the actions of their leader. On April 16, another negotiator asked Koresh if he would really come out. He answered by saying, "Yes, yes, yes. I never intended to die in here" (Wessinger 2000, 105).

In the end, Attorney General Reno became convinced by those informing her of the situation that no progress in negotiations had occurred. The only remaining plan was to use chlorobenzylidene malononitrile, "CS" gas, to drive out those inside. Just months earlier in January 1993, the US had signed an international treaty at the Chemical Weapons Convention in Paris that agreed not to use CS gas in warfare (OPCW 2005; Wessinger 2000, 80). On the morning of April 19, 1993, approximately 400 "grenades" of the chemical were inserted into the buildings at Mt. Carmel after tanks punched holes in the walls (Wessinger 2000, 78). The 1996 House of Representative majority report concluded that the use of this gas at Waco in an enclosed space "could have been a proximate cause of or directly resulted in some or all of the deaths attributed to asphyxiation in the autopsy reports." Furthermore, it reported "the FBI failed to demonstrate sufficient concern for the presence of young children, pregnant women, the elderly, and those with respiratory conditions" (House of Representatives 1996, 71–83; Wessinger 2000, 80). In addition, CS gas is also highly flammable, which contributed to the extreme nature of the fire.

It does not appear that the top authorities were unconcerned for those inside. At first, Attorney General Janet Reno had been highly reluctant to implement the gas plan, suggested weeks earlier by the FBI. They brought in an expert to evaluate the dangers of CS gas on pregnant women and children, who concluded on the basis of anecdotal evidence that the damage done would likely not be permanent.[35] President Clinton and the Attorney General discussed their concerns about the effects of CS gas on children at length. Reno had become convinced that the use of tear gas was necessary to drive the inhabitants out of the building. She told the President that *no progress had been made in negotiations* and "there were reasons to believe that the children who were still at the compound were being abused."[36] Reno gleaned these impressions from the chain of command that fed information to her. The Department of Justice report on Waco maintains that on April 15, Supervisory Special Resident Agent Byron Sage informed Webb Hubbell, Special Assistant to the Attorney General, that "further negotiations with the subjects in the compound would be fruitless." He further stated that "Koresh had been disingenuous in his discussions with Sage about the 'Seven Seals'," which he construed as a delay tactic.[37]

Reno mentioned evidence of ongoing child abuse to the president, probably an impression lingering from the BATF affidavit. However, she had to testify on April 28, 1993 to the House Committee on the Judiciary that the government actually had no evidence of ongoing physical or sexual child abuse occurring during the standoff.[38] The Department of Justice report maintains that the information on child abuse was only one factor in arriving at the decision to use CS tear gas, stating: "Ultimately, it made no difference whether the children were undergoing contemporaneous abuse, because the environment inside the compound was intolerable for children in any event."[39] Yet the "squalid" and "intolerable" conditions inside were imposed by the long, combative, and vigorous nature of the siege. Moreover, the manner in which the children died was agonizing, cruel, and terrifying. They faced a barrage of tanks, collapsing walls, gunfire, tear gas, and flames.

Clearly, by April 19, the Attorney General and her top advisors in the Justice Department genuinely believed that the tear gas plan was the only remaining option. As Wessinger has already suggested, the reasons for this position stemmed directly from the authorities inability, from the negotiators up to the Attorney General, to better understand religion. Several of the anti-cult "experts" and psychologists consulted by the BATF knew nothing about religion (Wessinger 2000, 21, 60, 72, 74, 75, 76). Those interpreting the situation for the government were not properly trained in the cultural context of communications coming from Koresh: apocalyptic interpretations of the Bible. Therefore, the government missed a major turning point in the group's psychological orientation on April 14.

## Apocalyptic beliefs of the Branch Davidians and David Koresh

The history of the Branch Davidians began in the 1930s, when Victor Houteff formed a splinter group off the Seventh Day Adventists. As a pre-millennialist, he held a fervent expectation that Christ would return soon and re-establish a physical Kingdom of David in Palestine where the right-eous would rule for 1,000 years. This view differed from the Seventh Day Adventists, who believe that the Kingdom of God is a spiritual and heav-enly one. Houteff held that the new "Israel" would be made of the members of the lost tribes, presently scattered about the world, who would be re-gathered in Palestine. He initially believed that this would occur after he led 144,000 purified members of the Adventists to Israel.[40]

After encountering resistance from the Adventist church, Houteff sub-seqently deemed them to be heathens. He then moved a few staunch believers to Mt. Carmel, Texas, in May 1935 to await the endtime, which he expected would occur in a year or so. This group was small but faithful. When confronted with the disconfirmation of a prediction, apocalyptic groups are far more likely to update their belief than to give it up. [41] Thus, the group continued on undeterred, even though the endtime never came.

After a few more leaders and a power dispute, Vernon Wayne Howell came to lead the group after claiming to have had a vision during a 1985 trip to Israel. To those familiar with Adventist and Branch Davidian doc-trine of the previous fifty-five years, Howell's theology would not have seemed all that strange. Like Houteff, Howell decoded the whole of Scrip-ture symbolically in terms of the Book of Revelation and current events. Like Seventh Day Adventist founder Ellen G. White, Howell accepted that revelation came progressively to him as a "present truth" or "New Light." Even his fantastic claim that he was the "seventh angel" of Revelation 10:7 simply updated Houteff's earlier claim about himself.

Under Howell's leadership, about 130 people came from all over the world to live separately from the world at Mt. Carmel. They didn't demonize the outer world, but they did believe it was a corrupting influ-ence on their children. Instead, they saw themselves as the most serious "students of the Seals," those who came to study the Scriptures, especially Revelation, in order to gain the deepest understanding of the prophesied events that were unfolding. They desired to live in a way they deemed to be pleasing to God, including running their own businesses (e.g., selling guns at gun shows), eating their own healthy food and participating together in worship and Bible study.[42] This lifestyle also included celibacy for all the men, except for their leader. Howell had polygamous relations with at least seven females of the group, some of whom were underage girls. Most of all, the congregation was eager to hear him expound his unique interpretations of the Bible, which he did for hours at captivating services. He also played guitar in the group's Christian rock band, a fact that would later cause them to interpret a "guitar shaped nebula" that appeared during the siege as an astral sign predicted in Revelation (Tabor and Gallagher 1995, loc. 181; Wessinger 2000, 73).

At the center of it all was Vernon Howell. By all Davidian accounts, he was a charismatic, perceptive, and passionate biblical exegete. His unique interpretations of Scripture explained that he and the group would play a pivotal role in the endtimes. Howell would often say that every part of Scripture referred back to the Book of Revelation. He saw himself as the "Branch of David" (Jer. 23:5–8, 10–20; 33:14–16; Ezek. 37:24–25; Hos. 3:5; Zech. 3:8, 6:1) and the "Lamb of God," a figure on the white horse in Revelation, who later has a marriage feast (Rev. 4–6; 19:7–19). He also claimed to have had a unique vision in the form of a heavenly ascent. In a vision, he went past the constellation Orion and entered into a UFO, a heavenly vehicle like the *merkabah* chariot of God described in Ezek. 1:3 and 8:10.[43] While up there, he was given a scroll to eat, as in Ezek. 3:3 and Rev. 10:10.[44] This event, he believed, opened up a period of divine revelation that came to him thereafter progressively.

However surprising his other beliefs, Howell did not claim, as the media widely reported, to be Christ or to be God. It is incorrect for the Justice report to the Attorney General to refer to his "near God-like status" and to say the group "worshipped" him, although the group highly revered him as an authoritative interpreter, leader and eschatological figure (Tabor and Arnold 1994, 14; DOD Waco 1993). In 1990, Howell legally took the name David Koresh. The symbolism conveyed that he was the prophesied descendant of David leading the elect remnant of Israel, the "Branch Davidians." The name Koresh was the Hebrew version of Cyrus, the Persian king whom the Book of Isaiah calls God's "anointed one" or God's "Messiah." In the Bible, "Messiah" is not a title only applied to Jesus. Howell's use of the name "Koresh" does not mean that he claimed to be "*the* Messiah" or "*the* Christ." Rather, he claimed to be "*a* Messiah," or in the Greek, "*a* Christ," which in the original Hebrew simply means one who is anointed by God for a special task.

David Koresh did not claim to be sinless like Jesus. He believed he was sinful, a trait that he saw prophesied in Psalm 40:12. Misunderstanding the symbolism, the media coined out of context the epithet "the sinful Messiah," which suggested to a non-Davidian audience that Koresh thought of himself as a blasphemous version of Jesus. Instead, David Koresh believed that he was a regular human, but appointed by God to be an eschatological figure, the Lamb of God of Revelation 4:6.[45]

Just before his name change, Howell had also received a controversial "New Light" revelation about sexuality in the group. He believed that only he was pure enough to have sex with young girls. Moreover, while other men in the group would remain celibate, Howell, as a duty to God, would have sex with their wives to father numerous children to rule the earth (Psalm 45:10–17; Isa. 53:10; Rev. 4:4).[46] He taught that all the members of the church, both male and female, were spiritually married to the Christ Spirit in him, which was the Shekhinah, the feminine presence of God (Wessinger 2000, 84). In God's kingdom, male and female would be united again in androgynous wholeness.

This "New Light" theology and its practice caused several members to leave the group, some of whom became vigorous opponents of Howell and who helped shaped the initial picture of the group for the BATF. Other members remained in the group and accepted the new arrangement based on his ability to interpret Scripture in support of his position. For instance, the biblical patriarchs had multiple wives, some of them young. After the transition in the group, Howell changed his name to Koresh. Many of the Branch Davidians considered their own last names to be "Koresh" as well. This showed how tightly knit the residual group had become, one big family with a divinely appointed role to play.

The disaffected members reported Koresh for child abuse. However, subsequent investigations by the Texas Department of Human Services never yielded an arrest because the remaining group supported and covered up his sexual relations with underage girls.[47] Complicating the case is the fact that in Texas a girl is legally allowed to marry at age four-teen with parental consent. Koresh legally married his first wife Rachel Jones under these conditions. However, he may have had other non-legal "spiritual marriages" with girls as young as twelve (Haldeman 2007, 44; Wessinger 2000, 63). The girls were told it was a privilege to bear children for Koresh, since the children would become the twenty-four elders of Rev. of 4:4 and 5:10. Many of them conceived; fourteen of Koresh's bio-logical children died in the fire.

Other than this destructive and idiosyncratic element, the rest of the Branch Davidian's theology is straightforwardly apocalyptic in the sense used in this book.[48] Koresh revealed to them *A Secret about this World, A Secret about the Righteous,* and *A Secret about the Future.* In Koresh's interpre-tation of Scripture and the Book of Revelation, the world is ruled by evil. "Babylon" is the government and the Branch Davidians are the elect of God. Although oppressed now, the Davidians will someday reign in God's kingdom. Using a host of biblical prooftexts, Koresh taught that he was the Lamb of God who would be slain in the land of Israel by a United Nations force led by the United States. After this, he would be resurrected to rule over the millennial kingdom of God alongside his biological chil-dren (Wessinger 2000, 85). Finally, Koresh believed that his special heav-enly ascent in 1985 had inaugurated his ongoing revelation and special interpretation of Revelation (see Rev. 4:1–2). He, as the slain Lamb of God, was the one chosen to open the Seals as in Rev. 5:2–14. Thus, not only did he possess *Authoritative Revelation/Interpretation* imparted by the authority of an ascent vision, he would also receive future interpretations of the Book of Revelation unknown to anyone else.

As long as the group remained in Texas, Koresh adhered to a delayed *Active Eschatology* that was not of a violent variety. He taught that the group would play a role in eschatological events only after they moved someday to Israel. Only then would they fight alongside Israel against UN forces while the Lamb, Koresh, would be killed and resurrected. The group never anticipated an "Armageddon"-like conflict to erupt at Mount Carmel.

However, the scale and intensity of the initial BATF raid led Koresh to change his eschatology. On February 28, he announced on the radio that the group was living in the time of the Fifth Seal, a time of persecution (Wessinger 2000, 91). Koresh began to believe that the six members who died on February 28 were those in the white robes from Rev. 6:9–11, who were slain by Babylon for the Word of God. They were told to wait "a little season," until their fellow servants and their brethren were also killed. Koresh began to consider the possibility that the additional brethren who would be slain by "Babylon" were the remaining Davidians at Mt. Carmel, who were about to be killed by US law enforcement.

The Justice Department somewhat understood in hindsight that the intensity of the initial raid drove Koresh to his reinterpretation. It wrote:

> The [Davidians] also believed the end of the world was near, that the world would end in a *cataclysmic confrontation* between themselves and the government, and that they would thereafter be resurrected. The February 28 BATF raid only reinforced the truth of Koresh's prophetic pronouncements in the minds of his followers.[49]

As the subsequent siege unfolded, Koresh communicated almost extensively through interpretations of biblical Scripture. However, the FBI agents were ill-equipped to understand what they termed his "Bible babble" (Tabor and Gallagher, 1995, locs. 107, 680, 1356, 1470, 2042, 2253, 3119). They failed to understand that decoding the "babble" was crucial for ascertaining Koresh's intentions. This key passage in Revelation regarding the "Fifth Seal" indicates Koresh's clear expectation of *passive martyrdom* as the fulfillment of his *Active Eschatology*. The verse does not imply *any* of the scenarios feared by the authorities, such as Koresh committing suicide, the Branch Davidians committing mass suicide or the Davidians attacking authorities.[50] It only anticipates an attack by authorities on the Branch Davidians and a willingness to die under those circumstances.

Koresh remained unsure whether this ultimate attack by Babylon had to unfold at Mt. Carmel or in Israel. The evidence suggests that until April 19, he still sought a peaceful end to the standoff. Since Koresh was following Revelation like an unfolding "script,"[51] he was trying to ascertain what would happen next. All that was clear was that those given white robes in Revelation are, by definition, those innocent persons who are killed by Babylon and who do not fight back (Rev. 6:9–11). Koresh, who read the Bible carefully, stuck to the original interpretation of the Book of Revelation rather than the violent medieval trope in which believers fight on God's side.

To fulfill his unfolding role as he saw it prophesied by Revelation, Koresh could not initiate violence or kill his people. As the "Lamb of God," Koresh believed he would eventually be slain like Jesus, a passive sacrifice unjustly killed. As the innocent, righteous martyrs in white robes, the Branch Davidians, who held suicide to be against the commandments, could never kill themselves or attack Babylon.[52]

However, since the authorities were not familiar with Davidian theology or the Bible, law enforcement missed the crucial turning point in which Koresh proclaimed that he would come out. Throughout the siege, with negotiators and on the radio, Koresh maintained that he was "waiting a little while" (Rev. 6:9–11) to be given the "Word from God," the full interpretation of the Seven Seals of the Book of Revelation. While his quest was unimportant to law enforcement, for Koresh this revelation was the very reason for the waiting period during which he refused to emerge from Mt. Carmel.

After CNN aired a segment in which Koresh challenged biblical scholars to come and debate the Bible with him, two took up the offer. James D. Tabor, a biblical scholar at UNC Charlotte, and J. Phillip Arnold, director of Reunion Institute in Houston, Texas, offered their services to the FBI because it seemed "urgent and vital that someone who understood the biblical texts become involved in the situation" (Tabor 1994, 1).

On April 1, Arnold and Tabor went on a radio program that the Davidians listened to. Arnold and Tabor used prooftexts from the Book of Revelation to argue that God did not want the Davidians to die at Mt. Carmel. By working within Koresh's own interpretive framework, the biblical scholars tried to offer Koresh alternative interpretations of his eschatology. They cited Revelation 10 and the image of an angel with "a little book" to suggest that Koresh should exit the compound and write down his revelations to share with the world (Wessinger 2000, 75).

It worked. On April 14, after Passover, a major breakthrough occurred in Koresh's position. He believed that he finally received the Word of God, namely, that God was permitting him to write the "little book." He wrote a letter that he gave to his lawyer, which stated:

> I am presently being permitted to document, in structured form, the decoded message of the Seven Seals. *Upon completion of this task, I will be free of my "waiting period."* I hope *to finish this as soon as possible and to stand before man to answer any and all questions regarding my actions....* As soon as I can see that people like Jim Tabor and Phil Arnold have a copy *I will come out* and then you can do you thing with this beast.[53]

To Koresh, the fact that he was permitted by God to write down the meaning of the Seven Seals was a monumentally important eschatological development. It was the end of the waiting period. Publishing this writing to the world would give everyone a chance to repent before the endtime. Koresh would be able to fulfill another role of the Lamb, the one who opens the Seven Seals through disclosing their meaning. Koresh promised to come out after finishing the writing, believing once again that he would only be killed and resurrected after the group ended up in Israel.

Within days, Koresh completed the exposition of the First Seal, which survived the fire on a computer disk in the jacket of a survivor. Speaking with the negotiator on April 16, Koresh again assured him that he would come out after writing the exposition of all Seven Seals. On one tape, the Davidians can be heard cheering in the background when Koresh states that they would come out soon (Wessinger 2000, 76). Wessinger estimates that at the serious pace at which Koresh was working on writing his "little book," it would have taken him twelve days (Wessinger 2000, 93–94). However, on April 19, he died along with seventy-three others.

The FBI entirely missed the significance of the "little book." They therefore disbelieved that Koresh's promises on April 14 and 16 to come out were genuine. On a negotiator's tape on April 18, just one day before the CS gas and fire, Koresh and the negotiator speak past one another in different languages:

DAVID (KORESH): Everyone in the tanks up there is playing …
HENRY (the negotiator): No, nobody is. People just want to see some
    progress.
DAVID: Look, some progress is being *made* – You don't realize what kind of
    progress is being made. There are people all over this world who are
    going to benefit from this book of the Seven Seals. You don't seem to
    understand … (Wessinger 2000, 110).

While Koresh preached to the negotiators repeatedly about his views of the Bible, sometimes for hours at a time, none of them were qualified to understand his communications. They dismissed it privately and publicly as "Bible babble" (Tabor and Gallagher 1995, locs. 107, 680, 1356, 1470, 2042, 2253, 3119). Worse, the Department of Justice report indicates that "law enforcement personnel at Waco were getting tired and their tempers were fraying."[54] Yet, however odd his beliefs, Koresh's religious framework was sincere, internally coherent, and comprehensible to those trained in understanding religion. Throughout the siege, he was trying to get the FBI agents to repent. With the exposition of the First Seal, directed at a non-Branch Davidian audience, he was trying to get the world to repent, thus fulfilling what he saw as his eschatological role (Tabor and Gallagher 1995, Appendix).

It does not take a Branch Davidian to understand this. Anyone who understands apocalypticism will easily grasp that Koresh's belief that he had received permission to write down the full meaning of all Seven Seals represents a definitive shift in his perspective. For Koresh and the Branch Davidians, receiving this "Word of God" was the whole reason they had been "waiting," as they said repeatedly. As the Lamb who opened the Seals, the waiting was over. Koresh could maintain his delayed *Active Eschatology*: no pre-ordained apocalyptic showdown would occur at Waco.

However, because the agents in charge failed to understand that Koresh's biblical discourses contained the key to his motivations, goals and decision to emerge, the authorities considered the writing of the Seven Seals to be insignificant. Since the FBI disbelieved his promises to come out, Attorney General Reno was never even informed of the contents of the April 14 letter. The letter didn't even make the daily chronology log, which was written by agents who did not understand the religious significance of what Koresh was saying. Instead, they made fun of his education, doubted he was actually working on anything, and simply noted that he had "established a new precondition for his coming out" (DOJ Waco 1993, 105; Tabor and Gallagher 1995, Chapter 1, footnote 35, loc. 2736). The position of the top authorities thus remained that no progress had been made in negotiations. This left them only with the last resort plan, to insert CS gas into the buildings on April 19.

Tabor gives several reasons why he believes that Koresh really intended to come out after writing the exposition of all Seven Seals. In addition to the promises to exit that Koresh made in the April 14 letter, Tabor notes that the "Exposition of the First Seal," a text that survived the fire, is a serious work that is purposeful, coherent, and "tangibly productive." The text was carefully planned in terms of structure and aimed at an audience outside of the compound (Tabor 1994, 15). Finally, Tabor notes that Koresh's last words in the manuscript are "Should we not eagerly ourselves be ready to accept this truth and *come out of the closet and be revealed to the world* as those who love Christ in truth and in righteousness?" (Joel 2:16, Tabor and Gallagher, 1995, locs. 294, 2330, 2331, 2555, 2650, 2667, 2671). After opening the seals through this writing, the group could "come out of the closet and be revealed to the world," that is, exit the dwelling.

One proposition from the formula for radical apocalypticism, *Redemptive Violence*, was largely absent from the worldview of the Branch Davidians during their stay in Texas. They were willing to endure persecution at the hands of "Babylon," but did not feel this martyrdom was necessary nor did they attempt to kill others in an act of piety. There is also no indication that they believed all others to be the *Concretization of Evil*. In fact, Wessinger notes that the Branch Davidians maintained missionary outreach beyond their circle until the very end, unlike violent groups, such as the People's Temple at Jonestown or Aum Shinrikyo, which became isolated. Indeed, the Branch Davidians never cut themselves off completely from the outside world. Throughout the siege, they offered to negotiate with family members and religion experts, people whom they thought would understand them, only to be turned down by the FBI (Wessinger 2000, 73–74, 101). Despite the firefight and assault, the Branch Davidians never devolved into an "us" versus "them" scenario. of Good versus Evil, but rather continued to work for the salvation of others. On April 18, Koresh told the negotiator, "You tell [them] we love 'em, we love 'em," apparently with reference to those involved in the siege (Wessinger 2000, 110). This was a possible in-road to communicating with Koresh, but it had to be conducted within his cultural framework.

Instead, the FBI ignored the advice of its own behavioral scientists. Pete Smerick and Mark Young rightly advised the FBI that greater tactical pressure would reinforce the Branch Davidians' worldview that the government was "Babylon" (Wessinger 2000, 70). Led by some of the same agents as at Ruby Ridge, the government responded much as it had back then. In fact, while the international Branch Davidians were not members of the Christian Identity church and were explicitly *not* racist, they did share traits in common with the Weavers at Ruby Ridge. These commonalities may be important for explaining the ways in which law enforcement initially regarded both groups.

Both the Weavers and the Branch Davidians were apocalyptic groups with a non-violent eschatology. Both interpreted "Babylon" of the Book of Revelation to be the government, which would definitely put governmental agents on the defensive. Both groups held a peculiar interpretation of Scripture that caused them to withdraw somewhat from society in preparation for the endtime. This aroused suspicions that they were antisocial, secretive criminals. Both groups lived an alternative lifestyle and sought to be self-sufficient, which was viewed as isolationism. David Koresh, like Vicki Weaver, received visions and felt he had an authoritative interpretation of Scriptures, especially of the Book of Revelation. Law enforcement considered this to be crazy. Both groups were armed and willing to defend themselves, leading to serious concerns from law enforcement over the threat that they posed. Just as the media had misunderstood and likely exaggerated the danger of Randy Weaver and his family, so too had it misconstrued David Koresh's self-identity and self claims. The media made him appear like a suicidal, psychopathic madman possibly willing to execute his whole group. In reality he was most likely far less of a threat, except as a repeat sexual predator of underage girls. Finally, when under siege, neither Vicki Weaver nor David Koresh would come out until they believed that God spoke to them and told them to do so. This is because both were ardent apocalyptic believers. The Weavers were under siege for ten days and the Branch Davidians for fifty-one days. In neither case did force cause them to exit.

Overall, this analysis shows that understanding "Bible babble" is crucial for conducting genuine negotiations with those who hold an apocalyptic Christian framework. It can aid in determining accurate threat levels, facilitate communication to move negotiations forward and shed light on goals and motivations. These insights were lacking at Waco. In fact, one of the FBI negotiators at Waco confided, "some of them initially thought the Seven Seals of the Book of Revelation, about which Koresh talked incessantly, were animals."[55]

These were well meaning and very intelligent agents, but they did not understand apocalypticism, the history of Adventism and the Branch Davidian theology, or the technical biblical exegesis through which David Koresh expressed his worldview. In other words, they simply didn't possess the cultural and religious knowledge needed in order to communicate effectively with Koresh. To their credit, they recognized this deficiency and the Department of Justice report lists numerous experts in religion who were consulted at various points during the siege. However, these experts did not correspond directly with Koresh except by way of notes or tapes passed along periodically. Their insights were not integrated systematically into the intelligence assessment. Finally, their explanations were subject to the judgment of those above them who did not possess religious expertise.[56]

Asking a religious studies expert about an isolated statement, phrase, or letter is not the same as conducting expert analysis of an entire worldview through the lens of the academic study of religion. Moreover, expert cultural knowledge cannot always be simply communicated to non-experts in a crisis situation. Subject matter expertise cannot be incidental to handling such a situation in order to be effective. An understanding of religion must be routinely integrated into law enforcement and intelligence analysis, understood and respected at the highest levels. The tragedy at Waco demonstrates that relegating religious expertise to a tangential opinion outside of the main chain of command results in missed opportunities and unintentional consequences.

For these reasons, several religion scholars, including Dr. Catherine Wessinger, Dr. Michael Barkun, and Dr. J. Phillip Arnold, reached out to the FBI to offer expertise. Leadership at the American Academy of Religion (AAR) and the Society for the Scientific Study of Religion (SSSR) made the organizations more available to law enforcement as well as to the media. The FBI sent a negotiator to the 1995 meeting of the AAR and asked Dr. Barkun to serve on the Select Advisory Commission for the FBI's Critical Incident Response Group. They also put in motion plans to bring in experts to train agents on millennialism and put "behavioral scientists on an equal footing with the tactical experts on the FBI crisis response team" (Wessinger 2000, 180). In 1996, their input improved the handling of the next major group standoff that received national attention, the Montana Freemen.

## How to manage a standoff – the Montana Freemen

In the Spring of 1996, an extremist small-government and militant group, the Montana Freemen, engaged in a heavily armed standoff with federal authorities at the Clark ranch in Jordan, Montana. Years of ongoing conflicts with public officials and the community had led up to it, including purposefully tying up the courts with Common Law suits and a false lien scheme to make money. In 1994, three-dozen armed Freemen took over the Garfield County courthouse, charged the judge with contempt, offered a reward for his capture, and apparently planned to try another judge and then hang him. Such actions earned them charges of threatening officials, impersonating officials, soliciting kidnapping, criminal syndicalism, armed robbery, and obstruction of justice. Several Freemen took up residence at the Clark ranch. The property had been foreclosed on earlier during the "Farm Crisis," when many farms and family ranches were lost to banks. They refused to leave. On March 25, 1996, a few leading members were arrested on a brief trip away from the ranch.

The remaining Freemen at the ranch renamed it "Justus Township," wrote up their own constitution, and claimed themselves to be free of federal laws. Inside the "Township" were "Wanted Dead or Alive" posters for public officials (Wessinger 2000, 158–217; Barkun 1997, 286–287; Daniels 1999, 171–198). However, instead of escalating the situation, the FBI patiently negotiated with the group for eighty-one days, reaching out to scholars of religion for advice. It was the longest standoff in US history and it ended peacefully.

The Montana Freemen were one group in a loose stream of various conservative Patriot groups that still proliferate today. The most hardcore of the groups, like the Montana Freemen, combine American patriotism, the legal system, early American history and Christian Identity teaching into an apocalyptic worldview. They believe that the God-given local government of "We the People," the "original" white people of America, are fighting the man-made laws of the federal government (Barkun 1997, 286; Wessinger 2000, 160). Rodney Skurdall, one of the main leaders of the Freemen, expresses it succinctly by writing, "This is a holy war" (Wessinger 2000, 165).

For the Freeman and those like them, the war is against a clear *Concretized Evil* – the federal government. This is the world of conspiracy theory, where opinions diverge regarding what evil force is truly controlling the feds: the Federal Reserve, the Council on Foreign Relations, alien overlords, Jews, Bildebergers, the Vatican, or the Illuminati. Regardless, they believe that the federal government enslaves white people in innumerable ways, such as trying people in a martial law admiralty court, as is revealed by the yellow fringe on American flags. Other instruments of enslavement are social security numbers, marriage licenses, driver's licenses, car registration, car insurance, building permits and inspections, and especially taxes. Their canon includes the Bible and legal documents from the earliest days of America, such as the (pre-civil war) US Constitution through the twelfth amendment, the Bill of Rights, the Magna Carta, the Constitutions of the states, the Articles of Confederation, rarely cited parts of the US Code and Uniform Commercial Code, and Ayn Rand's *Atlas Shrugged*.

The Montana Freemen and similar groups, such as the Wisconsin Posse (the Family Farm Preservation) and Michigan Militia, trace the origin of their model to the Posse Comitatus. That group formed in 1969 under the leadership of Henry L. Beach and William P. Gale as part of the "township movement." They named it after the 1878 US federal law of the same name, Posse Comitatus (18 US Code §1385), which prohibits the Federal government from using the military to enforce state laws. The symbolism conveys that the Posse group rejected all jurisdiction and government beyond the local level of Sheriff. They threatened federal judges with hanging and their symbol was a hangman's noose, which they wore as lapel pins (Daniels 1999, 174).

Ardent defenders of the right to bear arms, anti-federalists such as the Posse Comitatus and the Montana Freemen believe they are acting out their right to form a small army ruled at the county or state level. While they claim to revere the Constitution, they actually appear to operate more closely along the lines of the Articles of Confederation, which decentralized federal authority in favor of states' rights. Thus, they seem to reject laws at the federal level, such as exist under the full Constitution with Amendments (which was in fact created secretly in 1781 by governmental elites in order to secure a centralized government). Since they do not respect the authority of the federal level of government, they do not feel obligated to pay taxes, buy licenses, register their cars or guns or have insurance. Moreover, since these anti-federalists reject the Federal Reserve as an institution, they also feel free to manufacture their own currency by producing counterfeit money. This too recalls the Articles of the Confederation, which allowed each state (locality) to have its own army, currency, and banking.

The reality framework of the Freemen and like-minded anti-federalists is an apocalyptic one, scaled onto the history and locality of the "united States of America" (with a lower case "u," capitalization being significant in their thought system). They believe that the founding documents of the united States are God given. They also believe that white people are the true Israel, to whom God gave America as the place where they will inherit the blessings of the covenant. In this, they ignore the fact that Native Americans are the original inhabitants.[57] They believe that the county level of government corresponds to God, the state level to the Son (being of a lesser status), and the federal level to the Holy Spirit.[58] Their goal is a land in which Israel, the white race, is free from man-made laws and can live under biblical laws (Barkun 1997, 286).

When the Freemen took over the Garfield County courthouse, they viewed it as a church. They found deep meaning in correspondences they detected between the physical layout of a courtroom and a church: the flags are located where the cross is, the de facto judge where the preacher's pulpit is, the witness box where the church piano player would be, and so forth (Daniels, 1999, 189–198). Thus, their takeover of the courthouse was a religious statement, an enactment of *Active Eschatology*. By reclaiming the religious nature of the courtroom, they believed they were instituting God's rule in the region.

Similarly, when they declared the Clark ranch to be Justus Township, it tapped into the *Active Eschatology* of the whole loosely affiliated movement, including Patriot groups. Patriot leaders like Norman Olson, a former leader of the Michigan Militia, proclaimed that the Second American Revolution would emanate from the new Township (Daniels 1999, 183; Wessinger 2000, 167). This was the same eschatological vision that the CSA had disseminated through its *CSA Journal* and that McVeigh expected to erupt out of his attack. Extremists believe that this revolution will inaugurate the time of divinely blessed, blissful, and rightful rule of white people.

The Freemen announced on May 1, 1996 that they had promised Yahweh they would not surrender. They also believed that Yahweh had put an invisible barrier around Justus Township to protect them (Wessinger 2000, 179). It seemed to some in the movement that Armageddon was at last unfolding. *Redemptive Violence* was translating into concrete reality. While a few Patriot leaders distanced themselves, others, like Olson, sounded the cry all across the nation for members of the movement to prepare themselves to fight in a real, physical battle against the federal government (Wessinger 2000, 167).

All the ingredients for radical apocalypticism were abundantly present (and still are in the movements that continue). If any standoff with authorities could have ever turned violent, it should have been the FBI's standoff with the heavily armed Montana Freemen in 1996. If the standoff had turned violent, the event would have rippled throughout the world of the anti-federalist movements, which numbered in the tens of thousands, counting all Christian militias and Patriot groups.

However, the FBI had learned from the mistakes made at Ruby Ridge and Waco. They consulted scholars of religion, including Dr. Catherine Wessinger, Dr. Michael Barkun, Dr. Jean Rosenfeld, Dr. Phillip Arnold and Dr. Eugene Gallagher (Wessinger 2000, 178–201). After Waco, they had also consulted with Kerry Noble of the CSA, to see what had worked and what hadn't in their standoff with the government (Noble 1998, 205, 224). They brought in forty-five outsiders to negotiate with the Freemen, including family members and lawyers who could understand their language. They passed many letters to the Freemen from family members. Most of all, the FBI took seriously the Freemen's framework of reality, tried to negotiate with them in those terms, purposefully de-escalated tensions, and avoided any psychological warfare tactic that would entrench the Freemen further in their worldview of oppression.

Members of the group started to leave the ranch one by one. After eighty-one days, the remaining Freemen simply gave themselves up, in order to continue their battle in the place in which they were most comfortable – the law courts.[59]

Even more important than the peaceful surrender of the Freemen themselves was the message that it sent throughout the Christian militia and Patriot movements. Just a year earlier, some in those movements believed they had seen a great victory in Timothy McVeigh's terrorist act, which was retribution for Waco. The resolution to the Freemen standoff communicated that the government could respect the views of those on the Right and resolve conflicts peacefully.

## Countering ideologies

Members of utopian groups are more firmly committed in their self-identities to an ideology than they are to any specific group; hence, their membership affiliations may change (Burke and Reitzes 1991). The Christian Identity teaching, Township ideology, and conspiracy theories discussed in this chapter circulate fluidly amongst the organizations of the racist Christian Right. Members often jump from group to group in search of purer versions of the ideologies.

Ideological ties, rather than group affiliations, gave McVeigh the social world of support not just to inspire the Oklahoma City bombing, but also to help him see it as something good. Christian Identity teaching figured prominently in the Illinois-based Christian Patriots Defense League, which had an influence on leaders at the CSA camp. After they embraced Christian Identity influenced *Active Eschatology*, the leaders of CSA conceived of the Oklahoma City bombing as a way of starting the eschatological race war. CSA had strong ties with the racist murderer Richard Snell, whose execution occurred on the same day as the Oklahoma City bombing. Snell's close friend and spiritual advisor was the Reverend Robert Millar. In addition to being the spiritual advisor and anointer of James Ellison, leader of the CSA, he was also the founder of the Christian Identity camp called Elohim City. Timothy McVeigh called Elohim City twice on April 5, 1995 (Noble 1998, 81–83; Barkun 1997, 265, 269).

To combat ideological networks, law enforcement and intelligence first need to understand them well. The good news is that the FBI learned from earlier mistakes by taking steps to bridge the gap between academia, the intelligence community, and law enforcement. Yet, there are still further gains to make. Those religion scholars who volunteered their expertise are to be applauded, as are the intelligence community and law enforcement officials who recognized the value of their approach.

Unfortunately, the changes did not seem to permeate deeply at the time into the institutional culture and understanding of the FBI, or at least they did not do so systemically. Wessinger reports that subsequent to the Montana Freemen standoff, FBI negotiators told Jayne Docherty, an expert in conflict resolution, that "they found the Religious Studies advice to be irrelevant to resolving the Freemen standoff and that they found the Religious Studies scholars required 'high maintenance' because we kept asking for more data to analyze" (Wessinger 2000, 202). To their credit, Wessinger and the Executive Director of the AAR, Barbara DeConcici, continued to reach out to the FBI. Additional, sporadic meetings between scholars and the FBI occurred in 1998 and 1999 (Wessinger 2000, 202).

These positive steps occurred when I still was a graduate student. Unfortunately, by 2009, when I had the opportunity to lecture to the intelligence community on apocalyptic thought, those steps towards collaboration were no longer as evident. I found that, even after 9/11, hundreds of analysts in the room had very limited understandings of the religious worldviews of apocalyptic groups. I attribute this to the fact that while the FBI and other intelligence agencies continued to connect with the *social sciences* through programs such as START[60] they had not grasped until recently the value of the *humanities* and especially of the *academic study of religion* for addressing the root causes of terrorism and for effective counter-terrorism.

Greater, systemic cooperation between academics, law enforcement, and the intelligence community needs to occur. The contribution of the academic study of religion is still too frequently overlooked when conducting HUMINT or cultural intelligence, especially when dealing with terrorists motivated by religious ideology. In the final chapter, I discuss suggestions for improving this situation.

## Notes

1 Ties between the CSA and Elohim City included their top leaders. Richard Snell is buried there. James Ellison went there after his release from prison on April 15, 1995. Numerous sources, including FBI documents attained through the Freedom of Information Act, explain that just two days before the bombing, McVeigh telephoned Elohim City. He also possibly visited it at some point prior to April 19 (Ridgeway 2007); (Noble 1998, 206–216, 232). While those close to the CSA, including Kerry Noble, see a direct connection, no investigation of the link between McVeigh and Elohim City has led to a criminal indictment. See the interview with John Millar, son of Rev. Robert Millar, both leaders at Elohim City (Chapman and Kline 2012).

2 The bombing in the *Turner Diaries* used a truck packed with 5,000 lbs of ammonium nitrate fertilizer mixed with heating oil, aimed at the FBI Building in Washington DC. It killed 700 people (Pierce 2002, 35–41). The plan by the CSA, which probably was also inspired by the book, more precisely targeted the Alfred P. Murrah Building (Noble 1998, 209–212).

3 Various sources date the standoff as beginning anywhere from April 18 to April 21. However, because of its reverberations with other important dates, many on the radical Right tend to remember April 19 as the day of the FBI standoff with the CSA.

4 In August 2011, Governor Rick Perry solicited participation at The Response: A Call to Prayer, a religious rally organized by the New Apostolic Reformation Church (NAR). The NAR believes that demons inhabit multiple levels of reality, including individual persons, gay people, Jews, atheists, certain cities,

states and nations. One giant demon sits over the whole world. In their view, prayer causes the exorcism of these demons, and the return of Christ is contingent on a certain number of Jews being converted to their form of Christianity. The rally explicitly linked the Texas drought and state of the nation to prayer (Gross 2011).

5  At the time of writing, the Southern Poverty Law Center identifies thirty-seven locations of Christian Identity hate groups (SPLC 2015). The FBI has disavowed its former endorsement of the SPLC as a reliable partner and source. This was due to the imprecision of the characteristics for determining a "hate group" in general, which is not a legal term. However, the data on Christian Identity and KKK groups is trackable through each group's websites and the list of these groups appears to be accurate, although not exhaustive.

6  This trajectory of British-Israelism draws on the teaching of Edward Hine (Barkun, 1997, 11).

7  In 1948, he wrote for *Plain Truth* magazine that the founding of the land of Israel on behalf of the Jews, who were only Judah, was a human political mistake that did not yet fulfill biblical prophecy (Armstrong 1948, 10).

8  "Postmillennialists," by contrast, believe that Christ will return after the 1,000 year (or so) reign of the elect, which can be literal or metaphorical. Thus, the flourishing of the Church since the time of Jesus can be seen as a fulfillment of this period or it could be spiritualized as something occurring in heaven right now.

9  The CSA also rejected the rapture (Noble 1998, 67).

10  Michael Barkun has conducted the most thorough analysis of the apocalyptic thought of the radical Right in America. He has examined their belief in space aliens conspiring with Jews (Barkun 2003, 59–65).

11  Cooper explicitly says he does not believe in racism and he mentions his best friends who are non-white (Cooper 1991, 16, 68).

12  I appreciate this term coined by Barkun to indicate the complexity and macroscopic view of the conspiracy (Barkun 2003, 61).

13  Barkun divides the helpful category of "stigmatized knowledge" into forgotten knowledge, superseded knowledge (once known and then lost), ignored knowledge (found in low-prestige groups), rejected knowledge, and suppressed knowledge (Barkun 2003, 26).

14  Footage found in Wilson, 2008; this coheres with Noble's memory (Noble 1998, 85).

15  Really, I should say, "not yet." There is evidence that each group had the potential to change in either a violent or peaceful direction, depending on the evolution of their eschatological beliefs and experiences with outsiders.

16  The caveats are that I am only using open source material available to everyone and I am not privy to redacted or classified material. Also, I am only assessing the effectiveness of governmental actions through the lens of understanding radical apocalypticism, giving only minimal consideration to other concerns of law enforcement. I wish to state that I am not, in the assessment that follows, entirely placing blame on the government or exonerating all of the victims.

17  Although Kevin Harris admitted firing back in self defense, he was acquitted of charges in the death of US Marshal Degan.

18  From the testimony of Bo Gritz.

19  The Aryan World Congress shares Christian Identity teaching, but it should be noted that not all racist Right organizations subscribe to this teaching. For instance, Ben Klassen's World Church of the Creator, now the Creativity Movement, rejects Christian Identity and all of Christianity as a Jewish plot, instead urging the white race to adhere to the eternal law of Nature. In 1999 a member, Benjamin Smith, a close friend of then leader Matt Hale, went on a

two- state shooting spree that left two dead and nine injured, all non-white. The Creativity Movement exhibits many of the same radical apocalyptic elements as Christian Identity but in a different, non-Christian framework. It sells Ben Klassen's books as authoritative interpretations of the eternal Law, divides the world into white and non-white races, and believes that the white race is being persecuted to the point of extinction by "colored mongrels." Hatred available at: www.creativitymovement.net. Accessed May 29, 2015.

20 She writes of seeing an Aryan Nations cross burning as a child, and states "Looking back on it now, I shudder in horror that something so twisted can feel so right.... In my opinion, there was nothing Christian about it ..." (Weaver 2012, loc. 525, e-book).

21 The autographed edition of my used copy of *The Federal Siege*, while addressed to someone else, is signed by Randy Weaver and reads in part, "Freedom at Any Cost!"

22 The reasons for this omission could be an effort to not make Vicki look more radical or could be a discomfort with religion. After the events of Ruby Ridge, Randy seemed to grow less religious and Sara went in a much more mainstream direction, suggesting that the main religious force of Christian Identity in the family was really Vicki.

23 Sara indicates that, though fabricated, the name Ruby Ridge is "forever burned into the memories of many people" (Weaver 1998, 17–18).

24 The *Declaration of War* is printed in full in Noble 1998, 157–162. Upon reading it, law enforcements' interpretation of this quote as a threat is reasonable.

25 It is not only the radical Right that remains sympathetic to the Weavers and remembers Ruby Ridge. Listen to Old Crow Medicine Show perform Peter Rowan's moving "Ruby Ridge."

26 Eventually, it seems that the FBI did change its tone with regard to Sara Weaver. In her autobiography, she speaks about how healing it was for her to meet amicably with some agents of the FBI when they brought her the material remains of the family. She states that it was healing for her dad, Randy, and sisters, Rachel and Elisheba, as well. Sara, in particular, has written about the need to forgive the agents who attacked her family. This stems out of her new Christian beliefs, strongly dedicated, but more mainstream than those in which she was raised (Weaver 2012, loc. 1949, 2012, e-book).

27 This is excepting the possible child abuse that law enforcement first investigated, which alleged that underage girls were being married off in polygamous settings within the compound.

28 Early sources show confusion about the number of Davidians killed, because an eighteen-month-old child was covered in blood after the shoot-out, but was not in fact killed. (Wessinger 2000, 65; Tabor and Gallagher 1995, Note 8 to Chapter 1).

29 Any spark could have ignited the highly combustible CS gas that filled the buildings of Mt. Carmel on April 19. The government maintains that the Branch Davidians started the fire, a claim that the survivors vehemently deny. On April 18, microphones picked up plans to fight the tanks with fire, but, even if this is the case, it does not signal a mass suicide (Wessinger 2000, 79). Others believe that the government unintentionally started the fire (Gazecki 1997).

30 Daniels, citing Reavis, notes that the agency assigned "Public Relations Officers" that produced footage of the siege for local TV (Daniels 1999, 133–134; Reavis 1995, 31–38).

31 Michel and Herbeck 2001, 119–121 (capitalization in original), photo of McVeigh at Waco on p. 106g.

32 Representatives from CAN (Cult Awareness Network) and Rick Ross were both influential. Tabor and Gallagher discuss at length throughout their book how

law enforcement's early conceptual framework of the Branch Davidians as a Jonestown like "cult" informed their actions (Tabor and Gallagher 1995; Wessinger 2000, 59–60, 64).

33 Since some of these agents have received death threats, I have not included their names here.

34 For a careful amassing of details concerning the events that unfolded, including a timeline, the best source is Wessinger 2000, 56–104.

35 Dr. Harry Salem noted there were no lab tests on the effects of CS gas on children or pregnant women, but that anecdotal evidence suggested that the effects would not be permanent. Section XI. Planning and Decision Making between March 23 and April 19, 1993 (DOJ Waco 1993).

36 Section X. Role of the White House, also XI. Planning and Decision Making between March 23 and April 19, 1993 (DOJ Waco 1993).

37 Section XI. Planning and Decision Making between March 23 and April 19, 1993 (DOJ Waco 1993).

38 Section VII. Child Abuse (DOJ Waco 1993).

39 Section VII. Child Abuse (DOJ Waco 1993).

40 For a solid exposition of Houteff, Roden, and Koresh's apocalyptic eschatology, see Tabor and Gallagher 1995, locs. 460–488, e-book.

41 This is due to a psychological phenomenon called cognitive dissonance, which is especially strong in apocalyptic believers. When faced with two opposite claims, e.g., the date of the endtime and that date coming and passing, a fervent believer will most likely come up with a third proposition to ameliorate the dissonance, rather than just saying that he/she was wrong in the first place. A third proposition could be, for instance, that God decided to wait, or that there is a new interpretation of a later date that is more correct (Festinger 1957).

42 A rather unsentimentalized but sympathetic insider's view is provided by David Koresh's mother in Haldeman 2007, 88–95.

43 As reported by Clive Doyle to Phillip Arnold and by Koresh to FBI negotiators (Tabor and Gallagher 1995, Chapter 3, footnote 15, loc. 2939, e-book). In fact, UFOlogy as part of the interpretation of the Ezekiel's chariot is not as rare as one might think.

44 This important detail happens to be mentioned by Catherine Wessinger (Haldeman, 2007, 125, Chapter 1, footnote 21).

45 It is important to note that Wessinger, Tabor, and I all assess the communication from Koresh as indicating his genuine beliefs, however unique they were. Some FBI agents, who were not religion scholars, believed him to be a manipulative con man (Wessinger 2000, 85).

46 Section VII. Child Abuse (DOJ Waco 1993).

47 Former members also accuse Koresh of child abuse, claiming that he punished children with harsh spanking for infractions of strict rules. There is much less evidence for this than for statutory rape and polygamy (Section VII. Child Abuse, DOJ Waco 1993; Wessinger 2000, 62).

48 The Justice Department Report to the Attorney General refers to the "apocalyptic nature" of Koresh's preachings. The report does not use the term in the way that I or other biblical scholars do, but rather in a way that is synonymous with a dramatic, cataclysmic *eschaton* or endtime (DOJ Waco 1993).

49 Section VI. Attitudes of Koresh and Others in the Compound (DOJ Waco 1993).

50 Section VI. Attitudes of Koresh and Others in the Compound (DOJ Waco 1993) weighs evidence for and against thinking that the group intended suicide.

51 Tabor's use of this term is apt (Tabor and Gallager 1995, loc. 128, e-book).

52 See the negotiation tape with Steve Schneider in Wessinger 2000, 104, in which he states that suicide is against the commandments: "We're not a suicide bunch. We love life."

53 Italics added for emphasis, different from those edited by Tabor and Gallagher, 1995 loc. 223, e-book.

54 Section XI. Planning and Decision-making between March 23 and April 19, 1993 (DOJ Waco 1993).

55 As told by a FBI negotiator to Phillip Arnold, according to Tabor and Gallagher, 1995, loc. 1362, e-book.

56 Section IV. The Role of Experts During the Standoff (DOJ Waco 1993).

57 Thus, Wessinger classifies them as a "nativist" movement, Wessinger 2000, 159–1161.

58 See the Freemen document, "Our De Jure County Governmental Pursuant to the Word of Almighty God" (Daniels 1999, 189–198).

59 For details of the agreement and what unfolded in the courts, including some additional theatrics, see Wessinger 2000, 192–201.

60 The START consortium (National Consortrium for the Study of Terrorism and Responses to Terrorism) is an excellent resource for bringing hundreds of scholars in conversation with the intelligence community, see www.start.umd. edu, accessed May 29, 2015. Unfortunately, the humanities are barely represented, if at all. The controversial US Military Human Terrain System program has caused suspicion between academics and the US government. This program embedded anthropologists into local communities during the theater of war. This was an attempt to gain cultural knowledge during times of war to improve decision making and community relations. It was subsequently condemned by the American Anthropological Association (AAA), see the official Executive Board Statement at: www.aaanet.org/about/Policies/statements/ Human-Terrain-System-Statement.cfm. Accessed May 29, 2015. Since the advice of anthropologists occurred in combat situations, the temptation to use the knowledge to tactical advantage was too great. The AAA pointed out numerous cogent objections. These included that the anthropologists, as military contractors, could not always distinguish themselves from military personnel, might have conflicting responsibilities to their military units and the persons whom they study, that attaining "informed consent" from populations was compromised and that the counsel they gave could result in operations against those they study, violating the AAA Code of Ethics, and creating risks for non-HTS anthropologists and the people they study.

## Bibliography

Abanes, Richard. 1998. *Endtime Visions: The Road to Armageddon?* New York: Four Walls, Eight Windows.

ADL – Anti-Defamation League. September 21, 2004. "Letter to Wal Mart."

Armstong. Herbert W. June 1948. "Jews are a Nation Again," *Plain Truth magazine.* Accessed November 28, 2014, www.herbert-armstrong.org/Plain Truth 1940s/ Plain Truth 1948 (Vol XIII No 02) Jun.pdf.

Barkun, Michael. 1997. *Religion and the Racist Right.* Chapel Hill, NC: University of North Carolina Press.

Barkun, Michael. 2003. *A Culture of Conspiracy: Apocalyptic Visions in Contemporary America.* Berkeley, CA: University of California Press.

Burke, Peter J. and Reitzes, Donald C. 1991. "An Identity Theory Approach to Commitment." *Social Psychological Quarterly* 54, 3: 239–251.

Chapman, Lee Roy and Kline, Joshua. April 15, 2012. "Who's Afraid of Elohim City?" *This Land Press*. Accessed December 1, 2014, http://thislandpress.com/04/15/2012/whos-afraid-of-elohim-city/?read=complete.

Cooper, Milton William. 1991. *Behold A Pale Horse*. No imprint. (Self published).

Daniels, Ted, ed. 1999. *A Doomsday Reader: Prophets, Predictors, and Hucksters of Salvation*. New York: New York University Press.

DOJ Waco – US Department of Justice. October 8, 1993. *Report to the Attorney General on the Events at Waco, Texas (Feb. 28 to April 19, 1993)*. Redacted Version. Accessed December 1, 2014, www.justice.gov/publications/waco/report-deputy-attorney-general-events-waco-texas.

DOJ Review – US Department of Justice. Office of Inspector General. November 15, 2002. *A Review of Allegations of a Double Standard of Discipline at the FBI* Accessed July 11, 2011, www.justice.gov/oig/special/0211/final.pdf.

DOJ Ruby Ridge – US Department of Justice. *Report on Ruby Ridge Task Force*. June 10, 1994. Redacted Version. Accessed November 4, 2014, www.justice.gov/opr/readingroom/rubyreport40_84.pdf and www.justice.gov/opr/readingroom/rubyreport517_545.pdf.

Festinger, Leon. 1957. *Theory of Cognitive Dissonance*. Stanford, CA: Stanford University Press.

Gazecki, William, Director. 1997. *Waco: The Rules of Engagement*. Los Angeles: Fifth Estate Productions.

GCI – Grace Communion International. Updated 2015. "A Short History of Grace Communion International." Accessed December 15, 2014, www.gci.org/aboutus/history.

Goodrick-Clarke, Nicholas. 2002. *Black Sun: Aryan Cults, Esoteric Nazism, and the Politics of Identity*. New York: New York University Press.

Gould, Rebecca Kneale. 2005. *At Home in Nature: Spiritual Practice in America*. Berkeley, CA: University of California Press.

Gross, Terry. 19 August 2011. *Fresh Air:* "The Evangelicals Engaged in Spiritual War," on NPR. Accessed May 29, 2015, www.npr.org/2011/08/24/139781021/the-evangelicals-engaged-in-spiritual-warfare.

Haldeman, Bonnie. 2007. *Memories of the Branch Davidians: The Autobiography of David Koresh's Mother*. Waco, TX: Baylor University Press.

Hartzler, Joseph. April 24, 1997. "Opening Statement by Prosecutor Joseph Hartzler." Accessed November 26, 2014, http://law2.umkc.edu/faculty/projects/ftrials/mcveigh/prosecutionopen.html.

KIM – Kingdom Identity Ministries. 2014. "'Doctrinal Statement' and 'Seedline and Race'." Accessed June 18, 2009–20 December 2014, www.kingidentity.com/.

KKK– Ku Klux Klan. 2015. "Welcome to the Ku Klux Klan." Accessed January 27, 2015, www.kkk.com/.

Linder, Douglas. n.d. "The Oklahoma City Bombing and the Trial of Timothy McVeigh: A Chronology." Accessed December 10, 2014, http://law2.umkc.edu/faculty/projects/ftrials/mcveigh/mcveighchrono.html.

Marsden, Victor. 2011. *Protocols of the Elders of Zion*. RiverCrest Publishing.

Michel, Lou and Herbeck, Dan. 2001. *American Terrorist: Timothy McVeigh and the Oklahoma City Bombing*. New York: HarperCollins.

Noble, Kerry. 1998. *Tabernacle of Hate: Why They Bombed Oklahoma City*. Minneapolis, MN: Voyageur Press.

OPCW – Organization for the Prohibition of Chemical Weapons. Updated July 29,

2005 [31 August 1994]. *Chemical Weapons Convention* (CWC), Accessed January 2, 2015, www.opcw.org/chemical-weapons-convention/.

Pew Center Study. October 2006. Executive Summary of the "Spirit and Power – A 10-Country Survey of Pentacostals." Accessed March 11, 2008, www.pewforum. org/2006/10/05/spirit-and-power/.

Pew Research Center. July 14, 2010. "Jesus Christ's Return to Earth." Accessed October 2, 2010, www.pewresearch.org/daily-number/jesus-christs-return-to-earth/.

Pierce, William (aka Andrew MacDonald). 2002 [1978]. *The Turner Diaries.* 2nd ed. Hillsboro, WV: National Vanguard Books.

PALS – Portraits of American Life Study. 2006. "Religious Guidance and Religious Authority." Accessed October 23, 2010, http://palsresearch.net/.

Reavis, Dick J. 1995. *The Ashes of Waco: An Investigation.* Syracuse NY: Syracuse University Press.

Redfield, Robert. 1960. *The Little Community and Peasant Society and Culture.* Chicago: The University of Chicago Press.

Ridgeway, James. August 2007. "In Search of John Doe No. 2: The Story the Feds Never Told About the Oklahoma City Bombing." *Mother Jones News.* Accessed December 1, 2014, www.motherjones.com/politics/2007/07/search-john-doe-no-2-story-feds-never-told-about-oklahoma-city-bombing?page=7.

SPLC. 2004. "Wal-Mart drops Protocols, but the Controversy Lives On." *Southern Poverty Law Center Intelligence Report* Vol. 116. Accessed January 28, 2015, www.splcenter.org/get-informed/intelligence-report/browse-all-issues/2004/winter/selling-extremism.

SPLC – Southern Poverty Law Center. Updated 2015. *Active Christian Identity Groups.* Accessed December 2, 2014, www.splcenter.org/get-informed/intelligence-files/ideology/christian-identity/active_hate_groups.

Tabor, James D. 1994. "The Role of Biblical Scholarship at Waco: One Attempt to Avert Disaster." Accessed December 1, 2014, http://ccat.sas.upenn.edu/gopher/text/religion/koresh/Koresh%20Scholarship.

Tabor, James D. and Arnold, Phillip J. eds. March 1994. *David Koresh's Unfinished Manuscript on the Seven Seals; Events at Waco; Interpretive Log, Rethinking Waco: the Perspective of the Academic Study of Religion.* Accessed December 1, 2014, http://ccat.sas.upenn.edu/gopher/text/religion/koresh/Koresh%20Scholarship.

Tabor, James D, and Gallagher, Eugene V. 1995. *Why Waco? Cults and the Battle for Religious Freedom in America.* Berkeley, CA: University of California Press.

US House of Representatives. 1996. *Investigation into the Activities of Federal Law Enforcement Agencies toward the Branch Davidians: Thirteenth Report by the Committee on Government Reform and Oversight Prepared in Conjunction with the Committee on the Judiciary together with Additional and Dissenting Views.* Report 104–749. Washington, DC: US Government Printing Office.

US Senate Committee on the Judiciary. 1995. *Ruby Ridge: Report of the Subcommittee on Terrorism, Technology, and Government.*

Weaver, Randy and Sara. 1998. *The Federal Siege at Ruby Ridge: In Our Own Words.* Marion, MT: Ruby Ridge, Inc.

Weaver, Sara. 2012. *From Ruby Ridge to Freedom.* Overboard Ministries, Inc.

Wessinger, Catherine. 2000. *How the Millennium Comes Violently: From Jonestown to Heaven's Gate.* New York: Seven Bridges Press.

Wilson, Michael W. Director. 2008. *Silhouette City.* Social Satisfaction Media.

# 7 The humanpox versus green fire
## Eco-terrorists and eco-activists

In our decimation of biological diversity, in our production of toxins, in our attack on the basic life-support system of Earth, in our explosive population growth, we humans have become a disease – the Humanpox.
(Dave Foreman, *Confessions of an Eco-Warrior*)[1]

We reached the old wolf in time to watch a fierce green fire dying in her eyes ... I was young then, and full of trigger itch; I thought that because fewer wolves meant more deer, that no wolves would mean hunters' paradise. But after seeing the green fire die, I sensed that neither the wolf nor the mountain agreed with such a view.
(Aldo Leopold, *The Sand County Almanac*)[2]

At 1 p.m. on September 1, 2010, after the hottest summer to date for Washington DC, James Lee walked into the Discovery Channel building with explosives strapped to his body and a gun in his hand. Although the building of 1,900 people was quickly evacuated, Lee, aged forty-three, managed to hold three men hostage. Ominously, he told them, "Today is a good day to die." By 4:48 p.m., as he pointed a gun at one of the hostages, SWAT snipers killed Lee instead.

In the intervening hours, during negotiations with law enforcement, Lee explained why he had targeted the Discovery Channel and why he was insisting that they air his views. He posted his eleven demands that day on his website, www.savetheplanet.com. At first glance, his list of demands appeared to be the ravings of a sheer madman. He insisted that the Discovery Channel and affiliates have daily television programs, perhaps in a game show format, based on Daniel Quinn's novel *Ishmael* (Quinn 1992). Quinn's novel portrays a telepathic gorilla who describes the pernicious effects of human civilization. Lee's proposed new programming was supposed to convey how to improve the natural world and reverse human civilization. Lee wanted it to focus especially on how humans can avoid having "more filthy human children since those new additions continue pollution and are pollution" (Lee 2010).

The core theme that emerges in Lee's beliefs is the deep value placed on non-human species. This leads to a disdain for humans and their offspring because of our impact on these non-human species. He gives a long list of species that he imagines need protection, especially squirrels. Lee then writes, "The humans? The planet does not need humans" (Lee 2010).

As shocking as his position was, Lee was not alone in holding these views. Lee was a lone wolf who, through the internet and books, partook of a larger system of beliefs shared by other ecological extremists. His words betray deep familiarity with a system of beliefs that interprets the radical apocalyptic framework in tandem with certain environmentally centered philosophies. Vital elements of Lee's eco-apocalyptic view are shared by Theodore Kaczynski, "The Unabomber," scattered affiliates of ELF (the Earth Liberation Front), ALF (the Animal Liberation Front), and the recently closed campaign SHAC (Stop Huntingdon Animal Cruelty), along with numerous named and unnamed eco-anarchist groups.

According to the Federal Bureau of Investigation, one of the most serious domestic terror threats in the US is posed by "eco-terrorists" belonging to groups such as ELF, ALF, and SHAC. By 2008, these groups had committed over 2,000 crimes, causing over $110 million dollars in damage (FBI 2008). Their diverse acts of sabotage have included gluing locks, slashing tires, pulling up survey stakes to slow land development, tree-spiking (driving nails of various materials into trees to deter those who would cut them with chainsaws) and wrecking construction equipment. More seriously, they have sunk boats, destroyed power lines and attempted to carry out or actually carried out firebombing and arson. They act against a wide array of enterprises and properties that they believe harm the wilderness. These include: an animal experimentation lab at Michigan State University, a ski resort in Vail, Forest Services outposts, lumber companies, animal testing facilities, a tree farm that promoted hybrid poplars, meat packing plants, a wild horse corral, and power lines associated with nuclear energy facilities.[3]

These groups are a loose amalgamation of those in the "REAR" or Radical Environmental and/or Animal Rights movement.[4] The intelligence and law enforcement communities have serious concerns that some members of the movement may be escalating to act against humans, as did Lee. Killing three and injuring twenty-three, Kaczynski acted partly out of ideology concerned with defending the environment. However, he blended radical environmental ideology into his own anti-technological worldview. Law enforcement has to account for and track lone wolves, such as Lee and Kaczynski. Adding to that difficult task, law enforcement must also adequately assess established groups in the REAR movement. REAR operates with a model of "leaderless resistance," essentially a network of small, scattered, leaderless cells (Joosse 2007, Leader and Probst 2003).

However, some cells have been identified. The FBI's "Operation Back-fire" targeted The Family, a radical environmentalist cell sometimes affiliated with ELF. In the largest eco-terrorism case in history thus far, fifteen members of The Family have been indicted for over twenty crimes over six years, garnering property damages of $40 million. The arrest of the second of its leaders in 2012, Rebecca Rubin, was a major coup for the FBI. At the time of writing, two more Family members appear on the FBI's list of "Most Wanted Domestic Terrorists" (FBI December 7, 2012).

Currently, a vital difference exists between ELF, ALF, and SHAC on the one hand, and Lee and Kaczynski on the other. Unlike those lone wolves, ELF, ALF, and SHAC have thus far never intended to kill anyone. The very serious indictments against members of The Family include conspiracy to commit arson, destruction of an energy facility, use of a destructive device and arson. The charges do not include murder or attempted murder. Like the radical environmental group Earth First!, these groups have long espoused a principle to do no harm to any animals, including humans (Deshpande and Ernst 2012, 10–12; Foreman 1991, 113). This raises the question of whether the labels "eco-terrorist" and "domestic terrorist" effectively deter the direct actions of ELF, ALF, and SHAC or prevent a greater escalation of violence from offshoot groups and sympathizers.

Since the founding of the earliest REAR groups, ALF in 1976, Environmental Life Force in 1977, and Earth First! in 1980, numerous groups emerged that share their philosophy. These include ELF, SHAC, the Sea Shepherd society, various anarchist groups, and bio-regionalist groups, such as Mountain Justice and RAMPS (Radical Action Mountain Peoples Survival) in the Appalachia area and BMIS (Black Mountain Indigenous Support) in Arizona.

Some have engaged only in non-violent protests, while others have purposefully perpetrated damage to property, or "ecotage." The vast majority of these REAR groups have been non-violent towards persons, but it is unclear if this will always be the case.

Reliable estimates of the number of persons involved in the REAR movement are not available. In terms of demographics, the members of ELF are most often male, well educated, technologically literate, middle- to upper-middle class, between the ages of eighteen and twenty-five, and living in the US (Ackerman 2003, 148, 151; Loadenthal 2013, 35). Though diverse and geographically scattered, core ideology holds radical environmentalists together.

A fairly standardized "canon," a well-venerated, authoritative set of writings that inform a movement's ethics, worldview, and shared history, has emerged. Although the canon varies, it typically comprises works by the naturalist writers and poets Henry David Thoreau, John Muir, Aldo Leopold, David Abrams, and Gary Snyder, as well as the environmental writer Rachel Carson. It also includes philosophers, such as Arne Naess and Roderick Nash. Activists are often well versed in the major theses of population ecologists Anne and Paul Ehrlich, Gaia theorist and scientist James Lovelock, and the general conclusions of environmental and climate scientists. The *Earth First! Newsletter*, which published writings from a variety of activists, forms a canon of its own. Animal rights activists are also inspired heavily by the works of the bio-ethicists Peter Singer and Tom Regan, biologist Marc Bekoff who studies the emotional lives of animals, and the primatologists Jane Goodall and Diane Fossey, who studied primates in the wild and came to respect them deeply.

In addition to the standard canon, REAR activists frequently draw on an eclectic array of other works. A helpful list drawn up by Taylor includes: environmental philosophers, Native American scholars, environmental historians, environmental scientists and conservation biologists, anarchistic critics, social ecologists, bio-regionalists, critics of technology, eco-feminists, anthropologists, eco-psychologists, contemporary pagans, "New science" theorists and religionists (including "systems theorists," "complexity theorists" and "Gaia theorists"), New Age philosophers, other novelists and poets, other naturalists and anthropologists who provide a positive view of non-industrial life as an alternative to modern technological society.[5]

Just as diverse as this eclectic list of readings are the outlooks and practices of those in the REAR movement. Some are dedicated vegans, while others practice hunting, gathering, and survivalist skills. Some believe that each individual animal life is of supreme value, whereas others would put the protection of the wilderness as the top or only priority. And while many insist on entirely peaceful methods of protest and civil disobedience, others advocate doing property damage as a means of resistance against ecological damage. A few others still, in the tiniest minority of the movement, are also open to inflicting harm on humans.

All those affiliated with the REAR movement share certain core assumptions and concepts that are apocalyptic in the sense used in this book. These ideas are succinctly represented in the writings in the canon listed above, particularly in the still relevant views of Edward Abbey and Dave Foreman. Understanding the difference between peaceful apocalyptic and radical apocalyptic frameworks as they apply to the REAR movement is absolutely vital for determining which groups and individuals pose a genuine threat to human safety.

## The apocalyptic formula and the REAR movement

Radical environmentalism as well as animal rights activism begins with a basic shift in perspective: the secret about this world is that heaven *is* this world, and the secret about "the righteous" is that all creatures exist for their own sake and benefit. The ecological worldview applies directly to the first three apocalyptic reality propositions in our formula:

*A secret about the nature of this world*: The ordinary, mundane world is broken and unduly influenced by Evil of some kind, locked in a struggle with Good.
*A secret about the state of the righteous*: The righteous are oppressed, while the wicked flourish.
*A secret about another higher or future world. . . .*: There is a transcendent world in which justice, peace, and happiness reign. It is either a place somewhere out there that the righteous will go to someday, or it is a world that will someday come to the righteous ... and *a secret about the future*: At a special time the gap between the mundane world and the transcendent one will be closed.

In this radical environmental context, in the minds of peaceful and violent activists alike, *wilderness* is equivalent to the transcendent world. Wilderness is perfect when left in its pristine state. Even with the predators, natural disasters, and loss of individual animals, wilderness also contains luminescent waterfalls, sun-dappled trees, and exquisite creatures. By its own design, so to speak, wilderness and all the species in it have evolved just as they should, so long as we limit the scope of human impact. *Civilization*, on the other hand, is a (mundane) world governed by evil forces, including overwhelming materialism, polluting industrialism, the over-population of humans, and destructive technology.

In the REAR worldview, the animals, plants, ecosystems, and Mother Earth are "the Good" who have become the innocent victims of humans and our modern way of life. The wicked include a vast range of those responsible for environmental degradation, including timber and energy companies, land developers, the US Forest Service, and facilities experimenting on or exploiting animals. The wicked are also the vast human masses mindlessly perpetrating pollution and environmental degradation through habits of over-indulgence or simply using up the earth's resources through overpopulation. Altogether, this constitutes Evil.

The REAR movement deeply embraces a philosophy called biocentrism, or "deep ecology," a term first used by the Norwegian philosopher Arne Naess and expounded by Bill Devall and George Sessions (Naess 1973; Devall and Sessions, 1985). Biocentrism maintains that humans are no more intrinsically valuable than any other creature (Devall and Sessions 1985, 7, 70). In this view, a jellyfish or an oak tree is just as precious and worthy of protection and preservation as a human life. By de-centering humans in environmental preservation, REAR proponents differ from mainstream environmental conservation groups. Groups such as the Sierra Club, Nature Conservancy, Greenpeace, or the Humane Society would certainly privilege human preservation and, to varying degrees, human interests over efforts to protect wilderness and non-human species. Instead, they envision an ideal balance between civilized development and wilderness (Nash 2014, loc. 5647).

Dave Foreman, co-founder of Earth First!, states his biocentric perspective quite clearly: "An individual human being has no more intrinsic value than does an individual Grizzly Bear life" (Foreman 1991, 26). Foreman sometimes seems to privilege non-human life over that of humans: "Human suffering resulting from drought and famine in Ethiopia is tragic, yes, but the destruction there of other creatures and habitat is even more tragic" (ibid.). Similarly, environmental activist author Edward Abbey jokes that he was a "humanist" because he preferred killing a man over killing a snake (Abbey 1968, 17). While most REAR activists today do not wish harm upon humans, placing human interests on par with that of a squirrel's or a hawk's can make the activists appear misanthropic or dangerous.

In and of itself, the philosophy of biocentrism can be peaceful. Many naturalists, environmentalists, and philosophers have shared a biocentric perspective that stems from deep compassion (Abram 2006). The iconic *Earth First! Journal* simply attempted to build on the liberal tradition of Locke, Kant, and Rousseau in extending the idea that "every individual is of equal moral worth" to all creatures (Swartzendruber 2000, 14; Nash 1989). John Muir, the naturalist spokesperson for the Sierra Club and one of the first American eco-activists (Albanese 1990), penned this biocentric passage in his journal: "I have precious little sympathy for the myriad bat eyed proprieties of civilized man, and if a war of the races should occur between the wild beasts and Lord Man I would be tempted to sympathize with the bears" (Muir 1998, 122).

Biocentric views in the REAR movement can lead to direct actions, typically peaceful in nature, on behalf of non-human creatures. A peaceful example is the tree-sitting of Julia Butterfly Hill. She climbed up "Luna," a giant, 1,500-year-old redwood tree in a California forest. She remained in the tree for an astonishing 738 days to prevent the Pacific Lumber/Maxxaam Company from cutting it down. Hill forgave them and befriended loggers whose actions endangered her, while continuing to educate the public about Luna's value. With political and social pressure, her campaign of kindness and stubborn direct action eventually saved Luna as well as a twenty-foot buffer zone area around the tree (Hill 2000, 243).

One of the most controversial aspects of biocentrism is the call to halt human over-population (Ehrlich and Ehrlich, 1981, 2013). Many scientists and mainstream environmentalists share concerns about over-population and its impact on the planet. However, they also desire to ensure adequate future resources for so many humans. Thus, they advocate slowing population growth through education and increased availability of birth control, always putting human welfare first.

Some REAR activists call for more extreme measures to protect non-human species and the wilderness, such as limiting family size forcibly through establishing legal limits (Foreman 2011).[6] As we have seen in the case of James Lee, in extreme cases this outlook can lead to a virulent hatred of humans and children: "*Children represent FUTURE catastrophic pollution whereas their parents are current pollution. NO MORE BABIES!*" (Lee 2010, capitalization and italics original).

Hence, the biocentric approach to human over-population has engendered severe criticisms from within the environmental movement. Environmentalist writer Murray Bookchin, for instance, decries the proponents of deep ecology as being "barely disguised racists, survivalists, macho Daniel Boones, and outright social reactionaries," calling it the "same kind of crude eco-brutalism [that] led Hitler to fashion theories of blood and soil" resulting in mass murder (Bookchin 1988, 12–14).

Using the apocalyptic framework of analysis clarifies the governing logic, mood, and motivations that inform REAR positions, such as population control. Since REAR activists might actually identify more with the non-human world than with the human one (Abram 1996), the apocalyptic dualism of "us" versus "them" takes on new contours. For radical eco-activists, the "us" are those allied with the natural world against "them," those who profit from, degrade, or exploit the wilderness. The camp of "us" could be trees, a deer, sparrows, owls, coyote, a river, and the human who feels him/herself to be a part of them (Snyder 1969, 21–23, 41, 48). As a result of this strong identification with the non-human, the struggle to protect the natural world can easily rise to the level of Juergensmeyer's "cosmic war." Protection of the wilderness is most meaningful and represents a defense of basic dignity and lives. Losing the war is "unthinkable" (Juergensmeyer 2003, 164–166).

Radical environmentalists deeply feel this split between Good and Evil persons. The influential Dave Foreman posited that it may even have a biological basis. He speculated that Neanderthal DNA contains a "wilderness gene" long suppressed by the Cro-Magnon DNA that conquered it (Foreman 1991, 57). Drawing on Lovelock's Gaia theory, which views the whole earth or Gaia system as one organism, Foreman maintains that Gaia has retaliated by raising up the "eco-warriors" who possess this wilderness gene to fight back against the Cro-Magnons who lack it and endanger Gaia's welfare. Calling the masses of (Cro-Magnon) humanity the "Human-pox" and using the extended metaphor of humanity as a cancer, he states "Gaia has reached into the disease itself [humankind] for antibodies ... humans who love the wild, whose primary loyalty is to Earth and not to *Homo sapiens* ..." (ibid.). Foreman's wilderness gene theory illustrates how deeply he experiences the difference to be between radical environmentalists versus the rest of humankind: the two are literally different species.

If the radical environmental movement is indeed apocalyptic, then theoretically the transcendent world, the wilderness, will triumph over the mundane world of civilization. A core assumption of environmentalism is that the mundane world threatens the very integrity of the transcendent world. However, as in other apocalyptic systems, the oppression of the transcendent realm, the wilderness, and non-human realms, is only temporary. Ultimately, the wilderness will prevail.

All environmentalists urgently state that human degradation of the wilderness must be resisted to preserve the little biodiversity and the ecosystem stability left:

> mankind has become a locustlike blight on the planet that will leave a bare cupboard for its own children – all the while in a kind of Addict's dream of affluence, comfort, eternal progress – using the great achievements of science to produce software and swill.
>
> (Snyder 1969, 97)

One can argue that the concern over humanity affecting natural resources isn't ideology, it is conclusion based on experience.

Radical environmentalists' beliefs make them more akin to apocalypticists than to scientists: they have an apocalyptic secret that someday, in the future, regular human history will end and wilderness will be victorious. ELF websites and literature often quote the words of population scientists and conservation biologists Anne and Paul Ehrlich: "Nature bats last" (Ehrlich and Ehrlich 2013). The Ehrlichs urge us to avoid a collapse of global civilization in the face of climate change, overconsumption and over-population. Many radical environmentalists believe that industrial civilization is absolutely *destined* to collapse – and they may even welcome it. They believe that the world will revert to the age of the Pleistocene, a positive development. If any humans survive, they surmise, these people will live a primitive, pre-industrial hunter-gatherer lifestyle that would be paradise, since humans would finally live in harmony with the natural world (Foreman 1991, 28, 47–48).

For radical environmentalists, while the degradation of the environment and the loss of biodiversity must be mitigated, nature itself will eventually rectify the problem by eliminating industrial civilization. *Nature bats last.* Foreman puts it this way: "Our self-defense is damage control until the machine plows into that brick wall and industrial civilization self-destructs *as it must*" (ibid., 50). In Juergensmeyer's framework, a cosmic (global) war rages that may be unwinnable by earthly means, but assures victory for the Good side (Juergensmeyer 2003, 164–165). While battles to save certain species and ecosystems may be lost, the ultimate war can never be lost because Gaia will survive in some form or another.

This final phase describing a collapse of civilization is truly "eschatological" in that regular human history will be erased. For some radical environmentalists, the survival of the human species is incidental in the eschatological era of bliss (Foreman 1991, 26). Certainly, not all environmentalists favor the end of civilization. Last year, Nash penned his vision of "Island Civilization" in the fourth millennium. Technological advances allow humans to live in small, isolated circles of civilization on a primarily wild earth (Nash 2014, Epilogue). For many in the REAR movement, however, technology must fall and the call of "Back to the Pleistocene!" remains influential (ibid., loc. 8488).

What Rapoport dubs "messianism," I call "apocalypticism." His definition still applies to the context of radical eco-activism:

> One who believes in messianism is one who has faith that there will be a day in which history or life on this earth will be transformed totally and irreversibly from the condition of perpetual strife which we have all experienced to one of perfect harmony that many dream about.
>
> (Rapoport 1980, 197)

There may be no Messiah in the radical environmental eschaton, but there are certainly other parallels with apocalyptic traditions. Kaczynski recognizes this, quoting from the Book of Revelation and noting: "The revolution that anarcho-primitivists hope will overthrow civilization corresponds to the Day of Judgment, the day of destruction on which Babylon will fall (Revelation 18:2)" (Kaczynski 2009, locs. 3109–3111, e-book).

## When radical environmentalism becomes radical apocalypticism and eco-terrorism

The outlook of the REAR movement can be expressed either through peaceful resistance or by violent means. Eco-activists who maintain beliefs in biocentrism, the forcible curbing of over-population and the eventual collapse of industrial civilization are not necessarily going to become eco-terrorists. The subscription to the remaining reality propositions of radical apocalypticism distinguish those in the REAR movement with violent tendencies.

For violent radical environmentalists, the fourth reality proposition often results from a nature journey in which the person realizes the deep "truth" that wilderness is paradise.

*Authoritative Revelation/Interpretation Divine revelation*

A "divine revelation" is a direct, ultimately real, and transformative revelation from the transcendent world. Many leaders of the radical environmental movement have had a wilderness sojourn so profound and dazzling that it completely reorients the one who experienced it. Since that revelatory experience occurs whenever the person is in the wilderness, the person re-emerges from each journey with a deep, uncompromising commitment to protect nature.[7]

It is a matter of intensity. The journey is not just a lovely time in nature. Through immediate and deep communication, nature imparts a perspective so foreign that it changes the person's relationship to the non-human world. Frequently, there is a conviction that those without such journeys and encounters cannot attain the same true realizations or perspectives. Similarly, dedicated animal activists relate similar trans-formative experiences in their communions with non-human species, which Taylor dubs "eye to eye epiphanies."[8]

Abbey, Foreman, and other influential figures in radical environmen-talism often express their wilderness experiences in traditionally religious terms. Consider the statements by an author beloved by radical environ-mentalists, Edward Abbey. His iconic autobiographical *Desert Solitaire*, written in 1968, is replete with descriptions of the natural world as "Eden," "Paradise," or the *locus Dei*, the home of God:

> The only sound is the whisper of the running water, the touch of my bare feet on the sand.... Is this at last the *locus Dei*? There are enough cathedrals and temples and altars here for a Hindu pantheon of divin-ities ... I half expect to see not only the cottonwood tree rising over its tiny spring – the leafy god ... – but also a rainbow-colored corona of blazing light, pure spirit, pure being, pure disembodied intelligence, *about to speak my name.*
>
> (Abbey 1968, 176)

The experience is intensely intimate, expressed in religious terms as com-munion and epiphany. This is not pantheism, which sees the divine present and contained everywhere in creation. Rather, this is a revelatory experience conveying a realization that nature is the transcendent and ultimate reality, essentially God and heaven.

The religion scholar Bron Taylor describes Abbey's religious position as "Gaian naturalism" tinged with "naturalistic animism." Abbey's religious position is the view that the earth or Gaia is alive and sacred, combined with a deep awe and kinship for non-human life, and a skepticism of other metaphysical schemes beyond the concreteness of nature (Taylor 2010, 16, 23, 83). Biodiversity and evolution are thus functionally equivalent to the divine will. Although there may or may not be a god in this system, it is still deeply religious. Regarding the desert heat, sand, stone, and creamy flowers of the yucca plants around him, Abbey writes:

> God? ... who the hell is *He*? There is nothing here, at the moment, but me and the desert. And that's the truth. Why confuse the issue by dragging in a superfluous entity? ... I am not an atheist but an earthi-est. Be true to the earth.
>
> (Abbey 1968, 184)

Given this perspective, no cause – even protecting human life – could earn greater allegiance than the mission of protecting nature. Since for Abbey "the forests and mountains and desert canyons are holier than our churches," the nature of "Paradise" and of "the true original sin" are now clear:

> But the love of wilderness is ... an expression of loyalty to the earth, the earth which bore us and sustains us, the only home we shall ever know, the only paradise we ever need – if only we had the eyes to see. Original sin, the true original sin, is the blind destruction for the sake of greed of this nature paradise which lies all around us – if only we were worthy of it.
>
> (Ibid., 52, 167)

Like John of Patmos seeing the earth passing away and discovering another reality, Foreman swears: "Wilderness is *the real world*; our cities, our computers, our airplanes, our global business civilization all are but artificial and transient phenomena" (Foreman 1991, 27).

The experience conveys that wilderness is paradise or the real world, and carries with it a deep sense of bliss:

> If you want heaven – it is here.... If you seek total union with the cosmos, then float a river, drift into river time ... Heaven, Nirvana, Valhalla, everlasting life are here and now – in the *real world*. We need nothing more than this paradise in which we were born.
>
> (Ibid., 52–53)

For radical environmentalists, these realizations, like religion, are all-encompassing, wholly orienting, and uniquely realistic (Geertz 1973). Thus, scholar Bron Taylor is right to consider radical environmentalism a new religious movement, which he appropriately dubs "deep green religion" (Taylor 2010, 13).

When the other reality propositions of radical apocalypticism are present, this deep green religion can turn violent. For radical environmentalists, the realization that the wilderness is the "real world" and deserving of our protection readily results in an unbridled loyalty. This ecological fidelity can be expressed through another reality proposition:

> *Active Eschatology*: Our actions are key to ushering in the new stage of the coming good world.

If the "good world" is biodiversity that we must act to preserve in the face of the impending collapse of industrial civilization, then REAR activists such as those in ELF and ALF sometimes espouse an *Active Eschatology*. They believe in "direct actions" that protect nature until the collapse of civilization and they may even seek to hasten it.

One of the main differences between REAR activists and mainstream activists is a commitment to engage in illicit "direct actions" or "monkey-wrenching," acts of sabotage on behalf of the environment. Like other active eschatologists, they believe that only their measures will be effective. For members of ELF, ALF, and other groups, inspiration came from the fictional characters in Abbey's *The Monkey Wrench Gang*, who set fire to bill-boards, blew up bridges, and attempted to dynamite the Glen Canyon Dam because of the ineffectiveness of legal mechanisms. Foreman came to this same position after becoming disillusioned as a Washington environmental lobbyist, concluding that efforts through the legal system are too slow and overly tied to human-centric interest (Foreman 1991, 139).

Singularly focused on one goal, Foreman criticized issues that were normally "sacred cows of radical environmentalism, like non-violent disobedience and bioregionalism," when he thought they resulted in compromises that failed to protect the earth above all other concerns (Swartzendruber 2000, 13). From its inception, the founders of Earth First! instructed its followers that direct actions should be non-violent. However, members construed non-violence quite differently amongst themselves (Davis and Foreman 1991, 30, 257). By 1991, Earth First! had experienced a split between those who wished to engage in non-violent protests, such as picketing, blockading, or climbing up trees destined for destruction, and those who interpreted non-violence as including property damage (Loadenthal 2013, 30–31).

The more violent wing of Earth First! engaged in "monkeywrenching" or "ecotage," sabotage against objects in order to protect the environment. These acts took various forms: pouring karo syrup in the gas tanks of construction equipment or destroying the equipment outright; tree-spiking, nailing metal or ceramic spikes into trees (which destroys a chainsaw but not the tree and can injure loggers); and attempting to sabotage the power lines at a nuclear energy facility, a charge on which Foreman and three others were arrested.

By 1992, these actions inspired the formation of ELF, the Earth Liberation Front, which carried on the original direct action tactics and stepped them up to focus on arson. In addition to numerous other acts of ecotage, ELF arsons have been responsible for $26 million in damage to a ski resort in Vail, $900,000 in damage to a facility at Michigan State University, $3 million to a facility at the University of Washington, $700,000 in damage to the US Forest Service in Irvine, PA, and over $50 million in damage to a condo complex in San Diego (Deshpande and Ernst 2012, 9–11). These high property damages and risk to human life caused the FBI to spotlight ELF and ALF as one of the most dangerous domestic terror threats.

Yet, on ELF-affiliated websites, these actions are construed as non-violent, since they are not intended to cause harm to living beings.[9] Similarly, ALF describes itself as a "non-violent campaign," even though an affiliated website shows how to make bombs. A rejoinder on the website states that ALF only encourages the destruction of property used to abuse animals, not persons (who are also animals). With some insincerity, the website claims the bomb making instructions are included "for entertainment only" and are posted only because "they are part of the history of ALF" (ALF 2014).

Viewing property damage as a non-violent action is common in the REAR movement. Captain Paul Watson of the Sea Shepherd society considered himself "an ecological strategist" who was non-violent, since "we have never caused injury or death to a human." Yet his group was involved in ramming and disabling boats, destroying whaling stations, and "scuttl[ing] half the Icelandic whaling fleet" (Watson 1991, 34–35).

The majority of illegal direct actions by REAR activists are by the animal rights wing of the movement (Carson *et al.* 2012, 309). Between 2003 and 2010, animal rights activists were responsible for 5,578 crimes ranging from arson to cybercrime, including: "247 acts of arsons (4.4 percent), 0 assassinations (0 percent), 3,695 of vandalism (66.2 percent), 808 house visits (14.5 percent), 690 animal liberations (12.4 percent), 80 bombs (1.4 percent), and 58 cybercrimes (1 percent)" (Hirsch-Hoefler and Mudde 2014, 594). REAR crimes in the US "have been aimed overwhelmingly at property damage rather than causing injury or death to humans" (Carson *et al.* 2012, 304, 310).

However, some former REAR members feel that property damage and acts of ecotage are violent acts that pose a risk to human and non-human life. Arson in particular seems difficult to control. The former spokesperson for ELF, Craig Rosebraugh, eventually left the group and dubbed its actions as violent:

> Nonviolent ideology, as I interpret it, was the ability to display compassion, respect and decency toward the opponent. The opposition is supposed to be weaned from error by sympathy for the nonviolent activists who use their own suffering as the primary means of promoting change. ELF has not displayed any hint of compassion or respect toward its opponents ... [ELF's actions] can reasonably be construed as *violent* in its attempt to force or coerce.
>
> (Rosebraugh 2004, 248)

In part, Rosebraugh refers to ELF's use of threats and intimidation, including bomb hoaxes, harassing and threatening phone calls, and death threats against its perceived enemies (Deshpande and Ernst 2012, 11). In one case, an effigy of a University of California professor was burned outside of his home (Carson *et al.* 2012, 307).

The threats are worrisome. Although they haven't acted violently against humans yet, a few leaders in the REAR movement maintain that humans are legitimate targets of violence. These individuals accept the last two reality propositions of in our formula of radical apocalypticism:

> *"Othering"/Concretized Evil:* Those who are not with us are against us.
> *Redemptive Violence/Revenge:* Violence is somehow redemptive, whether it be self-martyrdom or the killing of others.

In the REAR movement, those who would ignore, degrade or exploit the wilderness are cast as the Evil "Other." To paraphrase Foreman, there are those willing to commit monkeywrenching on behalf of wild things and those who are not (Foreman and Haywood 1987; Foreman 1991, 139).[10]

Dr. Jerry Vlasak is a practicing trauma surgeon and spokesperson for several extremist animals rights groups, including ALF, the Animal Liberation Press, and the Animal Defense League. He takes direct action in a much more violent direction than does "Uncle Dave" Foreman.[11] Vlasak embraces direct actions against inanimate objects, facilities, and animal researchers. He bluntly answered the query of a reporter on an Australian television show by retorting, "Would I advocate taking five guilty vivisectors lives to save hundreds of millions of innocent animal lives? Yes, I would" (Vlasak 2004).

How could someone who has taken the Hippocratic oath to "do no harm" and whose day job is saving lives advocate the assassination of scientists? Vlasak's comments betray a process of "Othering" that is so severe that he considers vivisectors to be an evil that must be extinguished.

Moreover, Vlasak views the murder of scientists as "redemptive" because it prevents the further suffering and murder of animals. In a hearing before the US Senate Committee on Environment and Public Works, Vlasak said that murder of animal abusers would be "a morally justifiable solution" (Senate Hearings 108–764, 109–1005). Clarifying his reasons, Vlasak explained to Senator Frank Lautenberg, "Those [lives of the scientists] are not innocent lives" (Senate Hearing 109–1005). Like other radical apocalypticists, he framed this violence as necessary and defensive, saying:

> I think violence is part of the struggle against oppression. If something bad happens to these people [animal researchers], it will discourage others. It is inevitable that violence will be used in the struggle and that it will be effective.
>
> (Doward 2004)

He went on to say "I don't think you'd have to kill too many [scientists]. I think for 5 lives, 10 lives, 15 human lives, we could save a million, 2 million, 10 million non-human lives" (ibid. 2004). For making such comments, Vlasak has been banned from entering the UK. While he has not murdered anyone (yet), he certainly incites others to do so. He has indicated in interviews that the idea of him committing murder is not out of the question.

Similar to other radical apocalypticists, Vlasak's motivation for violence stems from an overwhelming sense of oppression, even though he is a practicing surgeon living in the lovely suburb of Woodland Hills, California. Since REAR activists espouse a biocentric view and identify deeply with animals and elements of the environment, they regularly experience persecution on their behalf. Violent REAR activists believe that they are fighting against an ongoing "genocide" being perpetrated against innocent lives that cannot defend themselves; furthermore, they feel a close kinship with those lives.[12] Although the politics are different, the same apocalyptic logic governs the ideological terrorism aimed at abortion clinics and providers, some of whom have been murdered.

In the writings of some REAR activists on social media, a virulent hatred of "the Other" is patently clear. Again, in radical apocalyptic thought systems, the "in-group" members demonize most the associates who fail to live up to the radical standards. For example, a website claiming to represent the legitimate ELF rails against both government informers formerly in ELF and more moderate eco-activists who claim to speak for ELF, such as Craig Rosebraugh. The anonymous author of the website states: "It is hard to choose who are the most contemptible: the growing number of snitches from within the ranks of ELF, or these two parasitic and opportunistic provocateurs bleating in front of networks camera crews" (ELF 2012).

Thus, two facts are equally clear. On the one hand, ELF, ALF, SHAC, and other REAR groups are dedicated to non-violence (as they construe it) and maintain an ethic to do no harm to animals, including humans. On the other hand, there is room in the thought system for the idea that violence against humans could be an acceptable form of defensive violence. James Lee and Theodore Kaczynski have already taken that second step. [13]

## From eco-activist to eco-terrorist: the case of Theodore Kaczynski, aka "The Unabomber"

From 1978 to 1995, mathematician, Luddite, and environmentalist Theodore Kaczynski sent sixteen mail bombs to universities and airlines, killing three persons and injuring twenty-three. Since Kaczynski's writings include many of the same ideas espoused by REAR activists, these worldviews should be considered carefully to explore how an eco-activist could become an eco-terrorist. His collected writings and ongoing correspondence with Dr. David Skrbina, which have been published, provide an insight into the ideology informing his terrorist actions.

Familiar with the activity of groups in the REAR movement, Kaczynski feels he is in a common cause with them, writing (always with the plural "we"): "since there are well-developed environmental and wilderness movements, we have written very little about environmental degradation or the destruction of wild nature, even though we consider these to be highly important" (Kaczynski 2009, loc. 588). In fact, he writes quite a lot about the importance of protecting nature, which he understands to be the perfect opposite of technology:

The positive ideal that we propose is Nature. That is, WILD nature: Those aspects of the functioning of the Earth and its living things that are independent of human management and free of human interference and control.... Nature makes a perfect counter-ideal to technology ...

(Ibid., loc. 1680, capitalization in original)

Kaczynski even advocates formally introducing a "wilderness religion" that could be a positive force. He feels such a religion would meet a human spiritual need through evolving into a low-technology life. He writes: "... there is a religious vacuum in our society that could perhaps be filled by a religion focused on nature in opposition to technology" (Kaczynski 2009, loc. 2132). Like Abbey and Foreman, he speaks of encounters with the wilderness, "Nature, our mother," in intimate, ultimate and religious terms:

Nature, our mother attracts and entrances him and offers him a picture of the greatest and most fascinating beauty. The destruction of the wild natural world is a sin that worries, disturbs, and even horrifies many people.

(Ibid., loc. 3972)

In even clearer language than in REAR activist literature, he advocates "love and reverence toward nature, or even worship of nature" (ibid., loc. 4048, also 2127).

An important difference between the ideology of the REAR movement and that of Kaczynski is that the protection of the wilderness did not primarily motivate Kaczynski, although it may have contributed to his violent actions. He incorporated the environmentalist perspective into a larger goal: to initiate the fall of technological society. Kaczynski anticipates that technology will not only destroy the wilderness, but also change human cognitive and social patterning to make us slaves and reduce our autonomy ibid., locs. 156, 168, 1354). He is ambivalent as to which is worse, the impending environmental catastrophe or the enslavement of humanity. Kaczynski feels that eco-activists like Earth First!ers fall short of being truly revolutionary because they are not "fully committed" to ending technological society (ibid., locs. 197, 4074).

Thus, it is not appropriate to call Kaczynski a member of the REAR movement per se, since he diverges on some important tenets. For instance, he urges revolutionaries (those who are actively trying to bring down technological society) to have as many children as possible (ibid., loc. 1803). He subsumes radical environmentalism to his ultimate goal of ending technology and human civilization as we know it.

Kaczynski's belief system should inform our approach to analysis of the REAR movement. To distinguish between peaceful and violent expressions of eco-activism, ascertaining the presence of the four reality propositions for radical apocalyptic thinking is more helpful as an indicator of threat than is ideology. Kaczynski's writings aptly illustrate his acceptance of all of these reality propositions. A few brief examples must suffice.

The conviction that he possesses an *Authoritative Interpretation* of the plight affecting humankind through technological society permeates his writings. Kaczynski undertakes a highly intellectual approach, even while in prison, by reading voluminous sources in several languages (which has earned him the approval of some intellectuals for his thought, but not for his crimes). He states his conclusions with utter confidence: "Only the collapse of modern technological civilization can avert disaster" (ibid., loc. 168). His authoritative understanding does not seem to be based on revelation, however, as much as on rigorous academic study and reflection. He stresses that his "is not an eccentric opinion" and carefully cites the thinkers who would agree with his position, expressing his argument in terms of facts and corollary propositions (ibid., loc. 173–177).

Kaczynski espouses an *Active Eschatology*, acting to end technological society. He calls explicitly for "a revolution":

> We therefore advocate a revolution against the industrial system. This revolution may or may not make use of violence; it may be sudden or it may be a relatively gradual process spanning a few decades.… Its object will be to overthrow not governments but the economic and technological basis of the present society.
>
> (Ibid., loc. 360, 581)

He does not expect a low-technology society to be a complete paradise.[14] However, he does speak glowingly of a time when we will realize the biocentric ideal and: "discard the technological ideal of human control over nature and replace it with reverence for the totality of all life on Earth – free and wild as it was created through hundreds of millions of years of evolution" (ibid., loc. 4196).

This is the "foundation for a revolution" for which Kaczynski fights (ibid., 4196). Incarcerated in a maximum-security prison and unable to communicate via any writings that advocate violence, he cannot explain how mail bombs to universities and airplanes would achieve this goal. *Active Eschatology* still evident, he repeatedly calls for a revolution to end of history as we know it, bringing about a more blissful time for the planet.

Kaczynski's writings also show that he subscribes to the process of "Othering" and accepts the idea of *Redemptive Violence/Revenge*. Kaczynski was dubbed "The *Una*bomber" because he sent mail bombs to those affiliated with Universities (Un) and airlines (a). While airlines represent technology, the ire for University faculty may seem out of place. Perhaps due to trauma experienced as a Harvard University student involved in unethical psychology experiments,[15] Kaczynski sees University professors as part of a destructive "System." The System is the all-encompassing industrial, economic and technological apparatus, which academics serve by falsely acting as if they are rebelling against it, without doing so (ibid., 3771–3777, 4196).

Like other radical apocalypticists who engage in "Othering," he feels that "those who are not with us are against us." He focuses his ire on those closest to him. In his mind, those professors *should* be able to lead a revolution and influence young people by revealing the truth of our technological dependence. They do not quit their University jobs after two years to retire to the woods, as did Kaczynski. And even though they are as educated and well read, as he is, they do not typically advocate the complete demise of industrial and technological society. Therefore, Kaczynski hates and targeted those who are most like him, yet who are not radical enough.

Kaczynski, like other radical apocalyptic thinkers, considers his violent actions to have been defensive in nature and in service to a higher good. In fact, he considers himself to be highly moral according to a cross-cultural, "natural 'morality'" (his quotation marks). He lays out these ethics in Six Principles (ibid., loc. 4290); the first and second read as follows:

1    Do not harm anyone who has not harmed you, or threatened to do so.
2    (Principle of self-defense and retaliation) You can harm others in order to forestall harm with which they threatened you, or in retaliation for harm that they have already inflicted on you.

While he cannot write from prison directly about his crimes for legal reasons, Kaczynski apparently views mailing the sixteen homemade bombs as an act of self-defense and just retaliation. This is akin to other apocalyptic bombers' belief in *Redemptive Violence.* Kaczynski's thought system demonstrates how flexible and dangerous the REAR ideology can be when blended with frameworks governed by radical apocalypticism.

## Preventing eco-terrorism

In determining how to prevent lone wolves or new cells in the REAR movement from becoming violent, we return to the question posed at the beginning of this chapter. Are the labels "eco-terrorist" and "domestic terrorist" effective deterrents for REAR-inspired violence? Since 9/11, US agencies' definitions of "terrorism" expanded to include the destruction of property, with many acts of ecotage now qualifying legally as terrorism. In the basic definition by the FBI, terrorism is "the unlawful use of force or violence against persons or property to intimidate or coerce a government, the civilian population, or any segment thereof, in furtherance of political or social objectives" (28 CFR Section 0.85).[16] FBI Domestic Terrorism Section Chief James Jarboe further defines eco-terrorism as "the use or threatened use of violence of a criminal nature against innocent victims or property by an environmentally oriented, subnational group for environmental-political reasons, or aimed at an audience beyond the target, often of a symbolic nature" (Jarboe 2002). Both definitions address intent, whether the desire to intimidate or coerce, or the effort to communicate with an audience through symbolism.

Legally, some acts of ecotage would not qualify as terrorist acts, if the worldview of the radical environmentalist were better understood. Is it the intention of every eco-arsonist to coerce the government or civilian population? Or might the intent be to destroy property or equipment in order to save a deer or a tree? If the radical environmentalist believes civilization is doomed, is the ecotage meant to influence people living in that society? The just prosecution of ecotage crimes requires a solid understanding of the worldview of the eco-activists or a change in definition.

According to Hirsh-Hoeffler and Mudde, a majority of scholars contest the use of "eco-terrorist" when applied to the REAR movement (Hirsch-Hoeffler and Mudde 2014, 589; Carson *et al.* 2012, 295–319). Terrorism researcher O'Kane states the matter strongly: "It is *wrong* (italics added) to call a group which directs action only at property a terrorist group" (O'Kane 2012, 22). Such scholars base their arguments on ethics and the history of the non-violent protest movement, regardless of legal definitions used by US agencies and the US code for "terrorism."

Asking whether the "eco-terrorist" label is legally appropriate or ethically warranted for acts of ecotage is a different question than asking whether the use of the label is effective for deterring violence from the REAR movement. As I have argued, when seen through the lens of radical apocalypticism, the greatest threat is not from ELF and ALF, which have a stated goal of avoiding harm to humans. The greatest threat comes from the much more violent offshoot cells or lone wolves, such as Lee and Kaczynski. Given the advanced educational level of many REAR sympathizers, the potential of a WMD or biological agent that only affects humans is especially concerning.

Overall, I agree with Taylor that there is little chance of ELF targeting humans (Taylor 2003). I disagree with Leader and Probst, who maintain that ELF as an organization "could easily switch to nuclear industry targets" (Leader and Probst 2003, 37, 44). Instead, the serious threat comes from spin-off cells and lone wolves in the REAR movement. Perhaps, as Taylor suggests, the serious threats come from anarcho-primitivist ideology adherents who wish to see the end of human civilization (Taylor 2003, 181). In this case, differentiating between activists, criminals and terrorists in the REAR movement becomes vital, as is the effort to avoid demonizing the movement as a whole. Carson, Lafree and Dugan recently computed that, according to the Global Terrorism Database, only 17 percent of criminal incidents committed by REAR activists between 1970 and 2007 could be classified as terrorist (Carson *et al.* 2012, 295).

However, the fringe violent element in the REAR movement is still a threat. Of special concern is nuclear terrorism, whether involving a plant, nuclear waste or weaponry. Nuclear imagery has played a huge symbolic role in the radical environmental movement. Since Abbey's writings have an iconic, canonical standing in the movement and directly inspired the practices of monkeywrenching, his statement on nuclear war is especially important:

> a constantly increasing population makes resistance and conservation a hopeless battle. This is true.... Wilderness preservation ... will be forgotten ... For my own part I would rather take my chances in a thermonuclear war than live in such a world.
>
> (Abbey 1968, 52)

Abbey's preference for thermonuclear war over the problems of over-population and the degradation of the environment sets a worrisome standard for those who look up to him.

The REAR movement has witnessed numerous ongoing anti-nuclear demonstrations and direct actions to protest nuclear weapons, energy, and waste. In 1987, three radical environmentalists in the self-named cell EMETIC (Evan Mecham Eco Terrorist International Conspiracy) planned to attack nuclear energy facilities: the Central Arizona Project and the Palo Verde nuclear generating station in Arizona, the Diablo Canyon nuclear power plant in California, and the DOE Rocky Flats nuclear facility in Colorado. Arrested through a FBI sting operation called THERMCON, named for a powerful explosive called thermite, the three received prison sentences ranging from thirty days to six years. Earth First! leader Dave Foreman was also charged $250.00 on a misdemeanor for handing out literature and giving a small donation to EMETIC (Leader and Probst 2003, 10).

Recently, numerous developments may be forming a perfect symbolic storm that could attract eco-terrorists to target either nuclear facilities or nuclear waste. After the events of 9/11 2001, the possibility of nuclear terrorism became more real after it was revealed that Al Qaeda sought to procure nuclear weapons (9/11 Commission 2004, 60, 109, 141, 342, 380). Since then, several notable events have highlighted the vulnerability of nuclear facilities to terrorism and the dangers of nuclear energy. Both could inspire an eco-terrorist. A partial list focusing particularly on the last few years includes the following:

- 2001 – the POGO (Project on Government Oversight) report relays that during a mock drill in 2000, "terrorists" were able to procure nuclear materials that would have endangered major population centers in the Southwest United States (Brian 2002).
- 2002 – an internal letter at the Department of Energy reveals that facilities are not adequately protected from terrorism due to budgetary

constraint. US Representative Edward Markey charges that terrorists could gain access to weapons grade nuclear material and construct a nuclear device (Vries, 2002). The media continues to report on mock drills in which "terrorists" were able to procure nuclear material at the Rocky Flats facility near Denver, Colorado and at Los Alamos National Laboratory (Pianin and Miller 2002).

- March 2011 – the Fukushima Daiichi nuclear power plant in Japan suffers serious damage in an earthquake and three of six reactors suffer meltdown. It leaks radioactivity for years.
- December 2011 – nine Greenpeace activists break into a nuclear power plant at Nogent-sur-Seine outside of Paris to unfurl a banner atop a reactor that reads "Safe Nuclear Power Doesn't Exist" (BBC News 2011).
- May 2012 – a Greenpeace activist paraglides into a nuclear reactor at Le Bugey, France to drop a smoke flare, while another enters the Civaux nuclear site and hides for an hour (Greenpeace 2014).
- December 2013 – novelist James Hall releases *Going Dark*, a fictional account of ELF terrorists targeting a nuclear power plant in Florida.
- March 2014 – fifty-five Greenpeace activists break into the Fessenheim nuclear plant to highlight weaknesses at France's oldest nuclear plant by climbing a reactor and unfurling banners (France24 2014).
- April 2014 – anti-nuclear protestors clash with police in Taiwan.
- November 2014 – radioactivity from the Fukushima nuclear plant disaster reaches the West Coast of the United States by November 2014.
- Fall 2014 – putting the French government on high alert, fifteen unexplained drones are spotted over nuclear facilities in France beginning in October. At least three are from anti-nuclear activists. Greenpeace denies involvement (De la Baume 2014; Lichfield 2014).

Overall, anti-nuclear protests have become more common in the US since 2005, when 40,000 protesters marched past the United Nations building in New York. Anti-nuke protests reignited by the meltdown of the Fukushima nuclear plant have also escalated around the globe. For those in the REAR movement, the continuing proliferation of nuclear weapons and plants is the greatest threat to biodiversity or animal life, except perhaps for climate change.

The vast majority in the REAR movement *fear* nuclear disaster and want to avert it, since it would cause harm to life and to ecosystems. However, some fringe elements have progressed towards accepting or even desiring harm to humans. If the apocalyptic elements of *active eschatology* and *redemptive violence* combine with commitments to biocentrism and the reduction of human over-population, a lone wolf or terrorist cell from the REAR movement could become a threat. They could decide to target nuclear facilities or waste materials, as the transport routes are easily discoverable on the internet. As in other radical apocalyptic systems, the loss of life and the impact on an ecosystem may be seen as an acceptable sacrifice to deter greater harm to global biodiversity.

Admittedly, this is a "black swan" event – a rare but high-profile event making a huge impact. However, by using an analytic perspective gleaned from an understanding of radical apocalypticism, such an event should not be a total surprise. Although unlikely, this possibility merits preparation and consideration to ensure that we do not make radicalization more appealing. Naming ELF and ALF as the one of the most serious domestic terror threats, as the FBI continues to do, is unhelpful because it obscures the real threat. Potentially misguided, the move increases the oppression of committed eco-activists, pushing them farther towards the fringes of society.

By labeling whole groups as "terrorists" and engaging with them through conflict, the US and its allies have unintentionally radicalized some of those who are drawn to extremist Islamist theology and Christian Identity ideology. We must avoid conceptually lumping together those in the REAR movement under the label "eco-terrorists" and aggressively targeting or harassing them. The person who trespasses at a factory site in protest or who lets animals out of a government laboratory should not be labeled in the same manner as someone who targets scientists for execution.

Law enforcement and the public must remember that out of all documented criminal incidents from the REAR movement, only 17 percent qualify as "terrorist" (Carson *et al.* 2012, 295). Yet, as Loadenthal notes, ELF activist ideology frequently conveys a perception of unjust persecution from law enforcement (Loadenthal 2013, 22). As in the other cases we have examined, a feeling of persecution by authorities only validates, strengthens and adds to the urgency of apocalyptic beliefs and lends support for the integration of theologies of redemptive violence. This can cause otherwise peaceful apocalypticists to transition into becoming radical apocalyptic terrorists. Instead, we should encourage engagement, such as community forums, intra-group dialogue, and grass-roots partnerships, amongst the REAR movement, law enforcement and local communities. Non-violence begins at the local level. A day in which local police and an eco-justice group volunteer together to clean up a river is a day spent preventing violence and misunderstanding.

As religion scholar Bron Taylor has suggested, we should view radical environmentalism as "a new religious movement that views environmental degradation as an assault on a sacred, natural world" (Taylor 2003). Intelligence analysis and law enforcement should strive to differentiate clearly between peaceful and violent members of the REAR movement. There is a vast difference between eco-activists engaging in civil disobedience, eco-activists engaging in criminal activity and eco-terrorists who intend to coerce and intimidate an audience other than the target. These differences should constantly be kept in mind during law enforcement dealings with ELF and other radical environmental groups and individuals.

## The real eschatological dilemma

Unlike the other cases of radical apocalypticism that we have examined, radical environmentalism has a twist: most of its basic presuppositions are supported by science. The fifth, most recent Intergovernmental Panel on Climate Change (IPCC) report sponsored by the United Nations Environmental Programme (UNEP) and the World Meterorological Organization (WMO) provides a dire outlook (IPCC 2014a, 2014b). The evidence for human influence on global warming is "unequivocal" and "unprecendented over decades to millennia" (IPCC 2014a). Furthermore, it warns: "Continued emission of greenhouse gases will cause further warming and long-lasting changes in all components of the climate system, increasing the likelihood of severe, pervasive and irreversible impacts for people and ecosystems" (IPCC 2014a, 18). The UNEP also concludes that we are losing between 150 and 200 species every twenty-four hours and that "this episode of species extinction is greater than anything the world has experienced for the past 65 million years … due, in large measure, to humankind's unsustainable methods of production and consumption" (UNEP 2010). In fact, according to scientists, we are living through the "sixth mass extinction." Their conclusions are as stark as REAR movement writings or Kaczynski's for that matter:

> Though it is true that life, so incredibly resilient, has always recovered (though after long lags) after major extinction spasms, it is only after whatever has caused the extinction event has dissipated. That cause, in the case of the Sixth Extinction, is ourselves – *Homo sapiens.* This means we can continue on the path to our own extinction, or, preferably, we modify our behavior toward the global ecosystem of which we are still very much a part. The latter must happen before the Sixth Extinction can be declared over, and life can once again rebound.
>
> (Elredge 2001)

As the environmental situation becomes more dire, eco-terrorism will likely become a more serious threat in the future. This calls for greater caution and nuance in how we interact with the REAR movement.

## Notes

1  Foreman 1991, 57–58.
2  Leopold 1968, 130.
3  See the Typology of REM (Radical Environmental Movement) Direct Action Tactics in Deshpande and Ernst 2012, 10–11.
4  Since there is significant overlap in the radical environmental movement and the animal rights movement, I have chosen to treat them together under the affiliation of REAR, as other scholars have done, such as Hirsch-Hoefler and Mudde (2014). However, other scholars have chosen to treat them separately. Since REAR or either movement is a loose affiliation of individuals and groups,

it is largely a matter of semantics, thus I examine them together as a whole where they overlap and attempt to differentiate between the radical environmentalists and animal rights activists where appropriate.

5　This excellent list is generated by Bron Taylor 2010, 75–76.

6　Recently, Foreman has tied this to caps on immigration in order to protect the American wilderness (Foreman 2011).

7　The premier magazine of animal liberation is titled *No Compromise*. Accessed May 29, 2015, www.nocompromise.org/.

8　Goodall and other biologists speak of eye to eye non-verbal communications with animals in which a whole other mind opens up to oneself. For Goodall, this occurred with the chimpanzee David Greybeard (Taylor 2010, 24–25; Goodall 1999, 29–81).

9　See, e.g., the website of ELF 2012, which advocates "non-violent direct actions" that will land activists in prison, while quoting the Hippocractic oath "do no harm."

10　Foreman riffs on Leopold's quote, "There are some who can live without wild things, and some who cannot. These essays are the delights and dilemmas of one who cannot" (Leopold 1968, *Almanac*, vii; Foreman 1991, 139).

11　This kindly self-epithet appears in the blog "Around the Campfire with Uncle Dave" on Foreman's website. Accessed May 29, 2015, www.rewilding.org.

12　Radical environmentalists commonly apply the label of "genocide" to both environmental degradation and the exploitation of animals (ELF 2012).

13　Hence, I agree with the findings of Taylor, who critiques Ackerman in "Beyond Arson?" for both his methods and for uncritically lumping together all radical environmentalists in his threat analysis (Taylor 2003; Ackerman 2003).

14　Kaczynski laboriously corrects the anarcho-primitivist writings on numerous points on the nature of pre-technological society (e.g., hunting-gathering is not more leisurely, there was neither racial nor gender equality) (Kaczynski 2009, locs. 457, 2337, 2958, 3017, 3111, 3116).

15　As a sixteen-year-old boy entering Harvard, Kaczynski and his fellow classmates were subjected to unethical psychological experiments in which they were humiliated by their professor, Dr. Henry Murray. Kaczynski seemed especially vulnerable to the stress of the humiliation, which lasted three years (Chase 2000).

16　This definition is different than that of the Department of Defense, which states that terrorism is "the unlawful use of violence or threat of violence, often motivated by political, religious, or other ideological beliefs, to instill fear and coerce governments or societies in pursuit of goals that are usually political" (JP 1–02 15 August 2014).

## Bibliography

9/11 Commission. 2004. *The 9/11 Commission Report: Final Report of the National Commission on Terrorist Attacks Upon the United States, Authorized Edition*. New York: W.W. Norton & Co.

109th Congress, 2005. April 2, 2012. "Oversight on Eco-Terrorism Specifically Examining the Earth Liberation Front ('ELF') and the Animal Liberation Front. ALF. 2014. "('ALF')." Accessed October 15, 2014, http://epw.senate.gov/hearing_statements.cfm?id=237836.

Abbey, Edward. 1968. *Desert Solitaire*. New York: Touchstone.

Abbey, Edward. 2006 [1975]. *The Monkey Wrench Gang*. New York: HarperPerennial.

Abram, David. 1996. *The Spell of the Sensuous: Perception and Language in a More-Than-Human World*. New York: Vintage.

Ackerman, Gary A. 2003. "Beyond Arson? A Threat Assessment of the Earth Liberation Front." *Terrorism and Political Violence* 15, 4: 143–170.

Albanese, Catherine L. 1990. *Nature Religion in America: From the Algonkian Indians to the New Age.* Chicago: University of Chicago Press.

ALF – Animal Liberation Front. 2014. "Timeless Myths." Accessed September 24, 2014, www.animalliberationfront.com/TimelessMyths.htm.

American Institute of Biological Sciences. Accessed November 3, 2010, www.action-bioscience.com.

BBCNews. December 5, 2011. "Greenpeace France Nuclear Action Prompts Security Alert." Accessed November 10, 2014, www.bbc.com/news/world-europe-16029572.

Bookchin, Murray. 1988 [1987]. "Social Ecology Versus 'Deep Ecology': Beyond Environmentalism." *Socialist Review* 18, 3: 11–29.

Brian, Danielle. September 24, 2002. "Testimony of Danielle Brian, POGO Executive Director: Preventing Nuclear Terrorism before the House Subcommittee on National Security, Veterans Affairs, and International Relations, Committee on Government Reform." Accessed July 27, 2014, www.pogo.org/our-work/testimony/2002/nss-npp-20020924.html.

Carson, Jennifer Varriale, LaFree, Gary and Dugan, Laura. 2012. "Terrorist and Non-Terrorist Criminal Attacks by Radical Environmental and Animal Rights Groups in the United States, 1970–2007." *Terrorism and Political Violence* 24, 2: 295–319.

Center for Respect of Life and the Environment (CRLE). 1997. "The Earth Charter: Benchmark Draft." *Earth Ethics* 8, 2–3: 1–23.

CFR – 28 Code of Federal Regulations, Section 0.85.

Chase, Alton. June 1, 2000. "Harvard and the Making of the Unabomber." *The Atlantic.*

Davis, John and Foreman, Dave. 1991. *The Earth First! Reader: Ten Years of Radical Environmentalism.* Salt Lake City, UT: Gibbs Smith.

De la Baume, Maia. November 3, 2014. "Unidentified Drones are Seen Above French Nuclear Plants." *New York Times.* Accessed November 5, 2014, www.nytimes.com/2014/11/04/world/europe/unidentified-Drones-are-spotted-above-french-nuclear-plants.html?_r=0.

Deshpande, Nick and Ernst, Howard. 2012. *Countering Eco-Terrorism in the United States: The Case of "Operation Backfire." Final Report to the Science and Technology Directorate, U.S. Dept. of Homeland Security, September 2012.* Accessed September 3, 2014, www.start.umd.edu/pubs/START_EffectivenessofLECountermeasuresOperationBackfire_Sept2012.pdf.

Devall, Bill and Sessions, George. 1985. *Deep Ecology: Living as if Nature Mattered.* Salt Lake City, UT: Gibbs Smith.

Doward, Jamie. July 25, 2004. "Kill Scientists, Says Animal Rights Chief." *Observer.* Accessed September 10, 2014, www.theguardian.com/society/2004/jul/25/health.animalrights.

Eagan, Sean P. 1996. "From Spikes to Bombs: The Rise of Ecoterrorism." *Studies in Conflict & Terrorism* 19, 1: 1–18.

Ehrlich, Paul R. and Ehrlich, Anne H. 1981. *Extinction: the Causes and Consequences of the Disappearance of Species.* New York: Ballantine.

Ehrlich, Paul R. and Ehrlich, Anne H. 2013. "Can a Collapse of Global Civilization Be Avoided?" *Proceedings of the Royal Society, Biological Sciences* 280: 20122845. Accessed September 10, 2012, http://dx.doi.org/10.1098/rspb.2012.2845.

ELF – Earth Liberation Front. 2012. Accessed September 10, 2012, http://earth-liberation-front.com/.

Elredge, Niles. June 2001. "The Sixth Extinction." American Institute of Biological Sciences: Action BioSciences. Accessed November 15, 2014, www.actionbio-science.org/evolution/eldredge2.html#primer.

FBI Counterterrorism and Cyber Divisions. 2004. "Tactics Used by Eco-Terrorists to Detect and Thwart Law Enforcement Operations."

FBI. June 30, 2008. "Putting Intel to Work against ELF and ALF Terrorists." Accessed September 10, 2009, www.fbi.gov/news/stories/2008/june/ecoter-ror_063008.

FBI. December 7, 2012. "Eco-Terrorist Surrenders." Accessed May 11, 2013, www.fbi.gov/news/stories/2012/december/eco-terrorist-surrenders-two-fugitives-still-at-large/eco-terrorist-surrenders-two-fugitives-still-at-large.

Foreman, Dave. 1991. *Confessions of an Eco-Warrior*. New York: Harmony Books.

Foreman, Dave. 2011. *Man Swarm and the Killing of Wildlife*. Albuquerque, NM: Rewilding Institute.

Foreman, Dave and Haywood, Bill, eds. 1987 [1985]. *Ecodefense: A Field Guide to Monkeywrenching*. 2nd ed. Tucson, AZ: Ned Ludd.

Fossey, Diane. 1983. *Gorillas In the Mist*. Boston: Houghton Mifflin.

France 24. September 4, 2014. "Greenpeace 55 Get Suspended Jail Terms over French Nuclear Protest." Accessed May 29, 2015, www.france24.com/en/20140904-greenpeace-55-get-suspended-jail-terms-over-french-nuclear-protest/.

Geertz, Clifford. 1973. *The Interpretation of Culture*. New York: Basic Books.

Goodall, Jane. 1999a. *40 Years at Gombe*. New York: Stewart, Tabori and Chang.

Goodall, Jane. 1999b. *Reason for Hope: A Spiritual Journey*. New York: Time Warner.

Gore, Al. 2006 [1992]. *Earth in the Balance: Ecology and the Human Spirit*. New York: Rodale.

Greenpeace Media. March 15, 2014. "Action at Le Bugey Nuclear Power Plant." Accessed September 11, 2014, http://photo.greenpeace.org.

Hill, Julia Butterfly. 2000. *The Legacy of Luna: The Story of a Tree, a Woman, and the Struggle to Save the Redwoods*. New York: HarperCollins.

Hirsch-Hoefler, Sivan and Mudde, Cas. 2014. "Ecoterrorism: Terrorist Threat or Political Ploy?" *Studies in Conflict and Terrorism* 37, 7: 586–603.

IPCC. November 1, 2014a. Fifth Assessment Synthesis Report. *Climate Change 2014. Synthesis Report: Approved Summary for Policymakers*. Accessed November 11, 2014, www.ipcc.ch/pdf/assessment-report/ar5/syr/SYR_AR5_SPM.pdf.

IPCC. November 1, 2014b. Fifth Assessment Synthesis Report. *Climate Change 2014. Synthesis Report: Longer Report*. Accessed November 15, 2014, www.ipcc.ch/pdf/assessment-report/ar5/syr/SYR_AR5_LONGERREPORT.pdf .

Jarboe, James. 2002. "The Threat of Eco-Terrorism." Statement before the House Resources Committee, Subcommittee on Forests and Forest Health Hearing on Ecoterrorism and Lawlessness on National Forests, February 12, 2002. Accessed October 30, 2014, www.fbi.gov/news/testimony/the-threat-of-eco-terrorism.

Johnston, Lucas F. 2013. *Religion and Sustainability: Social Movements and the Politics of the Environment*. Bristol, CT: Equinox.

Joosse, Paul. 2007. "Leaderless Resistance and Ideological Inclusion: The Case of the Earth Liberation Front." *Terrorism and Political Violence* 19, 3: 351–68, http://dx.doi.org/10.1080/09546550701424042.

JP 1–02 – Joint Publication 1–02. Department of Defense Dictionary of Military and Associated Terms. Accessed November 17, 2015, www.dtic.mil/doctrine/new_pubs/jp1_02.pdf.

Juergensmeyer, Mark. 2003 [2000]. *Terror in the Mind of God.* Berkeley: University of California.

Kaczynski, Theodore. 2009. *Technological Slavery: The collected writing of Theodore J. Kaczynski, a.k.a. "The Unabomber," with introduction by Dr. David Skrbina.* 2nd ed. Port Townsend, WA: Feral House.

Leader, Stefan H. and Peter Probst. 2003. "The Earth Liberation Front And Environmental Terrorism." *Terrorism and Political Violence* 15, 4: 37–58.

Lee, James. 2010. *My Demands.* Issued on September 1, 2010 at www.savetheplanet.com. Accessed October 31, 2014, http://media3.washingtonpost.com/wp-srv/metro/documents/leemanifesto.pdf?sid=ST2010090103923.

Lee, Martha. 1995. *Earth First! Environmental Apocalypse.* Syracuse NY: Syracuse University Press.

Leopold, Aldo. 1968 [1949]. *A Sand County Almanac: And Sketches Here and There.* New York: Oxford University Press.

Lewis, John. 2004. "Animal Rights Extremism and Ecoterrorism." Accessed April 5, 2012, www.fbi.gov/news/testimony/animal-rights-extremism-and-ecoterrorism.

Lichfield, John. November 9, 2014. "French Government on High Alert." *The Independent.* Accessed November 10, 2014, www.independent.co.uk/news/world/europe/french-government-on-high-alert-after-unexplained-drone-flights-over-nuclear-power-stations-9850138.html.

Liddick, Don. 2006. *Eco-Terrorism: Radical Environmental and Animal Liberation Movements* Westport, CT: Greenwood.

Loadenthal, Michael. 2013. "The Earth Liberation Front: A Social Movement Analysis." *Radical Criminology* 2: 15–45.

Lovelock, James. 2006. *The Revenge of Gaia: Why the Earth is Fighting Back – and How we can still Save Humanity.* Santa Barbara, California: Allen Lane.

Muir, John. 1998 [1916]. *A Thousand Mile Walk to the Gulf.* Mariner Books.

Naess, Arne. 1973. "The Shallow and the Deep, Long-Range Ecology Movement: A Summary." *Inquiry* 16: 95–100.

Nash, Roderick F. 1989. *The Rights of Nature: A History of Environmental Ethics.* Madison, WI: University of Wisconsin Press.

Nash, Roderick F. 2014 [1967]. *Wilderness and the American Mind*, 5th ed. New Haven, CT: Yale University Press.

O'Kane, Rosemary H. 2012. *Terrorism.* 2nd ed. Harlow: Pearson.

Pianin, Eric and Miller, Bill. January 23, 2002. "Nuclear Arms Plants' Security Lax, Report Says." *Washington Post*, A15. Accessed November 21, 2014, www.washingtonpost.com/wp-dyn/articles/A22106-2002Jan22.html.

Quinn, Daniel. 1992. *Ishmael.* New York: Bantam.

Rapoport, David C. 1980. "Messianic Sanctions for Terror." *Comparative Politics* 20, 2: 195–213.

Rosebraugh, Craig. 2004. *Burning Rage for a Dying Planet: Speaking for the Earth Liberation Front.* Brooklyn, NY: Lantern Books.

Senate Hearing 109–1005. n.d. *Eco-Terrorism Specifically Examining Stop Huntingdon Animal Cruelty (SHAC).* Hearing before the Committee on the Environment and Public Works, United States Senate, 109th Congress, first session. Accessed

November 1, 2014: www.gpo.gov/fdsys/pkg/CHRG-109shrg39521/html/CHRG-109shrg39521.htm.

Senate Hearing 108–764. May 18, 2004. *Animal Rights: Activism vs. Criminality.* Hearing before the Committee on the Judiciary, United States Senate, 108th Congress, second session. Accessed November 1, 2014, www.gpo.gov/fdsys/pkg/CHRG-108shrg98179/html/CHRG-108shrg98179.htm.

Snyder, Gary. 1974 [1969]. *Turtle Island.* New York: New Directions.

Swartzendruber, Michael. 2000. *Liberalism in the Wilderness: an analysis of Earth First! and the elusiveness of equality.* M.A. Thesis. Chicago: University of Chicago.

Taylor, Bron. 2010. *Dark Green Religion: Nature Spirituality and the Planetary Future.* Berkeley: University of California Press.

Taylor, Bron. 1998. "Religion, Violence and Radical Environmentalism: From Earth First! to the Unabomber to the Earth Liberation Front." *Terrorism and Political Violence* 10, 4: 1–42.

Taylor, Bron. 2003. "Threat Assessments and Radical Environmentalism." *Terrorism and Political Violence* 15, 4: 173–182.

UNEP – United Nations Envrionment Programme. 2010. "The State of the Planet's Biodiversity: Key Findings from the Millennium Ecosystem Assessment." Accessed November 3, 2010, www.unep.org/wed/2010/english/biodiversity.asp.

Vlasak, Jerry. October 12, 2004. Interview on "Tonight on Insight." Accessed November 10, 2014, www.youtube.com/watch?v=F4-PU5EGp9A.

Vries, Lloyd. April 23, 2002. "What Price Nuclear Security?" Accessed September 18, 2014, www.cbsnews.com/news/what-price-nuclear-security/.

Watson, Paul. 1991. "Tora! Tora! Tora!" *The Earth First Reader,* edited by John Davis and Dave Foreman, 33–43. Salt Lake City, UT: Peregrin Smith Books.

# 8  Bringing Armageddon
## Aum Shinrikyo

> I want the present world, which is so full of pain, to be extinguished.
> (Murai Hideo, Aum's no. 2 man, a scientist who created weapons of mass
> destruction and computer programs for Aum Shinrikyo)[1]

> Now, as the Bible explains, Armageddon is finally approaching.
> I will join the holy army to poa [murder] all wrongdoers.
> I will poa one evil, two evils, and more.
> Poa is world salvation.
> Poa is virtue.
> Practicing poa will lead me to the highest world.
> (From the Aum pamphlet, *Vajrayana* Resolution)[2]

Thus far, I have discussed the apocalyptic thought systems of a broad range of cross-cultural individuals and groups. Despite their many important cultural differences essential to an accurate portrait, I have argued that there are also broad similarities in apocalyptic worldview that turn out to be remarkably insightful predictors of violence.

In the courses that I teach, my students and I have run case studies on literally hundreds of apocalyptic groups, far too many to cover in one book. The apocalyptic formula is only one tool amongst many for thinking about these groups, but it is consistently accurate in explaining and predicting violence. As an educational exercise, we rank these hundreds of apocalyptic groups according to our estimates from "zero threat" up to a "severe threat" of violence. On our scale, Aum Shinrikyo always sits at the uppermost limit.

Surprisingly, many Americans have only the faintest familiarity with this group, although with prompting some will recall that a group put nerve gas on a Tokyo subway in the 1990s. If they know the name Aum Shinrikyo, they likely view them as an old, strange little Japanese doomsday cult that barely affected their lives. This lack of notoriety is odd for a group that was the first non-state actor to launch a chemical weapons attack on a major scale, that threatened the US as well as Japan, and that is still operational today (PSIA 1996, 6).

At its peak in the mid-1990s, Aum Shinrikyo (Aum for short) had over 40,000 members. Of those, 30,000 were in Russia, including 1,200–1,400 dedicated *shukkesha* or renunciants who left society to live the austere Aum life as a community of monks and nuns. Aum was officially registered as a religious organization in Japan. This book refers to it as such, despite its negative attributes and terrorist activities that have often earned it the label "cult" or "false religion" in Japanese media. The label "cult" obscures an understanding of the worldview that so powerfully attracted its members, which in turn limits our ability to anticipate similar developments.[3] In this particular case, this negative language also prohibits a fruitful line of communication with Aum's offshoot groups and inhibits the reintegration of former members back into Japanese society.

The Aum group owned and operated numerous large-scale facilities throughout urban Japan, in Tokyo, Fujinomiya, Kamikuishiki, Kyushu, Yokohama and in various cities in Honshu. The holdings included secret laboratories, a Clear Stream Temple that manufactured sarin gas, an Astral Hospital involved in punishing and murdering dissident members and numerous commercial enterprises, including computer manufacture and sales, a fitness club, a baby-sitting and dating service, real estate businesses, travel agencies, noodle shops, and a publishing house that produced voluminous amounts of media, especially *manga* (Japanese comic books) (Lifton 1999, 36). In addition, Aum had a sheep ranch in Australia, where it tested nerve gas on animals and/or also tried to prepare a haven from nuclear war. The sect also maintained a branch in Russia and offices in New York City, and tried to establish branches in Germany, Zaire, and Sri Lanka. The Aum group worked assiduously on a host of biological, chemical and technological weapons of mass destruction, and practiced releasing these repeatedly across Japan. The sect had apparently considered attacking the US, aiming above all to start a nuclear World War III between Japan and the US to trigger Armageddon. Aum Shinrikyo under the leadership of Asahara Shoko[4] represents the extreme limit of radical apocalyptic thought and *Active Eschatology*, fused with Japanese capitalism and slick marketing.

Today, the members of the movement are still active in two groups, Aleph, (the first letter of the Hebrew alphabet), and Hikari no Wa, "Circle of Rainbow Light." The former and, to a lesser extent, the latter, still maintains the beliefs and practices of Aum. For Aleph, this includes fidelity to their former guru leader, Asahara Shoko, now awaiting the death penalty by hanging.

## Aum attacks

On March 20, 1995, just about a month before the Oklahoma City bombing, five male members of Aum Shinrikyo put plastic bags of sarin nerve gas on subway cars on the Tokyo subway system, punctured them with sharpened umbrellas, and left. Twelve people were killed and about 6,000 were injured to various degrees, some of them severely and for life (PSIA 1996, 5; *Asahi Shimbun* 2011). Sarin gas, developed by the Nazis, is so lethal that inhaling even a single concentrated drop would kill a person (Lindsay 2012). Fortunately, the strain used by Aum was a third as strong as they intended or many more would have died.

The sarin chemical attack on the Tokyo subway resulted in arrests and eventual death sentences for thirteen members, including Asahara Shoko, as well as five life sentences for other members. A total of 180 members of the sect were arrested. However, the famous subway attack that brought the group to light was not their only attack. Beginning in 1988, Aum was likely responsible for the murder of some eighty persons under a variety of circumstances. This includes the famous murder of the Sakamoto family, a lawyer prosecuting Aum and his wife, both of whom were strangled, and their fourteen-month-old infant, who was suffocated. Their bodies were scattered to separate areas of Japan. The act earned them even greater condemnation in an ancestor-venerating culture, since this prohibited the baby from being with his family in death (Reader 2000, loc. 3577). We also know that Aum was responsible for at least fourteen biological and chemical attacks between 1990 and 1995, including relasing anthrax, botulinus toxin, sarin gas, VX (the most lethal nerve gas ever synthesized), and phosgene gas. They may have also attempted to procure the ebola virus and cholera, create a laser weapon, mine uranium, and measure plutonium (PSIA 1996, 6–7; Lifton 1999, 186–187).

On June 27, 1994 in the city of Matsumoto, about 100 miles from Tokyo, they released sarin gas, killing seven and sickening over 500. Unfortunately, the authorities did not definitively discover, until the Tokyo subway attack almost a year later, that the culprit was Aum. Asahara Shoko was formerly Matsumoto Chizuo, of the same name as the city (PSIA 1996, 6). After the Tokyo subway attack, the sect also attempted to release cyanide at the Shinjuku subway station, which could have killed tens of thousands save for the watchful attendants who had learned from the sarin gas attacks just months before (PSIA 1996, 5).

Aum aspired to carry out even greater destruction and acts of mass murder. In their fantasies, they explored purchasing a nuclear warhead. This was not as unrealistic as it may seem, since the group had $1 billion in assets and a global reach, including in Russia (Lifton 1999, 41; Wessinger 2000, 147).[5] Some theories hold that the attack on the Tokyo subway in March 1995 was only meant to be a dress rehearsal. The real attack was to be in November 1995. Members of the inner circle hoped to spray a total of 70 tons of sarin gas from a helicopter, purchased in Russia, with the aim of killing millions (Lifton 1999, 39–41).[6]

The Tokyo attack was probably aimed at the Kamusigaseki station because of its location under government buildings. Aum members who were not directly involved believed that the Japanese government had attacked itself or that the US had attacked Japan and World War III had actually begun, which the Japanese government was keeping secret (Juergensmeyer 2003, 111). Asahara may have orchestrated the subway attack to lead Aum disciples to this very conclusion or perhaps even to start World War III. Other analysts point to the fact that the attack occurred when the Aum leadership became aware of the police closing in on them for the Matsumoto attack. Thus, the action may have been a desperate lashing out, a form of group disintegration, a symptom of the guru's deteriorating mental state, an unconscious "outing" of the group, or a last minute attempt at achieving larger than life fame (Reader 2000, locs. 5035, 5083–5109; Juergensmeyer 2003, 111–113).[7]

Whatever the ultimate scope of their plans, they aimed at widespread destruction. Driving this intense activity was the radical apocalyptic worldview.

## Aum and the limit of radical apocalypticism

In order to explain how such a bizarre group could arise, analysts have often focused their attention variously on the personal history and psychology of the megalomaniac, charismatic guru Asahara Shoko, who held a totalistic grip on 1,300 or so monks and nuns. Some analyses examine the psychology and social dislocation of the disciples themselves or the unique cultural setting of Japan in the period after World War II up to the subway attack in 1995.[8] While all of these insights are valuable, in my view, the cultural approaches taken by the religion scholars Ian Reader, Erica Baffelli, Mark Juergensmeyer and Catherine Wessinger, as well as by the psychologist Robert Jay Lifton, have produced the most coherent explanations of the group's goals and the drama that unfolded. In this analysis, I wish to build on these earlier studies by focusing especially on Aum's radical apocalyptic attributes.

The worldview of Aum Shinrikyo was fashioned by its guru, born in 1955 as Matsumoto Chizuo. Matsumoto would later take the name Asahara Shoko, a combination of the words for "bright light" and "hemp" (Lifton 1999, 22).[9] He created the Aum philosophy by blending selected parts of Tibetan (Vajrayana) Buddhism, Shiva worship and yoga drawn from Hinduism, and New Age elements. By at least 1988, he subsumed these into an expectation of a coming Armageddon, drawn from the Book of Revelation and contemporary politics. Later Aum, dangerous Aum, was an eclectic patchwork collage of selected elements fitted carefully into a radical apocalyptic framing.

Matsumoto was born nearly, but not completely, blind. He bullied other children as one of the only partially sighted boys in a school for the blind.[10] Even as a child, he fantasized about attaining great power, including becoming Prime Minister (Lifton 1999, 14–15, 20). In his twenties, he was arrested for selling Chinese herbal cures without a license, already showing his propensity for skirting the law. In addition, he became a spiritual seeker who joined a few of Japan's new religious movements and learned to draw on an eclectic mix of yoga, Buddhism, Taoism, health food movements, and the writings of Nostradamus. This was not so strange, since post-World War II Japan saw a "rush hour of the gods," (Reader 2000, loc. 4116; McFarland 1967),[11] in which the state sponsored failure of the Shinto Emperor cult resulted in the rise of a host of new religious movements. One estimate is that Japan boasts 23,000 religious groups with 200 million members, many of whom belong to more than one religion (Lifton 1999, 262).

At age thirty, Asahara founded Aum Shinsen no Kai, "Aum Mountain Hermits Society," carrying the connotation of a circle of enlightened hermit monks (Reader 2000, loc. 1649). He then had a vision in which a deity appeared and anointed him as Abriaketsu no Mikoto, "the god of light who leads the armies of gods" in a war against darkness. This would bring about the utopian kingdom of Shambhala, which in Tibetan Buddhism signifies that an "enlightened sacred king would emerge to defeat the forces of evil and establish a new golden age of Buddhism" (Lifton 1999, 20; Reader 2000, loc. 2287). In Aum's early version of the belief, Shambhala would be established in Japan and spread across the globe for the salvation of all, with Asahara obviously leading the way (Reader 2000, loc. 2287).

As time went on, Asahara claimed that the deity who had appeared to him was Shiva, the Hindu god of destruction. This added an Indian flavor to the religion, a step that was quite unusual for a Japanese religion, as well as the theme of divinely ordained cosmic destruction and death. Asahara based his spiritual, social, and interpretive authority on this vision and on a subsequent spiritual experience in the Himalayas in 1986. In that spiritual experience, he maintained that he had become spiritually enlightened, like the Buddha himself. In 1987, he changed the group's name to Aum Shinriyko, meaning "Supreme Truth."

As Asahara shaped the worldview of the eclectic new religion, it came to exemplify in the extreme each of the reality propositions in our formula of radical apocalypticism.

> *A secret about the nature of this world*: The ordinary, mundane world is broken and unduly influenced by Evil of some kind, locked in a struggle with ultimate Good.

Since Aum is partly based on a Buddhist system, it envisions a universe with multiple realms. From lowest to highest, these include the realms of desire, form, and non-form. Humans exist in the realm of form, which itself has multiple realms, the lowest of which are hells. The aim of meditation and spiritual practice is to lessen one's negative karma in order to attain a better realm upon one's rebirth (after death). Only those who are the most enlightened, a state that Aum members hope to attain, are able to enter the realm of non-form. Hence, in the earliest stages, Aum tried to spread salvation to all by teaching practices they believed would aid people in reducing negative karma for a better rebirth (Reader 2000, loc. 569).

As Asahara's apocalyptic view deepened through exposure to the Book of Revelation in the late 1980s and early 1990s, he propagated belief in a dualistic battle between ultimate Good and Evil (Reader 2000, loc. 1793). Evil was represented in general terms by bad karma, by which every person outside of Aum was gripped. Asahara also began to identify certain key Evil figures that ran the world. Like believers in Christian Identity, he quoted from the "Protocols of the Elders of Zion." He claimed in an article called "Manual of Fear" that Jews operate a "World Shadow Government" using Freemasons as puppets, along with the "Black Aristocracy," the US government, the Japanese government, the wife of the Crown Prince, Masako, Emperor Akihito, the ambassador of the United Nations, and rival religious leader Ikeda Daisaku of Soka Gakkai, whom he tried to have assassinated (Wessinger 2000, 148; Lifton 1999, 42–43). He claimed that Jews had been behind several modern genocides and that they were plotting to destroy or brainwash the Japanese (Wessinger 2000, 148).

One innovation that Asahara made to the reality proposition of dualism was that he himself was the Good, the god of light. As one follower put it, the profound realization was that "the guru is the truth" (*guru wa shinri desu*). This suggests that the name "Supreme Truth," which contains the words for Aum (the sound of the universe) and Shinri (truth), is equivalent to Asahara himself (Reader 2000, loc. 914). The followers of Aum strove to merge with his Goodness through rituals, meditation, and other practices. They sought to become his clones (*guru no kuronka o sura*) by erasing their own brain waves and thought patterns (Reader 2000, loc. 616). They even meditated while wearing the "Perfect Salvation Initiation" or PSI headgear, a set of electrodes that emitted electric power that supposedly synchronized the Master's brainwaves with those of the initiate (Lifton 1999, 23–24, 51, 70–71). They considered Asahara to be so pure that they paid serious money not only to rent the PSI headgear for a month ($10,000), but also to drink his bathwater ($1,000) or even his blood, which it was claimed, had a unique DNA ($10,000).[12] Another way to merge with the guru was through having sex with him; several female members engaged in "Tantric initiations" with Asahara. Others in the community had to remain celibate.[13]

Even the righteous Aum members, however, could fall back into bad karma. In Aum philosophy, this required purification by the most extreme measures, lest the *shukkesha* become Evil too. Members who sinned by disobeying or even by having impure sexual thoughts or doubts about Aum Shinrikyo or Asahara were punished in harsh rituals. These included hanging upside down, being immersed in scalding hot or freezing cold water, or taking LSD or other narcotics in a Bardo or Christ initiation in which one confessed one's sins (Lifton 1999, 28, 51, 91–93, 98, 100; Murakami 2001, 297–300). These severe methods were thought to rid the body of pollution and cleanse the spirit, but the Christ ritual resulted in several deaths (Reader 2000, loc. 739, 1939, 4608). These were interpreted in Aum as the *shukkesha* reaching *samadhi*, a state of empty perfection and a goal of Buddhist meditation (Reader 2000, loc. 618–665). In fact, Reader reports that in some Aum publications, the Japanese ideogram for death, *shi*, was given the same reading as the Buddhist *samadhi* (Reader 2000, loc. 665–666). With such a lack of tolerance for disobedience or doubt, defectors were routinely kidnapped, tortured, imprisoned in cargo crates, subjected to electro shock, drugged in the Astral Hospital or killed outright (Wessinger 2000, 146–147).

> *A secret about the state of the righteous*: The righteous are oppressed, while the wicked flourish.

All radical apocalyptic believers experience oppression, but under Asahara the perception that enemies were persecuting Aum took on epic proportions. As early as 1993, Asahara claimed that Aum's enemies were poisoning its members in an elaborate conspiracy theory reminiscent of those that fuel the radical Right in the US, in which governments secretly run the world and attack the righteous. In early 1995, Asahara and others made a video called *Slaughtered Lambs* (*hofurareta kohistuji*) claiming that the group was being poisoned by the US and Japanese governments (Reader 2000, loc. 4565–4482). In addition to employing sacrificial Christian imagery, the video calls Aum's imagined enemies "Lucifer" and "the Devil" (Lifton 1999, 42, 165). In fact, Aum *shukkesha* did experience symptoms of sarin poisoning, either from accidental exposure while they were making it, or, as some followers later suspected, the leadership's purposeful poisoning of the group's own members (Lifton 1999, 180).

> *A secret about another higher or future world* ...: There is a transcendent world in which justice, peace, and happiness reign. It is either a place somewhere out there that the righteous will go to someday, or it is a world that will someday come to the righteous ... *and a secret about the future*: At a special time the gap between the mundane world and the transcendent one will be closed.

One of the powerful draws of Aum was a sense of bliss and contentment that members report having experienced during the meditations and rituals. Many early initiates joined Aum for its health and psychological benefits, believing it could cure disease as well as mental unease. Members report that they felt that they awakened to a transcendent world, achieving the Buddhist enlightened state of *satori*, absolute freedom, and happiness, *gedatsu* (Reader 2000, loc. 1000). In Aum's earliest days, the sect oriented its proselytizing towards a salvation plan (*kyusai keikaku*) that sought to transform the world spiritually through enhanced meditation resulting in the reduction of bad karma (Reader 2000, loc. 355). If this thought system had remained Aum's framework, it would have posed far less of a threat.

However, from at least 1988 onward, Asahara crafted Aum's belief system around a new center of gravity: the coming Armageddon, prophesied by the Book of Revelation and Nostradamus. Turning from world salvation, Asahara now claimed that his plan of salvation was to rescue Aum members from the coming nuclear Armageddon, in which the US would destroy Japan with nuclear weapons. The guru was clearly exploiting past memories of the atomic attacks on Hiroshima and Nagasaki. That tragic history plays into an uneasy cognitive dissonance experienced by many Japanese, who both benefit from a partnership with the US and suffer from the trauma of World War II.[14] Beginning in 1990, Aum had a renewed focus on apocalyptic scenarios and an inward-facing plan of salvation. This may have coincided with Aum's overwhelming defeat in political elections. The sect put up a series of candidates, including Asahara, only to suffer humiliating defeat (Reader 2000, loc. 864, 1664, 3511, 3544).

In a 1990 seminar held on the island of Ishigaki for 1,000 select members, the guru predicted from Buddhist scriptures and the Book of Revelation that after Armageddon would come Shambhala, a prophesied utopia of enlightened beings (Wessinger 2000, 139–140). In Asahara's interpretation, those enlightened ones would be the sole survivors of a nuclear attack. They would be able to live long lives by controlling their epinephrine through meditation, so that "it would not be impossible to live to the age of two hundred, three hundred, or one thousand" (Lifton 1999, 198). Hence, Shambhala had become the Buddhist equivalent to the Christian millennial kingdom (*sennen okoku*) (Reader 2000, loc. 4498). Asahara proclaimed himself to be the Lamb of God in a book entitled *Declaring Myself the Christ* (Reader 2002, 56–58; Wessinger 2000, 140).

As the group turned progressively inward after the Ishigaki "Armageddon" seminar, they attempted to prepare themselves physically and spiritually for salvation. They also retreated more and more from the world. Yet Asahara's message in the early 1990s still enshrined *passive eschatology*, preparation for an endtime that would come no matter what. Even though they envisioned Shambhala to be a kind of "survivalist Shambhala" in the mountains or underground or under the sea, a step that required lots of preparation, they could not trigger it. Instead, they thought they were preparing for it and happened to have a prediction of its date through the guru.

At first, Asahara predicted that World War III, Armageddon, would arrive in 1999. The group's goal was to purify their consciousnesses and to build "Lotus Villages" in preparation, including a nuclear fallout shelter in the mountains. This was a transformation of the concept of Shambhala. As time went on however, Asahara progressively moved the date closer, a move that may have been a mechanism for increasing commitment and loyalty in the group (Wessinger 2000, 142–143). By 1995, he claimed it would arrive that same year, in November 1995.

It was in a sermon in 1993 that the guru spoke publicly of Japan's need to create chemical weapons for self-defense, including sarin gas (Wessinger 2000, 138). The notion that Aum was being persecuted may have contributed to members cooperating in Aum's Ministry of Science and Technology. They secretly produced sarin and other chemical weapons at secret facilities, such as the building called Satian 7, or "Truth 7," translating the Sanskrit term "satyam" or "truth" (Reader 2000, loc. 479–481). The *shukkesha* also bought military-type gear that would protect them. The greatest protection, however, was spiritual: becoming a clone of the guru with a high enough enlightenment to survive or be reincarnated in the new world. As the psychologist Robert Lifton notes, this prophecy was the ultimate megalomaniac fantasy: an impure world is destroyed, leaving only the guru and clones of the guru (Lifton 1999, 11–43).

> *Authoritative Revelation/Interpretation*: Divine revelation or the authoritative interpretation of original revelation (e.g., the Bible, the Qur'an or *hadith*, the Constitution) is ongoing to our group's leaders.

> *Active Eschatology*: Our actions are key to ushering in the new stage of the coming Good world. I, as a righteous person, can trigger the end of the Evil age through my actions, especially through eliminating Evil on earth. (Note: this involves the presumption that "I am Good" or at least acting on the behalf of the Good). This will bring about divine intervention and the age of God/Goodness.

Since he claimed to be god, Asahara's will was absolute and his revelations were the only authoritative take on reality. Any doubt about his actions (such as when he gorged himself despite supposedly being ascetic), his judgment, or goals, such as ordering attacks and murders, was understood in the context of a *mahamudra* or test. In Vajrayana Buddhism, the term refers to clearing the mind of any confusion until it reaches a luminous state. Similarly, *shukkesha* were supposed to undergo a *mahamudra* when they doubted Asahara, thereby securing his will as the ultimate truth and revelation (Lifton 1999, 63). There was extreme shame for those who failed him, which included doubting him (Lifton 1999, 86). This also explains the group's acceptance of punishment for themselves, since it was interpreted as the Master clearing them of bad karma (Lifton 1999, 80). In other words, the phrase "Supreme Truth" or Aum Shinrikyo referred to Asahara himself, whose orders, reasons, and actions could not be questioned. And when doubts remained, torture and rituals such as the "Bardo [hell] initiation" were implemented to help the renunciant clear the confusion from his/her mind, including with the use of thiopental and LSD.

At some point in 1994, or perhaps earlier in 1993, Asahara introduced an *Active Eschatology* amongst his elite disciples. They were not only preparing for Armageddon, but also initiating it. By this point, Asahara had orchestrated a "foot in the door" approach for years with a select cadre. He gradually secured the inner members' loyalty and commitment until they were willing to commit sporadic murders of enemies of the group and produce and/or release anthrax, botulinus, cyanide, ebola, and other chemical and biological weapons. While the guru and 1,000 dedicated members were on the island of Ishigaki for the "Armageddon" seminar, certain elite members of the group tried to create Armageddon. They sprayed botulinus toxin manufactured by Seiichi Endo from trucks near the American naval stations at Yokohama and Yokosuka, as well as in Tokyo, and at the Naraita airport (Lifton 1999, 187).

As an Aum pamphlet proclaims, "Armageddon is finally approaching. I will join the holy army to poa [murder] all wrongdoers. I will poa one evil, two evils, and more ... Poa is world salvation" (Lifton 1999, 88). As early as 1990, Asahara himself and a few devotees may have already possessed an *Active Eschatology*, or what Lifton calls "forcing the end," (Lifton 1999, 59–88). Through *poa*, including the subway attacks, Aum would rid the world of evil and bring the endtime closer. If Asahara was acting consistently within the radical apocalyptic framework and a gradually coalescing *Active Eschatology*, his goal in attacking the Tokyo subway in 1995 may well have been to start World War III by making it appear that the US was attacking Japan.

> *Othering/Concretized Evil:* Those who are not with us are against us. Our group knows the identity of the people that are "Evil" vs. "Good," and those not in our group belong to "Evil." It is the people themselves that are Evil, not just the forces behind them, and through the revelation that we have received, we are able to identify them. Evil people are irredeemable, while we represent the side of God/the Good.

> *Redemptive Violence/Revenge:* Violence is somehow redemptive, whether it be self-martyrdom or the killing of others. We know when and how the Good world is going to come about and our violence is necessary for bringing this about. Our enemies have wronged us and our revenge is God's will. Our vengeance serves a higher purpose.

Asahara justified his will through claiming spiritual superiority and "proving it" through the scriptures, but in a distorted form. This proving of spiritual superiority was similar to other radical apocalyptic leaders. The central doctrine that he employed was *poa*,[15] which in Vajrayana Buddhism refers to a fully enlightened person killing another creature and absorbing its karma so that it may be reincarnated to a better life. However, in that tradition, the concept is invoked most carefully in a parable describing the act of a fully enlightened person eating a fish. The point is practically the reverse of Asahara's interpretation. The traditional interpretation reveres life: a fully enlightened person is rare indeed and only that person can kill a less sentient life form such as a fish. In that case, he should do so with the utmost kindness and in a meditative state that absorbs the fish's negative karma (Lifton 1999, 74–76).

Hence, Aum's interpretation of the act of *poa* has a most insidious twist, fusing *poa* with the radical apocalyptic ideas of redemptive violence, piety, and the "Othering" of one's enemies. The guru marshaled *poa* against the entire world. According to Asahara, everyone has negative karma except himself and since he is pure, he could *poa* everyone (Lifton 1999, 68).

The *shukkesha* who participated in *poa* were not passive puppets carrying out the guru's will, but saw themselves as active participants in the new plan of salvation, which was extermination. *Shukkesha* interviewed by the psychologist Robert Lifton considered it a sacred honor to "preside over the destruction and re-creation of humankind" (Lifton 1999, 81). In the words of one Aum nun, the special people of Aum, who were spiritually advanced, should:

> for the sake of salvation kill those beings who commit bad deeds and who cause Aum to commit bad deeds.... A spiritual achiever can *poa* another being to a higher world. That's why it's all right and a merit for him.
>
> (Lifton 1999, 81)

Ian Reader reports that Asahara asked a crowd of followers if it was right to *poa* all spirits and they exclaimed "yes!" (Reader 2000, loc. 4530). The disciples' role was not a passive one. Rather, the fusion of Buddhism, worship of Shiva, science, and an apocalyptic framework was deeply compelling to them and held explanatory power for their experience of reality.

Members of the inner circle could convince themselves that murder meant they were helping to "crush the karma of all people in order to save them" (Reader 2000, loc. 4534). There was a strong sense of "Othering" driven not only by compassion, but also by spiritual elitism and disgust. One group member stated, "Aum occupies holy space while the present world is a garbage dump" (Lifton 1999, 121). As we have seen, such language of filth and dirt, especially when contrasted with images of extreme purity for the in-group, often appears in the words of radical apocalypticists who view their victims with hatred, vengeance, or disgust. A year before the subway attacks, Asahara claimed to have received another message from Shiva, as related by Reader: "the time for war had come ... only he could purify this polluted world. This was his mission and that of his true victors: to confront the polluted world and eradicate its evils"

(Reader 2000, loc. 4549). Thinking of victims as evil and pollution depersonalizes them, a requisite for committing violence against them.

Hence, in Aum "Othering" took the form of an unusual mixture of hatred and compassion: disciples believed that by murdering others, they were ridding Aum of its enemies, ridding the world of evil, and bringing Armageddon closer, yet at the same time they were aiding the victims to achieve a higher rebirth. Asahara had succeeded in fully melding the reality propositions of "*Othering /Concretized Evil*" with "*Redemptive Violence*" and a sense of piety. Killing meant the redemption not just of the Aum group in this life, but also of the victims in the next. The words of a renunciant named Hiroyuki Kano, who at the time of his post-subway disaster interview with Murakami was still a distant member of Aum, clearly expresses this logic of redemptive violence: "If by killing another person you raised him up, that person would be happier than he would have been living his life. So I do understand that path."[16]

In addition to this highly idiosyncratic interpretation of Buddhism, which would be rejected by most other Buddhists,[17] peculiar interpretations of the Bible were also employed to validate the violence in Aum's philosophy. The guru offered eschatological interpretation of images such as Noah and his family surviving the flood.[18] Nothing in the Bible could support a violent eschatology more than the Book of Revelation. Asahara decoded the book technologically, theologically, and politically. His goal was to create a vast laser and plasma weapon that could cut the world in half, an idea drawn from his hero Nikola Tesla. Aum scientists labored vigorously on the device. Asahara explained that the weapon was prophesied: it was the very sword of truth from the Book of Revelation (Lifton 1999, 191).

Asahara saw himself as the Lamb of God and also interpreted Shiva's appearance to him as the appearance of the Son of Man on the throne in Revelation. In a 1989 Aum *manga* entitled *The Day of Perishing*, Asahara "opens" the Seals (like so many Christian apocalypticists, from Hal Lindsey to David Koresh) by interpreting them in terms of contemporary events. The martyrs' robes dipped in blood are revealed to be Aum members in their uniforms undergoing the blood initiation, in which disciples literally drank the Master's blood. Asahara also made predictions, such as the eruption of Mount Fuji, according to the imagery in Revelation's Seals. His radio broadcast prediction in January of 1995 of the Kobe earthquake secured the group's belief in his absolute omniscience – which he parlayed to secure their allegiance in carrying out the Tokyo subway massacre. In reality, his prediction had relied on "Hirota," an Aum scientist who implemented an astrological computer program for earthquake detection. That fact shook, embarrassed and shamed the scientist when it happened to occur nine days later on January 17, 1995 (Lifton 1999, 47, 131–132). At the center of it all was Asahara's interpretation of Armageddon, revealed to be a nuclear war initiated by the US and the Russians. Images of divine fire were equated with images of nuclear holocaust.

## The role of disciples in radical apocalypticism: fostering commitment in utopian societies

Given Aum's extreme interpretations of all seven reality propositions of radical apocalypticism, Asahara gradually and effectively led his inner circle to the ultimate, logical horrific conclusion of radical apocalypticism: they themselves would initiate the destruction of the world. Yet the dance of guru and disciples includes not just a charismatic interpreter with brainwashed puppets at his command, it also requires receptiveness on the part of intelligent people who find that the propositions create a meaningful and compelling view of reality.

In the aftermath of the "Aum affair" (*Oumu jiken*) (Reader 2000, loc. 330), several authors (including Murakami, Lifton, Bafelli, and Reader) interviewed surviving and former members of Aum. Those interviews shed unparalleled light on the dynamics that made the radical apocalyptic worldview attractive in the first place. More of this kind of work needs to be done, in a systematic way, with former and current members of other radical apocalyptic terror groups (Chandra *et al.* 2010, 10–12; Cohrs *et al.* 2013, 590–600).

One thing that becomes apparent to me as a scholar of religion when reading these first-hand accounts is that, even after disciples leave a group such as Aum, the apocalyptic worldview still holds a clear fascination for them. The disciples were motivated by an experience of the ordinary world as devoid of meaning or joy. As the number two man in the group, Murai Hideo, expressed, "I want the present world, which is so full of pain, to be extinguished" (Lifton 1999, 121). This led to a fascination with the end of this world and for some, a commitment to bring that about. Consider Murakami's interview of Namamura Akio, a former member who had already begun to distance himself from Aum at the time of the gas attacks:

> NAMAMURA: I want to see with my own eyes what will happen at the end. I'm interested in doomsday religions.
> MURAKAMI: When you say "the end," is that when the present system will be wiped out?
> NAMAMURA: I prefer to think of it as being reset. It's the desire to push the reset button on life. I imagine it as a catharsis, very peaceful.
> (Murakami 2003, 276)

Although Namamura squarely blames Asahara for the gas attacks and speaks openly of what went wrong in Aum, the attraction of apocalyptic eschatology is still clearly present for him. The same can typically be said for other former members of radical apocalyptic groups.

Apocalypticism has proven to be so "sticky" for thousands of years precisely because it answers a lot of existential questions that plague the human psyche. It affirms the pain of living, identifies a clear culprit, suggests that suffering throughout life has a higher purpose, imbues the participants with a profound and rewarding sense of specialness and promises an eventual rescue and victory. It is powerful stuff to resist, and even more difficult to undo.

In addition to revealing an apocalyptic framework, the interviews and analyses of Aum illuminate other processes at work in securing the loyalty of disciples. In seeking to understand why disciples find fulfillment in subsuming their will to radical apocalyptic groups and their leaders, I have found studies of "commitment" mechanisms in social utopian groups to be especially pertinent, even though the studies were not originally applied to this data set.

Radical apocalyptic groups both promise an ultimate utopia – the Kingdom of God, Shambhala, ascent to a better planet, the Pleistocene in which humans and nature live in harmony, ascent to heaven – and attempt to create a temporary sense of utopia amongst followers. While to an outsider the conditions in the innermost circles of a radical apocalyptic group such as Al Qaeda, ISIS, the CSA, or Aum may seem rank, dirty, oppressive, or harsh, to the insiders of a radical apocalyptic group there is a taste of Paradise. The physical conditions might be horrific (think of Aum in dirty roach-infested rooms and cells with people being tortured, or the hot, buggy climate in Jonestown, Guyana, or the difficult, bare bones existence of a survivalist family in the mountains of Idaho). However, the spiritual and conceptual framework placed around this reality, coupled with the social mechanisms at play, lead followers to describe their lives as hard, but, at the same time, like Paradise.

The sociologist Rosabeth Moss Kanter studied utopian communities and the commitment mechanisms that fostered loyalty amongst their members. She correlated types of commitment mechanisms with the ways in which a person was oriented to engagement in the social organization of the community, concluding that: Commitment mechanisms of mild *sacrifice* and *investment* foster commitment to Continuance in a social organization, in which individuals are committed to continuing in a social system role. Commitment mechanisms of *renunciation* of ties and *communal sharing* foster Cohesion within a social organization, so that individuals are committed to other members of the group through cathetic bonding. Commitment mechanisms of *mortification* – "the submission of private states to social control" – and *surrender* of the decision making processes foster commitment to the group in a way that fosters group Control, such that members are committed to obey *the group's authority* (Kanter 1972, 1, 36; Kanter 1968, 500–12, 510).

Asahara led initiates through each phase of the commitment mechanisms, tightening his grip and fostering more and more commitment at each level. To begin with, interested members simply responded to health seminars or yoga classes. Fostering their commitment to Continuance in the group, they paid money (a mild sacrifice) and made small lifestyle changes (additional investment), such as eating differently, buying audio and video tapes, maintaining celibacy, and perhaps renting the PSI headgear. Aguilar has shown that many utopian communes use sacrifices such as austerity and food choices, as well as investments of time and money, to foster commitment at the level of Continuance (Aguilar 2008). Tens of thousands of people in the Aum movement found this satisfying. Given enough time, some of those people would move to a stricter level of social organization and become a *shukkesha* or renunciant.

Successful groups also require Cohesion, the *shukkesha* practiced greater renunciation of family, jobs, and place of residence, in order to live communally with other renunciants. They were only allowed to bring two suitcases into the commune. Vast sums of Aum's money derived from the savings of such members, who gave it to Aum to share communally. The logic behind Aum member's uniforms, similar schedules, shared meals, and shared rooms is that communal sharing contributes to affective bonds, known as Cohesion (Kanter 1968, 507–508). In Kanter's framework, drinking the guru's bathwater and blood are also forms of communal sharing that foster Cohesion. At this level of social organization, the members wore the PSI often, also communally sharing (as they thought) the guru's brainwaves, synchronizing everyone as a clone or incarnation of the guru.

Another mechanism of renunciation is "free love or celibacy," which Kanter notes are "experientially opposite but functionally alternative organizational arrangements which forbid individualistic ties" (Kanter 1968, 508). By maintaining group celibacy except in his family, Asahara placed himself above all others while fostering cohesion in the rest of the sect. This arrangement demonstrates that the one who controls sexuality in the group has social control over the group. It is familiar in other groups that we have examined, e.g., with David Koresh and, with modification, James Ellison of the CSA.[19]

The majority of the 1,200–1,400 renunciants remained strongly bonded, exhibiting the potent group loyalty that results from tight Cohesion felt amongst group members. Even after the "Aum affair," some found it difficult to leave and stayed with Aleph, the newly renamed Aum.

Eventually, some *shukkesha* progressed to doing very intensive rituals, such as the underground *samadhi* ritual performed by Joyu Fumihiro. This involved being buried in an airtight container, meditating, and slowing the breathing in order to survive (Reader 2000, locs. 1893, 2918, 2924–2958). This ritual dramatically demonstrates that the guru exercised total control over both the bodies and minds of these high-ranking members. There were many other initiations involving bodily mortifications, including the so-called "Bardo [hell] initiation" and "Christ initiation." These involved the use of thiopental and LSD, rigorous physical postures (such as hanging upside down for extended periods), food deprivation, and severe conditions, including extreme heat and cold.

Clearly, the most elite disciples operated at a social organizational level of Control. Asahara exercised his control over recalcitrant disciples to the point of commanding one renunciant who sinned to eat his own feces, which he did (Lifton 1999, 144, 172). By using the theological excuse of imposing a *mahamudra* and with the interpretive authority due a god of light, the guru exercised full physical and psychological control over his inner circle.

However, this kind of control does not occur simply because the guru is *actually* powerful and able to exercise physical control over his pawns. Instead, psychological and social "commitment" is a relationship in which both guru and disciples participate. A disciple willingly binds his/her individual interests to the group because it is fulfilling (Kanter 1968, 499–500). Nuancing Kanter's thesis, John Hall found that "other-worldly sects," such as Aum, are one of the best types of organizations for solving commitment problems effectively. This is done by exercising social control through a clear spiritual hierarchy and an atmosphere of confession (Hall 1988, 682). Whereas outsiders would be inclined to think that the guru's extreme spiritual claims and rigorous rituals would be a deterrent to retaining members, they were in fact quite effective at securing internal and social commitment and at erasing doubt in the minds of the *shukkesha*.

In other words, the image of disciples as just naïve, brainwashed puppets must be challenged. This is the case in Aum Shinrikyo or the suicide religions of Jonestown, Order of the Solar Temple and Heaven's Gate. Aum targeted intelligent, educated young professionals who felt a sense of social dislocation, were experiencing transitions or needed to wean themselves from their families. Amongst the inner circle were graduate students in astrophysics and virology, a young chemist, a medical student, a top physician, and a telecommunications specialist with a position in the Japanese space agency (Lifton 1999, 28–31).

Such well-educated disciples would not subsume their will to the guru for random reasons or because they were weak-minded.[20] Understanding the potency of commitment mechanisms and the apocalyptic framework helps explain why intelligent people would allow themselves to be treated as they were and to act in a manner contrary to human decency. To offset the obvious costs of being in Aum, there had to be significant payoffs in terms of community and meaning. Moreover, the apocalyptic framework has an appealing simplicity that probably appeals to people at the very roots of human evolution: identifying friend vs. foe.

The identity theory approach to commitment suggested by Burke and Reitzes is a vital addition to Kanter's thesis. These social psychologists suggest that commitment connects an individual first and foremost to an *identity*, which includes an ideology or a "stable set of self-meanings" (Burke and Reitzes 1991, 239–251). Thus, persons are only committed to a social organization when the identity fostered by that group remains stable. When members find the ideology to be preached and practiced most "purely" in another organization, they might float to another group to preserve their identity. This often happens with REAR activists and members of the racist Christian Right, who have a strong ideological commitment but loose or multiple group affiliations. Burke and Reitzes maintain that it is a stable identity that produces "consistent lines of activities" (ibid., 239).

In Aum, members took on a powerful identity that bonded them together: all were incarnations of the perfect Master, the god of light, involved in ending and recreating the world. Thus, the identity imparted to them through participation in Aum was a divine one. *Shukkesha* who did not commit atrocities, but nevertheless turned a blind eye to the torture, suppressed their own doubts or silenced their concerns because they were committed to their self-identity as a practicing Aum disciple (Reader 2000, loc. 5418–5452). The violence within Aum grew in part due to their complicity.

Understanding commitment mechanisms is a highly valuable tool for grasping the reactions of Aum members after the Tokyo gas attacks were made public. Although many members left Aum after the attacks, some could not cognitively give up their commitment to the group and/or to its ideology. By April 1998, Aum membership still consisted of roughly 500 *shukkesha* and 600 lay members, with an untold number of sympathizers and members in Russia. The group's income remained around £30 million pounds a year, drawn mainly from its computer businesses (Maekawa 2001, 181; Baffelli 2014, 32). Of those who left the group, none who were interviewed four years later by Lifton had left directly on account of the attacks themselves (Lifton 1999, 215). Instead, they at first rejected the notion that Aum was responsible. When the evidence was too overwhelming (such as when Aum members confessed), they found ways to justify the actions within the ideology of the group, such as thinking that the attack was a *mahamudra* for the world (Lifton 1999, 63, 84, 86–87, 170, 172, 203). A few years after the attack, Murakami found that those who remained in Aum, those who left and those who had lost faith in Asahara continued to find an "unwavering conviction in the group's 'correctness of aims'" (Murakami 2001, 360). As one member said in court, "The results were bad, and we regret them. However, the basic aims of Aum Shinrikyo are not flawed, and we don't feel there's any need to reject them outright" (ibid.).

Clearly, the inner circle of *shukkesha* in Aum Shinrikyo operated at the extreme social organizational level of Control under Asahara, as Kanter helps us to understand. This was the case even after Asahara was fully discredited when he began to act like a psychotic, mumbling madman in court (Reader 2000, loc. 1061). Still, about half of the *shukkesha* remain loyal to the ideology of Aum nearly ten years later. As Burke and Reitzes point out, the *shukkesha* were above all committed to an identity, which they have retained by forming a new group around the same radical apocalyptic worldview.

In 2000, Aum Shinrikyo changed its name to Aleph, the first letter of the Hebrew alphabet, which they claimed signified a fresh start. It was also necessary because, after 1999, they were not legally allowed to use the name "Aum Shinrikyo" due to bankruptcy proceedings (Baffelli 2014, 33). Although the members issued an apology to the victims of the gas attack and their families, the overall Aleph philosophy remains much the same as in Aum (ibid., 35). In 2002, Aleph gained new leadership when Joyu Fumihiro, the handsome former spokesperson of Aum, got out of jail. He made the move to keep most of the traditional Aum teachings but to dispense with what he calls "dangerous" teachings.

Quite understandably, Aleph has aroused tremendous opposition from neighbors in its new home in Iriya, Adachi Ward in Tokyo. This led to a 2010 local "Adachi Ward Ordinance Regarding the Regulation of Antisocial Groups," which allows the government to inspect the facilities and requires Aleph to issue reports (ibid., 31, footnote 3).[21] Indeed, several facts arouse suspicions that Aleph is simply carrying on in the mindset of Aum. These include: leading roles for members of Asahara's family, a refusal to disavow Asahara as spiritual guru, a lack of public statements about Asahara since Joyu's departure, the use of videos of Asahara in training, neighbors' reports of scalded red feet (suggesting the ongoing use of the "thermotherapy" hot water rituals), and the presence of suspicious shipping containers formally used to imprison and torture defectors (Baffelli 2014, 35; Marshall 1999).

In 2007, Joyu and 200 followers, including only 60–70 *shukkesha*, broke away from Aleph to form Hikari no Wa, "Circle of Rainbow Light" (Baffelli 2014, 35). Joyu had become highly critical of Aleph. Whereas Aleph did not formally disavow Asahara as "spiritual leader," Hikari no Wa has done so and has urged members of Aleph to leave and to disavow him also (ibid., 34). Nevertheless, the Japanese Public Security Intelligence Agency remains suspicious of both Hikari no Wa and Aleph (PSIA 1996).

On closer inspection, Hikari no Wa's publicly stated theology is a point by point rejection of the radical apocalyptic principles accepted by Aum Shinrikyo and Aleph. A textbook distributed to attendees of a seminar in August 2010 outlines Hikari no Wa's (that is, Joyu's) reformations to the group's theology and practices. They state that it is "necessary to reject any kind of absolutism regarding both the leader and the teachings," which undermines absolutist interpretations and guru worship. They also reject "the absolute distinction between good and evil [which] was the cause of the tension between Aum and the larger society" (Baffelli 2014, 37). Joyu instead states, "absolute evil and absolute good do not exist" (ibid.). Since there are no evil persons, there is no need to withdraw from society. Hikari no Wa is thinking of opening its training and practices to anyone. Most importantly, this breakaway group now rejects "beliefs in the end of the world, and prophecies ... and *poa*-related beliefs" (ibid., 38).

These changes would seem to strip Hikari no Wa of the radical apocalyptic framework of Aum and Aleph, including beliefs in the specialness of the righteous, oppression by Evil, a coming end of the world, active eschatology, authoritative revelation, and redemptive violence (ibid.). If this publicly stated theology is the real theology operating at all levels of the new group, it would seem to remove an apocalyptic mindset from Hikari no Wa altogether, returning it back to purer Buddhist and Hindu roots. However, the group will still be faced with overcoming the stigma of being led by a former member of Asahara's inner circle, despite Joyu's present disavowals of his former guru.

## A thicker description of Aum

The radical apocalyptic worldview framed Aum's violent philosophies and allowed Asahara's megalomaniac, power-hungry fantasies to find a coherent expression. However, in addition to recognizing the pattern of the radical apocalyptic thought system, a full analysis of any specific group requires including additional culturally specific qualities until a "thick description" is reached (Geertz 1973).

Aum's translation of the radical apocalyptic paradigm arose in a peculiarly Japanese context, which has been thoroughly explored by other studies. Numerous possible cultural factors may have contributed to the Aum gas attacks, including: the trauma of post World War II Japanese self-identity, the failure of the Emperor cult, the historical precedent of an entire nation pledging loyalty to a single Emperor, the vast proliferation of New Age religions and syncretistic new religions in Japan, the rapid rise of Japanese prosperity and "Western-style" capitalism, Japanese identity as a post-atomic catastrophic society, Japanese acquiescence to hierarchy, and a cultural pattern of silence regarding past traumas and atrocities such as occurred in World War II (Reader 2002; Lifton 1999, 232–270; Murakami 2001, 224–250).

In addition, Aum exhibited characteristics worth mentioning, not just to fill out this "thick description," but also because they also sometimes occur in other radical apocalyptic groups. These "secondary characteristics" are not exemplified by all radical apocalyptic groups and, hence, they do not appear as part of the formula that I have used throughout this book. However, it is worth noting that they appear not just in Aum, but also in the thought systems of very different individuals and groups that share apocalyptic orientations. They are as follows:

• a charismatic leader/guru whose authority is secured through mystical experiences and visions (e.g., Asahara Shoko, James Ellison, Abdullah 'Azzam);

- an appeal to forgotten or esoteric knowledge (e.g., Aum's New Age interest in Chinese herbalism/astrology/Nostradamus; Christian Identity and its theory of the origins of the races/UFOlogy; Al Qaeda's use of medieval *hadiths* unknown to most others);
- an appeal to the validating authority of science (e.g., Aum's reliance on science, technology, and the inventions of Nikola Tesla; radical environmentalists' use of climate science to justify their claims; Ted Kaczynski's appeal to science as an authority);
- expression through theater and drama, as well as other performance media (e.g., Aum produced videos and its brief political campaign exhibited great theatricality, which included dancing in Asahara masks; Jim Jones had his followers perform "White Night" dress rehearsals of their mass suicide; David Koresh performed in a Christian rock band for the Branch Davidians; CSA acted out Armageddon in Silhouette City; ISIS/ISIL makes slick propaganda videos);
- an appeal to science fiction or fiction as a legitimate basis of reality (e.g., Aum saw prophecy in an animated series *Voyage of the Space Battleship Yamato* and even created technology based on that in the show; the UFO-suicide group Heaven's Gate modeled themselves on *Star Trek*; Timothy McVeigh saw his life paralleled in *Star Wars*; Christian Identity groups see reality depicted in *The Turner Diaries* and *Atlas Shrugged*);
- ascetic lifestyles as a means of fostering sacrifice and commitment, especially in terms of limited food and conformity of uniforms (e.g., Aum's austere diet and uniforms; CSA's simple food and military fatigues);
- an ethos of communal confession (e.g., Aum's *Bardo initiation* and other punishments for doubting Asahara; CSA's talking chair in which a member made confessions of sin or doubt);
- explicit militarization of the organization, especially in connection with the Book of Revelation (e.g., Aum's "Armageddon Warriors"; CSA's Christian militia; Montana Freemen as an army).

While these characteristics are not ubiquitous amongst radical apocalyptic groups, they appear with enough frequency as to merit our attention.

Understanding the draw of Aum, as difficult and horrific as its actions were, is essential for understanding the global rise in radical apocalyptic fascination that we have seen in this century and especially in recent decades. In the last chapter, I suggest some practical avenues for combating radical apocalyptic terrorism in ways that foster real and lasting peace.

## Notes

1  Quote attributed to Hideo Murai, in Lifton 1999, 121.
2  Ibid., 88.
3  Note: this is not a definition of religion, but rather a list of attributes character-istic to many religions. Reader is making his point over and against those who would label Aum a "cult" (Reader 2000, loc. 864–931).
4  Following the example of Ian Reader, and in keeping with Japanese conven-tions of nomenclature, I am listing Japanese names with the family name first and personal name last.
5  As found in Hayakawa Kiyohide's notebooks, according to Reader 2000, loc. 5033 . While various sources list their assets quite differently, this figure follows the PSIA (1996, 7).
6  Realistically, this order given by the guru was too large to fulfill, but it speaks to the group's intent (Lifton 1999, 39–41).
7  Reader finds the claims that the attack was a precursor to an Armageddon style attack to be ludicrous, noting that they depend largely on grandiose fantasies in one member's journal (Hayakawa).
8  Lifton gives an unparalleled psychologist's view of both the guru and the dis-ciples, and also explores the cultural setting of Japan and the similarities to apocalyptic movements (Lifton 1999). Murakami interviews survivors of the attack as well as a few members of Aum, giving an oblique but cutting portrait of Japanese culture at the time of the attack (Murakami 2001). Reader argues that Aum should not only be understood in its Japanese context, but also in the millennial/apocalyptic one (Reader 2000).
9  Lifton 1999, 22. Wessinger instead states that Shoko is an offering of incense, and Asahara a classy Japanese last name (Wessinger 2000, 127–128). Also, I am following Reader's example of using Asahara when speaking of the religious persona, instead of using Matsumoto as the courts did. See Reader 2000, loc. 268 of 7752.
10  In this detail and what follows, my account of the biography of Asahara's early years mostly follows Lifton 1999, 11–43. I am deeply indebted to his psychologi-cal analysis and first-hand interviews of members.
11  This term comes from the title of McFarland, and has since been coined by Yulia Mikhailova to describe the rise of new religions in Russia that erupted with the fall of communism. This also fits Aum, with its 30,000 adherents there. (Reader 2000, loc. 4116; McFarland 1967).
12  Disputing this with a test at Kyoto University led to the murder of the Sakamoto family (Wessinger 2000, 139; Lifton 1999, 36).
13  This caused a few men to become bitter, such as "Isoda" (Lifton 1999, 97). The women reacted differently (Murakami 2001, 340).
14  In psychological terms, Festinger's "third proposition" that ameliorates the dis-sonance is that the prosperity coming from a friendship with the US and the spread of American values is all a huge Luciferian /Jewish/Masonic plot to destroy Japan (Festinger 1967; Lifton 1999, 195–196, 255–259; Reader 2000, loc. 1407, 2259, 3354).
15  Although *poa* is a noun, "killing," and the verb is *poa sum*, I am using *poa* alone as a verb, since it appears that Aum members did (Reader 2000, loc. 262).
16  This interview, which occurred after the Tokyo subway attack, reflects the mem-ber's cognitive dissonance. While agreeing in principle with *poa*, he adds that no one in the group had achieved the level of enlightenment to discern the victim's transmigration and rebirth, except for Asahara. Yet the killings were perpetrated by five members, not by Asahara, and were clearly indiscriminate (Murakami 2001, 251–264).

17 I have tried here, as elsewhere, to avoid calling Aum a false form of Buddhism, although it is obviously highly idiosyncratic. Juergensmeyer points to the fact that while religions have violence avoiding ideals, they are also violent, and even Buddhism also has some violence affirming doctrines (Juergensmeyer 2003, 113–120).

18 In fact, there is a long history of eschatological interpretation of the Noah story, beginning in early Judaism. See *1 Enoch* 54, 65–67.

19 Ellison took two wives, whereas other men in the CSA had only one. When Noble briefly tried to adopt the same practice, it caused irreparable mental dissonance to him, his wife and the group, in part because Ellison was using it as a mechanism of fostering control.

20 Other investigators have stressed the "relational" aspects of charisma, which benefits both guru and disciple (Reader 2000, loc. 5431 of 7752; Tabor and Gallagher 1995, 142).

21 (Baffelli 2014, 31, footnote 3). For those who read Japanese, the Adachi Ward Ordinance is at: www.city.adachi.tokyo.jp/008/do180064.html. Accessed May 29, 2015. Aum was not banned under the Anti-Subversive Activities Law (the *Haboho*) (Reader 2000, loc. 5167).

# Bibliography

Aguilar, Jade. August 20, 2008. *Activism or Escapism: Making Sense of 21st Century Communes.* Ph.D. Dissertation, University of Colorado.

*Asahi Shimbun.* November 21, 2011. "Death Sentence upheld, ending all Aum Shinrikyo trials." Accessed December 10, 2014, http://ajw.asahi.com/article/behind_news/social_affairs/AJ201111210054.

Baffelli, Erica. 2014. "Hikari no Wa: A New Religion Recovering from Disaster." *Japanese Journal of Religious Studies* 39, 1: 29–49.

Baffelli, Erica and Reader, Ian. 2012. "Impact and Ramifications: The Aftermath of the Aum Affair in the Japanese Religious Context." *Japanese Journal of Religious Studies* 39, 1: 1–28.

Burke, Peter J. and Reitzes, Donald C. 1991. "An Identity Theory Approach to Commitment." *Social Psychological Quarterly* 54, 3: 239–251.

Chandra, A., Acosta, J., Meredith, L.S., Sanches, K., Stern, S., Uscher-pines, L., Williams, M. and Yeung, D. February 2010. *Understanding Community Resilience in the Context of National Health Security: A Literature Review.* Prepared for the Office of the Assistant Secretary for Preparedness and Response, U.S. Department of Health and Human Services, WR-737-DHHS: 10–12.

Cohrs, J.C., Christie, D.J., White, M.P. and Das, C. 2013. "Contributions of Positive Psychology: Toward Global Well-being and Resilience." *American Psychologist* 68, 7: 590–600.

Festinger, Leon. 1956. *Theory of Cognitive Dissonance.* Stanford, CA: Stanford University Press.

Geertz, Clifford. 1973. *The Interpretation of Cultures.* NY: Basic Books.

Hall, John. October 1988. "Social Organization and Pathways of Commitment: Types of Communal Groups, Rational Choice Theory, and the Kanter Thesis." *American Sociological Review* 53, 5: 679–692.

Hofstader, Richard. November 1964. "The Paranoid Style in American Politics." *Harper Magazine.* 77–85.

Japanese Public Security Intelligence Agency (PSIA). 2011. *Annual Report 2010.* Accessed October 3, 2014, www.moj.go.jp/content/000072886.pdf.

Joyu, Fumihiro. 2000. "Outlook on the Aum-related Incidents." Accessed November 10, 2010, http://english.aleph.to/pr/01.html.

Juergensmeyer, Mark. 2003 [2000]. *Terror in the Mind of God: The Global Rise of Religious Violence.* Revised edition. Berkeley: University of California Press.

Kanter, Rosabeth Moss. 1968. "Commitment and Social Organization: A Study of Commitment Mechanisms in Utopian Communities." *American Sociological Review* 33: 499–517.

Kanter, Rosabeth Moss. 1972. *Commitment and Community: Communes and Utopias in Sociological Perspective.* Cambridge: Harvard University Press.

Kisala, Robert J. and Mullins, Mark R., eds. 2001. *Religion and Social Crisis in Japan: Understanding Japanese Society through the Aum Affair.* New York: Palgrave.

Lifton, Robert Jay. 1999. *Destroying the World to Save it: Aum Shinrikyo, Apocalyptic Violence, and the New Global Terrorism.* New York: Holt.

Lindsay, James M. March 20, 2012. "Lessons Learned: Tokyo Sarin Gas Attack." Accessed December 30, 2014, http://blogs.cfr.org/lindsay/2012/03/20/lessons-learned-tokyo-sarin-gas-attack/.

McFarland, H.N. 1967. *The Rush Hour of the Gods: A Study of New Religions in Japan.* New York: Macmillan.

Maekawa, Michiko. 2001. "When Prophecy Fails: The Response of Aum Members to the Crisis." In *Religion and Social Crisis in Japan: Understanding Japanese Society through the Aum Affair,* edited by Robert J. Kisala and Mark R. Mullins, 170–201. New York: Palgrave.

Marshall, Andrew. July 14, 1999. "It Gassed the Tokyo Subway, Microwaved its Enemies and Tortured its Members. So Why is the Aum cult Thriving?" *Guardian.* Accessed February 8, 2008, www.theguardian.com/theguardian/1999/jul/15/features11.g2.

Murakami, Haruki. 2001. *Underground: The Tokyo Gas Attack and the Japanese Psyche.* New York: Vintage.

PSIA – Permanent Subcommittee on Investigations of the Committee on Governmental Affairs, United States, 104th Congress, First Session. 1996. *Global Proliferation of Weapons of Mass Destruction.* Part I. October 31 and November 1, 1995. Accessed August 7, 2014, https://archive.org/stream/globalproliferat01unit#page/n5/mode/2up.

Rapoport, David C. 1992. "Some General Observations on Religion and Violence." In Mark Juergensmeyer, ed. *Violence and the Sacred in the Modern World,* 118–140. London: Frank Cass.

Reader, Ian. 2000. *Religious Violence in Contemporary Japan: The Case of Aum Shinriyko.* Honolulu: University of Hawai'i Press.

Reader, Ian. 2002. *A Poisonous Cocktail? Aum Shinrikyo's Path to Violence.* Copenhagen: Nordic Institute of Asian Studies.

Stern, Jessica. 2003. *Terror in the Name of God.* New York: Ecco.

Strozier, Charles B., Terman, David M., Jones, James W. and Boyd, Katherine A. May 2010. *The Fundamentalist Mindset: Psychological Perspectives on Religion, Violence, and History.* Oxford Scholarship Online. Accessed November 5, 2014, http://dx.doi.org/10.1093/acprof:oso/9780195379655.001.0001.

Tabor, James D and Gallagher, Eugene V. 1995. *Why Waco? Cults and the Battle for Religious Freedom in America.* Berkeley, CA: University of California Press.

Wilkinson, Gregory. 2009. *The Next Aum: Religious Violence and New Religious Movements in Twenty-First Century Japan.* Ph.D. Dissertation, The University of Iowa. Accessed May 29, 2015, http://ir.uiowa.edu/etd/272.

Wessinger, Catherine. 2000. *How the Millennium Comes Violently: From Jonestown to Heaven's Gate.* New York: Seven Bridges Press.

# Part III
# Conclusion

# 9 Creating peace in an apocalyptic moment

Sadly, during the final editing phases of this book, the dreadful Paris attack on *Charlie Hebdo* was carried out on January 8, 2015; two gunmen, the Kouachi brothers, attacked the satirical magazine that had published controversial cartoons, including depictions of the Prophet Muhammad. They killed twelve people before they themselves were killed in a standoff following a lengthy chase. As that tragedy unfolded, so did another attack on a Paris kosher grocery store, Hyper Cacher. At least one gunman, Amedy Coulibaly, held hostages and killed four of them.

*Figure 9.1* International flags fly in Brezovica, Kosovo (photo credit: Frances Flannery).

Additional accomplices were charged with providing logistical assistance, giving rise to concerns that a sleeper cell was activated in France. More than one cell could be involved. Al Qaeda in Yemen has claimed responsibility for planning the *Charlie Hebdo* assault, but not the grocery store attack, which may have been ISIS/ISIL inspired (Schmitt *et al.* 2015). In the two weeks following the *Hebdo*/grocery store attacks, law enforcement is still tracking and arresting potential terror suspects across Belgium, Germany, the UK, and France. This leads many to believe that a series of Islamist extremist sleeper cells are operative throughout Europe (Sanchez *et al.* 2015), perhaps in the US and other allied nations as well. ISIS/ISIL has continued to take and kill hostages, even threatening to behead President Obama and make the US "a Muslim state" (Khan 2015).

These events are terrible, but not surprising, considering the potency of the radical apocalyptic worldview. The attacks may signal a change or addition in tactics by extremist Islamists. Moving away from complex, orchestrated operations such as 9/11 and towards smaller-scale targets, they attack in a manner that creates mayhem and sends a symbolic message. Combating the latter style of terrorism is all but impossible through law enforcement efforts alone, as imperative as they are. In addition to such short-term measures, a *preventative* response is required.

Such a response may have already begun to emerge spontaneously from the French people. Just after the *Charlie Hebdo* attacks, up to 3.7 million gathered in the streets of France for a "rally for unity" that had a joyous and defiant tone. Marchers brandished signs reading "Je suis Charlie," (I am Charlie). In Paris, up to 1.6 million people marched behind forty world leaders linked arm in arm. Noticeably, top US officials did not participate, prompting an official apology by the White House after the fact. The event was unprecedented, the largest demonstration in French history (*Chicago Tribune* 2015).

It was also groundbreaking in terms of the world's united response to terrorism. For the most part, this was not a march against terrorists. That negative tone would have had a mood of revenge and perhaps even violence. It was a march *for* unity. World leaders entrenched in bitter conflict came together to march arm in arm as a united, peaceful force. This included unlikely compatriots, such as Israeli Prime Minister Benjamin Netanyahu and Palestinian President Mahmoud Abbas, Ukrainian President Petro Poroshenko and Russian Foreign Minister Sergey Lavrov. Although brief, it was a breathtaking moment that points to the ideal of showing mutual respect despite our differences. In a conversation with Ambassador Ahmet Shala of Kosovo months earlier, he had suggested to me this very idea that crystallized in France – a demonstration *for peace and for our values* would be much more effective than a protest *against terrorism*. What he insightfully recognized is that the mood and the motivation matters in shaping how the movement goes forward. As the saying goes, love is stronger than fear.

After the Unity march, however, some felt in hindsight that "Je suis Charlie" could be a slogan signaling future divisions in French society. Perhaps it meant sympathy with a satirical paper over and against identification with the Muslim community. As Jack Miles argues, the paper had not shown "religious etiquette" in featuring images of a naked Prophet Muhammad rolling around on the ground and asking, "Do you like my butt?" Miles notes that "Cartoons like that seem to say to Muslims, Charlie Hebdo despises you – we despise your prophet and we despise you." Thus, as Miles reminds us, the "Je suis Charlie" event could seem to convey the same message, that "we too despise you, we too scorn you just as the cartoonists of Charlie Hebdo did" (Gross 2015).

Censorship is certainly not the answer, since satirists purposefully offend in order to perform a vital function in pointing out the absurdity of Fundamentalism. But in the wake of religious and societal tensions after terrorism, there eventually needs to be wide societal space for expressing discontent and discomfort on all sides (Brooks 2015).

In 2000, the National Intelligence Council predicted that by 2015 terrorists would strive for greater lethality, more attacks on critical infrastructures, cyberattacks, and the use of weapons of mass destruction (WMDs) (NIC 2000). Some of these predictions may be coming true. On January 3, 2015, a week before the terrorist events in France, Boko Haram executed an attack in Baga, Nigeria, that resulted in far greater casualties than ever before, possibly up to 2,000 villagers of all ages. Since fall 2014, MI5 has warned that the threat of terrorism in the UK is severe or "highly likely" (MI5 2014).

In this apocalyptically infused moment, we need to rethink the problem of terrorism. We should carefully consider the circumstances in each social setting that give rise to and sustain the ideology of apocalyptic terrorism. We need to side with secularism in France as well as with the Muslims of Europe. The challenge is to be able to say empathetically: I am Charlie, I am a Jew, I am a Muslim, I am a Christian, I am a Buddhist, I am a Hindu, I am a secularist, I am a person in solidarity with other people around the globe.

## Directions for US counter-terrorism

It is imperative that we break our current, short cycle of combating individual terrorists, only to raise up another generation of terrorists a decade later after virtually ignoring the humanitarian aspects of our military intervention. With the Oklahoma City bombings in 1995, the 9/11 attacks in 2001 and the surprise emergence of ISIL/ISIS, two main approaches have presented themselves as options in counter-terrorism. Can the problem of terrorism be solved by eliminating terrorists? Or can it only be solved by addressing the ideology that spawns terrorism? This juncture in US counter-terrorism policies against ISIS/ISIL suggests that both options have their support at the present time.

As did President Bush after 9/11, President Obama promised to "hunt down" terrorists after ISIS/ISIL issued the first two beheading videos of James Foley and Steven Sotloff (Obama September 10, 2014). After noting, "we can't erase every trace of evil in the world," President Obama continued by saying, "we will hunt down terrorists who threaten our country, wherever they are" (ibid.). This is the language of cosmic war once again. Although the official name for the US strategies against ISIL/ ISIS is "Operation Inherent Resolve," a quick media search in autumn 2014 shows that the phrase "War on ISIS" is far more popular. This terminology resulted from key members of the administration repeatedly announcing "We are at war with ISIS," even if the president himself carefully avoided the term in his speech on ISIS (Alexander 2014; Obama September 10, 2014).

However, the rise of ISIS is the very case study that illustrates the inefficiency of the strategy of "hunting down" terrorists. ISIL/ISIS rose out of AQI, Al Qaeda in Iraq, which grew as a consequence of the Iraq war, according to the determination of the 2010 National Intelligence Estimate. Despite repeated executions of extremist Islamist leaders, including al-Zarqawi, al-Masri, and al-Awlaki, the Al Qaeda network and ISIL/ISIS continue to proliferate.

President Obama outlined a four-prong strategy against ISIL/ISIS in September 2014 that includes: (1) a systematic campaign of airstrikes, (2) American support forces on the ground in a non-combat role to train Iraqi and Kurdish forces and to equip and train moderate Syrian rebel forces, (3) counter-terrorism efforts to prevent ISIL attacks, and (4) humanitarian assistance for the displaced (Obama September 10, 2014). Prongs 1–3 are short-term and medium-range options that aim to "degrade and destroy" the military capability of ISIL/ISIS, to eliminate terrorists (ibid.).

Prong 4 is the only item that addresses the root causes that make the ideology of radical apocalypticism appealing in the long-term. Humanitarian assistance for the displaced is not only a sound moral choice; it is a practical one that avoids the creation of another discontented generation susceptible to extremism.

In fact, the White House appears to be broadening its scope of terrorism understanding and heading in this long-term, comprehensive direction. Military strategies include combating ideology and providing humanitarian relief (US Army FM 3–24). The president's speech on October 14, 2014, made to the Chiefs of Defense at Joint Base Andrews, was much broader in its understanding of the problem and is worth quoting at length:

> this is not simply a military campaign. This is not a classic army in which we defeat them on the battlefield and then they ultimately surrender. What we're also fighting is *an ideological strain of extremism that*

*has taken root in too many parts of the region.* We are dealing with sectarianism and political divisions that for too long have been a primary political, organizational rallying point in the region. *We're dealing with economic deprivation and lack of opportunity among too many young people in the region.*

And so one of the interesting things to hear *from our military leadership* is the recognition that this cannot simply be a military campaign. This has to be a campaign that includes all the dimensions of our power. *We have to do a better job of communicating an alternative vision for those who are currently attracted to the fighting inside Iraq and Syria....* And so, in addition to denying ISIL safe haven in Iraq and Syria, in addition to stopping foreign fighters, in addition to the intelligence gathering and airstrikes and ground campaigns that may be developed by the Iraqi security forces, we're also going to have to pay attention to communications. We're going to have to pay attention to how all the countries in the region begin to cooperate in rooting out this cancer. And we're going to have to continue to deliver on *the humanitarian assistance* of all the populations that have been affected.

(Obama October 14, 2014, italics added for emphasis)

This is the direction that could finally begin to turn the tide in the fight against terrorist ideology. That ideology will continue to grow despite, or perhaps because of, the number of terrorists killed. It is a promising direction, if military, intelligence, policy and diplomatic strategies are all brought into alignment with this long-term vision.

As the President's speech made clear, this is "an ideological strain of extremism" (Obama October 14, 2014). At this time, more than ever, it is vital to understand the central themes of religion, culture, and radical apocalypticism in strategically planning our counter-terrorism. Over a decade since 9/11, the analysis of religion is surprisingly not a routine practice in the mainstream intelligence collection process. It is often assigned to non-specialists who equate religion with beliefs and practices, rather than with a comprehensive worldview. Much is missed when the task of analyzing religion is a formality, coming from experts focused on intelligence analysis, political science, international relations, or history.

Each of those disciplines has tremendous insights to offer, but they should not replace the subject matter expertise of someone trained in the academic study of religion. As early as 2006, the importance of integrating specialists in religion was stressed by former Secretary of State Madeline Albright to the American Academy of Religion. Yet not much has been accomplished to systematically incorporate religious scholarly insights into diplomacy, law enforcement, and intelligence analysis. In addition, specialists in religious studies must also be willing to engage in this discourse (Schneider 2011).

## Winning the war, losing the peace

The analysis presented in this study suggests that apocalyptic ideology only strengthens under oppression. To be successful, a long-term counter-terrorism effort must avoid perpetuating the explanatory power of the oppressor myth. Admitting those instances in which the US and its allies have done so is a risky political venture that will garner criticism from those who find taking responsibility to be a weakness. However, at some point, terrorism could become enough of a perceived threat that politicians might have to unite and accept responsibility as a country.

To increase our international credibility and combat the appeal of apocalyptic terrorist ideology, the US should continue to confront its past practices and policies condoning torture. Those practices occurred despite torture being illegal within US territory and being prohibited under FM 3–24. We should also have a vigorous and respectful national debate about present policies concerning Guantanamo Bay and the drone program. Both of these programs serve to energize the *jihadist* resentment of America and increase suspicion amongst the radical Right in the US. In his campaign for presidency, Barack Obama expressed grave concern over the detention of inmates without due process at Guantanamo Bay. He called it an embarrassment and noted that it sent the wrong signal about American justice. As president, he promised to close the facility by signing an executive order on January 22, 2009 to close Guantanamo Bay Detention Facility within one year, "to restore the standards of due process and the core constitutional values that have made this country great" (Wagner 2013). However, the President has not been able to close the facility due to Congressional opposition over relocating prisoners in domestic prisons and fears that freed inmates will re-engage in terrorism (which they have done at rates of around 16–27 percent) (ODNI 2013).

Despite these hurdles, an open Guantanamo has become a rallying cry for the discontented, especially for radical Islamists. Opposition to Guantanamo Bay reached a crescendo in 2013, when desperate prisoners held hunger strikes for at least six months (Sutton 2013). Rather than let them die from starvation, staff force-fed the strikers, a controversial procedure that received international attention.[1] While the issue of Guantanamo is complicated, resolving the closing of this facility should be a top priority for the US as a counter-terrorism strategy.

Similarly, the drone program that has been much embraced by President Obama and his Cabinet has serious pros and cons. Undoubtedly, it has reduced the operational capacity of the core of Al Qaeda by killing top leaders. One such leader was the American Anwar al-Awlaki, dubbed the "bin Laden of the Internet," who motivated domestic radical Islamist terrorists in America through his fiery sermons, blog, YouTube videos, and the Al Qaeda magazine, *Inspire*.[2] However, as we have seen with the *Hebdo* attacks in the name of al-Awlaki and with the rise of ISIS, the termination of leaders does not stop terrorist ideology from spreading. In an information age such as ours, it could even unintentionally increase the appeal of the ideology through the creation of a martyr and heighten the sense of persecution amongst extremists, further entrenching the radical apocalyptic worldview.

Part of the Obama administration's calculus has been that while drones do sometimes kill civilians, ground wars such as that in Iraq kill many more. The drone program has significantly reduced US troop casualties and facilitated the withdrawal of troops from Iraq and the drawdown in Afghanistan. However, drones also kill and maim civilians, including children, and these statistics are finally known. In Pakistan alone, hundreds of child and adult civilians have been unintentionally killed by drones.[3] The habitual accidental killing and maiming of innocents as acceptable collateral damage, as well as the psychological anxiety of a population "living under drones," brings into grave question the costs, wisdom and morality of the program.

Moreover, analysts and policy makers must begin to appreciate the extent of the motivational *symbolic power* of these tragedies, which reverberates for a long time in the affected cultures. Across the world, resentment and anger toward America is steadily building amongst the next generation on account of our drone program (Living Under Drones 2013b). David Kilcullen, a former advisor to US General David Petraeus, puts it plainly, saying "every one of these dead noncombatants represents an alienated family, a new desire for revenge, and more recruits for a militant movement that has grown exponentially even as drone strikes have increased" (Kilcullen and Exum 2009). Sherry Rehman, Pakistani Ambassador to the US, expressed that the drone program "radicalizes ... entire villages in our region" (Imtiaz 2012).

Recently, the Obama administration has begun to recognize the need to reassess the conditions under which drones are employed, minimize accidental casualties, arrive at legal parameters of the program and reduce the number of drone strikes. This is a small but significant step in the right direction. In addition, the administration should weigh the long-term effects of the program on societies and consider long-term effects on radicalization. In the meantime, at minimum, there needs to be a far greater US response to the accidental deaths of innocent bystanders, particularly children. It should be conducted in a manner that expresses genuine empathy for the loss of the families, as if they were American lives.

It is simply impossible to calculate how much damage a single *jihadist* who loses a child to drone attacks or who witnesses the drone deaths of children could do. In bin Laden's case, he claimed that it was watching American sponsored Israeli strikes on Lebanon and the deaths of the Lebanese children that drove him to conceive of 9/11.[4] It is such grievances and experiences of suffering that often inspire terrorism.

Thus, it is pragmatic for any policy decisions about terrorism to be made with *the next generation* in mind. Some policies will come out favorably in this light and others, including reappraisals of Guantanamo Bay and the drone program, should be reconsidered. At each step, policy makers must ask a simple question, "Does the policy make radical apocalyptic ideology more or less attractive to marginalized populations and children in the future?" One out of ten children in the world today lives in a zone affected by armed conflict (UNICEF 2015). There is a definite "youth bulge" in the countries most at risk for radicalization, in which children make up as much as half the population.[5] Since children grow up, this makes it a prudent as well as an ethical choice to look after the welfare of these children and promote positive relations amongst all peoples.

## Counter-messaging

In a sense, these long-range, multi-targeted efforts to work for better governance of marginalized populations and resilient societies are a step towards effective counter-messaging that can challenge the terrorist narrative. In the meantime, we can also engage in more direct counter-messaging through better communications. For instance, in African regions where Al Qaeda is shoring up social support, recent defectors from Al Qaeda affiliate groups have complained that there is a racial disparity in how *mujahideen* are treated in Al Qaeda affiliate groups. Light-skinned Middle Easterners typically function as leaders, while dark skinned Africans are placed on the front lines and therefore suffer the most casualties (Huckabey 2013). Bringing this hypocrisy to light can effectively counter the narrative of Al Qaeda, which claims that the group members are the "defenders of Muslims everywhere" who fight for blacks.[6]

President Obama and his aides seized the opportunity to counter Al Qaeda's message during his July 2010 visit to Africa. During this trip, he stated to the South African Broadcasting System, "they do not regard African life as valuable in and of itself. They see it as a potential place where you can carry out ideological battles that kill innocents without regard to long-term consequences for their short-term tactical gains" (Tapper 2010; Huckabey 2013). To make the remarks even clearer, a top aide added:

> al Qaeda leadership specifically targets and recruits black Africans to become suicide bombers because they believe that poor economic and social conditions make them more susceptible to recruitment than Arabs ... al Qaeda is a racist organization that treats black Africans like cannon fodder and does not value human life.
>
> (Huckabey 2013)

The president was speaking specifically of Al Shabaab's attack at the World Cup in South Africa, which killed seventy-four spectators, but he had many incidents from which to choose. When Al Qaeda bombed the US Embassy in Dar es Salaam and killed eleven people, none of whom were American, bin Laden commented on the deaths of the Muslim Africans there by saying, "even if this involved the killing of Muslims, this is permissible under Islam" (9/11 Commission 2004, 70). Some local African *mujahideen* who join Al Qaeda in the Islamic Magreb, or Boko Haram, or Ansaru are pious Muslims who believe that they are fighting against evil infidels on behalf of a purified vision of Islam (although some appear to be attracted to thuggery, revenge, and power). When confronted with the reality of an organization that raises funds through the illegal drug trade (against which bin Laden railed) (Forest 2011), some pious extremists who are thinking of joining can grow disillusioned and become de-radicalized.

At home in the US, Canada, Australia, New Zealand, and Europe, a campaign that explains the true nature of ISIL/ISIS is vital. Several US teens, such as nineteen-year-old Shannon Conley, joined extremist groups and later stated that they did not understand the true nature of what they were joining (Sanchez 2014). The president's plain remarks describing ISIL/ISIS' actions are thus constructive:

> Let's be clear about ISIL. They have rampaged across cities and villages – killing innocent, unarmed civilians in cowardly acts of violence. They abduct women and children, and subject them to torture and rape and slavery. They have murdered Muslims – both Sunni and Shia – by the thousands. They target Christians and religious minorities, driving them from their homes, murdering them when they can for no other reason than they practice a different religion. They declared their ambition to commit genocide against an ancient people.
>
> (Obama August 20, 2014)

This fact-based information campaign is different, however, than calling terrorists names, such as "a cancer." Those pejorative labels only succeed in putting potential recruits in a defensive posture (Obama September 10, 2014).

A major, new venue for counter-messaging terrorism is social media, not just on mainstream sites such as Facebook and Twitter, but also on lesser-known sites such as Friendica and Quitter. The State Department Center for Strategic Counterterrorism Communications (CSCC) has tried to counter-message ISIS/ISIL using a variety of the same social media platforms that the group employs, including Twitter and videos. Some of their attempts employ fear tactics and some, not very successfully, have employed humor or trolling, trying to irk the terrorist group (Brown 2014). Given the radical apocalyptic framework that inspires *jihadists*, mockery and annoyance are not likely to be effective strategies and could well backfire.

Furthermore, the benefit of censoring *jihadist* social media sites is unclear. While much has been written on the presence of ISIL/ISIS and Al Qaeda on social media platforms, *jihadist* blogs and sites may be less of a factor in recruitment than previously thought and arguably may let off some social steam. Ramsay points out that while a few terrorists have been radicalized through social media, thousands of *jihadists* who participate in such platforms have not turned to violence (Ramsay 2013). The issue is complex and deserves further scrutiny.

I thus favor two approaches to counter-messaging. The first is to encourage counter-messaging campaigns that come from members of larger, peaceful communities with which a terrorist seeks to identify. A powerful example is the British Muslim NGO that has used Twitter at #Notinmyname to convey that the messages of ISIL/ISIS are unislamic. Similar voices from Christian leaders consistently rejecting Christian Identity teaching and anti-federalist terrorism and from the ecological and climate change movements condemning eco-terrorism are much more effective in preventing radicalization than are messages from the government.

The second is a fact-based, informational approach that publicizes an extremist group's "sins" within its own theological context. For instance, Al Qaeda has attempted to procure chemical, biological, and even nuclear weapons, although bin Laden condemned the US for bombing Japan in World War II (9/11 Commission 2004, 60, 109, 141, 342, 380; Ibrahim 2007, 36, 49, 204, 205, 211). By 1998, bin Laden even proclaimed that he might have a nuclear bomb, declaring: "it is the duty of the Muslims to prepare as much force as possible to terrorize the enemies of God" (US Indictment S (10) 98, 21, 21, 34). Even some hardened extremists may be de-radicalized by such evidence, since Islam forbids the killing of innocents. While hundreds or perhaps thousands of Muslims may have joined ISIS/ISIL after the publication of their beheading videos, over a billion and a half Muslims have been repulsed by them.

When confronted with the plans for 9/11, a schism erupted amongst the senior Al Qaeda leadership regarding whether it was just within Islam to attack America in its own borders. Mullah Omar, Sheikh Saeed al Masri, Sayf al Adl, and Abu Hafs were all weighty figures in Al Qaeda who reportedly opposed the actions. Abu Hafs even wrote Bin Laden a refutation of the 9/11 plans based on the Qur'an (9/11 Commission 2004, 252).

Even in the case of some radicals, there are opportunities to nuance the dualistic portrait of "us vs. them" through positive counter-messaging. This is particularly important in the case of US relations with Muslim populations. Under President Clinton, a US-led coalition conducted military strikes from 1993 to 1995 that ended the Serbian genocide against the predominantly Muslim population of Bosnia-Herzegovina, although it arguably took far too long. When Serbia then attacked Kosovo in 1999, Clinton was much quicker to take action, which dramatically cut down the deaths that would have resulted from this second genocide (Flannery 2014). This moderate nation, which is approximately 93 percent Muslim, displays a markedly pro-American attitude, evidenced by the US flags that fly everywhere next to the Kosovo flag. The capital also boasts Bill Clinton

Boulevard, bedecked with a golden statue of the past US President, arm raised and smiling.[7]

A golden statue may be deserved in this case. A close look at the recently released CIA archive containing, amongst other documents, meetings with the Principals (major advisors of the president) shows that the Clinton administration was consistently concerned for the humanitarian welfare of the Muslim population in Bosnia, Kosovo, and Albania. This was the case even when there was no clear US interest (Flannery 2014). This was particularly true of then US Ambassador Madeline Albright (CIA, 2013, 1993–02–05) and Vice-President Al Gore, who suggested allying with the core of the Muslim world as a diplomatic strategy (CIA, 2013, 1993–02–05, 1993–04–14). The suggestion was not taken up at the time. It is impossible to know how differently relations between the US and the Muslim world might have unfolded if this direction had been taken in 1993. Over twenty years later, this is still an important insight and a piece of US and the Balkans' history that should be recovered to counter-message the oversimplified history propagated by extremist Islamists (Flannery 2014).

## A comprehensive cultural counter-terrorism strategy

While the US and allied governments are readjusting to a new conception of fighting terrorism, so must the rest of us. Instead of a "war on terrorism" approach in which we expect the government to solve the problem of terrorism for the US, Canada, and Europe through intelligence and law enforcement, we need new, comprehensive solutions.

An effective long-term counter-terrorism effort to promote peace will require a change in approach. The old paradigm has been stretched to its limits (Kuhn 1962). We need a broad-based network that includes governmental agencies, NGOs, grass-roots organizations, and faith-based humanitarian programs working together and with local partners to address the contexts of discontent in which terrorism finds its appeal. The public in the US and allied countries need to be aware that outreach is not just ethical concern for people in far-away places, but also a pragmatic action to protect people "at home." Such "cultural counter-terrorism" eliminates the appeal and explanatory power of terrorist ideology.

This direction requires the creative reorganization of current resources. For instance, Arthur Lundahl proposes creating a wholly transparent "White Center" that would marshal intelligence resources for humanitarian issues. It would utilize the digital mapping resources of the National Geo-spatial Intelligence Agency (NGA), the supercomputers of the National Security Agency (NSA) and the epidemiologists at the National Center for Medial Intelligence (NCMI) to predict humanitarian crises, direct rescue efforts in national disasters, predict environmental catastrophes and predict the spread of disease (Bamford 2015).

In the remainder of this chapter, I present a few examples of other organizations that are rethinking the approach to terrorism and peace. This sampling is only meant to be illustrative of the creative, new approaches taking place amongst hundreds of thousands of innovative academic centers, NGOs, grass-roots organizations and faith-based humanitarian programs. None of these efforts alone can solve the problem, but together they could form a potent comprehensive counter-terrorism strategy that focuses on preventing radicalization.

## Academia engaging government

In an op-ed in the *New York Times*, journalist Nicholas Kristoff wrote an op-ed entitled "Professors, we need you!" in which he urged academics to come down from their ivory towers to engage in public policy discussions (Kristoff 2014). Considering the vast wealth of academic prowess in the US, Canada, Europe, Australia, and New Zealand, there is still too large a gap between subject matter experts in academia, public policy officials and the intelligence community. For a decade or more, many in the intelligence community have participated in outreach to academics,[8] but there is still no generally accepted mechanism for bringing these fields together. Furthermore, the endeavor has been hampered by past abuses[9] and misunderstanding from conflicting expectations and modes of communications (Bourdieu 1990, 53).[10]

If the goal is to promote new paradigms for addressing the challenges posed by terrorism, we still have vast, untapped resources. Several universities have centers for the study of terrorism, which usually employ an intelligence analysis/social sciences approach to national security issues and terrorism.[11] However, the input from the humanities (including religion) has been minimal at best[12] and reliance on government funding has generated suspicion from other academics concerned about academic freedom and integrity.[13] Outside of university settings, academic experts play an important role at think-tanks, especially around Washington, DC. While benefitting from a team approach, these think-tanks tend to be partisan, producing consensus opinions that are often to be expected. An analyst or policy maker knows which think-tank to consult in order to support an a priori conclusion, in time producing an echo-chamber effect around the DC Beltway.

To overcome some of the challenges outlined above, I founded the Center for the Interdisciplinary Study of Terrorism and Peace (CISTP) at James Madison University. While relatively new, CISTP could provide another model of interaction for academia, public policy and the intelligence community. CISTP takes an interdisciplinary team approach by bringing together twelve subject- matter experts from the humanities, social sciences, natural sciences, intelligence analysis, and education. These scholars offer expertise to intelligence analysts and public officials on a range of topics that challenge peace. We are non-partisan and do not strive to provide a consensus opinion. Instead, we perceive our diversity to be our strength, with the goal of expanding the range of perspectives from which a situation may be considered.

As a team, we began with the recognition that terrorism arises and is sustained in contexts of discontent. We wish to address the roots of terrorism and also envision a long-term approach to solving terrorism by thinking about the second-, third-, fourth-, and even fifth-order effects of policy actions. Our interdisciplinary team approach is valuable for identifying blind spots and previously unquestioned assumptions. Our conversations led us to embrace two paradigm shifts in thinking about terrorism and peace.[14]

The first shift was redefining peace. Instead of thinking of peace in terms of national security, we define peace as encompassing "the physical, psychological, material, traditional/cultural, and ecological well being of peoples" (CISTP 2015). The absence of terrorism alone is not peace. Terrorism can be temporarily halted through intimidation and interventions that rob populations of civil liberties and inflict psychological, cultural or ecological harms. However, in such situations, terrorism eventually returns.

Social resilience has been defined as the "timely capacity of individuals and groups – family, community, country, and enterprise – to be more generative during times of stability and to adapt, reorganize, and grow in response to disruption" (Threshold Global Works 2015). The theory of social resilience recognizes that national and regional resilience depends on the health of smaller communities and individuals (Echterling and Stewart 2008). At minimum, to achieve social stability, we need to remove terror and insecurity, through better governance and culturally positive counter-terrorism strategies that promote sustainable peace.

The second paradigm shift emerges from the recognition of a blind spot inherent in the overarching "red team vs. blue team" or "us against the enemy" approach to analysis. Since terrorists inflict harm on innocent targets (Hoffman 2006, 34), this "us vs. them" framework naturally emerges in the analysis of terrorism in the media, intelligence analysis and policy arenas. Yet, an "us vs. them" construction of the universe is the very starting point of terrorist ideology itself. Therefore, CISTP wonders if there might be another framework. We propose that a narrative of inclusion might better address the complexity of the situation in numerous instances (CISTP 2015).

A narrative of inclusion prompts us to ask, "How can our 'community' be redrawn, rethought, or acted in differently so that more persons feel included?" In multiple contexts, we need to widen whom we include in the conceptual category of "us." One way to do so is to widen our scope of empathy. This is not just an abstract idea; it is a compassionate and pragmatic stance that results in concrete changes. For instance, we might mandate counseling instead of punitive justice for young people who have just been radicalized, but who have not yet committed a terrorist act. Jail time reinforces feelings of being "the Other" who must be punished and ostracized. Instead of promoting reform, prison often results in more entrenched radicalization and the spread of radicalization. Counseling is an attempt to de-radicalize those on the fringes and include them back in society someday as a contributing citizen. We wouldn't do this to be nice. We would do this to stop making terrorists.

Humanitarian partnerships between government and local organizations are another important model of inclusion that can prevent terrorism in the long-term. This should occur domestically and internationally. For instance, educating children in refugee camps is often a low priority behind the immediately pressing needs of securing immediate safety, lessening overcrowding, ensuring sanitation, preventing disease, and procuring adequate clean water and food. However, with sixty million children living in armed conflict zones and millions of refugee children living under long-term displacement (UNICEF 2015), proper educational support is absolutely crucial. UNICEF has just announced its most ambitious appeal of $3.1 billion due to the extreme need of children globally at the present time, particularly in conflict zones (ibid.). Its programs involve working with sixty NGOs, including World Vision International and SOS Children's Villages, to create stable and resilient local communities (UNICEF – NGO 2015). These efforts are more than social justice initiatives; they should be recognized as long-term counter-terrorism measures.

## Supporting non-governmental, grass-roots and faith-based organizations as a strategy for counter-terrorism

Hundreds of thousands of excellent NGOs, grass-roots organizations, and faith-based humanitarian organizations struggle in a live or die cycle of grant writing and procurement and the solicitation of donations.[15] Americans are generous – altogether we gave $335.17 billion to charities in 2013 (NPT 2015).[16] By contrast, annual spending for the US military is still well over 600 billion per year, despite a recent drop due to drawdown in the Middle East (Walker 2014). I grew up in a military family. I feel a great deal of respect and admiration for the military and the men and women who dedicate their very lives to protecting national interests. If I were convinced that terrorism could be solved through military intervention, I would not in principle have an objection to this vast military spending. However, as I have shown in this book, hunting terrorists potentially exacerbates the radical apocalyptic ideology that fuels much of terrorism. Hence, I am convinced that a broad-based, humanitarian approach to social justice causes around the world must be a part of a comprehensive national strategy of counter-terrorism. For this reason, I would advocate shifting some funds from military spending to humanitarian efforts, including those of NGOs, grass-roots organizations, and faith-based humanitarian organizations. This paradigm shift simply envisions that a happy, well-cared-for, educated child with a bright future in a stable and resilient community will very likely never become an extremist.

One example of an NGO doing stellar work in preventing extremism, even though they do not necessarily think of it in that way, is the International Center for Religion and Diplomacy (ICRD). Based in Washington DC, the ICRD understands that facilitating a better understanding of religion lies at the heart of resolving many conflicts around the world. Recently, ICRD has begun working with a local NGO in Yemen to facilitate conflict resolution training amongst Yemeni tribal leaders, training "local peacebuilders to work across religious, ethnic, and tribal identities to meet basic social service and infrastructure needs, thus diminishing the influence of violent extremist groups who otherwise seek to take advantage of desperate conditions for their own ends" (ICRD 2015).

In another of its many programs, ICRD worked for eight years to reform the madrasas (religious schools) in Pakistan, including those that gave birth to the Taliban. Its goals in doing so were to expand the curriculums to include the physical and social sciences, with a strong emphasis on religious tolerance and human rights (especially women's rights), and to transform the pedagogy to promote critical thinking skills among the students. During that period, it engaged more than 2,700 leaders from 1,600 madrasas in the most radical areas of the country – a successful track record that stands in marked contrast to the failed attempts of others, including the government of Pakistan.

ICRD's approach is an exemplary model to emulate. The success of the madrasa program was a function of conducting the project in such a way that the madrasa leaders felt it was their own reform effort, not something imposed from the outside. This gave them significant ownership of the change process. Working within the religious and cultural framework of the madrasas, ICRD inspired them by appealing to their own history as institutions of higher learning formerly without peer in the medieval world. Most importantly, ICRD grounded all suggested changes in Islamic principles, so that madrasa leaders engaged in the program could genuinely feel they were becoming better Muslims. ICRD has since turned the project over to an indigenous NGO. The total number of madrasa leaders who have been engaged in this process has now reached more than 4,500.

The value of the peacebuilding that results from their innovative programs in the most challenging regions is patently obvious. As noted by ICRD's President, Douglas Johnston, "by dealing with the ideas behind the guns, the work we have done with the madrasas is every bit as strategic as anything else that has taken place either on or off the battlefield. Bombs and bullets have their place, but more often than not, they spawn more terrorists. Respectful engagement, on the other hand, becomes contagious" (Johnston 2015). Yet when I asked him to name their greatest challenge in trying to implement programs around the world, he simply replied, "securing the necessary resources to support our efforts" (ibid.).

Grant opportunities from various foundations are available, but they are highly competitive and time consuming to pursue. Faith-based organizations can turn to the White House Office of Faith-Based and Neighborhood Partnerships, established in 2001, which alerts qualifying organizations to federal grant opportunities (White House 2015). These small programs can have leave lasting social impressions by impacting individual lives.

Direct engagement with religious communities is key. One example is the Interfaith Peace Camp in Virginia in which Jewish, Christian, and Muslim children spend a week together learning about one another's traditions and cultures. I saw children eating food from one another's cultures, learning about one another's religious history, respectfully visiting houses of worship together, making art together around themes of peace and playing games that foster cooperation (EMU 2015). I feel confident in saying that none of the children in that camp would grow up to hate another religion and consider it to be the "Other."

Similarly, across the world, Jewish and Palestinian kids attend school together in "Hand in Hand" Jerusalem School. This is the largest joint Jewish–Palestinian school and the only primary and high school in the capital city with this approach (Sales 2014). In one of the most strained and conflict-ridden zones in the world, "students attend classes in Hebrew and Arabic, celebrate Jewish, Muslim, and Christian holidays, and engage in a weekly current events dialogue. They learn both the Israeli and Palestinian historical narratives" (Sales 2014). This is the sort of grass-roots humanization that prevents the process of destructive "Othering" and that reverses "Other deindividuation." Whether in Virginia or in Jerusalem, these kinds of interfaith programs help children find meaningful, positive self-identities in their local communities and create a sense of belonging in a global culture that promotes tolerance and dignity.

Numerous such programs operating simultaneously and strategically could stem the long-term rise of radicalism. An incomplete list includes programs that: promote greater dialogue within religions; promote intra-religious dialogue; create policies that promote humanitarian support for developing moderate, democratic societies (including in the form of Muslim democracies); facilitate grass-roots friendships amongst individuals in different religious communities through shared activities and projects; address problems of hunger, social inequality, disease, and displacement; and provide education for displaced children. It is also vital to address phobias of the "Other" through intra-group dialogue and education. Consider the long-term effects if all public school children in America, Western Europe, Canada, New Zealand, and Australia learned just a few positive things about each of the world's major religious traditions, as do the Jewish and Palestinian children at the Hand in Hand school in Jerusalem.

This broad, slow, systemic approach to terrorism is quite different than the "War on Terror." It recognizes that all the collective tiny steps of governmental agencies, NGOs, and faith-based organizations to promote the physical, psychological, material, cultural, and ecological well-being of peoples add up to a long-term counter-terrorism strategy. Especially by thinking of children's welfare first, cultural counter-terrorism works by weakening the explanatory power of the radical apocalyptic worldview that posits an evil "them" against an embattled "us." This is accomplished through eliminating the roots of discontent and by reimagining inclusive relationships amongst nations and peoples. Nations are really just imagined communities, since none of us have met everyone else in our nation (Anderson 2006). More children across the world need to feel that they are a part of a global community that supports them.

Finally, no model of inclusion can be successful in a political climate that is bitterly divided. In the US, we must heal the embarrassing partisan differences that have become extreme. We need to foster respectful debate and discussion so that we can begin to live up to our own values and ideals. Instead of Republicans and Democrats fighting one another, we should unite against our common enemies: the suffering of children, societal injustice, and radical apocalyptic extremism. Can we converse respectfully if we understand what is at stake?

## Rethinking our modern apocalyptic moment

It is impossible in this study to say whether the past half-century has witnessed a rise in apocalyptic fascination, but it seems fair to say three things. One, we are living in an historical era in which apocalyptic movements proliferate (as they have in certain other key periods, such as around 1000 CE, the mid fourteenth century, and the mid-1800s). Two, secular apocalyptic themes permeate popular culture. Three, some of the apocalyptic movements of these last few decades have been responsible for the most dramatic episodes of terrorism, with the greatest numbers of casualties (Hoffman 2006, 86–88).

Why is apocalyptic thinking popular now? There is at least one meta-explanation that deserves consideration. As I have tried to show in this book, "worlds" are social projects, collective conceptual constructions (Berger and Luckmann 1967). Many academics believe that we are living in a post-modern period. The world we had known since around 1500 CE has passed away (Aho 1997). Since the late nineteenth century, we have experienced the flaws in a variety of institutions or developments in which vast numbers of people had placed great hope: Victorian England, the Ottoman Empire, democracy, communism, the Industrial Revolution, and the rise of technology. The shadow side of each of these developments has readily made itself known (e.g., through colonialism, corruption, the tyranny of the mediocre majority, inefficiency and oppression, pollution and exploitation, the A-bomb, and so forth).

To complicate matters more, the sociologist James Aho argues that today the self is increasingly displaced as the "disruptive consequences of modernization ... affect people nearly everywhere on earth. Contact with strangers and with strangeness has become planetary, and with it the unsettling sense of being knocked off center, of losing footing and plunging into anomie" (ibid., 66). This doesn't apply just to the materially downtrodden, it applies to anyone in society who searches for an anchored sense of meaning, like the middle-class Japanese scientists who were attracted to Aum Shinrikyo. Aho argues that one reaction to this state of affairs is Fundamentalism, the attempt to cling to modernity through a ret-rojected fantasy that supports a saving paradigm. Fundamentalism in general imagines some idealized past with concrete, absolute values that orient all of reality (ibid., 67–69). It envisions salvation.

In this sense, apocalypticism may be viewed as a Fundamentalist[17] response to disruption and a loss of meaning. Cosmic dualism, which posits a universe in which Good battles Evil, makes simple sense of an increasingly complex world. The academic "linguistic turn" of postmodernism and relativism cannot impose this coherency, especially for those actually living in chaos (ibid., 68). Apocalypticism secures meaning by reconstructing social history through various dualisms, whether as the Crusaders vs. the West, the white children of Seth vs. the children of Cain, civilization vs. nature, or Japan vs. America in World War III. This simplicity appeals strongly to the very root of our evolutionary development, the lizard-like level of functioning in our brains that simply wants to know: Friend? Or Foe?

I would argue that we are presently experiencing the slow collapse of modernity worldwide. Vast numbers of people live someplace between the extremes of pure relativism (with its infinite world centers) and Fundamentalism (with its one center). Most of us maintain hope of some kind in various grand, salvific schemas (science, technology and artificial intelligence (AI), the global economy, national exceptionalism, democracy, socialism, and/or religion). The challenge is to embrace humility, complexity, and ambiguity within each framework and be willing to amend them as we are confronted by the chaos of our present age.

We are living at a tender moment in human history that is experiencing change at an increasingly accelerating rate (Kurzweil 2005). Given the tenaciousness of apocalyptic terrorism, it is necessary at this moment to rethink apocalypticism, even of the peaceful variety. It is mostly up to the adherents of the major Abrahamic religions to do so, once the connection between apocalyptic thinking and terrorism is openly admitted. The major religions must reclaim their full interpretive freedoms to challenge and transform the apocalyptic framework.

There are interpretive options in religion for reimagining apocalypticism in a peaceful key. We could return to the original message of Revelation and accept that only divinity can exercise judgment. We could conceive of the *eschaton* as the end of human conflict and the rise of a collectively created utopia, which affirms the basic claim of the apocalyptic worldview: hope for the recovery of a broken world. We could open up to interpretations, found in each Abrahamic religion, of a "realized" eschatology that stresses that the presence of the divine is available now, not only in the eschatological future. We could open ourselves up to a universalist apocalyptic fantasy, as did Derridas, by hoping that everyone gets invited to the eschatological banquet (Derridas 1983, 42). We could resist the temptation to shed ourselves of living well on this planet because of an expected *eschaton*. To do this, we would remember that the endtime is known only by God and reaffirm that most of the major religions envision humans as the caretakers of this world.

Or, given the injury that the apocalyptic framework has caused throughout human history, we could reject it altogether. We could choose to imagine a world without end.

## Notes

1 Much of the publicity occurred when rapper Mos Def agreed to be force-fed under the same conditions for a journalistic piece by a human rights charity. He quit the experiment early, weeping before completing the feeding. The video has received over five million viewings on YouTube (*Telegraph* 2013).

2 Al-Awlaki also appears to have inspired Nidal Hasan, who was charged with killing thirteen soldiers at Ft. Hood on November 5, 2009.

3 As of the time of writing, studies on the numbers of drone strikes and civilian casualties in Pakistan vary widely. The visual interactive by Pitch Interactive estimates 175 children or 5.6 percent amongst the casualties, which include 535 civilians and 2391 others, out of a total of 3,149 casualties in Pakistan. *The Long War Journal* reports that drones have killed 2,396 "leaders and operatives from Taliban, Al Qaeda, and allied extremist groups" since 2006, along with 138 civilians. New America Foundation's *Year of the Drone* project reports that somewhere between 1,584 and 2,716 "militants" and between 152 and 191 civilians have been killed in Pakistan since 2004 (plus 130–268 "unknowns"). The London based non-profit *The Bureau of Investigative Journalism* reports that drones have killed between 474 and 881 Pakistani civilians since 2004, out of 2,562 to 3,325 total deaths (Living Under drones 2013a).

4 Osama bin Laden, "Your Fate is in Your Hands Alone," in Ibrahim 2007, 215–216.

5 For instance, in Pakistan in 2003, seventy-three million out of 176 million people were children (UNICEF 2003).

6 As stated in a recent Al Qaeda *Inspire* magazine article on Trayvon Martin. Huckabey further notes that the *Inspire* article had a quote from Malcolm X along with the caption "field negro" under Trayvon Martin's photo, illustrating their awkwardness in communicating a message that they understand to be aimed at African-Americans. "Islam: The Solution to Racism," Spring 2013, *Inspire*, Al-Malahem Media, 29. Along the same awkward lines, al-Zawahiri

called President Obama a "house negro." "Transcript: English Translation of Zawahiri Message," Nov. 19, 2008. *FoxNews.com.* Cited in Huckabey 2013.

7 Kosovo is bi-partisan when it comes to US politicians, since the cross streets for Bill Clinton Boulevard are a smaller George Bush Street and Robert Dole Avenue.

8 A leader in this area is IAFIE, the International Association for Intelligence Educators.

9 In addition to controversies in the past, such as the U.S. government's use of the work of anthropologists like Margaret Mead, the more recent Human Terrain System project has garnered the opposition of the American Anthropological Association: www.aaanet.org/about/Policies/statements/Human-Terrain-System-Statement.cfm. Accessed May 29, 2015.

10 I recognize how difficult it is for people from different cultures to communicate effectively. Academia, public policy and intelligence analysis are all different "fields." Bourdieu pointed out that "fields" are autonomous social structures with their own "structuring structures," including their own language, implicit and explicit rules, power structures, habits, expectations, gestures and customs. Yet as he also states, fields are constructed dynamically and they can interact. I suggest that since a field is determined in part by an agent's *habitus,* the participation of professors in intelligence analysis necessarily changes it. The intelligence community is not just a "structuring structure," but also a "structured structure" (Bourdieu 1990, 53).

11 The excellent scholarly research from the Center for the Study of Terrorism and Political Violence at The University of St. Andrews deserves mention as an exemplar of the contribution that academics can make to terrorism studies.

12 The largest list of subject matter experts available for consultation with the intelligence community is available at START, the National Consortium for the Study of Terrorism and Responses to Terrorism, at www.smart.umd.edu. Out of hundreds of experts, almost none have a specialty in the humanities.

13 This is especially the case in anthropology and sociology because of the Human terrain systems project.

14 Paradigm shifts can inform scientific revolutions that change societies (Kuhn 1962).

15 In fact, in 2013 there were 1,536,084 charitable organizations in the US, including religious congregations (NPT 2015).

16 This figure includes individual donations (72 percent of the total), foundations (15 percent), bequests (8 percent), and corporations (5 percent) (NPT, 2015).

17 This use of the term is distinguished from Christian Fundamentalism, which holds a different set of precepts but partakes of this general orientation.

## Bibliography

9/11 Commission. 2004. *The 9/11 Commission Report: Final Report of the National Commission on Terrorist Attacks Upon the United States, Authorized Edition.* New York: W.W. Norton & Co.

Aho, James. 1997. "The Apocalypse of Modernity." In *Millennium, Messiahs, and Mayhem: Contemporary Apocalyptic Movements,* edited by Thomas Robbins and Susan Palmer, 61–72. New York: Routledge.

Alexander, Peter. September 12, 2014. "Obama Administration: Yes, We are at "War" with ISIS." Accessed October 15, 2014, www.nbcnews.com/watch/nightly-news/obama-administration-yes-we-are-at-war-with-isis-328718915879.

Anderson, Benedict. 1991. *Imagined Communities: Reflections on the Origin an=d Spread.* London: Verso.

Bamford, James. January 29, 2015. "Big Brother Doesn't Have to be a Bully." *Foreign Policy.* Accessed January 30, 2015, http://foreignpolicy.com/2015/01/29/big-brother-doesnt-have-to-be-a-bully-surveillance-to-save-lives/?wp_login_redirect=0.

Baudrillard, Jacques. 1981. *Simulacra and Simulations.* University of Michigan Press.

Berger, Peter and Luckmann, Thomas. 1967. *The Social Construction of Reality: A Treatise in the Sociology of Knowledge.* New York: Anchor.

Bourdieu, Pierre. 1990. *The Logic of Practice.* Stanford, CA: Stanford University Press, 1990.

Brooks, David. January 9, 2015. "I am not Charlie Hebdo." *New York Times,* A23.

Brown, Hayes. September 18, 2014. "Meet the State Department Team Trying to Troll ISIS into Oblivion." Accessed October 30, 2014, http://thinkprogress.org/world/2014/09/18/3568366/think-again-turn-away/.

*Chicago Tribune.* January 12, 2015. "White House admits error: U.S. should have sent high-level official to Paris." *Chicago Tribune.* Accessed January 12, 2015, www.chicagotribune.com/news/nationworld/chi-white-house-admits-error-20150112-story.html.

CIA. Released October 1, 2013. *Bosnia, Intelligence and the Clinton Presidency.* Archive. Accessed October 1, 2013–14 April 2014, www.cia.gov/library/publications/historical-collection-publications/bosnia-intelligence-and-the-clinton-presidency/index.html.

CISTP (Center for the Interdisciplinary Study of Terrorism and Peace). 2015. James Madison University. Accessed February 1, 2015, www.jmu.edu/cistp.

Derridas, Jacques. 1983. *D'un Ton Apocalyptique.* Edition Galilée.

Eastern Mennonite University Center for Interfaith Engagement. 2015. "Interfaith Peace Camp." Accessed February 2, 2015, www.emu.edu/interfaith/ipc/.

Echterling, Lennis G. and Stewart, Anne L. 2008. Resilience, in *Twenty-first Century Psychology: A Reference Handbook 2,* 192–201. Thousand Oaks, CA: Sage.

Esposito, John L. and Voll, John O. 1996. *Islam and Democracy.* New York: Oxford University Press.

Flannery, Frances. 2014. "Towards a New Social Memory of the Bosnian Genocide: Countering Al-Qaeda's Radicalization Myth with the CIA 'Bosnia, Intelligence, and Clinton Presidency' Archive." *The Role of Intelligence in Ending the War in Bosnia in 1995,* edited by Timothy R. Walton, 111–132. Lanham: Lexington Press.

Forest, James J.F. 2011. "Al-Qaeda's Influence in Sub-Saharan Africa: Myths, Realities and Possibilities." *Perspectives in Terrorism* v, 3–4: 63–80.

Gross, Terry. January 29, 2015. Interview with Jack Miles: "Editor Picks Religions for the First Norton Anthology of World Religions." *Fresh Air.* Accessed January 29, 2015, www.npr.org/2015/01/29/382388786/editor-picks-religions-for-the-first-norton-anthology-of-world-religions.

Hoffman, Bruce. 2006. *Inside Terrorism.* Revised and expanded edition. New York: Columbia University Press.

Holbrook, Donald. 2012. "Al Qaeda's Response to the Arab Spring." *Perspectives in Terrorism* 6, 12. Accessed February 12, 2013, www.terrorismanalysts.com/pt/index.php/pot/article/view/228/html.

Huckabey, Jessica M. Summer 2013. "Al Qaeda in Mali: The Defection Connections," *Orbis* 57, 3. Accessed July 5, 2013, www.fpri.org/articles/2013/07/al-qaeda-mali-defection-connections.

Ibrahim, Raymond ed. and trans. 2007. *The Al Qaeda Reader*. New York: Broadway Books.

ICRD – International Center for Religion and Diplomacy. January 13, 2015. Facebook page. Accessed February 5, 2015, www.facebook.com/ICRD1999.

Imtiaz, Huma. July 10, 2012. "Drone Program is Counterproductive for Pakistan's Goals: Rehman." *Express Tribune*. Accessed July 12, 2012, http://tribune.com.pk/story/406195/concerns-over-drone-strikes-cannot-be-brushed-aside-sherry-rehman/.

Johnston, Doug. January 13, 2015. Personal correspondence with Frances Flannery. International Center for Religion and Diplomacy.

Khan, Maria. February 1, 2015. "ISIS Threatens to Behead Obama and 'Transform America into a Muslim Province'." *International Business Times, UK* Accessed February 1, 2015, www.ibtimes.co.uk/isis-threatens-behead-obama-transform-america-into-muslim-province-1485636.

Kilcullen, David and Exum, Andrew McDonald. May 16, 2009. "Death From Above, Outrage Down Below." *New York Times*. Accessed May 17, 2009, www.nytimes.com/2009/05/17/opinion/17exum.html?pagewanted=all.

Kristoff, Nicholas. February 16, 2014. "Professors, We Need You!" *New York Times*. Accessed February 16, 2014, www.nytimes.com/2014/02/16/opinion/sunday/kristof-professors-we-need-you.html?_r=0.

Kuhn, Thomas. 1962. *The Structure of Scientific Revolutions*. Chicago: University of Chicago Press.

Kurzman, Charles. 1998. *Liberal Islam: A Sourcebook*. New York: Oxford University Press.

Kurzweil, Ray. 2005. *The Singularity is Near*. New York: Viking.

LeBlanc, Kim and Waters, Tony. March 2005. "Schooling in Refugee Camps." *Humanitarian Exchange Magazine* 29. Accessed January 2, 2015, www.odihpn.org/humanitarian-exchange-magazine/issue-29/schooling-in-refugee-camps.

Living Under Drones project. International Human Rights and Conflict Resolution Clinic at Stanford University and the Global Justice Clinic at New York University School of Law. 2013a. "Living Under Drones: Death, Injury and trauma to Civilians from US Drone Practices in Pakistan." Accessed August 13, 2013, www.livingunderdrones.org/numbers/.

Living Under Drones project. International Human Rights and Conflict Resolution Clinic at Stanford University and the Global Justice Clinic at New York University School of Law. 2013b. "U.S. Drone Strike Policies Foment Anti-American Sentiment and May Aid Recruitment to Armed Non-State Actors." Accessed August 14, 2014, www.livingunderdrones.org/report-strategy/.

MI5. August 29, 2014. "Threat level to the UK." Accessed February 2, 2015, www.mi5.gov.uk/home/news/news-by-category/threat-level-updates/threat-level-to-the-uk-from-international-terrorism-raised-to-severe.html.

NIC – National Intelligence Council. December 2000. *Global Trends 2015: A Dialogue about the Future with Nongovernment Experts*. Accessed February 3, 2015, www.dni.gov/files/documents/Global%20Trends_2015%20Report.pdf.

NPT – National Philanthropic Trust. 2015. "Charitable Giving Statistics." Accessed February 1, 2015, www.nptrust.org/philanthropic-resources/charitable-giving-statistics/.

Obama, Barack. September 10, 2014. "Statement by the President on ISIL." White

House. Accessed on September 10, 2014, www.whitehouse.gov/the-press-office/2014/09/10/statement-president-isil-1.

Obama, Barack. October 14, 2014. "Remarks by the President after Meeting with Chiefs of Defense." The White House, Office of the Press Secretary. Accessed October 15, 2014, www.whitehouse.gov/the-press-office/2014/10/14/remarks-president-after-meeting-chiefs-defense.

ODNI – Office of the Director of National Intelligence. March 4, 2013. "Summary of the Reengagement of Detainees Formerly Held at Guantanamo Bay, Cuba." Accessed June 15, 2013, www.dni.gov/index.php/newsroom/reports-and-publications/193-reports-publications-2013/814-summary-of-the-reengagement-of-detainees-formerly-held-at-guantanamo-bay-cuba.

Pitch Interactive. n.d. "Out of Sight, Out of Mind." Accessed March 1, 2013, http://drones.pitchinteractive.com.

Ramsay, Gilbert. 2013. *Jihadi Culture on the World Wide Web*. New York: Bloomsbury.

Sales, Ben. November 25, 2014. "Amid rising tensions, Arab-Jewish school in Jerusalem struggles for balance." *JTA*. Accessed November 26, 2014, www.jta.org/2014/11/25/news-opinion/politics/jerusalem-coexistence-programs-persist-amid-rising-tensions.

Sanchez, Ray and Cabrera, Ann. September 10, 2014. "Colorado teen pleads guilty in plan to join ISIS." *CNN*. Accessed 10 October 2014, www.cnn.com/2014/09/10/justice/colorado-jihadist-guilty-plea/.

Sanchez, Ray, Smith-Spark, Laura, and Mullen, Jethro. January 16, 2015. "Terror Cell Warning as Europe Scrambles to Handle Threats." *CNN*. Accessed January 16, 2016, www.cnn.com/2015/01/16/europe/europe-terrorism-threat/.

Schmitt, Eric and Mazetti, Mark and Callimachi, Rukmini. January 14, 2015. "Disputed Claims over Qaeda Role in Hebdo Attacks." *New York Times*. Accessed January 14, 2015, www.nytimes.com/2015/01/15/world/europe/al-qaeda-in-the-arabian-peninsula-charlie-hebdo.html.

Schneider, Nathan. November 21, 2011. "Why the World Needs Religious Studies." *Religion Dispatches*. Accessed December 9, 2011, http://religiondispatches.org/why-the-world-needs-religious-studies/.

Sutton, Jane. July 31, 2013. "Hunger Strike at Guantanamo Bay weakening." *Reuters*. Accessed December 12, 2014, www.reuters.com/article/2013/07/31/us-usa-guantanamo-hunger-idUSBRE96U1FZ20130731.

Tapper, Jake. July 13, 2010. "President Obama, White House: Al Qaeda Is Racist." *ABC News Political Punch*. Accessed January 21, 2015. http://abcnews.go.com/blogs/politics/2010/07/president-obama-white-house-al-qaeda-is-racist/.

*Telegraph*. July 9, 2013."US hiphop artist Mos Def force-fed in Guantanamo Bay video." *Telegraph*. Accessed July 10, 2013, www.telegraph.co.uk/news/world-news/northamerica/usa/10170261/US-hip-hop-artist-Mos-Def-force-fed-in-Guantanamo-Bay-video.html.

Threshold Global Works. 2015. *Social Resilience Model*. Accessed October 8, 2014, www.thresholdglobalworks.com/about/social-resilience/.

UNICEF. February 24, 2003. Pakistan: Statistics. Accessed August 14, 2013, www.unicef.org/infobycountry/pakistan_pakistan_statistics.html.

UNICEF. January 29, 2015. "UNICEF launches US$3.1 billion appeal to reach more children in emergencies." Accessed January 29, 2015, www.unicef.org/media/media_78952.html.

UNICEF – NGO. Updated 2015. "NGO Committee on UNICEF." Accessed January 3, 2015, www.ngocomunicef.org/about/.

US Army. 2006. Army Field Manual 3-24, Marine Corps Warfighting Publication 3-33.5, "Counterinsurgency." December 15.

US Indictment S (10) 98 Cr. 1029 (LBS) against Osama bin Laden, Muhammad Atef, Ayman al Zawahiri, Saif al Adel, Mamdouh Mahmud Salim, Abdullah Ahmed Abdullah, Muhsin Musa Matwalli Atwah, Khalid al Fawwar, Wadih El Hage, Anas al Liby, Ibrahim Eidarous, Adel Abdel Bary, Fazul Abdullah Mohammed, Ahmed Mohamed Hamed Ali, Mohamed Sadeek Odeh, Mohamed Suleiman al Nalfi, Mohamed Rashed Daoud al-'Owhali, Mustafa Mohamed Fadhil, Khalfan Khamis Mohamed, Ahmed Khalfan Ghailani, Fahid Mohammed Ally Msalam, and Sheikh Ahmed Salim Sedan. '

Wagner, David. January 28, 2013. "Obama's Failed Promise to Close Gitmo: A Timeline." *The Atlantic.* Accessed August 14, 2013, www.theatlanticwire.com/global/2013/01/obama-closing-guantanamo-timeline/61509.

Walker, Dinah. July 15, 2014. "Trends in U.S. Military Spending." *Council on Foreign Relations.* Accessed February 1, 2015, www.cfr.org/defense-budget/trends-us-military-spending/p28855.

White House Office of Faith-based and Neighborhood Partnerships. 2015. "About." Accessed February 2, 2015, www.whitehouse.gov/administration/eop/ofbnp/about.

# Index

Made in the USA
Columbia, SC
10 January 2021